The Sacred Remains

RICHARD J. PARMENTIER
The Sacred Remains
Myth, History, and Polity in Belau

THE UNIVERSITY OF CHICAGO PRESS
Chicago and London

RICHARD J. PARMENTIER is assistant professor
of sociology and anthropology at Smith College
and research fellow at the Center for
Psychosocial Studies (Chicago).

The University of Chicago Press, Chicago 60637
The University of Chicago Press, Ltd., London
© 1987 by The University of Chicago
All rights reserved. Published 1987
Printed in the United States of America
96 95 94 93 92 91 90 89 88 87   5 4 3 2 1

Library of Congress Cataloging-in-Publication Data
Parmentier, Richard J., 1948–
    The sacred remains.

    Based on the author's thesis (doctoral—University
of Chicago, 1981)
    Bibliography: p.
    Includes indexes.
    1. Ethnology—Palua.   2. Palau—History.
3. Palau—Social life and customs.   I. Title.
GN671.C3P37   1987   996'.6   87-6051
ISBN 0-226-64695-5
ISBN 0-226-64696-3 (pbk.)

Contents

Illustrations

FIGURES

MAPS

PHOTOGRAPHS

Tables

Belauan Texts

Foreword

Here's a fascinating story. Here are, in fact, many fascinating stories. Here is Parmentier the ethnographer, with all his academic paraphernalia, being apprenticed to one of Belau's master archivists and antiquarians, a font of Belauan historical wisdom whose oral archive Parmentier and now we are privileged to experience. Here are the people of Ngeremlengui district, coping with a couple of hundred years of imperial and colonial intervention that proves crucial to the course of their ongoing history, which is its own re-"writing." Here is the goddess Milad, giving birth to her four children (and their afterbirth) so as to determine, for temporal orders to come, the quadripartite sociopolitical order central to the thinking of participants in Belauan society. And here are many, many more protagonists and outcomes connected in minutely narratable detail.

They all take their places in this lucid and orderly book in whose story, as its reader, you are now about to figure. For Parmentier has assembled these stories and brought us to them with the consciousness that culture, what anthropologists profess themselves to be interested in, is profoundly "historical" in character, and that history, what historians take as their province, is in a fundamental sense perspectivally local and therefore inherently "cultural."

To be sure, Parmentier's theme is quietly and soberly announced in the specifics of his gradually more inwardly based account of the historical culture / cultural history of Belauan politics. Let me be a bit louder and more expansive in blowing the conch shell, as it were, on behalf of Parmentier's accomplishment; for this work is, in exceedingly good Belauan fashion, "path"-establishing all the while protesting too much its adherence to normative convention.

For ultimately the book is an extraordinary inside account of the deadly serious business of chiefly political theory Belauan style, where deploying, capturing, and even concealing history is the name of the game. And vice versa: history in Belau conversely resides in what we might term the "game of names." Names. Endless names of *olangch* 'historicizing objects/signs': names of places, names of houses, names of village stones, names of titleholders, names of pavement stones, names of kinsmen, names of valuables, etc., etc. These will parade before you as they figure in the emplotment of recountable events, configurated temporarily like unstable *tableaux vivants*. Each has its own arrangement of names, yet each implies also its own type of dynamic of their priority and subsequentiality that locates the instability (hence mutability) of the situation in hierarchies of value. Somebody's, and hence certain interested parties', hierarchies of value.

Each configuration of nameables is representing in its order of social process a structure of actualized and potential interrelationships of the people, the objects, and the categories of such that the names denote. Such configurations are inscribed in and by the social relations that connect people and things to each other in locatable events. But every event is, in effect, hyperdetermined by many alternative configurational readings that actors may understand the instance to be realizing. So it is precisely the configurationality of events coded in the codes of nameables—i.e., what "history" they instantiate—that is subject to contingent play.

This is the deadly serious "play" by and for the protagonists, who conceptualize events as affected by and as effecting the configurated values of names and their denotata. So the kinds of effectiveness of events—what and whom they affect, and with what import—are grounded in the kinds of configuration understood to have brought about the relationships of nameables instanced in the event, which in turn has the potential for affecting the configurations. History ceaselessly "repeats" itself in the minimal sense that the roles of nameables in events represent (re-present) the events as the coming-into-being of their understood values; in the maximal sense that the coming-into-being of value (from which power derives in the "real" or practical world) has the same epistemological contours, qua events, as what we can experience in the practical world with our (Belauan) historical consciousness. These two poles of contrast in the sign-values of named *olangch* Parmentier characterizes by the characteristics *signs of history* and *signs in history*, respectively.

Conceptualizing whole trajectories of such mutable configurations of names and their denotata, moreover, presupposes a framework, a topology if you will, for understanding how all the systems of names/*olangch* have gotten to—and are going—where they are. This topology of trajectories, this schematic of emplotments, turns out to look like a historical topography of Belau itself, a reticulated hierarchy of sets of names/*olangch* that gives the geographical landscape human meaning and connections.

Seen this way, the dynamic of conceptual and topographical re-distribution of *olangch* in a spatialized polity of actors, constituent corporate entities, and physically embodied values (powers) constitutes the local cultural concept of sociopolitical "time." It is not a "cardinal" time, conceptually measurable in infinitely divisible gradations along a single linear dimension; it is an "ordinal" time, conceptually measured in relative historical priorities that are themselves a function of the multi-dimensional arrangements of named things that emerge in the stories about them and the events involving them.

The validity of this point emerges especially clearly from the semiotic point of view underlying Parmentier's study, that is, from the point of view of the study of sign systems in general. For, uniquely in such a perspective, it seems to me, the Belauan material discussed in this book can be seen as a species of the more generic problem of culture and history once again becoming a central issue of reflection in many quarters. And it is in the exact *how* of connections of sign systems that the fascination lies for us, how the texture of time is, in fact, a cultural property.

How is "time" spatialized in this society's cultural concepts? How are the political institutions of Belauan society relatable to the orders of time (eras or epochs) that interested parties use to represent historical priority and destiny? How are such representations mapped into the interests of protagonists in exercising power in the contemporary context? How does such exercise of power rest on a person's ability to balance the jeopardy to which historical representations, put into play, become subjected, against the authoritative security of historical representations as these may be strategically withdrawn from play? How is chiefly politics, finally, a kind of thrilling confidence game of the authority of names, both in political jeopardy and removed from it? And how, then, is political history in Belau the irreversibly cumulative shifts in the configurations of names and their denotata as a master *olangch* of the causal effectiveness of the game of power?

The account of the encompassing cultural system that makes all this possible is what Parmentier presents in this volume. He carefully interweaves such documentary evidence left by European encounters with Belau, with his own ethnographic and oral archive materials, to show that the dynamics of Belauan politics over the course of some centuries

is in fact to be interpreted within the cultural system. The cultural account is the prerequisite to being able to make consistent sense of all
these various documents, European and Belauan alike. Most importantly, he shows that this cultural system can be understood when we understand the texts through which Belauans articulate it as the practice-
laden theory of their own polity. Hence, for Parmentier, there is always
a return to the text, the artful arrangement and exegesis of which constitutes much of the following text, deployed as the story of these wonderful stories.

The achievement here liberates us, then, from the curious (though,
to be sure, culturally congruent) beliefs of many writers in such phan-
tasms as "cold" societies, that is, societies without any effective sense of
history, even as a particular cultural variation on a more generally universal theme. It liberates us from the universal imputation of epistemological topologies of cyclicity (and hence, ultimately, of stasis) of
events as underlying all but modern European (and derived) societies.
It liberates us from seeing culture as merely a static framework of symbolic possibilities endlessly realizable in pulsating social-functional configurations. It liberates us from having to attribute to the encounter of
the benighted natives with people of "real" history the unique causality
that pushes the natives' social system into realtime (as opposed to myth-
time, or dreamtime, or whatever) or pulls it into what we might term
worldsystemtime. It liberates us from needing contact with foreign
culture—such contact, at least, having the structure of causally contingent eventhood—as our logical deus ex machina in comprehending
the plot of cultural change in a particular society. All of these positions
are amply illustrated in the anthropological and ethnohistorical literature, even from the pens of some of our otherwise sophisticated
theorists.

Parmentier's achievement recalls for us the more fruitful course of
theorizing, which might be analytically reconstructed as follows. If we
ask what are the conditions in the systems of signs of a culture that
would give us evidence for something analogous to what we see as
"history," we must be prepared to see differences of particulars within
an overall framework of similarities. Hence, we might ask of such sign
systems, Are they representational? Are they representational in a context-
specific or context-independent way? Do they represent some unique
asymmetric cumulativity of contingent causality in terms of which
social life is understood? If so, in what medium or media of representational signs? If context-dependent, how does deployment (or
instantiation) of the code of representation interlock with the condi-

tions for deployment? What modes of authoritative deployment differentiate people by their "possession," as it were, of history?

The account thus fits within the modern trend in the comparative semiotic analysis of cultures, rejecting the extremes of nihilistic relativism and of asemiotic functionalisms, in favor of seeing how far our comparatism can be pushed so that the analysis of one culture has the potential to illuminate the problem of Culture itself, and vice versa.

Yet, within this trend, as we understand more of the complexities of the social life of signs, the more we realize that the condition of culture is, in fact, history, and that history in any useful sense can only be cultural.

Any culture is profoundly historical as an object of apprehension and study, and cannot with any plausibility be minutely studied *as* a so-called synchronic system (factoring out a so-called diachronic aspect) without abstracting so much away from the data that it is no longer a particular culture we are describing, but Culture, some universal abstract realm. Such have been the excesses of both structural-functional and symbolic-structural analysis.

For people experience their own lives as events with differentially efficacious causal contingencies connecting them. The implicit dimensions of efficacy, causality, and contingency—not to say of eventhood itself—of this experience are precisely what the anthropologist sets out to capture in some systematic way in an ethnographic account of a people's culture. To suppose that anthropological description can be done without seeing that such historical consciousness is precisely what culture motivates and explains as its implicit framework, is to engage in some other form of study, perhaps an attempt at social "Science."

But the systematicity with which we can determinately embed local historical consciousness from our outsider's analytical perspective is in principle incomplete: it rests always on yet one more "story," as it were. And this incompleteness demonstrates the logical limits to which the nonhistorical must come in understanding another culture.

But, conversely, history, both as folk concept and as specialized discourse in our academy, is a particular construal of a realm of events as differentially efficacious, causally contingent individuables, or particulars, in whatever order(s) of eventhood we may be considering. So the critical prerequisite to having (a) history, to knowing historically the way things were, are, or will be, is being able to individuate some eventlike abstract entities, and to understand the dimensionalities along which we can discern measures of efficacy and of contingent causal connection.

It is obvious that, put this way, there are as many "histories" as there are ways of having epistemologies of individuable eventhood. That is, there would seem to be as many cultures-of-history, or cultural variations on the sense of history, as there are differing cultural schemata for event individuation. And, once we rest the matter on individuation, we reach the verbal-logical plane of names, the semiotic plane of indexical signs, and their intersection in the conceptual space of asymmetric contingency we might as well call "time."

Parmentier has, it seems to me, illuminated the empirical landscape of this paradigm in the concrete example of Belauan historicities. He has done so by focusing on "the sacred remains," both verbal-literary and lithic-objectual, to which he was introduced during long and intensive field research centering in Ngeremlengui district on Babeldaob island in Belau. The connections he makes in this particular cultural milieu across the planes I indicated above locate Belauan "time" for us, and demonstrate its particular experiential properties in the political consciousness of those living in its contours.

What is that experiential texture, and how does its analysis illuminate the more general problems of culture/history? To get a sense of this, I invite the reader to submit to the compellingly interesting stories that follow.

MICHAEL SILVERSTEIN

Preface

Several stylistic conventions which are followed in the text require a brief explanation. I have attempted to illustrate the discussion as often as possible with translations from stories, chants, and exegeses I recorded in the field and to cite parallel accounts from published literature and archival sources. In translating these materials I have tried to strike a balance between the Belauan idiom and intelligible English; where this has proved impossible I have tended to give greater weight to the former rather than to the latter. Unless specifically noted, translations from archival materials are taken from the original sources. All annotations presented in brackets within translated texts are my own interpolations. Also, paragraphing of lengthy narratives often does not correspond to any particular discourse marker in the originals.

Four Belauan terms are frequently left untranslated, either because available English terms do not fully cover the meanings or because adequate glosses would be cumbersome: *kebliil*, "house affiliation network, principal house, multivillage alliance of related houses, set of related local lineages"; *kelulau*, "whispers, rhetoric of chiefs, political strategy, foreign policy"; *olangch*, "physical marker, historical sign"; and *rubak*, "titleholder, chief, village elder, leader." A list of recurrent English expressions that are used in the text to render Belauan terms and phrases is provided in the glossary.

Proper names are always a major problem in writing about Belau, and I apologize at the outset for their proliferation in the text. As the early ethnographer J. S. Kubary (1885:65) states, "This abundance of names, the understanding and use of which presupposes an exact knowledge of local conditions, makes difficult the comprehension of strangers and easily leads to misunderstandings. Yet the knowledge of names is essential, for they are constantly met with in all the old traditions and in everyday conversation." In almost every case names are meaningful expressions, and where these meanings are relevant I give a rough gloss in parentheses. To add to the volume of proper names the variety of spellings given in various published and unpublished sources would be unpardonable, so I have taken the liberty of respelling all proper names and terms according to the rules set down in Josephs's *Palauan Reference Grammar* (1975). One exception to this practice is that I have retained various spellings of the names of the islands, such as Panlog, Palu, Pellow, Pelew, Belao, Pelhow, Palau, Belau, because the names are themselves often important historical markers.

As will be immediately apparent, spatial relations play an important part in the argument of many of the chapters. It would be helpful for the reader to spend a few moments with the maps of Belau and Babeldaob in order to become familiar with the names and relative positions of the islands, districts, and principal villages. Locations mentioned more than once are listed under "Place Names" following the Glossary. One of the specific difficulties for English readers is that place names look alike, since many begin with the locative prefixes *nger-* or *i-*. It is helpful to concentrate on the rest of the word. Also, there is an unfortunate disjunction between pronunciation and orthography; the spelling *ch* represents a glottal stop (formerly pronouced with a Germanic *ch* sound).

The writing of this book began in 1980, when I drafted the first version of my doctoral dissertation at the University of Chicago. Encouraged by the criticisms of Marshall Sahlins, I rewrote the entire manuscript in 1981 to clarify my theoretical approach to the problem of semiotics and history. Between 1981 and 1984 I reworked and refined many of the specific arguments for journal articles and completed a new revision of the manuscript. Further modifications and additions followed in 1986 in light of detailed comments by two reviewers and in response to lectures on the anthropology of history by Michael Silverstein at the International Summer Institute for Semiotics and Structural Studies held at Northwestern University.

Belau is not only one of the most studied island groups in the Pacific, but it is also one of the best studied. The prospect of writing an ethnography dealing to some degree with "traditional" Belau in the shadow of the magisterial studies by J. S. Kubary and Augustin Krämer is certainly daunting. But in addition to these classics, Belau has more recently been the home for ethnographers such as Machiko Aoyagi, Homer Barnett, Maryanne Force, Roland Force, Gary Klee, Mary McCutcheon, Robert K. McKnight, Robert E. Ritzenthaler, DeVerne Reed Smith, John Useem, and Arthur Vidich. It is an honor to work in such company, and I hope that this book continues the high standards set before me.

Finally, it is important for me to state at the outset that this book is not about Belau in general, but about Belau from the vantage point of Ngeremlengui. Accordingly, the myths and stories I report should not be taken as definitive or authoritative. In a hierarchical and factionalized society like Belau, there are bound to be multiple perspectives, each part of the overall cultural picture. During my two years in the field I rarely left Ngeremlengui, and with the exception of two brief but informative visits to Ngerdmau and Melekeok, I restricted my formal data collection to my own district. The decision not to travel widely within the archipelago was a combination of the incredibly fortunate working conditions I found in Ngeremlengui and a desire to replicate (to a small degree, to be sure) Kubary's intimate knowledge of Melekeok (on the other side of the island) rather than Krämer's encyclopedic, but often shallow, survey approach.

❦

Acknowledgments

To enumerate the personal and professional debts I have incurred during my stay in Ngeremlengui and for the seven years since my return from the field would require a lengthy document. And to think that thanking a handful of individuals here absolves this debt would be an insult to Belauan friends and professional colleagues. Whatever in this book advances our understanding of Belauan culture does so only to the extent that it builds on the solid foundation constructed by scholars in several fields who preceded me and then only to the degree that the people of Ngeremlengui entrusted me with their "sacred remains." In writing this ethnography, I have not always found it possible to satisfy at the same time the demand for accuracy, completeness, and criticism I recognize as an anthropologist and the sense of respect, pride, and affection I feel for the people of Ngeremlengui. Professional and Belauan readers will doubtless find excesses in both directions, for which I alone am responsible.

While I have taken care to conceal the names of contemporary Belauans in the body of the text, I trust that if I mention the personal names of several who assisted my research as family, friends, teachers, tutors, bureaucrats and boatmen, those mentioned will not feel embarrassed that their names are given here without titles and those unnamed will not be offended that their names are missing. I take this opportunity to thank the following people in Ngeremlengui whose patient help I enjoyed for two years (in alphabetical order): Chebil, Dirratengadik, Dudiu, Heinrich, Humio, James, Johanna, Klung, Lakius, Lorens, Madalutk, Maidesil, Maireng, Malsol, Moded, Ngiltii, Ngiraikelau, Ongos, Rengolbai, and Ucheliei. To the following Belauans outside Ngeremlengui I also extend my thanks: Dr. and Mrs. Anthony Polloi, Ramona Polloi, Tudong, Kathy Kesolei, Tina Rechucher, Kempis Mad, Thomas Remengeseau, Moses Sam, Francis Toribiong, and Deborah Toribiong Fambro. I wish to acknowledge also the generous assistance, advice, and support offered by Miles Grabau, Eli Halpern, Beth Halpern, Lewis Josephs, Ben Lee, Laurie Lucking, Robert K. McKnight, Mr. and Mrs. Amory J. Parmentier, Jr., DeVerne Reed Smith, Rebecca Stephenson, and Sue Toribiong. To Paula Wissing, who joined me in Ngeremlengui for three months and whose support made my fieldwork possible, I owe a special debt and expression of thanks. Finally, it is a pleasure to acknowledge the help of Nina Kammerer, who has lived with this manuscript for several years now, and who has been a constant source of encouragement and expert council.

The fieldwork project in Belau was made possible in part by a Research Fellowship from the Center for Psychosocial Studies in Chicago (1978–1980); to Bernard Weissbourd and all my colleagues at the Center I extend my warmest appreciation. The William Rainey Harper Memorial Fellowship at the University of Chicago (1980–1981) sustained me during the write-up. My work in Chicago was greatly aided by the computer expertise of William Sterner, by the intellectual stimulation of my dissertation committee (Marshall Sahlins, David Schneider, Michael Silverstein, and Valerio Valeri), and by the linguistic sensitivity of Anita Skang Jordan. Funds for the acquisition of research materials and for technical support were provided by the Committee on Aid to Faculty Scholarship at Smith College. John Graiff of the Interlibrary Loan Office at Neilson Library located obscure materials in places from Tokyo to Tasmania. Additional support for preparing the final manuscript was provided by a sabbatical leave (spring semester, 1986) and by the Jean Picker Fellowship at Smith College (1986–1987). The maps were prepared by Allison Bell.

An early version of chapter 3 appeared as "Diagrammatic Icons and Historical Process in Belau" and is reprinted by permission from the *American Anthropologist* 87 (1985), no. 4, © American Anthropological Association 1985. A portion of chapter 6 appeared as "Tales of Two Cities: The Rhetoric of Rank in Ngeremlengui, Belau," *Journal of Anthropological Research* 42 (1986), no. 2, and is reprinted by permission of the editor. A greatly condensed version of chapter 5 appeared as "Mythological Metaphors and Historical Realities: Models of Transformation of Belauan Polity," *Journal of Polynesian Society* 95 (1986), no. 2. To the many friends, colleagues, and reviewers who commented on these articles in their original forms and to the audiences who discussed them at various professional meetings, seminars, and colloquiums I extend my thanks.

I dedicate this book to Malsol Ngiraibuuch Ngiraklang of Ngeremlengui (photograph 1). Combining a brilliant, encyclopedic comprehension of traditional Belauan culture with an equally astounding inquisitiveness about things new and changing, he embodies the tensions which are the subject of this book. But more importantly, I am fortunate to have spent two years of my life calling him "father." *Chedam, ak telkib el medengei e ng di ngar er ngii a meduch,* "Father, I may know a bit, but there is one who is an expert."

The Sacred Remains

Introduction

OF STORIES AND STONES

One of the rewarding experiences in the course of anthropological field-work is the realization that something which at first appeared to be entirely fortuitous is in fact regular or predictable. For me an example of this was when I finally saw that the informants I was working with and the district where I was living were not selected for me at random. After I declared my intention to learn, among other things, myths and historical narratives, my initial hosts in Belau arranged for me to visit Ngeremlengui, a district on the west coast of Babeldaob island, to meet an elderly man widely known to be an expert in these and other matters. While I did anticipate that the kind of stories I would hear would be structurally determined by the social position of my informants and by the political position of the district, I did not at first acknowledge that my being there to record them was also determined. Perhaps anthropologists like to feel that they select their field sites carefully and rationally and that they control the sorts of data they collect—that beyond this everything else is a matter of good luck. In my case, I can only accept the good luck part of these conditions, since I had little or not input into where I would live and who would be my teachers.

So it was my self-perception of fortuitously being in the right place at the right time that proved false; I ended up at the proper place for the work I had set out to do. The stories I taped during the two years I lived in Belau depict Ngeremlengui as the highest-ranking district in the archipelago and posit the superior status of my principal informants, who held titles belonging to the district's capital village, Imeiong. These stories are, in short, the view "from the top down," since they identify the history of Belau as a whole with the history of

Ngeremlengui district, the history of Ngeremlengui with the history of Imeiong village, and the history of Imeiong with the history of its four high-ranking houses. Now one response to the obvious ideological skewing that characterizes the narratives I collected is to attempt an equally ideological correction, that is, to try to filter out this bias in order to construct a neutral account. I say equally ideological because this method presumes that there is a true story hiding behind the subterfuges of history-work, just as according to Freudian theory there is a psychologically significant latent dream behind the masking activity of "dream-work." A second option, and the one upon which this book is based, is to try to uncover in the narratives and myths themselves the principles of this skewing and, rather than filter them out, make them the focus of analysis. Fortunately and predictably, this enterprise was facilitated by the fact that people from lower-ranking villages in the district told stories in systematically different ways, so I was able to grasp the relationship between these two narrative perspectives. But in the end, the history remains the account told by high-ranking people, for the differential power to construct history is a fundamental feature of hierarchy.

Many of the stories I learned focus on several types of stones, including backrests of chiefs, village boundary markers, gravestones, anthropomorphic monoliths, and various classes of exchange beads. At first these stories set in "ancient times" and the stones located on abandoned sites seemed to have little relevance for contemporary villagers and their difficult transition from inherited to elected leadership and from traditionally defined to legislatively apportioned districts. The time-consuming task of taping, transcribing, and studying mythological accounts of the origin of the islands, the birth and rebirth of the Belauan people, and the fashioning of district polity was, to my mind, a fascinating supplement to more clearly defined investigations into the contemporary district's sociopolitical life. In fact I regarded research into mythology and megaliths as a much-needed break from the stress of other ethnographic work. Weekend hikes to photograph the roads, platforms, and graves of abandoned villages and the anthropomorphic stones and other monoliths which dot the landscape also provided me with a ready topic of conversation with my friends and teachers, who regarded my persistent quest for these "reminders of the past" (*ngesechel a cherechar*) and "matters of ancient times" (*tekoi er a irechar*) with only nodding approval.

It soon became apparent, however, that this compartmentalization of "ancient" and "contemporary" research was an artifact of my own false assumption that villagers, too, had a largely antiquarian interest in these stories and stones. Gradually I realized that many of the factional disputes between rival chiefly houses and between high- and low-ranking villages were replaying patterns well documented in myths, chants, and narratives. I also incorrectly supposed that failure to explicitly mention or be actively interested in some archaic god, sacred stone, or ancient path of relationship implied that people were not engaged in constructing their social reality on the basis of these categories. But before I left the field, I had concluded that my ethnographic writing must first lay out these traditional lines of political tension and the general cultural principles for understanding the past before the contemporary scene could be described, while realizing that the two tasks would have to be closely intertwined.

So in addition to listening to stories, I also spent much time systematically exploring the territory of the district in search of abandoned village sites, stone remains, overgrown taro swamps, and paved paths. It was during a violent rain squall in 1978 that I first wandered into Ngerutechei, an abandoned village a short distance from Imeiong. Clusters of towering bamboo and betelnut trees lining the elevated stone path through the low-lying swampland marked the location of the site. Since on this initial visit I was traveling alone, I did not know the names of the house platforms, gravestones, and upright monoliths that I could detect beneath the underbrush. After making a sketch map of these various stoneworks, I retraced my steps and made my way out of the village. Crossing a tree-trunk bridge over the stream separating Ngerutechei from the hillside to the west, I climbed up the trail toward Imeiong until I reached a broad stone square named Chemeraech (Morning Star), a resting spot which affords a spectacular view of the terraced hillsides of Ingesachel and Uluang, the looming Roismlengui range, and the densely forested lowlands surrounding Ngerutechei.

My standard procedure on such hikes was to be as observant as I could and then, upon returning to Ngeremetengel village where I was living, to ask my friends what it was I had seen. On this particular occasion I asked about Ngerutechei, thinking that perhaps I could elicit some stories about the history of this place or even record genealogies of people who had lived there. To my surprise, my principal informant, a man originally from Imeiong now living at lower-ranking Ngeremetengel, told me that Ngerutechei was a "holy" (*chedaol*) village, that in ancient times a group of gods called the Ruchel met at a stone pavement named Uchuladebong (Origin Point from Which We Go Forth) and there distributed titles to the four chiefly houses of Imeiong, and that because of this the "sacredness" (*meang*) of all Belauan villages remains to this day in Imeiong. At first this seemed to be a strange claim, since Imeiong village is presently much smaller than Ngeremetengel, and the important chiefs of the district live in Ngeremetengel rather than in Imeiong. I was also informed that at the rocky peak of Roismlengui range, clearly visible on my walks, a goddess named Milad (Was Dead) landed after a great flood, and that she gave birth to four children in the form of stones at the foot of the mountain. These four children were to become "cornerposts" of the Belauan political order—in fact, Milad's eldest son was Imeiong, the capital of the district where I was living.

For two years I pursued these matters in greater depth, in order to find out what it meant to talk about the Ruchel gods, why they met at Ngerutechei, who the four chiefs were whose titles were instituted there, what kinds of political relations were entailed by the notion that the "sacred remains" at Imeiong, and what the link was between the four-part order established by Milad in the pan-Belauan context and the four-part order constituted by the Ruchel gods for Imeiong village. The sacred remains of Ngeremlengui include not just individual stones and stories, however; a entire political order gradually emerged from these studies. This polity organized interdistrict relations such as warfare and alliance and legitimized itself in myths about Milad. But this quadripartite political order was not the only one mentioned in the narratives I collected. An archaic order of villages founded by another goddess, Chuab, predated the era of Milad, and was based on a linear linkage, or "path," of villages located along the eastern side of the archipelago. I found these stories and associated lithic evidence fascinating, since standard ethnographic descriptions of Belauan polity mention, rather, a dualistic opposition between two federations combining, respectively, villages on the eastern and western coasts.

So, although my original intention was to write an ethnography about changes in the language of social relations and in the system of ceremonial exchanges among houses, I decided to complete *The Sacred Remains* first, since this study of myth, history, and polity is the necessary foundation for understanding events in the ethnographic present.

TOWARD AN ANTHROPOLOGY OF HISTORY

In grasping the importance of relating these stories and stones to contemporary political institutions and activities, I realized that the textual and lithic evidence I was assembling suggested the need for rethinking more generally the term "history" as an anthropological category. This section sketches the theoretical rationale for the semiotic framework used in the chapters which follow. I take history to be a universal cultural category differentially manifest in societies, in which the relationship between past, present, and future states of a society is expressed by signs in various media which are organized by locally valorized schemes of classification. This definition is designed to take advantage of the triple ambiguity of the English word "history," which can mean (1) what happened in the past, that is, historical *events;* (2) records from the past surviving into the present that are necessary for reconstructive knowledge, that is, historical *evidence;* and (3) narratives or other representational vehicles constructed in the present about the past, that is, historical *discourse.* This definition is also intended to open up three areas of discussion to cross-cultural understanding: (1) the different ways history is connected to notions of time, (2) the distribution within a given society of power to control the significance of events by creating or destroying historical evidence and by constructing historical discourse for specific ideological ends, and (3) the variety of representational media for coding historical consciousness.

Rather than setting up a rigid substantive definition of what history is, derived from our own scientific tradition, and taking that as the universal standard for labeling some societies as "without history," I am suggesting that what is needed is the ethnographic study of the modalities of history along the dimensions enumerated above. Essential to this enterprise is the assumption that historical consciousness is not a phenomenon restricted to observers or analysts, but is also an indigenous category relevant to the thoughts and actions of social actors that cannot be ignored even in the most objective external accounts of a society's past. As the American historian Becker points out,

> The actual event contributes something to the imagined picture; but the mind that holds the imagined picture always contributes something too. This is why there is no more fascinating or illuminating phase of history than historiography—the history of history: the history, that is, of what successive generations have imagined the past to be like. It is impossible to understand the history of certain great events without knowing what the actors in those events themselves thought about history. (Becker 1955:336)

But to this it is necessary to add that a culturally sensitive account of history must include not only the study of what "actors in those events" thought, but also how subsequent generations recorded, remembered, reconstructed, and reinterpreted what the original actors did or said.

I have specifically avoided using the term "ethnohistory" for this enterprise, for several related reasons.[1] It is unfortunate that, in contrast

1. See McBryde 1979 for an excellent survey of definitional and disciplinary aspects of ethnohistory.

to parallel forms such as ethnoastronomy and ethnobotany, the term ethnohistory does not normally indicate indigenous forms of knowledge, discourse, or social practice. In fact, the term is widely taken to mean exactly the opposite of an "emic" category, and in two distinct senses. On the one hand, some historians consider ethnohistory to be the utilization of oral traditions, rigorously filtered through the tests of source criticism and washed of ideological bias, as independent confirmation of the true historical record (see Cohn 1981:246): "And here the historian using oral traditions finds himself on exactly the same level as historians using other kinds of historical source material. No doubt he will arrive at a lower degree of probability than would otherwise be obtained, but that does not rule out the fact that what he is doing is valid, and that it is history" (Vansina 1965:186).[2] But in order for ethnohistorical material to be admitted as historical evidence, the poetic, stylistic, or semiotic constitution of these linguistic and nonlinguistic phenomena must be selectively deformed, and oral traditions in particular must be separated into myth and history (see MacGaffey 1978). On the other hand, ethnohistory is sometimes viewed as the history of the asymmetrical contact between societies that produce historical records and those that do not. For the Pacific historian Dening (1966:25), ethnohistory is "the description of illiterate societies by literate observers at the time when contact between the two had not changed or destroyed the illiterate society. On every continent this period of contact and change has been caught in the journals and letters of explorers, administrators, traders and missioners."[3] This view implies the additional assumption that contact situations are in principle distinct from the ways societies experience themselves through time in the absence of imposed, Western forces.

2. It is not the case that Vansina simply ignores the existence of history outside the world of the historian; in fact, he insists that such indigenous "historiology" must also be submitted to the tests of evidence: "It follows that oral traditions are not just a source about the past, but a historiology (one dare not write historiography!) of the past, an account of how people have interpreted it. As such oral tradition is not only a raw source. It is a hypothesis, similar to the historian's own interpretation of the past. Therefore oral traditions should be treated as hypotheses, and as the first hypothesis the modern scholar must test before he or she considers others. To consider them first means not to accept them literally, uncritically. It means to give them the attention they deserve, to take pains to prove or disprove them systematically for each case on its own merits" (Vansina 1985:196).

3. In his distinguished history of the Marquesas, Dening (1980:42) is just as adamant in rejecting the status of history as a cultural category: "The *historical* reality of traditional societies is locked together for the rest of time with the historical reality of the intruders who saw them, changed them, destroyed them. There *is* no history beyond the frontier, free of the contact that makes it."

I would rather rehabilitate the term "history" and stress that the inclusion of the intensions and intentionality of people who create and interpret their own past is essential, rather than supplementary, to adequate ethnographic study. And the fact that "history" would then label a cultural category as well as an established scholarly discipline should be an indication both that our own historical discourse participates in broader cultural principles and assumptions, and that the historical study of other cultures is always the study of historicizing activities within those cultures. That the discipline of anthropology has, in general, failed to recognize the cross-cultural relevance of history is strange, especially in light of the fact that many other familiar Western categories such as kinship, economics, and religion are all too frequently found fully instantiated in other societies. As Rosaldo points out,

> The anthropologist's failure even to perceive history in pre-agrarian societies is in part an artifact of synchronic analysis. But a more subtle factor has also influenced the received wisdom of anthropology, for certain theories have held that because so-called primitives lack Western historical consciousness they have none at all. The latter stance is curious in light of the anthropological insistence on the universality of such institutions as marriage, the family, and incest. Indeed, in many other cultural realms— including ideas of the person, shame, kinship, rites of passage, sacrifice, witchcraft, and religion—wide variations in form and content are acknowledged at the same time family resemblances across cultures are also recognised. Why should the sense of history be an exception to this general rule of anthropological analysis? (Rosaldo 1980:92)

Perhaps one reason for this situation is that, for many Western scholars, historical inquiry is in fact a quest to eradicate the confining influence of the past, or more generally, to insure our immunity from any form of culturally transmitted limits to individual perception and consumption (Gross 1981–82:66; Sahlins 1985b:52–53). Freedom becomes release from the past, as is argued by the British historian Plumb:

> Each one of us is an historical being, held in a pattern created by Time, and to be unconscious of our historical selves is fraught with dangers. History, however, is not the past. The past is always a created ideology with a purpose, designed to control individuals, or motivate societies, or inspire classes. Nothing has been so corruptly used as concepts of the past. *The future of history and historians is to cleanse the story of mankind from those deceiving visions of a purposeful*

past. The death of the past can only do good so long as history
flourishes. (Plumb 1971:17; emphasis added)

But even those who view the past as more than a "deceiving vision"
are prone to deny the existence of history outside of the Western tradition. One of the most blatant examples of this is the work of the philosopher Collingwood, who establishes on purely logical grounds what
history is, and then, not surprisingly, fails to find it instantiated in the
cultures of the world outside the Greco-Roman tradition. For Collingwood (1956:9–12), history is the inquiry into those actions performed
by human beings in the past of which we do not presently have adequate knowledge, by means of examination and interpretation of evidence existing in the present, for the purpose of self-knowledge. In
imposing this definition on the ancient Sumerian civilization, for example, he rules that their stelae and official inscriptions are not strictly
speaking historical, first, because these monuments and writings lack
the "character of science," and second, because the events recorded are
deeds of gods rather than men. Similarly, Roman pottery acquires historical character only because modern-day scholars use it as evidence in
scientific reconstruction (Collingwood 1965). So "history proper,"
that is, the rigorous rethinking in "incapsulated" manner of the purpos-
ive thoughts that produced evidence surviving from the past, did not
actually emerge until the twentieth century (Collingwood 1970:115–
16).

On the positive side, Collingwood's contribution is to have ex-
panded the range of evidence which can be used by historians in their
studies. He saw worth, for instance, not only in surviving written documents but also in artifactual and folkloristic remains. But since he refuses to see history as belonging to the consciousness and discourse of
social actors who create, modify, and invent these remains, this openness to anthropological evidence becomes merely a revival of the
Tylorian doctrine of "survivals," whereby evidence from "primitive
culture" is used by others for tracing the inevitable path of progressive
rationality.

The reason why anthropology is an important study for civilized
men is not, as might have been thought in the heyday of
imperialism, because civilized men have to rule over savages and
must learn, therefore, to understand them. It is because the
civilized man contains a savage within him, in the special sense in
which any historical present contains within itself its own past, and
must therefore study this savage—not savages in the abstract, but
the savage that he himself in this sense is—for the same reason for

which all history is studied, namely to make possible a rational human life in the present day. The problem of anthropology is a special case of the problem of self-knowledge; and history is the only way in which man can know himself. (Collingwood, in Van der Dussen 1981:186)

By restricting the sphere of historical thought to a reflexive modality of the present consciousness of people who did not create or preserve the original historical evidence or who are not part of an indigenous continuity of historical reconstruction, this approach clearly dismisses two of the most interesting problems in the study of other cultures: what kinds of categories operate in the cultural construction of history, and how historical knowledge is recorded, transmitted, and manipulated.

If Collingwood sees history as a form of reconstructive self-knowledge, yet refuses to admit the existence of such consciousness in the cultures of the world which do not share our scientific worldview, Lévi-Strauss's approach to the subject of history takes an inverse position, namely, of combining a sense of the relativity of scientific thinking with the exclusion of history from the set of possible forms of cultural categorization. Lévi-Strauss is primarily interested in discovering (some would say inventing) variations in cultural schemata which are unconscious structures revealed in the course of historical transformation. There is thus an implicit distinction between synchronic structures, that is, patterns which remain stable through time, and events, the "irreducible contingency of history," which impinge on these structures in the course of their contextual realization.

All systems, linguistic and otherwise, are in constant imbalance with themselves; this is the driving force of their internal dynamism. However, in my view, this is not exactly history, or at any rate not all history. It is the dimension that we call diachronic in our jargon, it has to do with the evolution of structures, and everybody accepts the existence of this dimension. But beyond this there is something else that we can never handle through reduction. History stands before us as something absolute before which we must bow. (Lévi-Strauss, in Lévi-Strauss, Augé, and Godelier 1976:50)

So although all structures are inherently synchronic, and "the degree of historicity" (Lévi-Strauss 1983:1218) confronting them is a constant, societies can be graded along a continuum according to the degree to which they remain impervious to the singularities of causal conjunction or else interiorize history as "the motive power of their development" (Lévi-Strauss, in Charbonnier 1969:39; cf. Friedman 1985). The former "cold" societies, exemplified in the so-called totemic groups of aboriginal Australia, deny the cumulative effect of historical contingency by applying atemporal, static, or cyclical forms of classification— though Lévi-Strauss does claim that these societies value the past as the template for understanding the present. The latter "hot" societies explain themselves as the product of cumulative, evolutionary processes by means of cultural codes such as calendars anchored in the linearity of absolute chronology (Lévi-Strauss 1966:258).

As should be apparent from this sketch of his position, Lévi-Strauss makes two contradictory analytical divisions, the first between classification as a universal cultural propensity and history as the residual, acultural facticity of social phenomena; and the second between atemporal and temporal types of intensional categorization of this first distinction, that is, myth and history as two ways of looking at the past (see Beidelman 1971).[4] I think that this confusion is indicative of a more fundamental problem concerning the relationship between cultural schemata and their social implementation. For Lévi-Strauss, it seems that classificatory schemata categorize some "stuff" which is itself irrelevant as far as anthropological analysis is concerned. That is, the events, words, and practices so organized are necessary to the contextual realization of the "savage mind" in us all, but these manifestations are merely the meaningless content of synchronic, paradigmatic principles. But additionally, cultural schemata are implicit, unconscious structures not subject to valuation by actors operating according to their dictates. Conscious models born of actors' intentional awareness are dismissed as ideological smokescreens blocking analytical penetration.

In contrast, the argument advanced in this book depends on seeing, first, that cultural patterns in Belau classify tokens which themselves have important contextual meanings that are grounded in their indexical properties and realized in social processes; and second, that classificatory models do acquire symbolic valuation, so that their application or instantiation in a given instance can have strategic or rhetorical effect. To put it simply, adequate anthropological analysis requires locating the reciprocal meaningfulness of abstract schemata and their contextual content.

---

4. Lévi-Strauss also wants to argue that history, considered now as a form of analytical discourse, functions as a modern mythology in that it locates events in a "natural" order of things (see White 1975:51).

SIGNS OF HISTORY, SIGNS IN HISTORY

In particular, this book tries to understand the eventfulness of Belauan culture precisely as one of its intrinsic qualities and, in so doing, looks for modalities of history in signs other than strictly linguistic ones. For Belau, as well as for other cultures, the investigation of the coding of historicity is a matter of studying classes of signs—physically manifested vehicles that bear culturally endowed meaning. Signs function in two ways: as *signs of history* and as *signs in history*. Here the expression signs of history refers to representational expressions which, through their iconic, indexical, and residually symbolic properties, record and classify events as history, that selective discourse about the diachrony of a society. These signs of history can originate either in the spatiotemporal context of the events to which they refer or, at any later time, as the self-conscious reconstruction of the past. Duby (1980:8–9) illustrates a clear example of the former case in medieval Europe: "They would carefully save some object that, during the rites of investiture, one hand had placed in another . . . to signify the transmission of a right—such as those boughs, knives and rocks occasionally found in the archives attached to some parchment . . . , the object appearing as a more appropriate commemorative monument than the written word to a world that could neither read nor understand Latin." The "aura" (Benjamin 1968:221) derived from their contiguity with the original ritual context makes these objects appropriate signs of history.[5] These signs signal that some event of note occurred but do not offer any intensional description or categorization of what kinds of events, actors, or processes are at issue (White 1972:9). This is the primary function of the second variety of signs of history, for example, the composition of an epic poem depicting events from earlier centuries or the minting of a postage stamp commemorating the centennial of a famous person's birth or death.[6] In both of these varieties, the importance of the sign lies more in the value of what it represents than in the material quality of the signifying vehicle.

And the phrase signs in history refers to those signs of history which,

---

5. C. S. Peirce (1977:35) calls these historical signs "vestiges" and points out that these objects (e.g., the "boughs, knives and rocks" of the example above) not only carry meaning derived from their context-specific origins but also come to take on the character of resembling some quality or feeling associated with the events in question.

6. I note with sorrow a report in the *New York Times* (1 September 1986) of the minting in Belau of a postage stamp as a memorial to Haruo Remeliik, the assassinated president of the Republic of Belau.

as objects, linguistic expressions, or patterns of action, themselves become involved in social life as loci of historical intentionality *because* of their function as representational vehicles. These objects are frequently considered to be concrete embodiments or repositories of the past they record, that is, to be endowed with the essentialized or reified property of historicity. In our own tradition, the distinction between signs of history and signs in history is syncretized only in special contexts. Imagine a struggle between bureaucrats of New York and Philadelphia over ownership of the original copy of the Declaration of Independence. In these rare or marked cases, social action focuses on an object whose value derives from its function as being itself a token embodiment of historical discourse. In general, we tend to carefully preserve our signs of history, especially those of the first type, by putting them in hermetically sealed environments—time capsules, archival vaults, guarded museums—so that future events or generations cannot intentionally or unintentionally change their physical shape. In a sense, their indexical quality of being derived from the context of past events is maintained as emblematic of historicity only through the preservation of their semiotic form in a decontextualized environment; so formal stability guarantees their continued legitimacy as authentic signs of history.

But in Belau and in many preliterate societies, signs of history are frequently at the same time signs in history. That is, they are extensionally deployed in social action, and by encoding the layered course of historical change they make possible an intensional sense of cultural continuity through time. When functioning as historical signs, several kinds of objects and expressions are labeled by the general ethnosemiotic term *olangch,* "external sign" or "mnemonic marker." These include carved narrative pictures, named ceramic and glass valuables, anthropomorphic monoliths, prescribed seating patterns, names and titles, ceremonial protocols, stone grave pavements, and oral narratives. Skill at reading signs is divided into two arts, the first involving knowledge of "external signs" (*olangch*) and the second involving predictive interpretations of "prophetic signs" or "portents" (*ulauch*). An informant clarified these two terms by distinguishing the epistemic status of their respective signifieds. For *olangch* we already know what it stands for; for example, a drawing of a boat stands for the boat itself, which is something we know clearly; similarly, a chief's personal hammered turtleshell piece (*cheluib*) is the *olangch* of his good faith and can be used as a pledge for a financial loan. *Ulauch,* on the other hand, are secret and represent things which might be the case: "We wait for it to occur, and when it occurs we say 'so there!' The words of a person are the *olangch* of his thoughts, not the *ulauch*." Not only do these signs code historical events, but they can also come to play a vital role in social action, because they are constantly modified, manipulated, contested, and concealed. There is, in other words, a constant interplay between the "sedimenting" power of contexts of action and the "typifying" function of historicizing representation; and it is this dialectical reconstruction that I mean when I refer to history as a cultural category.

A famous comparative example of this latter syncretic pattern is the Golden Stool of the Ashanti people of Africa described by Rattray (1923:287–93) and Fortes (1969:138–91). When it "descended from heaven" amidst celestial rumbling and dark clouds during the reign of the fourth Ashanti king around 1700, the Golden Stool was pronounced by the king's high priest to represent the "soul" of the nation. The stool was then endowed with historicizing function by the practice of adding various objects to it. When it first descended to earth, the king affixed four bells to the sides; then chiefs and members of royalty removed body hair and fingernail fragments, which were made into a paste that was smeared directly on the stool. During the reign of the tenth king additional regalia were attached to the Golden Stool. And then later, after a pivotal battle, golden masks formed from the stool of the defeated chief were hung on the sides. Representing the permanence and continuity of the Ashanti as a nation, the Golden Stool also indexed the historical depth of the chiefly line. Lineage stools functioned as signs in history as well.[7] Carried in ritual, anointed with sacrificial blood, and guarded in consecrated houses, these stools symbolized the juropolitical constitution of the Ashanti lineage system and marked the genealogical legitimacy of succession to lineage headship.

A second illustration of the link between signs of history and signs in history comes from Tahiti, where a system of elevated stone pavements called *marae* served as local ancestral temples and as centers of cultic worship. The iconic linkage between segments of localized ramages and these *marae* structures is analogous to the system of lineage shrines described by Fortes for the Tallensi. As Sahlins (1958:165) describes the Tahitian case:

> The ramage system was reflected in the system of ancestral temples (*marae*). Each family had a temple. The largest temple in a district, that of the senior family, was considered the parent temple from

7. The British learned this in 1900 when the Ashanti silently prepared for war after Sir Frederic Hodgson reportedly said, "Why am I not sitting on the Golden Stool at this very moment?"

which the others branched off. . . . When a household divided and
lands were partitioned, a stone from the old temple was used as a
cornerstone for the new. The latter was reconsecrated to the same
god as the old, while the head of the segmenting group took an
hereditary title associated with the older temple.

This practice of actually removing a piece of the stone foundation to
mark ramage segmentation is also found in the expansion of religious
cults from one island to another. At the ancient cultic center of Taputapuatea on the island of Ra'iatea, eight boulders representing eight
chiefs who ruled the land stood at the *marae*. Called "stone memorials
of kings," these pillars were lined up in squares parallel to the main
structure. Together these stones iconically represent the linkage between political segments. Their historicizing function was noted by the
missionary Orsmond (in Henry 1928:135), who observed simply,
"Several squares were thus sometimes formed showing the antiquity of
the *marae*." And when the cult dedicated to the god Oro spread from
the western portion of the group of islands to the large island Tahiti, a
stone was taken from the religious center at Ra'iatea to be the cornerstone of the new *marae,* also called Taputapuatea, which Captain
Cook visited in 1777.

   In each of these ethnographic examples, physical objects, rather than
linguistic discourse, function as both signs of history and signs in history. Furthermore, both examples illustrate the important point, stressed
especially by Prague School theorists, that synchronically manifested
signs can represent the sedimentation of diachronic processes. But in
addition to linguistic and material signs, history can be recorded by the
structure of society itself, as Fortes (1945:224) so elegantly demonstrates in his work on Tallensi clanship: "We see how the lineage structure at a given time incapsulates all that is structurally relevant of its past
phases and at the same time continually thrusts its growing-points forward." In this passage Fortes moves significantly beyond Evans-Pritchard's earlier effort to define the relationship between temporality
and the interaction of social groups for the Nuer. For Evans-Pritchard,
certain sets of social relations such as age sets and lineage segments
provide a convenient reference point for the Nuer's concept of "structural time," just as the cyclic movements of nature provide a reference
point for "oecological time" (1940:95). But Fortes notes that structures of social relations are not just reference points for some previously
defined notion of time but are the "incapsulating" signs of history that
code a definite kind of temporality.

   And it is here that we encounter a central concern of Belauan history as well, that continuity, permanence, and invariance are a principal modality of the society's—or at least the dominant segment of the society's—understanding of the relationship between event and structure. In our own notion of history, the focus is frequently on the efficient causality of events in transforming society from state A to state B (Benjamin 1968:263); on the representational transparency between historical discourse and "real" depicted events (Barthes 1986:138–39); and on the relative position of events along an absolute linear framework of temporality, a continuum itself external to the events so categorized, which are thought to be "in time" (Collingwood 1926:150). The problematic of Belauan history is different: how can events, with their context-dependent and pragmatically valued quality, be recorded so that, on the one hand, the structure of society—in particular the hierarchical arrangement of its parts—can be invariantly reproduced, and so that, on the other hand, this repeated structure gains value from the cumulative weight of layered events. In other words, the trick of history is to maintain both the invariance of structure (for example, that the position of the capital village in a district is a matter of timeless, cosmologically grounded legitimacy), and the value of temporal precedence (for example, that the chiefly line traces its migration back to a point prior to that of other, lower-ranking lines). As will become clear, these two dimensions are played out rhetorically and politically in instances of Belauan historical discourse.

THE CLOSELY GUARDED STORY OF NGEREMLENGUI

The present volume is in part an attempt to understand a single sign of history, namely, a text recorded in the Belauan language in 1971 as part of the historical research program conducted by staff members of the Palau Community Action Agency (PCAA, Ngeremlengui File). This document summarizes the position of Ngeremlengui in Belauan polity and links certain customary practices and concepts to the social changes of the modern period. Since the narrator of this text became, seventeen years later, my principal informant, I was in a position to return to it again and again over the course of my two years in the field. Now I do not believe that a single document can be said to encapsulate the essence of a culture, a village, or even an individual, but it proved to be such a powerful source of insight and puzzlement for me that it can function also as the stepping-off place for the ethnographic analyses of this book.

The story of Ngeremlengui has been closely guarded, since the old
people told us: do not discuss the internal affairs of the village, for
then every village would know it. Ngeremlengui is a district
composed of thirty-eight villages. When all these villages are
combined together we call it Kerngilianged (Dwelling As In
Heaven). Kerngilianged refers to all the villages combined
together, and it implies that they are all of one spirit, and that these
villages share common laws which were instituted by [the goddess]
Milad and by the Ruchel [messenger gods].

I too have guarded the story of this village, but I can no longer
keep it concealed because we are now recording Belauan stories.
Today we are approaching the final turning point for this village,
so now I can inform others about Ngeremlengui.

The reason that Ngeremlengui has been at peace up until the
present day is that we have never discarded these laws, for we know
that the sacredness of Melekeok, Oreor, and Imiungs remains here
in this village. That is, we obey the person who carries the position
of leadership, and we also remind him of those things which are
mistaken with reference to our human existence. But today the
things that are going wrong stem from this very point: the most
important factor which keeps this village at peace and harmony is
that we do not respect high-ranking people or brave people.
Rather, we hold the greatest respect for the sacredness which is in
the village, and this is the very same respect we hold for the general
public of Ngeremlengui. No matter how far away we go, we will
still respect it because this sacredness is the real original cause for
the life of this village and for proper behavior in it. But it is very
difficult to conceal something which a person does not know
about, since no one ever told him so he could possibly know about
it. They just locked it up. This was not a lie, though, for they
knew: keeping the village together begins with respect.

Our primary respect is for the public, because we know that the
sacredness of Melekeok, Oreor, and Imiungs are all located here.
So we address the four leaders of Ngaraimeiong council [in
Imeiong village] as Chuong (Respected), since they are to be
greatly respected. And here [in Imeiong] there are no female
titleholders but rather the wives of the [male] titleholders are to be
respected. When these four wives of the Chuong are gathered
together, the senior women from Ngerturong house or the senior
women from Klang house will guard the seats where they are
sitting, for this is something which was pronounced by the Ruchel
[gods]. The Ruchel declared these wives of the Chuong to be
taboo and their every need will be seen to by the senior women.

This is something which has been cherished up until the present day.

Something else which really makes this village well behaved is the law of marriage, whereby a low-ranking person is permitted to become the spouse of one of these Chuong titleholders. When a child from one of the Edeuteliang (Three at the Other End) villages is born, they instruct her: if you are well behaved, you can become the wife of a Chuong. The significance of this is that, should she become the wife of a Chuong, then she would also become respected. They also instruct the children: the important thing is not just that you marry into Imeiong but that we all become thereby respected.

Now you have no doubt heard it said that this word *kuoll* (to be respected) is an expression which no longer has any significance. But when we respect the public, then we will respect the households and the children. You absolutely cannot scold a child or step over a sleeping child, since you do not know if this child will come to have sacredness or not. And those people who speak for the village should be obeyed, for the people know that sacredness has fallen upon a person who speaks for the village. And those speaking for the village who follow their own will in respect to this law will always be brought to ruin, or else they will fall from the office which concerned this very sacredness, about which they exercised their own personal judgment.

And Ngeremlengui does not stand alone, for we also respect the two other sacrednesses [of Melekeok and Oreor], which are united with the sacredness of Ngeremlengui. And these villages and the people in them know that their sacredness remains (*meang a medechel*) in Ngeremlengui, and should there be a violation they will be cursed by their own sacredness. This does not imply, then, that Imiungs will be cursed. Rather, the village that violates the sacredness itself will be cursed. If this principle is rejected, it is not the words of the people of Imiungs that are being rejected.

I truly believe that this sacredness really exists. And I truly believe these stories and have thought very carefully about what I have just spoken. (PCAA, Ngeremlengui File; my translation)

Clearly for this narrator, the telling of this story for the record is no simple recitation of historical recollections but is itself a sign of an important transition in Ngeremlengui's relationship with the changing Belauan political world.[8] This narrative is thus a directional marker

8. Cf. the remarkable indigenous account by a Fijian chief of the principles of that society's "custom," in Milner 1952:351–61.

(*olangch*) by which we can set our path through the complexities of the district's history: rank, respect, and sacredness; titleholders, leaders, and senior women; districts, villages, and houses; Imiungs, Melekeok, and Oreor; Kerngilianged, Ngeremlengui, and the Edeuteliang; Milad and the Ruchel gods—these will be our guideposts in the task of unraveling the meaning of the sacred remains.

The chapters that follow take up these and other themes relating to the issues of signs and history, events and structures, stories and stones. The order of chapters is designed to be a demonstration of the importance of uncovering indigenous categories of history: many of the same topics are covered twice, first from the perspective of externally imposed categories and second from various perspectives internal to Belauan culture. In chapter 1, Belau is situated in terms of the Pacific geographical context, the Austronesian cultural context, and the Western historical context. Chapter 2 continues this contextualization by synthesizing ethnographic material about traditional political institutions, including the organization of villages and districts, the functioning of titled chiefs and their political councils, and the manipulation of valuables in intervillage activities involving warfare, concubinage and collection ceremonies. Chapter 3 marks a turn toward analyzing Belauan historical categories and presents a detailed account of the relationship between four models or diagrams (to use the convenient Peircean vocabulary) which organize social relations, namely, "paths" linking elements in a linear order, "cornerposts" joining four terms in a coordinated structure, balanced "sides" combining similar, yet opposed, members of symmetrical pairs, and "large/small" gradations placing elements in hierarchically ranked series. The cultural understanding of these four diagrams reached in chapter 3 is then explored in greater depth in the next three chapters. Chapter 4 links three of these diagrams to mythological narratives about the transformation of Belauan polity: the progression of political eras, such as the "polity of Chuab" and the "polity of Milad" noted above, as well as a third era based on an ideology of two "sides of heaven" factions, is shown to correspond to the rhetorical application of models of paths, cornerposts, and sides. Chapter 5 is a case study of the political organization of Ngeremlengui district, in which the ranked relationship between capital village and member village turns out to correspond to the differential valuation of these same cultural diagrams, with the high-ranking village stressing the quadripartite order and lower-ranking villages the linear model of paths. Implications of this distinction in political rank are discussed again in chapter 6, where contrasting narratives of village foundation are analyzed. Rather than reducing narrative variants to arrive at a neutral account of district history, chapter 6 shows how different positions in rank correspond to different narrative strategies. Finally, chapter 7 deals with narratives and explications of a complex sequence of events in which all these models, institutions, and principles are played out in the context of interdistrict political relations among Belau's capital villages.

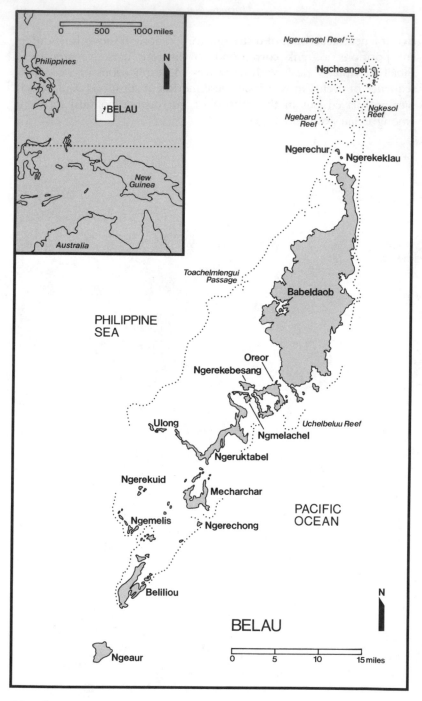

MAP 1

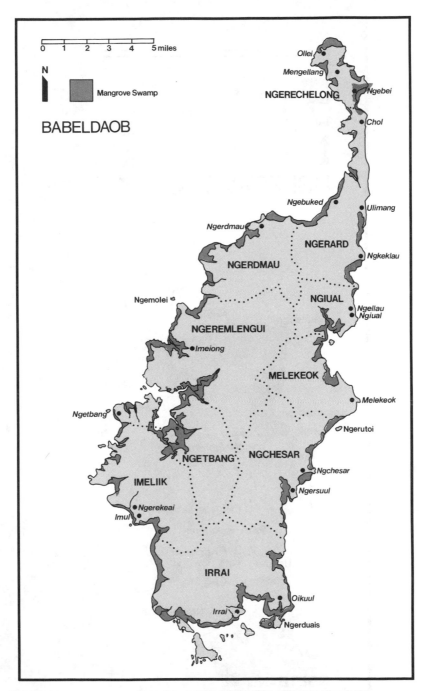

0 1 2 3 4 5 miles

N

Mangrove Swamp

BABELDAOB

Ollei
Mengellang
NGERECHELONG
Ngebei
Chol

Ngebuked
Ulimang
Ngerdmau
NGERARD
NGERDMAU
Ngkeklau
Ngemolei
NGIUAL
Ngellau
Ngiual
NGEREMLENGUI
Imeiong
MELEKEOK
Melekeok
Ngetbang
Ngerutoi
NGETBANG
NGCHESAR
IMELIIK
Ngchesar
Ngersuul
Ngerekeai
Imul
IRRAI
Oikuul
Irrai
Ngerduais

MAP 2

MAP 3

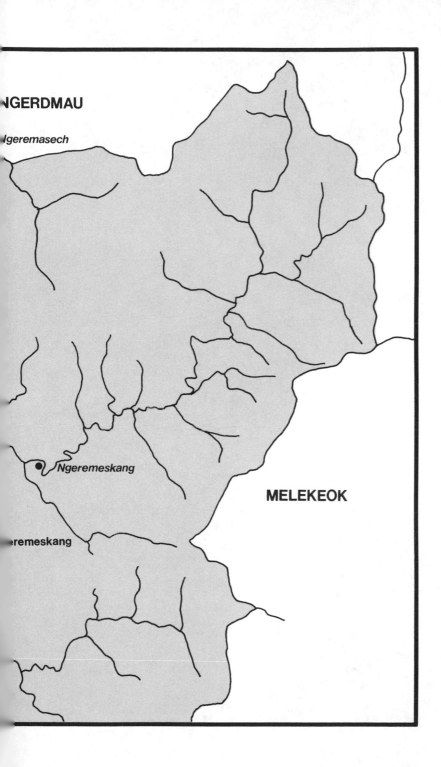

NGERDMAU

Ngeremasech

● *Ngeremeskang*

eremeskang

MELEKEOK

CHAPTER

1

Contexts of Belau

This chapter establishes the ethnographic and historical context for subsequent analyses of Belauan mythology, history, and political organization. Three complementary sections each look at Belau from a different perspective. The first section reviews the archipelago's position in
the Pacific geographical context, with brief consideration of geo-
morphology, resources, and climate. The discussion then turns to the
connection between certain aspects of Belau and related Austronesian
cultures that have been useful in charting the islands' settlement history.
As the data presented in these two sections show, Belau seems to occupy a cultural niche mediating between island Southeast Asia to the
west and Oceania proper to the east. Finally, the history of contact with
Western explorers, traders, missionaries, soldiers, and colonial administrators is rapidly sketched. None of these sections is intended to be
comprehensive, and the information reported and concepts utilized are
largely derived from Western sources, a bias which holds to some degree in the next chapter as well. Subsequent chapters reverse this general orientation and focus on presenting indigenous understandings of
history and political organization.

PACIFIC GEOGRAPHICAL CONTEXT

Belau is an Austronesian culture occupying an archipelago of more than
two hundred islands in the extreme western corner of the Pacific Ocean
between 6 and 8 degrees north latitude and 134 and 135 degrees east
longitude. Stretching approximately 125 miles along a northeast-to-
southwest axis, the archipelago represents the exposed crest of the
Palau-Kyushu Ridge. Belau is the westernmost island group of the Caroline Islands, one of four conventionally applied divisions of Microne-

sia (Alkire 1977:2). The Marianas, Yap, and Belau constitute the islands of Western Micronesia, since they appear to have been settled directly from island Southeast Asia, in contrast to the other Micronesian islands in the Carolines, Marshalls, and Gilberts (Kiribati), which were populated by people sailing north and west from Melanesia. The archipelago's geographical isolation—with the nearest large land masses being Mindanao (approximately 550 miles to the west), New Guinea (600 miles to the south), and Guam (725 miles to the northeast)—is countered by its cultural centrality, since it is surrounded by disparate Indo-Pacific cultures located in the Philippines, northern Indonesia (Halmahera), western New Guinea (West Papua), and Micronesia (Yap). Evidence from archaeology, comparative linguistics, and ethnography suggests that the Austronesian culture of Belau derived from multiple sources and that it developed its distinctive shape over one or perhaps two millennia of relative isolation. The islands themselves display a range of geological types and ecological conditions, from high volcanic islands such as Babeldaob and Ngerekebesang, high limestone islands such as Ngeruktabel and Iilmalk, platform limestone islands such as Beliliou and Ngeaur, small reef islands such as Ngemelis and Ngerechong, and low atolls such as Ngcheangel and (now submerged) Ngeruangel (see map 1). Babeldaob, the largest high island of the group, covers approximately 140 square miles. Like other islands west of the andesite line marking the end of primarily continental rock types (Thomas 1968:9), Babeldaob shows great diversity of ecological zones, from heavily wooded central mountains, to rolling hillsides covered with weathered volcanic breccia and infertile soil supporting only sparse vegetation, to alluvial flats where numerous mineral-rich rivers flow into lagoons and bays. Rich in water for irrigating taro swamps, in wood for house construction and fuel, in stone for platforms and roads, and in clay for pottery making, Babeldaob contrasts sharply with the ecologically poorer rock islands in the central zone, which have no large rivers, no clay, and little flat land for agriculture and residence.

The barrier reef which encircles most of the archipelago nourishes plentiful marine resources in the lagoons and limits the entrance of ships to a few channel openings such as Toachelmlengui, in front of Ngeremlengui district, and Toachelmid, leading to Oreor, contemporary Belau's most populous village. The difficulty in finding clear passage to Babeldaob was probably a factor in routing arriving canoes and ships to the islands of Ngeaur, Beliliou, Oreor, and Ngcheangel.

The climate of Belau is tropical, with humidity constant around 80 percent, mean temperature at 81 degrees, and rainfall ranging from 126 inches per year at Ngeaur to 168 inches on central Babeldaob. The seasonal shift from summer westerly-to-southwesterly monsoons and winter easterly-to-northeasterly trades is recorded in the traditional calendrical system as the alternation of the "year of west wind" (*rekil a ngebard*) and the "year of east wind" (*rekil a ongos*), each season lasting approximately six lunar months.[1] Because this wind shift cuts across the general north-to-south axis of the main island Babeldaob, villages on the east coast (*desbedall*) and villages on the west coast (*kiukl*) experience different tides, sea swells, rains, and winds, all influencing fishing and other subsistence activities. The year of west wind corresponds roughly to the months of May through October, with heaviest rainfall reported from July to August; the year of east wind corresponds to the months of November through April, with lowest rainfall reported for the period from February to April.

These daily constants of temperature, rainfall, and humidity and the seasonal alternation of winds are interrupted by devastating typhoons which regularly pass near the islands. Extensive damage to houses, boats, and farms is reported for 1862, 1866, 1868–69, 1906, 1912, 1919, 1927, 1928, 1965, and 1967. Traditions also mention a typhoon or tidal wave which "simultaneously" destroyed the reef islands of Uchelbeluu (east of Oreor) and Ngibtal (off the east coast of Babeldaob), as well as the now-submerged atoll of Ngeruangel (northwest of Ngcheangel). People from these three islands are said to have escaped the inundation of their homelands and to have sought refuge in various villages on Babeldaob and Oreor, where they established a network of high-ranking, wealthy houses which still dominate social life (Takayama 1979).

AUSTRONESIAN CULTURAL CONTEXT

In light of Belau's strategic position at the crossroads of several Austronesian cultural traditions or as the "stepping stone" into the Pacific (Osborne 1958), and in view of the evidently perplexing quality of the prehistoric data discovered thus far, it is understandable that students of Belau—and I am no exception—find it difficult to resist speculating on the significance of their research for broader comparative questions. It is not within the scope of this book to consider in detail the evidence, arguments, and conclusions of specialized investigations in archae-

---

1. Sources differ in assigning Western months to the Belauan calendar; see Klee 1976:240; Osborne 1966:14; Krämer 1917–29, 3:323–26. The interrelationship between wind direction and rainfall is clear from the climatic table in Palau District Planning Office 1977:11.

ology, comparative linguistics, and physical anthropology, but it is
hoped that some of the ethnographic analyses presented here may contribute to this overall enterprise. A few general observations about
Belau's position in the Austronesian context are in order, then, as an
introduction to some of the specific analytical questions addressed in
later chapters.

According to the prehistorian Bellwood (1983), the origin of Austronesian peoples of the Indo-Pacific world lies with rice-cultivating,
megalithic societies of Southeast Asia. The people that gradually ex-
panded into the Pacific were expert seafarers and pottery makers and
lived in societies with systems of social stratification based on fraternal
rank: "Thus, by 5500 years ago expansion had taken place from the rice
cultures of southern China into Taiwan, by 5000 years ago it had continued into the Philippines, and central Indonesia was perhaps well-
settled by 4000 years ago. By 3000 years ago the expansion had reached
Malaya at one extreme, Samoa at the other, and by 1500 years ago
Madagascar and Easter Island—210 degrees of longitude apart" (Bellwood 1983:80). Bellwood's map charting this expansion of Austronesian settlement labels the Western Micronesia area at 4000–3000 years
B.P. (cf. Golson 1972:18). These dates have to some extent been confirmed by archaeological research. Carbon 14 dating clearly places the
settlement of Western Micronesia not later than the first or second millennium B.C.: Tarague, Guam: 1455 ± 70 B.C. (Kurashina et al.
1981:66); Rota: 640 ± 85 B.C. (Oda 1981:123, citing Takayama);
Pemrang, Yap: 360 ± 80 B.C. (Takayama 1982b:91); Ngcheangel,
Belau: A.D. 40 ± 70 (Takayama 1981:88); and Ngulu: A.D. 190 ± 80
(Intoh 1981:77).

The distinction between Babeldaob and the rock islands has more
than geological significance, because local traditions, as well as archaeological evidence, point to a general cultural drift from the southern
islands of the "lower sea" (*eou el daob*) to the larger northern islands of
the "upper sea" (*bab el daob*). Myths frequently place the origin or invention of customary practices, subsistence patterns, or social groups in
the lower sea. These stories trace the migration of individual families
and entire villages from sites in the rock islands, Ngeaur, and Beliliou to
villages on Babeldaob, Oreor, and Ngerekebesang, many of which
came to have village names, chiefly titles, local deities, and tabooed
species associated with the original sites. This evidence also suggests,
however, that the region of the lower sea and the region of the upper
sea were in continuous contact—through reverse migration, trade in
pottery and valuables, and warfare—for an undetermined period
culminating in the final abandonment of most rock island villages sever-

al centuries prior to Western contact (Osborne 1979:235–41; Takayama 1979).[2]

The settlement history revealed by recent archaeological research appears, however, to be more complex than this simple south-to-north movement. According to the tentative synthesis proposed by Masse, Snyder, and Gumerman (1984), there is a puzzling temporal and spatial discontinuity between the radiocarbon dates from the extensive terraces found on the high islands (A.D. 200–1200) and from sites of historically attested village complexes on these same islands (from A.D. 1500) (cf. Lucking 1984:160). Evidence that major rock island village sites have dates falling roughly between these two periods (i.e., A.D. 1200–1600)[3] leads to the hypothesis that there have been two major internal population movements, the first from the high islands to the rock islands at the end of a period of agricultural intensification around 1200, and the second from the rock islands back to villages on Babeldaob and Oreor during the sixteenth and seventeenth centuries. Curiously, while the migrations of this second movement are well recorded in Belauan narratives (some of which are analyzed in later chapters), there are no extant traditions describing the abandonment of terraced villages for southern rock island sites (Krämer 1917–29, 2:5–8; Osborne 1966:425).

It is not known whether the original Austronesian settlers established themselves on the relatively inhospitable islands of the lower sea or on the more fertile sites of the upper sea, or if these first settlers came from ancestral high or low islands.[4] And there is no published evidence

2. The frequently made claim that the rock islands were universally abandoned prior to 1783 needs slight modification in light of the report of John Duncan, who accompanied Oreor's war party against Beliliou. Duncan notes (in Keate 1788:202) that the warriors attacked an occupied but unnamed island between Ulong and Beliliou, burning down the houses and destroying taro gardens and coconut trees.

3. Masse, Snyder, and Gumerman (1984:117) summarize their speculations as follows: "The reasons for both the establishment and the eventual abandonment of the villages in the rock islands between Oreor and Beliliou are poorly understood. Palauan legends indicate that warfare among the rock island villages and between the rock islands and the volcanic islands was endemic during this period. Certainly the seemingly defensive posture of the rock island villages lends support to these oral traditions. Both warfare and starvation are mentioned in the legends as contributing to the abandonment of the rock island villages, but these hypotheses have yet to be tested archaeologically."

4. Takayama (1979:94–95; cf. 1982b:96) concludes that the evidence for Belau does not support Goodenough's (1957) generalization that first settlers came to high islands before low islands because of their richer resources. His uncertainty is revealed in the following summary: "In theory, it may be safe to assume that the initial colonisers, possible agriculturalists with pottery, came to the Palaus from an unknown homeland at an undetermined date." Cf. Alkire 1984:10 n. 1; Kurashina and Clayshulte 1983:120.

from archaeology, linguistics, or ethnography that a hunter-gatherer population occupied the islands prior to the arrival of Austronesian-speaking horticulturalists. In this respect, Belau resembles Oceanic islands to the east rather than island Southeast Asia to the west, where groups such as the Negritos of Luzon and the Semang of Malaysia were established millennia prior to the Austronesian migration.

A problem which immediately arises is that historical and ethnographic evidence cannot be assumed to be directly comparable to an original Belauan culture. The Belau observed by the crew of the *Antelope*, which ran aground at the reef near Ulong island in 1783, was already very different from the picture which emerges through archaeological study. First, as has been noted, most rock island villages had been abandoned by the time of contact, and the bulk of the people, population estimates of which range from Semper's (1982:290) guess of 40,000 to Krämer's (1917–29, 2:291–96) more conservative estimate of 20,000, resided on Babeldaob. Since the first complete survey of villages was completed by Krämer in 1910, over a century after Captain Wilson's visit in the *Antelope* and after massive depopulation, it is impossible to tell how many of the 151 villages listed as extinct were also uninhabited in 1783. Second, by the time of contact, two of the most visually spectacular features of the landscape, terraced hillsides and megalithic constructions, had become inexplicable reminders of the past for both Belauans and Westerners.

Babeldaob and several neighboring high islands are dotted with extensive, man-made terraces situated on mountain slopes and coastal hillsides (e.g., Osborne 1966:157, fig. 49). Of unknown function and antiquity, these terraces have puzzled foreign observers for over a century. One of the earliest references is a journal entry by Andrew Cheyne, a trader who lived in the islands in the mid-nineteenth century.

> All the hills of the Pelew Islands that are clear of timber are terraced and crowned with a square fort, having a deep and wide ditch round it, evidently done by the hands of another race— probably Chinese—long ago exterminated by the savage invaders who now occupy the soil. The Pelew Islanders when questioned about the terraced hills and forts say it was either done by the gods, or by the sea at the flood. (Cheyne 1863–66: 29 June 1864)

Cheyne's assumption that those terraces topped with what Osborne has termed "crown and brim" earthworks were defensive structures suggests parallels with the forts of New Zealand and the artificial hilltops of Rapa Iti in Polynesia (Bellwood 1979:406–413; Davidson 1985:269, fig. 5.9; Heyerdahl 1958:336; Yawata 1930). But if the terraces were constructed for defensive purposes, it is curious that folklore, while replete with detailed accounts of warfare, does not mention their strategic use. Also, the design of many of the terraces seems to facilitate, rather than impede, access to the top. Furthermore, this hypothesis cannot help to explain the existence of elongated, stepped terraces without crowns. Krämer echoes Cheyne's inquiry into the terraces: "The natives deny that the shape of the mountains is the result of artificial construction. They say that the elevations are what remained after the great flood and that this explains the terraced formation. I have seen similar formations on the east coast of New Ireland, which for want of time I did not inspect" (Krämer 1917–29, 2:238–39). This association of the terraces with a great flood, mentioned by both Cheyne and Krämer, is an allusion to the story of Milad (see chapter 4) in which a massive inundation of Babeldaob marks the transformation of Belau's political organization.

An alternative hypothesis, evaluated in detail by Osborne (1966: 152–55) and Lucking (1984:163), is that the terraces were primarily agricultural, and that their construction was perhaps the result of the inability of lowland taro swamps to sustain a growing population or massive immigration.[5] But the absence of evident irrigation works and the fact that the available planting areas are composed of latosols, which rapidly become infertile, make this alternative as problematic as the defensive one. And the obvious solution that the elongated, back-slanting terraces are ancient rice terraces like those found in northern Luzon is countered by the fact that there is no evidence of prehistoric rice cultivation in Belau, in contrast to the case throughout Indonesia, the Philippines, and perhaps the Marianas.[6] The staple crop most frequently mentioned in folklore is wetland taro (*Colocasia esculenta*), which is grown today, as in ancient times, in alluvial swamps and is still the most important ceremonial-exchange food (McKnight and Obak 1960; Sproat 1968; Vessel and Simonson 1958).

A final theory, that the terraces were ancient village sites, is supported by Yawata (1930) on the grounds that their sheer size is disproportional with their being only temporary fortifications, and that traditions describe stone carvings now standing in modern villages as having been brought from these elevated village sites. But given that

5. On the general problem of terraces see Spencer and Hale 1961; Wheatley 1965; for a discussion of taro cultivation see Spriggs 1982.

6. On this question see Osborne 1966:155; Spencer 1963; Craib and Farrell 1981. The absence of ancient rice cultivation in Belau is consistent with other cases in which Austronesian rice cultivators, migrating from island Southeast Asia, turned their energies to taro cultivation when they arrived at islands without significant dry seasons (Bellwood 1980).

foundations, walls, and other massive stone structures found uniformly in ancient and contemporary villages are generally absent from the terraces, that elevated villages were built on mountain tops (like Roisbeluu in Ngeremlengui and Rois in Ngeaur) rather than on terraced slopes, and that sacred stones need not necessarily mark village sites, Yawata's theory cannot be accepted on the meager evidence he presents.

In contemporary, as well as ancient, village sites stand several kinds of stone structures, including meetinghouse foundations (*cheldukl*), elevated roads (*rael*), defensive walls (*cheluatl*), and burial pavements (*odesongel*), as well as a range of smaller carved and natural stoneworks such as anthropomorphic faces (*klidm*), sitting posts (*btangch*), ceremonial display tables (*oleketokel*), and village-boundary markers.[7] The huge stone pillars at Bairulchau in Ngerechelong and the foundation stones at Beluuraklngong in Ngeremlengui suggest comparison with the famous *latte* stones of the Marianas and with the stones found on Malekula in the New Hebrides, while the design of stone face carving may relate to that of New Britain or central Indonesia (Bellwood 1979:287; Layard 1942).[8] Within Belau there seems to be, in fact, a systematic stylistic distinction between the rough-hewn andesite and andesite-conglomerate stones, the carved faces of which feature circular recessed eyes and upturned mouths (called "Great Faces" by Osborne),

7. Belau's stone carvings have been well studied and illustrated by Hidikata 1973b and Osborne 1979. Chapman (1968:69) summarizes Hidikata's contribution: "Hijikata feels the upright monolithic images originally served to insure basic needs such as reproduction, good fishing, and so forth, but that after passing through various hands as the result of wars and raids, they came later to be associated with the particular aims of families and villages. The older skeletal style belonged to a people who cleared the hills for terraces and platforms, and left potsherds of a rather fine quality." Hidikata's association of monoliths and terraces, however, is not entirely supported by more recent archaeological research. When he visited Ngeremlengui Hidikata was not permitted to see several of the most remarkable stoneworks in the area, for reasons which will be noted later.

8. The Beluuraklngong site, as yet unstudied, lies on the northeastern slope of Usas cape. Although it must be close to Osborne's site B3 (which I never did locate), Beluuraklngong's stones are smoothly finished and precisely laid-out foundation supports forming a rectangle approximately 42 feet by 10 feet. Osborne (1979:178–79) points out a possible connection between the structures at Badlrulchau and Yapese men's clubhouses; he also points to a comparison with the parallel rows of basaltic pillars described by Gifford and Gifford (1959:154). The style of anthropomorphic carvings is only vaguely like the parallels which have been suggested; see Raven 1926 and Riebe 1967. Not mentioned in the literature is the parallel between the stone mortars illustrated, for example, in Kaudern 1938 and the round stone named Imiungselbad, which is the sacred stone of Imeiong village (see photograph 5). For a general review of the problem of megalithic culture see Heine-Geldern 1945; cf. Glover, Bronson, and Bayard 1979.

and the smaller, more smoothly fashioned elongated stone faces with long straight noses and small eyes. It is possible to speculate that this distinction correlates with the distinction between the archaic mega-lithic architectural style manifested at the Bailrulchau site and later In-donesian-type carpentry characteristic of historically documented meetinghouses (cf. Osborne 1979:178–79). Villagers today give expla-nations for these stones similar to those recorded by Cheyne, Krämer, and Hidikata: that the Belauan people are incapable of these monu-mental feats of construction, that gods or men from a foreign race (Chi-nese or Portuguese) built them in ancient times, and that the stone faces are the bodies of their original creators. Although the practice of stone carving is thought to belong to a distant cultural era, evidence from archaic and contemporary society indicates that, as sacred objects, stones continue to be highly valued repositories of magical, religious, and political power. In fact, the casual indifference some scholars have reported to be the local attitude toward these stones can be seen as a profound unwillingness to discuss these objects with Westerners. In Belau, high cultural value need not correspond to an attitude of active or obvious interest.

Finally, red-ocher petroglyphs called "Orachel's drawings" have been reported for six sites in caves and cliffs on the rock islands, Oreor, and southern Babeldaob (McKnight 1970:5). These paintings are huge murals—the one at Ulong island is sixty-six feet long—consisting of human figures, boats, abstract designs, and handprints executed in a bold "stencil-like" style.[9] Stylistic and technical variation among the sites and an apparent lack of exact comparative parallels in rock-paint-ing art from other Pacific islands make it difficult to use these paintings to link this rock island culture to the historic culture on the high islands of Belau or to establish linkages between Belau and possible external source traditions.[10] Attempts have been made, nevertheless, to connect the more fully formed figures with mythological characters such as the culture hero Orachel, the spider Mengidabrutkoel, and the trickster god

9. The best set of reconstructed illustrations of rock paintings is McKnight 1970; four color photographs are reproduced in Henrickson 1968; a quantitative comparative style analysis by Gregory appears as appendix 4 in Osborne 1979; additional illustrations are given in Simmons 1970.

10. Using the same data, McKnight (1970:22) stresses the dissimilarity of sites, especially those on Ulong and Taberrakl, while Osborne and Gregory (Osborne 1979:299) note stylistic similarity. My own inspection of the various reproductions tends to support McKnight's position.

Medechiibelau, and to suggest stylistic parallels with Indonesian and New Caledonian examples (Osborne 1979:313–14).[11] But as Osborne and Gregory point out, the style of these paintings does not seem to be consistent with the style of either the stone carvings from the high islands or the highly refined wood carving practiced today.

The abandonment of rock island sites, the presence of extensive unused terraces, and the stylistic discontinuity of artistic traditions support the general conclusion that the culture recorded at the time of Western contact was the outcome of a long and complex development involving multiple sources of influence, as well as adjustment to diverse and changing local ecological conditions. More specific evidence to place Belau in the broader Austronesian context is found in three additional phenomena which have received increasing ethnographic and comparative attention: language, pottery, and exchange valuables. And for each of these three kinds of data, study of the contemporary culture supplements the historical and archaeological records.

The Belauan language is spoken with little dialect variation throughout the archipelago, except for the Southwest Islands of Tobi, Merir, Pulo Ana, and Sonsorol, where languages related to that of the Carolinian atoll Ulithi are spoken (McKnight 1977:13). Linguists are in agreement that the three westernmost languages of Micronesia—Belauan, Chamorro, and Yapese—cannot be placed in the nuclear Micronesian family, which includes among others the languages of Truk, Ponape, Kosrae, and the Marshalls.[12] This differentiation of Micronesian languages into nuclear and non-nuclear is consistent with evidence that the islands of nuclear Micronesia bear a closer cultural relationship with island Melanesia to the southeast, while non-nuclear or western Micronesia shows greater similarities to Indonesia, Taiwan, and the Philippines (Alkire 1977:12–13; Bellwood 1979:282). There is disagreement, however, over the precise relationship among the three non-nuclear languages, their relative position with respect to reconstructed Proto-Austronesian, and their linkage to Austronesian languages spoken in the Philippines, Botel Tobago, Indonesia, and Taiwan (Pätzold 1968). According to Dyen's (1965) lexicostatistical study, Belauan forms one of the many coordinate subgroups of the Malayopolynesian linkage and outside Micronesia is most closely relat-

11. Neither Osborne nor Gregory seems to have noted the ship motif which parallels the "scarlet haematite" paintings from Niah Cave in Borneo (see Harrisson 1964:184, upper photograph; McKnight 1970: pl. 9). Some of the human figures resemble those found in the Philippines (Peralta and Santiago 1979).

12. Basic sources on the position of Micronesian languages include Bender 1971; Izui 1965; Matthews 1949–50; Murdock 1948, 1968; Sakiyama 1979.

ed to the language of the Baree people of Sulawesi. In Blust's
(1979:216, 1980a:11) more recent formulation, Belauan is included
along with Austronesian languages of the Philippines, western Indonesia, Charmorro, Chamic, and Malagasy as the Western Malayo-Polynesian subdivision of Malayo-Polynesian.

The use of linguistic data as evidence for theories of early Austronesian migration has to date produced strikingly different results in the
hands of comparativists. Basically, one line of reasoning places the
homeland of Austronesian languages in the islands of Melanesia and
then proposes a series of westerly migrations through eastern Indonesia
to western Indonesia and through Belau to the southern Philippines,
northern Sulawesi and Borneo; Taiwan was then settled from the Philippines and western Indonesia from Borneo (Murdock 1968). The argument is that since western Melanesia (New Guinea, Bismarck
archipelago) displays the richest diversity of languages it must be the
point of linguistic dispersal.[13] The second and more widely accepted
argument contends that the migration of Austronesian speakers was
from an original homeland on Taiwan (settled initially by pre-Aus-
tronesian speakers from southern China) to the Philippines and then in
two divergent lines, first to Borneo, Java, and Sumatra, and second to
Sulawesi, southern Halmahera, and western New Guinea (Bellwood
1980; Shutler and Marck 1975:977; Tryon 1984:154–55). In this
view, Belauan and the other non-nuclear Micronesian languages derive
either directly from the Philippines (ca. 4500 B.C.) or at a later date (ca.
4000 B.C.) from an offshoot of the general movement from southern
Halmahera toward New Guinea. But whichever path turns out to be
correct, far from being a stepping-stone for the movement of Austronesian speakers into the Pacific, Belau appears to be a minor sidestep or a
dead end. The languages of nuclear Micronesia, on the other hand,
resulted from northwestern movement of Oceanic speakers, whose
homeland was in the New Ireland–New Britain area (Pawley and
Green 1984: fig. 1). Data from Belau and neighboring Yap will undoubtedly play a central role in any future determination of the relative
strength of these two theories, and nonlinguistic data will have to be
fully integrated before conclusions can be drawn.

The linguistic differentiation noted above between nuclear and non-
nuclear Micronesia is supported by the fact that pottery is found exten-

13. As Blust (1976:36) points out, this theory implies that many aspects of Austronesian society (taro and rice cultivation, writing systems, and knowledge of pig and iron)
derived at a later date from Southeast Asia; Blust himself argues from comparative
linguistic evidence that there is no need to postulate borrowing for words referring to
these and other features.

sively in Belau, Yap, and the Marianas in western Micronesia, but only
rarely in central or eastern Micronesia (Osborne 1966:62; Bellwood
1979:286; Athens 1983).[14] But beyond this, little evidence has been
found in the analysis of Belauan pottery to tie it to either Marianas Red
Ware described by Spoehr (1957) or to the pottery of Yap (Gifford
and Gifford 1959). The sherds found in abundance by Osborne in
Belauan sites from all island types show extreme uniformity, and thus it
is difficult to make inferences about internal cultural sequence. The pottery is generally unslipped and sherd-tempered, with paddle-anvil fin-
ishing and only rare instances of decoration, incision, or painting
(Kubary 1895a:199). Belauan potters, normally women, produced a
variety of vessels, including cooking pots, large storage jars, special pots
for boiling coconut syrup, and clay lamps.[15] Similarities with the two
most likely candidates, Marianas Red Ware and Lapita Ware of island
Melanesia, are not evident. And Bellwood (1979:286), basing his comment on Osborne's data, goes so far as to conclude that there are in fact
"no known outside parallels" for this tradition.

Osborne describes several exceptional sand-tempered, decorated
sherds which have connection with or were actually produced in the
Philippines; but other than this the search for external connections has
proved as elusive as the attempt to construct an internal sequence (Takayama 1982a:100). On a more recent field trip in 1968–69, Osborne
obtained radiocarbon datings which vary so widely that little confidence can be placed in the results (Masse, Snyder, and Gumerman
1984). But the negative conclusion still stands: Belauan pottery bears
little resemblance to the pottery of its Western Micronesian neighbors,
Yap and the Marianas;[16] and its unique simplicity and stylistic continuity suggest a long period of cultural isolation and panarchipelagic
uniformity.[17]

14. As Takayama (1981) explains, pottery found recently on atolls such as Ulithi,
Lamotrek, Ngulu, and Kapingamarangi was imported from high, volcanic islands; these
linkages are thus evidence for a degree of prehistoric interisland contact.

15. According to Takayama (1979:88), clay lamps were manufactured only after
Western contact and in imitation of foreign models.

16. On the basis of the discovery of pottery of the Belauan type on Ngulu atoll
(dating before ca. A.D. 800) Takayama (1982b:94) speaks of the existence of a "Palau
Empire," that is, a trade-and-tribute network in western Micronesia parallel to the well-
documented system linking Yap and the Carolinian islands to the east. While Belauan
folklore does mention contacts with the people from Yap, Ulithi, and Ngulu, I am not
familiar with any evidence for an institutionalized trading system.

17. The pottery found by Gifford and Gifford (1959:200) on Yap, however, has been
recognized by Spoehr as identical to Marianas Plain Ware.

In addition to language and pottery, scholars have used money or valuables (*udoud*) to place Belau in the Indo-Pacific context.[18] At the time of first Western contact, islanders were using varieties of ceramic, stone, and glass beads and bracelet sections to purchase goods and services, to pay fines, tribute, and brideprice, and to manipulate political alliances. The cultural significance of these valuables will be considered later; here it is sufficient to point out first that as a general rule these valuables were not manufactured locally but rather came to the archipelago from the Philippines, Indonesia, or Yap at some time prior to Western contact. In addition to these immediate sources, almost every early encounter between Western ships and Belauans involved the exchange or theft of beads, glass, plates, and other objects resembling those valuables already in use (see below). Second, the separation of valuables into classes according to criteria of color, shape, design, and material corresponds to functional differentiation in customary exchange. That is, the valuables are not based on an absolute cross-class scale of value (although such a scale was imposed by later colonial powers); they function, rather, like family heirlooms or royal treasure. The most highly prized pieces, those cut from yellow and red ceramic and glass rings (*bachel*), bear individual names; and the value of a given piece is dependent on the story of its exchange history as well as on its membership in a certain class. Third, ownership of these valuables and esoteric knowledge of their names, classes, and exchange histories are essential to the maintenance of the pervasive social stratification between high-ranking or chiefly families and low-ranking commoner families. Because Belauans considered the money supply to be fixed and the existing pieces to be endowed with inherent efficacy, chiefs did not expend much energy in the acquisition of these loci of value (as is the case in other Austronesian societies [Hayden 1983]), but rather in the monopolization of their use.

Attempts to trace an original place of manufacture for the various classes of valuables have postulated origins in Rome, Greece, China, India, and Southeast Asia (Beauclair 1963; Force 1959). But since beads and other valuables were traded extensively in the Indo-Pacific world and appear in Metal Age burial sites in the Philippines (Fox 1979:239–40), these efforts have little to offer beyond what Krämer

18. The basic ethnographic sources for the study of Belauan money from the point of view of origins and materials include Force 1959; Krämer 1917–29, 3:156–73; Kubary 1895b; Osborne 1966:477–94; and Ritzenthaler 1954.

stated about their origin.[19] After noting that beads similar to those in use in Belau have been found in Borneo and Indonesia, he concludes:

> We thus arrive at the following explanation for the origin of the money of Palau—as in the Sudan, in Indonesia and elsewhere, valuable stone and glass beads were imported along the trade routes and when the supply was exhausted and the trade service was given up, they became standards of value due to their age, rarity, and durability. Thus they assumed the role of money. (Krämer 1917–29, 3:157)

The presence of these opaque and translucent glass beads and bracelet sections may thus be explained by supposed trading contact with Chinese, Malay, Philippine, or even Arabic merchants.[20] In fact, folklore records specific instances of ships visiting or wrecking at Belau near Ngeaur, Beliliou, Ngerechelong, and Ngeruangel, and even mentions the name of one sailor, Ngirabaliau, who, after settling in northern Babeldaob and obtaining a chiefly title, manufactured bracelet sections (*bachel*) which became the most valuable class of money, and which have been conclusively identified with bracelets from Cebu and Jolo in the Philippines (Force 1959). In the colonial period, extensive contact between Belau and Yap, in which Yapese mined aragonite stone money on sites near Oreor, resulted in considerable movement of Belauan money between the two island groups (Beauclair 1963; Lessa 1980:13).[21] The fact that there are a large number of similar beads in a limited number of classes suggests further that these foreign contacts were intermittent but substantial.

Equally important, however, are stories which attribute the origin of valuables to a magical "money bird," Delarok, stories which describe the discovery of the valuables inside fruit or in the ground, and which tell of their descent from a heavenly city where valuable replace stones. There is an important connection in Belau, as elsewhere in the Aus-

19. Plates illustrating beads from the Indo-Pacific area are useful for this comparative enterprise; see Ch'en 1968: figs. 76–79; Colani 1935, 2: aquarelle I and II; Heekeren 1958: pl. 13; Hose and McDougall 1912: pl. 130; Seligman and Beck 1938; and Solheim 1964: pl. 45.

20. A yellow glass bead found in the context of a fourth-century Philippine boat indicates a link between maritime trade and valuables (Peralta 1980).

21. A further ramification of this mining arrangement noted by Alkire (1980) is that the Yapese lack of navigational skills necessitated the use of central Carolinian experts. Although the extensive tribute network between Yap and the islands to the east operated at a net loss for Gagil village on Yap, it enabled this village to obtain valuable stones from Belau, which in turn gave it considerable political advantage vis-à-vis other villages.

tronesian world, between the notion of foreign provenance and the idea of sacred power (Barraud 1979:211; Liep 1983; Sahlins 1985b:82; Walleser 1913:610). Valuables are, in fact, essential signs of social rank and political power. Possession of certain famous pieces marks a house as high-ranking (*meteet*), and titleholders from these houses manipulate the system of fines to recover important pieces that come into the hands of titleless commoners (*chebuul*). Of interest also are scattered references in folklore to a form of money in use prior to the advent of ceramic valuables, based on the use of small black teeth of a kind of mullet fish found in large groups near the rock islands. The people of the rock islands are said to have purchased food and goods from the village of Ngchemliangel on Beliliou with this "teeth money" (*udoudungelel*).[22]

This rapid survey of terraces, megaliths, petroglyphs, language, pottery, and valuables supports the same conclusion as the previous discussion of geographical and cultural position: Belau occupies both a central and an isolated position in the Austronesian world. Not only has it been difficult to establish direct and specific linkages with external cultural sources, but it has been equally difficult to join together data about these six phenomena to make a statement which would integrate the problem of prehistoric derivation with the question of internal cultural sequence. On the other hand, in a general typological sense all these phenomena are found in various places throughout the Pacific, so claims that Belau's specific manifestations are "without parallel" must be converted into the conclusion that, in the end, its culture has molded and been molded by diverse external influences. In this sense, then, there is at least a theoretical continuity between the question of Belau's prehistoric origin and the question of its fate in the hands of modern colonial powers. The ability to integrate the external, to adapt to changing circumstances, and to impose consistency upon heterogeneous elements are powers of culture in general and of Belauan culture in particular. The next section concludes this contextual introduction by taking up the history of Belau's contact with Western voyagers, traders, missionaries, merchants, soldiers, and colonists. This account will provide a backdrop for our analysis of Belauan perspectives on these events in later chapters.

WESTERN HISTORICAL CONTEXT

It was, then, a geographically diverse but culturally homogeneous Belau which European ships repeatedly "discovered" in the sixteenth and

---

22. My information confirms that collected by Osborne (1966:404), but his gloss of "*udaud ungelel*" (*sic*) as "fish, its money" does not appear to be correct.

eighteenth centuries.[23] This early contact, aptly characterized by Hezel and del Valle (1972:26) as a "period of gradual familiarization of European and Carolinians before the rapid acculturation of the nineteenth century," was at first unintentional and fleeting. Only later did the systematic goals of exploration, trade, and missionization motivate European voyagers to come to Belau. Lessa's (1975) conclusion seems valid: Sir Francis Drake's *Golden Hind* was the first ship to sight Belau, on 30 September 1579. An initially ordered exchange of fish for beads broke off when the Belauans' eagerness to appropriate marvelous foreign goods was interpreted as malicious thievery. Experiencing the wonders of Western firepower for the first time, the terrified islanders took shelter under their canoes, only to return the next day with renewed enthusiasm and an altered strategy, which met with even more severe consequences.

> Notwithstanding other new companies (but all of the same mind) continually made resort unto us. And seeing that there was no good to be got by violence, they put on a show of seeming honesty, and offering in show to deal with us by way of exchange; under that pretence they cunningly fell a filching of what they could, and one of them pulled a dagger and knives from one of our men's girdles, and being required to restore it again, he rather used what means he could to catch at more. Neither could we at all be to rid of this ungracious company, till we made some of them feel some smart as well as terror: and so we left that place by all passengers to be known hereafter by the name of the *Island of Thieves*.[24] (Drake, in Lessa 1975:55; spelling modernized)

Subsequent to Drake's passage through Belauan waters, the next contact with the West was the result of Micronesian, rather than Euro-

23. An authoritative history of Western contact has not been written. Since such a project would require investigation of English, Spanish, German, French, Russian, and Japanese archival sources—in addition to sources in the Belauan language—it may never be written. An excellent chronology of events based primarily on Western sources is contained in the multivolume *A History of Palau* (PCAA 1976–78); Krämer (1917–29, 1:10–180) provides detailed accounts of early voyagers and traders; Hezel (1979:1–14) lists foreign ships at Belau up to 1885; and Hezel (1983:66–81, 170–90, 266–81) focuses on several colorful eighteenth- and nineteenth-century encounters between Westerners and Belauans.

24. Lessa (1975:57–58) also cites a passage from the second deposition of Drake's voyage: "The Indians embarked in canoes which were very well made, with short oars with which they rowed very well; they were naked and carried darts and stones. They took from each other the beads and things which were given to them in payment: the strongest remained in possession while the quarrelling went on the whole time."

pean, navigation. In 1669, Father Francisco Miedes, a Jesuit living on the island of Siau (north of Sulawesi) encountered four men from one of the atolls in the central Carolines (Jacobs 1980). These men had been blown off course and landed in the Talaud Islands and as slaves came to Siau. Father Miedes managed to converse with them, and they eventually produced a rough diagram of the islands within their rather extensive geographical knowledge. Not only did they locate and name many of the atolls in the central Carolines, but they clearly listed both Yap and Palu (Belau). The official report announcing this vast unmissionized area did not, however, attain the status of another missionary letter written in 1697 by Father Paul Klein, who met a large group of men and women who had drifted from Fais atoll all the way to the Philippines. These islanders too had wide knowledge of the islands of western Micronesia and listed Belau, as Panlog (Krämer 1917–29, 1:31) or Palu (Blair and Robertson 1906:49), and Yap as high islands with plentiful water.[25] The end result of these two accidental contacts was to stimulate Jesuit missionization of the islands east of the Philippines; the efforts led directly to the arrival of the next ships which touched at Belau (Lessa 1962:316).

The next recorded contact took place over a century after Drake's voyage, on 11 December 1710, when the *Santisima Trinidad,* captained by Francisco de Padilla, passed through the southern zone. The events that took place in the next two days almost perfectly reproduced the events during Drake's visit. From the canoes which paddled out to meet the ship, several Belauans climbed aboard. But when efforts to carry off every available piece of iron were answered with the firing of warning shots, they quickly jumped back into the water—but not before receiving, among other things, "a string of glass beads" (Somera, in Lessa 1975:103). Undeterred by these shots and hoping to attract the ship to their island, the men in canoes communicated to their foreign visitors that the inhabitants of a nearby island to the north were likely to kill them (Calderon, in Krämer 1917–29, 3:65). This is the first Western notice of the interdistrict and interisland rivalry which will occupy much of our attention in following chapters. And it provides an excellent example of the way in which this struggle involved the encompassment of external sources of power, whether valuables, firearms, castaways, or trade.

---

25. The islands of Micronesia were generally referred as "Palaos," from the Malay term *proa,* "canoe." The historian Jacobs (1980:396) unfortunately conflates this generic label with the similar name Belau and states that these people came from the "Palau Islands."

On 15 February 1712, the *Santo Domingo* arrived at the northern tip of Babeldaob island, and when several canoes approached, a brief trade of nails for food ensued. As in previous encounters, Belauans appeared overly anxious to seize what they could, so Captain Don Bernardo de Egui ordered several to be placed in stocks. During the next day, while the ship sailed down the coast of Babeldaob, one of their captives indicated by signs:

> That the natives on some small islands, which we discovered near the large island, were cannibals and that they (the natives of these islands) were at war with the natives of the large island. He said that they were good friends of the natives on the other small islands which are further to the south, near the large island. (Krämer 1917–29, 3:83)

This evidence suggests that the central islands of Oreor and Ngerekebesang were at the time enemies of allied villages on Babeldaob, Ngeaur, and Beliliou.

Seventy years elapsed between the brief visit of the *Santo Domingo* and the next recorded contact. This long hiatus is largely due to the fact that Belau lay too far south to be sighted by ships traveling along the Spanish galleon route from Acapulco to Manila (Hezel 1983:32). Later, however, when the East India Company began sailing to China, repeated contact with the islands became inevitable (Delano 1817:71). Captain Henry Wilson "discovered" the islands on 10 August 1783, when the packet *Antelope* ran aground on the western reef near Ulong island (see map 1). Ten months prior to this, a Chinese trading vessel had wrecked at Beliliou, and at least one of its Malay crew came ashore to live under the protection of Ibedul, the chief of powerful Oreor village (Hockin 1803:17). This proved historically fortuitous, as well as "an unlooked for source of consolation" for the shipwrecked Englishmen, since Captain Wilson was able to establish communication with his hosts using two translators, his Malay-speaking linguist Tom Rose and the Belauan-speaking Malay castaway (Keate 1788:24–26).[26]

Due to the fact that Ulong was at that time under the jurisdiction of chief Ibedul of Oreor, Wilson quickly became embroiled in a series of Ibedul's military campaigns against his enemies, Melekeok and Beliliou, in support of which Wilson contributed men, firearms, and displays of miraculous firepower (Cheyne 1971:239; Hockin 1803:41–42). One

---

26. A story from Ngeremlengui gives this Malay the Belauan name Ngirabaliau and notes that his Chinese ship wrecked near Ngeruikl on Beliliou.

indirect consequence of this intimate involvement with ongoing political affairs is that Wilson and several of his crew were able to record in their journals the first detailed account of local customs, political relations, and geography.[27] Although Wilson abandoned his original idea of making a detailed survey of all of Babeldaob's villages, he did accompany a party of important chiefs to Imeiong village in Ngeremlengui district. His description of the customary transactions that took place there, as well as several of his passing observations, provide us with an invaluable historical marker, as will be seen in chapter 7. On the Belauan side, the benefits of this lengthy visit accrued to those brave individuals who swam off with glass and bottles from the wrecked ship, since some of these items became instantly converted into exchange valuables. In particular the benefits accrued to the men of Oreor, whose successful monopolization of Western power enabled them to mount victorious military campaigns against their enemies.

News of the generous hospitality received by the crew of the *Antelope* spread rapidly, not only through the publication of Keate's *Account of the Pelew Islands* in 1788, but also by the visit to England of Lee Boo (Lebu), the "second son" of chief Ibedul of Oreor. Under the paternal eye of Captain Wilson, the young boy attended school at Rotherhithe, explored the wonders of London, and demonstrated an active fascination with English customs, arts, and artifacts. Despite every precaution, however, Lebu caught smallpox and died in 1784. From his deathbed his thoughts did not swerve from matters of Belauan value: exchange valuables and rank.

> He then enumerated the presents which had been made him, and expressed his wishes that Mr. Sharp would distribute them, when he returned to Pelew, amongst the chiefs, recommending to his especial care, the blue glass barrels on brackets, which he particularly directed to be given to the king [Ibedul]. (Keate 1820:122)

27. The published account of Wilson's visit, written by his literary friend George Keate on the basis of personal interviews and journals of the ship's crew, reveals a romantic, moralizing tone obviously intended to redeem the image of the "primitive" through the concept of the "noble savage" (Smith 1960:98–99). It is, however, a simple task to extract important ethnographic and historical data from behind this ideological veil. Unfortunately, I have not been able to locate positive reference to the existence of Captain Wilson's original journal and log. The list of logs extant at the India Office as of 1986 cites Wilson's *Antelope* log, but it ends on 5 June, two months prior to the *Antelope*'s wreck at Belau; Mander-Jones (1972:147) notes that "in 1860 there was a general destruction of journals and books other than the logs."

Between the departure of crew of the *Antelope* and the turn of the century, several additional English ships called at Belau, many continuing Wilson's policy of giving trading privileges, ceremonial recognition, and military assistance to the "King" at Oreor (Delano 1817; Hockin 1803; McCluer 1790–92; Meares 1790; Wilson 1799). Encouraged by the friendly reception extended to Captain Wilson, the East India Company thought that Belau might become a convenient stopping place for its trading ships. The continued presence of Englishmen pleased the leaders of Oreor, who willingly provided shelter, water, and food in return for guns and ammunition. And as was the case with each earlier instance of contact with visiting ships, various sorts of beads were exchanged for supplies, as noted for the *Snow Panther* in 1791: "The vessel from day break till sunset was surrounded with canoes, but not a man permitted to come over the gunwale, except the principal men who sat down peaceably in the deck. The appearance of our large China beads roused up the spirit of invention among them, and industry was introduced among them for awhile" (McCluer 1790–92:115). The flow of beads was at times so great that the chiefs were unable to control their distribution to commoners: "The old man [Ibedul] told me, I had so much enriched his country by so many beads and other things, that the people would all grow foolish, and would not obey his orders, which would oblige him to take all their beads from them" (McCluer 1790–92:122; cf. Browning 1833–36:300; Delano 1817:191; Hockin 1803:26, 40, 122; and Ward 1966:146).

This mutually advantageous compact between the English and the Oreor leaders established an enviable precedent for other villages, which soon realized that greater benefit could be gained by treating foreign ships with guarded hospitality rather than by thievery. So, for example, when the American whaler *Mentor* wrecked at Ngeruangel reef in 1832, the people of Ngerechelong district in northern Babeldaob were quick to entertain the survivors and to volunteer to build a new ship—actions performed in self-conscious imitation of Oreor's helpful attitude toward Wilson and the crew of the *Antelope*. Upon hearing of the arrival of these sailors, Ibedul of Oreor sent an English castaway as his emissary to Ngerechelong to convince the Americans that their chances of reaching home would be greater if they put themselves and the contents of their ship in the hands of Oreor.[28]

---

28. Ibedul's efforts to control the fate of shipwrecked sailors was repeated several years later when he arranged to transport the crew of the *Dash* from Babeldaob to Oreor (Browning 1833–36:221–22).

He stated that his name was George, that he was an Englishman, that he had been on the islands about twenty-five years, that he came by the order of the King and Chiefs to invite me and my crew to go to Oreor, that they would build a boat to take me from the islands, that the Chiefs and warriors were on a small island and the next day they intended going to the wreck and wished to know what was in the ship. I informed him. He was very particular to inquire the number of muskets and where they were. After getting all the information he wanted and pressing me to go with him, which I would have gladly done but feared the consequences, he said they would not hurt me but might kill him. But I declined the attempt, and he left me to rejoin his party on the island with the promise that he would call on his return. (Barnard 1980:21; spelling and punctuation modernized)

Although Captain Barnard refused to abandon his situation in Ngere-chelong, Ibedul did not give up his efforts to manipulate the crew of the *Mentor* for his own benefit.[29] When the boat was completed, the Americans agreed to take three Belauans on board and to leave behind three of their group as security for a future gift of firearms (Holden 1836:71; Paullin 1910:733).

These hostages became pawns of interdistrict political struggle three years later, when Ibedul persuaded Captain Aulick of the man-of-war *Vincennes* to use his might to ransom the Americans. On the other side, the Ngerechelong leaders, using the services of a castaway named Charlie Washington, offered to give them up in return for two hundred muskets (Browning 1833–36:227). The eventual solution to this impasse pleased neither side: Oreor did not get to see the destruction of Ngerechelong (as they had witnessed the destruction of Melekeok fifty years earlier), and Ngerechelong received only iron tools in return for the Americans. These events indicate clearly the increasing involvement of individual Westerners in internal political affairs. Usually functioning on behalf of local chiefs, these beachcombers and castaways reappear continually during the nineteenth century as translators, negotiators, traders, emissaries, and general symbols of foreign power (Hezel 1978:262–65).[30]

29. Not satisfied with this response, the Oreor party proceeded on to Ngcheangel, the island nearest the wreck, where they hung the high chief from a coconut tree until he surrendered six muskets, a compass, and a sextant (Barnard 1980:22).

30. A partial list of these individuals, with the approximate dates of their arrival in Belau, includes: Madan Blanchard (1783), John McCluer (1791), Charlie Washington (1801), George (1807), Dick (1822), John Davey (1833), Johnson (1855), and James Gibbons (1856 or 1860).

The dominant feature of Western contact between 1840 and 1900 was the development of commercial enterprise by traders such as Andrew Cheyne (1863–66, 1971), Edward Woodin (1861–63), Alfred Tetens (1958), and David O'Keefe (Klingman and Green 1950), who established operations for the extraction of trepang, pearl, and tortoiseshells, and later copra.[31] By himself, Cheyne managed to have local chiefs sell him an estimated 10,000 acres of land in several districts by the early 1860s, with the explicit aim of settling Chinese laborers there to begin extensive planting of rice, sugarcane, tobacco, and cotton. The growth of trading stations throughout the islands did little, however, to stimulate productivity which might have benefited the local villagers. As a British captain acutely observed in 1882: "A great change for the worse seems to have taken place amongst them since their intercourse with traders who in many cases treat them very badly: give them but little and that frequently bad for their produce and charge them exorbitant prices; this the natives are not slow in finding out and it is not surprising that they take the first opportunity to make reprisals" (East 1882).

The attempted monopolization of this trade by Oreor chiefs led to the increased power of its leader Ibedul, who was pronounced "absolute sovereign" in the 1861 "Treaty of Commerce" signed by the chiefs of Oreor for the benefit of the merchant Cheyne (Semper 1982:194). From his base on Yap, O'Keefe sent trading vessels to Belau in order for Yapese workers to quarry huge aragonite stones; these were then transported back to Yap, where they became valuable pieces of money. To the importation of firearms, increased rivalry over chiefly titles, aggressive competition for access to Western goods, and the enlarged role of foreigners in internal political affairs must be added the dramatic depopulation which took place in the nineteenth century. From an estimated precontact population of between 25,000 and 40,000, the population fell to less than 4,000 by 1900 as a result of dysentery and influenza epidemics (Robertson 1876–77:45). The resulting loss of manpower in local men's clubs, the abandonment of ancient family and village sites, and the inability to fill positions of leadership by lineal recruitment are among the political consequences of this depopulation.

This period of exploitation of Belau's resources by individual European traders, in which their commercial rivalry became intertwined

31. Meeking (1846–47: 2 October 1846) notes that the collection of trepang was becoming increasingly difficult due to scarcity, but other sources suggest that the villagers were being diverted from collection of trepang by other agricultural activities. Traders lived in several villages during this period: Sims in Melekeok and Ngeaur, Braun in Imeiong, Woodin in Ngebuked, Cheyne in Ngerekebesang, and Kondon in Ngchesar.

with shifting district alliances, title disputes, and warfare, changed toward the close of the century to a situation of international competition between Spain, Germany, and England. Neither Germany nor England recognized Spain's rights in the Caroline Islands, and each country attempted to protect its local interests, punish offenses against its representatives, and prevent its rivals from gaining the upper hand. During this period Belauans learned graphically the destructive potential of foreign power, as several military vessels came to the islands to collect indemnities for commercial damages, to execute chief Ibedul as punishment for the murder of Andrew Cheyne, and to burn villages as retribution for offenses against resident missionaries (East 1885). After Pope Leo XII acknowledged Spain's claim to the Caroline Islands in 1885, a group of Capuchins finally established a mission station on Belau in 1891. The early missions were under the auspices of Ibedul, chief of Oreor, and Reklai, chief of Melekeok village on Babeldaob (Hezel 1971). During the short period of Spain's control of the islands from 1885 to 1899, these missionaries were the principal colonial agents, working to eradicate native religious beliefs and practices, to suppress the practice of concubinage, and to end headhunting and intervillage warfare (Valencia 1892).

Germany's purchase of Spain's Pacific island possessions in 1899 marked a return to primarily economic colonialism. Working through local leaders when convenient, the German administration (1899–1914) concentrated on regulating the society for maximal extraction of phosphate on Ngeaur (Firth 1973:26), copra on Babeldaob, and trepang and shells in the lagoons. By restricting traditional men's club activities that took time away from more "productive" labor, the administration was able to encourage the planting of coconut trees, a policy which led to the fragmentation of land holdings and the weakening of matrilineal kinship ties. Public projects involving local labor, including construction of roads, docks, government buildings, and commercial facilities, were perhaps not as significant as the forceful banishment of native religious practitioners, whose power had steadily increased during the nineteenth century, the continuation of Capuchin efforts toward religious indoctrination and baptism, and the institution of a pan-Belauan council of village chiefs to transmit official regulations.[32]

---

32. The German administration used the services of James Gibbons, the son of a Jamaican castaway, to assemble the high chiefs into session once a month and to "confer with them on all measures, just as it was handled from the beginning on Yap" (Germany, Reichstag 1903).

The German role in Micronesia was brought to a halt in 1914 at the outbreak of World War I, when the Caroline Islands (except Guam) were occupied by Japanese military forces. At the close of World War I, the League of Nations awarded Germany's Pacific possessions in Micronesia to Japan as a Class C Mandate. Under this arrangement, "The Mandatory shall promote to the utmost the natural and moral well-being and the social progress of the inhabitants of the territory subject to the present mandate" (Clyde 1935:64). But Japan did not come to Belau for the first time in 1914. Early in the German period, Japanese trading companies established operations in Micronesia, and while Germany held political control over the islands, Japanese firms handled the bulk of export trade in copra, trepang, and shells (Yanaihara 1940:26; Purcell 1967). When the Japanese navy arrived in 1914, it was in part to protect these established commercial interests and in part to secure the islands for future economic expansion and settlement.

The history of the Japanese period from the expulsion of the Germans to the American invasion of Beliliou during World War II can be summed up by saying that Japan, in contrast to England, Spain, and Germany before, tried to make the islands an "integral portion" of her empire, and in doing so brought about changes in the social and economic fabric of the society which did little to promote the "well-being" and "social progress" of the local people (Purcell 1967; Vidich 1949: 64–77). In 1922 the Japanese military authority was replaced by the civilian South Sea Bureau, which governed all Japan's Micronesian mandated territories from its headquarters on Oreor. An elaborate bureaucratic system bypassed traditional chiefs, some of whom were replaced by more cooperative, if less legitimate, leaders, and utilized local "magistrates" (*soncho*) appointed by the administration to communicate District Office rulings to the local villages (Goodman and Moos 1981: 38–39):[33] "Political leadership and authority at the indigenous level were emasculated to a point where they virtually did not exist. Hereditary chiefs became leaders in name only. The body of senior chiefs from each of the districts in Palau became known as the *waisei* ("yes") congress because of its inability to do more than simply agree with whatever policy was suggested by the Japanese administrators" (McKnight 1975).

33. Purcell's (1967:213) conclusion is that, except for the appointment of nontraditional leaders and the seizure of control over land, "The Japanese political system cannot be said to have been oppressive. There were, with few exceptions, no policies implemented which caused fundamental changes in native political and social patterns." The weight of published evidence and the overwhelming testimony of Ngeremlengui people combine to refute this conclusion. The seizure of land, the overstepping of local leaders, and forced labor surely cannot be treated as "exceptions," as Purcell suggests, in the study of an hierarchical island society.

The imposition of artificial leaders and foreign laws, along with strong restrictions placed on customary exchange activities, created a climate conducive to the spread of Modekngei (Let Us Go Forth Together), a local religious movement which stressed indigenous, as opposed to Japanese, medicine, education, religion, and authority (Vidich 1949). The Japanese persecution of Modekngei leaders only accelerated its growth, and by 1937 the movement counted among its believers both high chiefs, Ibedul and Reklai.

In order to further its overall aim of developing the export of mineral, marine, and agricultural resources, the administration took drastic steps, such as the seizure of over eighty percent of clan- and village-held land on Babeldaob (Kaneshiro 1958:388; Toomin and Toomin 1963:257–59), the establishment of rotating forced labor in Ngeaur's phosphate mines, the expansion of bauxite extraction operations in Ngerdmau, and the restriction of customary activities which interfered with production schedules. Only to the extent that efforts furthered these economic goals were expenditures made for native education in Japanese language, technical training, public health, and recreation. The overall economic orientation of the Japanese presence dovetailed with the already well-defined cultural focus on financial exchanges using Belauan money. As one of the first social scientists to visit the islands after the war observed,

> The Japanese influence was not primarily that of an Oriental culture, but more that of a colonial capitalistic one. Hence, its imprint on native society is more discernible in terms of the motivations and aspirations of a nascent capitalist social order than of any other form. The pivotal values of Palau society are now oriented around the norms characteristic of western capitalism: Namely, improvement in levels of living, acquiring property and wealth, technical efficiency, occupational skills, etc. (Useem 1946:65)

A policy of massive immigration brought the Japanese residential population equal to the Belauan population by 1935, although the colonial community in Oreor (with a population of 23,767 by 1940) was almost completely isolated from village life on Babeldaob. The population figures are more significant when it is realized that the Japanese population grew by over 21,000 from 1930 to 1940 (Oliver 1951:31). Stimulated by increasing immigration, Oreor quickly grew into a bustling Japanese town.[34]

34. A revealing photograph of the town in 1935 is printed in Vincent 1973:151; Ehrlich and Mekoll 1984:41 reproduces a map dated ca. 1938.

Oreor itself was a thriving hub of cosmopolitan activity: the
governing center with visiting dignitaries from Japan and other
islands of Micronesia; an active port with a vigorous fishing fleet
and with marine industries and research; and a commercial center
with score upon score of small shops, theaters, a rollerskating rink,
and even a "geisha lane" with its teashops, bars, and houses of male
entertainment. Though not a large town . . . Oreor was thriving
and exciting with all the attractive seductions implied by "city
lights." (McKnight 1978:9)

In 1940, the town of Oreor was the site of the enshrinement ceremony
of the Shinto shrine Kampei Taisha Nanyo Jinja, dedicated to the future of the "New East Asian Order" of Japanese imperial expansion
(Shuster 1982b). Although the elaborate rituals and processions were
of concern primarily to local Japanese followers of Shinto, the event
undoubtedly provided impetus for the reemergence after World War II
of the anti-Japanese Modekngei movement. And even prior to these
economic and political changes, the Japanese had begun the secret fortification of the islands, expressly forbidden under the terms of the
mandate agreement and repeatedly denied by local officials at the time.
Airfields, gun emplacements, munitions buildings, and naval bases were
quickly erected, and approximately sixty thousand troups were charged
with defending what had been for over three decades an "integral portion" of the Japanese empire (Price 1944).

World War II reached Belau in 1944, when United States forces
began intensive air strikes on Japanese military and industrial installa-
tions. A bloody amphibious assault on Beliliou in September and October secured the southern portion of the islands for the United States
forces, and continued bombing of the northern islands drove starving
Japanese soldiers and Belauans into mountain caves in central Babeldaob. Shocked to learn that the people they had come to admire, the
culture they emulated, and the government they respected had been
defeated, Belauans emerged from the forests to face yet another group
of Westerners (rechad er a ngebard), who for over two hundred years
played out their commercial, religious, scientific, and now military interests on their territory. The Japanese policies of direct rule, forced
acculturation, and economic exploitation—what an acute Belauan leader labels the "Okinawaisation of Micronesia" (Salii 1973:41)—had not
been interpreted as oppression or suppression. Even the recollection of
Japanese brutality did not prompt expressions of hostility in 1948,
when the anthropologist Barnett (1970:21) noted that "they [two old
men from Chelab village] recounted the now familiar stories about the

abuses of Japanese soldiers and the American war superiority; and as is always the case they laughed in telling about Japanese cruelty to them. I have never seen an expression of hatred on their faces." So the American takeover, which began with the leveling of most of the Japanese-built infrastructure of roads, schools, factories, farms, and harbors, and which instantly terminated the social, educational, and recreational activities of the imposed "custom" (*siukang*), was not received with the enthusiasm expected by the "liberators."

An interim Naval Administration for Micronesia ended in 1947, when the islands of the former mandated territory passed to the United States as a unique "strategic trusteeship" under the United Nations (Coulter 1957:173–77; McHenry 1976:540; Nufer 1978).[35] Committed under this agreement to "foster the development of such political institutions as are suited to the trust territory," to "promote the development of the inhabitants . . . toward self-government or independence," and to "promote the economic advancement and self-sufficiency of the inhabitants" (Clark and Roff 1984:4), the American administration of the new Trust Territory of the Pacific Islands in fact did little in terms of economic aid and political development during the early years to exercise their "virtually complete control over the territory" (McHenry 1976:6). The entire Trust Territory, covering the vast north Pacific Ocean from Belau and Yap in the west, to the Marianas in the north, and to the Marshalls in the east, operated with a budget ceiling of approximately $7 million, and the United States was content to leave the islands as a protected "zoological park" (Keesing 1941:81), by not rebuilding the destroyed infrastructure and by restricting all but local Micronesian commercial enterprise (Meller 1969:16). The bulk of United States expenditures in the Trust Territory was focused on other island groups, including Guam, the Marianas, and the Marshalls, which were sites of new military facilities, intelligence activities, and nuclear testing (Manhard 1979:4). This deliberate neglect contrasted dramatically with the aggressive acculturation of the Japanese period. And many Belauans, apparently more eager to continue the developments instituted before the war than their conservative Yapese neighbors, feared that a "golden age" had indeed come to a close (Useem 1947:65).

But by the 1960s the United States, embarrassed before world opinion at still being a colonial power and cognizant of the strategic military

---

35. Ten trusteeships were created after the war, but only Micronesia became a "strategic trusteeship." This meant that the islands fell under the jurisdiction of the United Nations Security Council (where the United States held veto power) rather than under the General Assembly, and that the United States was permitted to fortify the islands for security reasons (Goodman and Moos 1981:70).

position of the Pacific islands, suddenly shifted this policy to accelerate the level of social and political development, primarily through improved educational and health services (Vitarelli 1984) and the promotion of local democratic legislatures. In a succession of chartered bodies starting with the Palau Congress of 1947, Belauans learned to exercise political decision making in a democratic context with increasingly differentiated customary authority resting with traditional leaders and the legislative powers of elected representatives (Force and Force 1965:4). At the village level this new attention was manifest primarily in the availability of Western commercial goods (clothing, food, tools, and construction materials) and in the ubiquitous presence of Peace Corp volunteers, who were among the first foreigners to live in Belau alongside local villagers without coercive authority or overtly self-interested motives.

Belau was thus initially cast back on its own traditional resources during the first two decades of the trusteeship. Subsistence fishing and agriculture and local chiefly rule regained their importance, and the Japanese period's changes quickly became a nostalgic memory of paternalistic security. With the new political climate of the late 1960s and the 1970s, however, Micronesia once again became the focus of far-reaching plans for social and economic development. The United States, in fact, desired to transform the status of strategic trusteeship into a more intimate form of political relationship. The renewed interest of the United States in Belau has been linked to the need for a military base as a fallback for Subic Bay and Clark Air Force Base in the Philippines, for a deep-water tanker port, and for a potential site for dumping nuclear waste. As the so-called Solomon Report commissioned by the government in 1963 recommended, rapid increases in spending on educational and medical programs was a good way to encourage a positive attitude toward this new political status. Both parties brought to the rounds of negotiations which were held during this period multiple agendas concerning the future political status of Micronesia. After flirting with affiliation with the pan-Micronesian entity which eventually emerged in 1978 as the Federated States of Micronesia, Belau chose to negotiate independently for both increased capital investment, direct economic assistance, and social services and for recognition as a self-governing constitutional republic.[36] The United States, on the other hand, balanced its offers of financial aid with requests for land, power

36. Belau voted 55.1 percent against membership in the Federated States of Micronesia on 12 July 1978, thereby committing itself to futher bilateral negotiations with the United States or other foreign powers (Iyechad and Quimby 1983).

of eminent domain, and other guarantees to enable the construction of large-scale military facilities in the islands.[37] These negotiations climaxed in January 1981 when, after a long internal factional struggle, Belau finally ratified its first constitution, and the newly elected democratic government of the Republic of Belau took office (Shuster 1980, 1982a, 1983).

The public celebration over this new measure of self-determination concealed the fact that strong factional divisions continued to split the islands. Generally this division separated those who favored total independence under the terms of the newly ratified constitution and those who argued for strong economic relations of "Free Association" with the United States—even if that association required the suspension of several emotionally charged articles of the national constitution, including the archipelagic definition of Belau's territorial boundaries, the explicit prohibition against the transit of nuclear-powered vessels in national waters, and the declaration that the power of eminent domain shall not be used for the benefit of a foreign entity. The conflict between the desire for self-governance proclaimed in the constitution and the need for massive economic assistance provided in the Compact of Free Association continued to dominate political struggles in the early 1980s. A plebiscite in February 1983 expressed the depth of this ambiguity: voters both approved the free association compact (62 percent), and failed to approve by the three-quarters required margin necessary changes in the constitution (Ranney and Penniman 1985). Again in September 1984, 66 percent of Belauan voters approved the Compact of Free Association with the United States in a national referendum; this agreement involves financial aid of $500 million over five years in return for limited military privileges. Whether this referendum marks the end of the long period of political struggle or only another stage in its development cannot be determined at a distance.

This brief survey of Belau's political relations with the colonial world has been based almost entirely on sources external to the islands and has been organized by analytical categories, such as voyages of discovery, periods of colonial rule, and political development, which are foreign to Belau's own understanding of these events and processes. Not only does the preceding narrative presume that the history of the islands begins with Western contact in 1579 or 1783, but it also fails to pene-

37. In Round V of these negotiations in 1972, the United States requested anchorage rights in Ngmelachel harbor, a military airfield in Irrai, and two thousand acres of exclusive use and thirty thousand acres of nonexclusive use of land on Babeldaob for the purpose of ground force training and maneuvers.

trate the inside of history, that is, history from the perspective of local actors and their cultural categories. This sketch of prehistoric migrations from multiple Austronesian sources, a lengthy period of relative isolation and internal development, and a sequence of externally imposed colonial eras ending in constitutional self-governance assumes, moreover, that the significance of these events is given to the culture by objective circumstances (migration, geographical location, ecological setting) or by imposed force (foreign trade, colonial domination, and missionary ideology).

But as the chapters which follow make clear, the growth of Belauan polity cannot be understood apart from indigenous cultural notions about space, time, hierarchy, relation, and motion, or apart from institutional arrangements which are engaged in specific events. Turning to local sources such as myths, chants, warfare narratives, genealogies, migration stories, pictorial carvings, stone monuments, naming patterns, and the discourse and actions of contemporary informants in order to uncover these categories and institutions does not imply, however, that Western archival, journalistic, and scientific sources are of no help in trying to grasp the "inside" of this history. Often even the most objective foreign report containing information about village names, political meetings, and exchanges of valuables can contribute significantly to a fuller understanding of which political institutions are operative and which events these cultural categories are coding.

CHAPTER
2

Traditional Political Institutions

The political system of Belau should be of great interest to students of comparative Austronesian society, for the islands were settled at an early time, remained relatively isolated for centuries, if not millennia, and did not experience an overlaying of Indic or Islamic institutions (cf. Geertz 1980 on Bali). Moreover Belau did not develop many of the features Claessen (1984, 1986) identifies in "early states," so we get a rare glimpse of a fairly large-scale polity without a single overarching system of kingship. This chapter describes several institutions and forms of intervillage relations in traditional Belau. By "traditional" I refer to those customary practices described by my informants as "authentic" (*mera el tekoi*) or "ancient" (*tekoi er a irechar*), uncorrupted by foreign influence. Generally this correlates with the polity described in Western documents for the early nineteenth century. This introductory material is collected here so that later chapters will not be weighed down by disconnected and ad hoc ethnographic explications. Beginning with the village itself as the basic political unit, the discussion considers four levels of multivillage association: *village complexes,* consisting of satellite hamlets surrounding a dominant village; *districts,* which group together member villages around a focal capital village; *subdistrict* divisions within a single district; and shifting *federations* of villages from different districts. The system of titles and councils is then characterized as the primary means of decision making and as a clear expression of the principle of social rank. This largely typological discussion is then filled out by ethnographic descriptions of social mechanisms which channeled intervillage cooperation, friendship, exchange, competition, and hostility.

Villages, Districts, and Federations

One of the striking aspects of Belauan society so richly described in Krämer's multivolume ethnography based on data gathered between 1907 and 1910 is that the formal consistency of spatial organization of villages is matched by the fluidity of actual site occupation. Krämer recorded a total of 253 villages for the entire archipelago, of which only 84 were inhabited in 1910; of these, only 57 possessed the minimal number of men's clubs, chiefly councils, and residential houses to be counted as viable political entities.[1] From Captain Wilson's description of villages he visited in 1783, from Kubary's extensive analysis of the organization of Melekeok in the late nineteenth century, from Krämer's detailed maps of all extant major villages, and from my own study of Ngeremlengui's occupied and abandoned villages, it is clear that a similar formal pattern has characterized village organization for at least two hundred years.

In contrast to the dispersed homesteads and isolated hamlets found in many Pacific island societies (such as nearby Yap), the Belauan village is a concentrated group of residential houses (*blai*) and club and chiefly meetinghouses (*bai*), all built upon elaborate stone foundations and linked together by elevated stone pathways which fan out from a central paved square. Even the earliest documented village sites in the rock islands appear to be composed of concentrated networks of residential house platforms; Masse, Snyder, and Gumerman (1984) counted twenty-four platforms at Ngemelis island, twelve at Uchularois island, and thirty-six at Mariar on Ngeruktabel. Houses of high-ranking titleholders tend to be located near the chiefly meetinghouse (*rubakbai*) on the central square, while lower-ranking houses line paths at the periphery of the village. At the central square are arranged the backrest stones (*btangch*) of the high-ranking titleholders; usually arranged in a quadripartite order, these stones (called *ongeluluul*, "place for whispering") were occupied when titleholders met to discuss affairs of state or to make announcements to young men of the village.[2] The permanence of a village's stone structures is in part a result of the fact that taro cultivation in large irrigated lowland swamps provides the most important food staple (McCutcheon 1978). The stone roads of larger villages lead directly from the residential area to nearby taro patches, fed by

1. Kubary (1873:215) counted seventy extant villages in 1872.
2. Kusakabe (1979: fig. 2[6]) illustrates the spatial relationships among backrest stones, meetinghouses, and residences for Melekeok. A case study of the village layout of Imeiong is presented in chapter 5.

freshwater streams flowing from sources at the base of interior mountains toward the coast. Second only to taro cultivation in importance is the exploitation of plentiful marine resources at adjacent lagoon and reef fishing areas, rights to which are under the exclusive control of the local village council.

Tied to its taro swamp complex, built upon permanent stone foundations, and controlling a specific section of lagoon and reef, the Belauan village epitomizes the locative force of the basic existential verb *ngar,* "to be, to be located at," which forms the first syllable of the names of many villages and houses: for example, Ngeremetengel, from *ngar er a Metengel,* "at the descent"; Ngeremid, from *ngar er a Mid,* "at Mid sea passage"; and Ngerekiukl, from *ngar er a kiukl,* "on the west Coast." The word for village, *beluu,* is clearly cognate with Proto-Austronesian **banua,* as well as with Proto-Polynesian **fanua* (Dempwolff 1934–38, 3:23; Walsh and Biggs 1966:8). Like many of its widespread cognates in Oceania and Indonesia, *beluu* ranges in meaning from "land," "soil," "earth," to "inhabited area," "residential unit," and "political division." In the story of the creation of the islands, the first solid land that emerges from the formless primordial sea is called *beluu,* and the first creatures to rise up from the sea to dwell on this new land are organized into politically integral units also called *beluu.* As these examples indicate, a variety of English glosses can be used to translate the many meanings of *beluu,* including land, village, hamlet, district, municipality, state, nation, and country. A particular village is called *beluu er a Ngeremetengel,* "village of Ngeremetengel"; the United States is called *beluu er a Merikel;* and the Christian heaven is called *beluu er a eanged,* "country in the heavens." The title of the recent national constitution is *Uchetemel a Llach er a Beluu er a Belau,* "the foundation of the laws of the Republic of Belau." When the *Antelope* wrecked near Ulong island in 1783, Captain Wilson first became acquainted with the word *beluu* when his Oreor hosts indicated that they were going to sail back to their *beluu,* "village," which Wilson misunderstood as the *name* of their village, "Pelew."

Surface archaeology and historical narratives show that the contemporary pattern in which villages are located near the coastline at riverbanks, mangrove channels, and bays is the result of a gradual movement away from elevated inland sites (Robertson 1876–77:46). For example, the three currently occupied villages of Ngeremlengui district are located just inside the thick mangrove swamp that rings the west coast of Babeldaob, and all three had former locations on higher ground where stone roads and house platforms are still visible. But more significantly, these three villages are only the modern remnant of a large ancient district called Kerngilianged, consisting of over forty villages stretching across the Ngeremeskang drainage in central Babeldaob (see map 3). The villages comprising Kerngilianged were situated on inland riverbanks, lofty terraced hillcrests, and mountainous ridges, and one even sat atop a narrow ledge beneath the peak of Chetiruir mountain. As several stories detail, the impregnable location of many of these dispersed inland villages was linked to the constant threat of attack by raiding parties from hostile districts; and it was only with the final abolition of warfare that these villages were able to relocate at more convenient coastal sites.

This movement toward the coast was accompanied by an increasing consolidation of smaller villages into village complexes, like those Krämer observed in Ngeremlengui, Ngetelngal, and Oreor, with a dominant capital village being the seat of the highest-ranking chief of the district, surrounded by subordinate member villages. Often the name of the capital village became recognized as the name of either the cluster of member villages or of the entire district under the political control of the chiefs at the capital. Thus, Ngetelngal district on the east coast was led by the capital village of Melekeok, which is now the name of the whole district; similarly, Oreor village became the capital of Ngerekldeu district, which today bears the name Oreor.

And finally, during the colonial periods these larger village complexes once again shifted away from their ancestral stone foundations to relocate on level river flats or along beach strips in order to accomodate western-style roads and to be close to improved docking facilities. The village of Ngiual, in fact, was entirely rebuilt following the linear pattern of a rural Japanese village, with houses, trees, and decorative shrubs neatly lined up on two sides of a straight path. The relocation of villages on coastal areas has to some extent made more explicit the opposition between "affairs of men" (*tekoi el sechal*) oriented toward the lagoon and reef and "affairs of women" (*tekoi el dil*) oriented toward the taro swamp and gardens.[3] When villages were located on high ground, the taro swamps usually lay in alluvial flats between the village and the coast, and frequently the main stone path leading from the coast to the village square passed through the middle of the swamp along a raised dike. But today, with villages hugging the coast, women's work takes place largely "behind" the village and men's work "outside" the village.

These generalizations are intended to point out an apparent contra-

3. This gendered opposition correlates with the expressions "words of the fishing area" (*tekoi er a kereker*) and "words of the taro patch" (*tekoi er a cheluis*), and with the complementary opposition between the protein food (*odoim*) and starchy food (*ongraol*) essential to a complete meal.

diction between the village as a source of ideas of temporal permanence, structural stability, and spatial order, and the village as the locus of constant political, ecological, and demographic change. The key to understanding why this is only an apparent contradiction is the fact that both stability and change are coded historically by stones. Major villages are symbolized by sacred stones placed at significant positions in the central square or on paths connecting villages to the outside world. These stone markers are not, however, merely passive records of the political order, since they may be transported, exchanged, stolen, destroyed, or concealed in the course of political activity.

The village is more than a collection of residential houses, an entity of political jurisdiction, and a unit of economic cooperation. It also instantiates various conceptual forms or spatial models, such as the "path" (*rael*), "cornerpost" (*saus*), "side" (*bitang*), and the graded continuum of "large"/"small" (*klou/kekere*), the importance of which will emerge in later chapters. The village is conceived of as an enclosed space approached through an entrance (*siseball*), left through an exit (*tebedall*), and linked to other villages by paths across the hillside and lagoon. The entrance and exit or a large village is often marked by a broad road terminus pavement (*bdelulechang*) where travelers rest before continuing on their journey and where members of local men's clubs assemble to protect their village from attack. Two types of stones are frequently found at these pavements. First, a group of upright backrests arranged either in a circle or at four corners of a raised square functions as the outdoor chambers of the village's chiefly council; second, various types of sacred stones (*meang el bad*) stand guard against the penetration of evil or upsetting influences into the village (see, e.g., photograph 2). The road terminus marks the transition between the world "outside the village" (*ikrel a beluu*) and the world "inside the village" (*chelsel a beluu*), and movement between these two zones must pass along established paths, both physical and conceptual. Careful distinctions are drawn between different modalities of movement of people, things, events, and words which "move toward the village," "pass through the village," "enter the village," "pass by on the outside of the village," "originate within the village," or "go out from the village." Each type of movement is differentiated according to its place of origin, intentionality of motion, difficulty of entrance, duration of stay, and final destination. As the beginning and ending points of movement, the village is not conceived of as a semipermeable membrane where particles drift randomly back and forth across a wide area of articulation, but rather as an opening at the end of a tunnel or across a narrow bridge where particles must follow well-defined channels.

As was noted above, villages are grouped into several types of political associations which will be provisionally glossed as village complexes, districts, subdistricts, and federations. Political history as described in the writings of early European visitors and in indigenous narratives and chants is largely the story of the changing composition, organization, and function of village districts, the shifting alliances among village chiefs, and the gradual consolidation of the archipelago into several large federations with the assistance of Western arms.[4]

Village complexes are groups of satellite hamlets surrounding a dominant capital village. These smaller hamlets are not themselves fully autonomous villages, in that their component houses are affiliated with the principal or chiefly houses in the capital village. They frequently have only one meetinghouse and one clubhouse, in contrast to the full complement found in the capital. And they are not internally partitioned into two balanced "sides of the channel," each with its own landing place. These satellite hamlets are often founded by immigrant groups who are permitted to build houses in the "suburban" perimeter of the capital or by overflow from overpopulated principal houses. A clear example of this arrangement in Ngeremlengui district is the case of Imeiong with its hamlets Nglabang and Ulechetong, which form a geographically continuous unit along the same mangrove channel. Settled after Imeiong and dependent upon its high-ranking houses for all political relations with other villages, Nglabang and Ulechetong have in recent years become populated by families from Imeiong, who established residences away from their ancestral house pavements. In this and similar cases, satellite hamlets function as inland border guards or as coastal landing places for the capital, which often lies on more inaccessible high ground. This clear-cut differentiation in social rank and political power between hamlets and the capital village is aptly coded in the expressions that the satellites are the "children of the mother village," and that they are "side villages" (*bita el beluu*) of the capital.

Districts (*renged*, from *merenged*, "tie together"), the second type of multivillage association, are far more important than village complexes for understanding political history, since it is at the interdistrict level that institutions such as tribute, concubinage, warfare, ceremonial dancing, and financial exchanges took place.[5] Despite the testimony of

4. Basic ethnographic sources on political relations include Cheyne 1863–66; Hockin 1803; Keate 1788; Kubary 1873 and 1885; McCluer 1790–92; Semper 1982; Tetens 1958.

5. I use the politically neutral term "district" to refer to what were called "municipalities" during the Trusteeship period and what are referred to as "states" in the contemporary constitutional period.

historical narratives and surface archaeology that the district polity observed by European visitors after 1783 was only the latest phase of a dynamic process of development, the fact remains that most of Belau's districts have retained their political identity and geographical integrity for at least two hundred years. Like village complexes, districts consist of dependent villages affiliated with a dominant capital village. But in the case of districts, member villages are fully distinct entities with titleholders, houses, and clubs that are not merely subservient to the corresponding institutions at the capital. Furthermore, villages in the district maintain political relationships of various sorts with villages in other districts, ties that do not necessarily pass through the capital. Kubary (1885:116–17) even mentions a case in which a member village kept up peaceful relations with a village in a neighboring district which was at war with its capital village.

Member villages were dispersed throughout the territory of the district, although there was some tendency for villages to cluster around the capital. District boundaries can be correlated with geographical divisions to some degree. The districts of Ngcheangel, Beliliou, and Ngeaur occupy separate islands bearing the same names; only the district of Ngerekldeu in the central portion of the archipelago encompasses a large number of islands. On Babeldaob island, district boundaries tend to follow natural divisions created by major rivers, watersheds, and mountain ridges (see map 2). As in the better known Polynesian polities on the high volcanic islands of Tahiti and Hawaii, this arrangement implies that each district has access to major resource zones (wooded mountains, river valleys, barren hillsides, and coastal lagoons) and that exchanges distribute produce such as fish and taro more regularly within a district than between districts. Interdistrict trade, however, was extensive and included not only daily necessities such as lamp oil, pottery, wooden implements, palm syrup, and canoe sails, but also specialized goods such as turmeric powder, tortoiseshell ornaments, beaded women's skirts, red-ocher dye, and dugong bracelets.[6]

Because district composition and extent were subject to change due to defeat in warfare, abandonment of ecologically precarious village sites, or the instability of political alliances, it is impossible to fully represent Belauan district polity in a single map or chart. Maps 1 and 2 shows the location of fourteen districts which Kubary and Krämer both recorded as extant during their periods of research, but since most of

6. The production of pottery is said to have been confined to the villages of Oikull (in Irrai), Chelab (in Ngerard), and Ngersoes (in Ngetbang).

TABLE 1. DISTRICTS OF BELAU

Contemporary Name	Poetic Name	Archaic Name	Capital
Ngcheangel	Ngedebuul		Ngerdimes
Ngerechelong	Rteluul	Olokl	Mengellang
Ngerard	Kerradel	Ngerringal	Ngebuked
Ngerdmau	Ongedechuul		Urdmau
Ngeremlengui	Imiungs	Kerngilianged	Imeiong
Ngetbang			Ngeredubech
Imeliik		Ngerbungs	Ngerekeai
Irrai	Kedelukl	Ngerechumelbai	Irrai
Ngchesar	Oldiais		Ngchesar
Melekeok	Olekeok	Ngetelngal	Melekeok
Ngiual	Kiuluul		Ngiual
Oreor	Cherenguul	Ngerekldeu	Oreor
Beliliou	Odesangel		Ngeredelolk
Ngeaur	Edeaur		Ngerbelau

these districts are also mentioned by late-eighteenth-century visitors, it can be assumed that the map represents at least a century-long arrangement, that is, from 1783 to 1910.[7] And with only the loss of Ngersuul as an independent district and several name changes, these same districts would appear on a map of contemporary Belau. Table 1 summarizes this "classic" political order; the districts are listed in a relatively neutral format: starting with the northernmost district of Ngcheangel, the list circles counterclockwise around Babeldaob and then adds the two southern island districts.

The territorial stability of these districts is further confirmed by the careful study made by Krämer of the traditional processes by which the districts attained their modern shape. In almost every case fluidity of district membership and alliance took place within the confines of the modern district boundaries. Krämer records, for example, accounts of a succession of archaic village groupings within the limits of Ngerechelong district at the northern end of Babeldaob. A grouping called Ukall (a lumber tree) consisted of the (now-extinct) villages of Ukall, Ngertol, Dubech, and Ngerekeam; a second grouping called Delbirt was composed of the village of Ollei along with five extinct villages, Kiok,

7. Both Kubary and Krämer comment that the district of Ngersuul, once a populous land, fell under the sway of powerful Ngetelngal district to the north. I have not been able to locate references to either Ngersuul or Ngiual in eighteenth-century Western records.

Ngerechebab, Ngchui, Ngetmel, and Melekei; a third grouping called Eoaltaoch (Four Mangrove Channels) included Ollei, Kiokukall, Ngeremetong (or Ngeremetuker), and Ngeiungl; and finally a fourth grouping named Euiderchelong (Seven of Chelong) was composed of the capital Mengellang (with its side-channel hamlet Ngriil), Ngeiungl, Ngeremetong, Ngebiul, Iebukl, Ngerebau, and Ollei (Krämer 1917–29, 2:9–15). At no point in this traditional picture of Ngerechelong's history does a village from Ngerechelong's southern neighbor Ngerard enter into one of these four archaic groupings. And at no point does a village "secede" to join another district. Note finally that a given village enters into several successive groupings within Ngerechelong: Ollei is listed as a member of Delbirt, Eoaltaoch, and Euiderchelong.[8]

This grouping of villages within a district often took the form of structured opposition between two opposed subdistricts, each controlled by a different chiefly house at the capital or by two chiefs from cocapital villages. In several cases the existence of named subdistricts points to a previous stage of political consolidation before the emergence of a single district chief and a dominant capital village. Ngerekldeu district, for example, is divided into subdistricts named Ngerusekluk or Ngos (East) and Ngeremenganged or Ngebard (West). According to one account, the chiefs Kloteraol, head of the eastern group of villages, and Rubasech, head of the western group, were in constant competition until their opposition was successfully mediated by a wise person from Oreor village, to whom they yielded overall authority and for whom they invented the new title Ibedul (Head) (Kubary 1885:68–69).[9] A parallel tradition exists for Ngetelngal district, according to which chief Reklai united competing subdistrict factions of "upper" Melekeok under the leadership of Renguul and "lower" Melekeok under the combined leadership of Tmekei and Secharuleong. The subdistrict division of Ngerechumelbai (modern Irrai) is particularly interesting, since the two sections correspond to a split allegiance to capital villages of different districts: Kiukl er a Irrai (Irrai on the West Coast) under the leadership of Ngirikiklang was loyal to Oreor,

8. A more ambiguous example would be Ngerard district, whose formation, organization, and history have been studied by Krämer (1917–29, 2:45–73), Barnett (1949:175–78), and Aoyagi (1979:19–38). These scholars, however, give differing accounts of Ngerard's district organization.

9. This mediation, however, was apparently short-lived, since other traditions note that the dualism of subdistricts was reinstituted, but this time as the split between Ibedul on the eastern side and Ngiraikelau on the western side (PCAA, Oreor File).

while Desbedall er a Irrai (Irrai on the East Coast) under Ngiraked was loyal to Melekeok.[10]

Based on these comments on the dual structure of several districts and on the overarching control by chiefs at the capital, it is possible to overstate the level of political integration of districts. First of all, rank differentiation of capital and member villages was not accompanied by an inclusive or linear ranking of all the district's villages, nor was there a cross-district system of village rank as found, for example, in Yap (Labby 1976; Lingenfelter 1975; Schneider 1949). Rather, in Belau member villages stood in a coordinated relationship around the capital in much the same way that, in the intravillage context, lower-ranking houses surround chiefly houses. For example, Aoyagi (1979:35) cites evidence from Ngerard district that the four member villages of Chelab, Chol, Ngkeklau, and Ulimang are said to be the "four cornerposts" supporting the capital village, Ngebuked. And the villages of Ngeremlengui district are organized into a two-valued hierarchy, with the capital Imeiong referred to as the "big village" (*klou el beluu*) and the member villages of Ngeremetengel, Ngchemesed, and Ngereklngong classed together as Edeuteliang (Three at the Other End).

Second, there is little evidence from stories and chants that there existed a districtwide council of chiefs over and above the ruling council at the capital. In the most detailed published accounts of district organization, namely Aoyagi's study of Ngerard and Kubary's study of Ngetelngal, no mention is made of a district council. And my own field data from Ngeremlengui likewise indicate that there was no council whose authority transcended that of Ngaraimeiong, the chiefly council at Imeiong. Data from Ngerekldeu district, on the other hand, do suggest that Ngarameketii council, representing the capital Oreor and standing at the geographical midpoint between eastern and western subdistricts, consisted of titleholders whose ancestral ties link them to separate member villages within the district (Krämer 1917–29, 2:216; PCAA, Oreor File). But even this does not argue directly against the claim that there were no district councils, since in the cases of Ngarameketii and Ngaraimeiong councils, titled representatives from member villages joined the higher-ranking chiefs as part of a largely honorific secondary council and sat silently while the capital village's titleholders conducted business and issued directives. In the modern period, how-

10. Parallel divisions are reported for Ngcheangel district (into Ngerdilong and Ngerdimes), Ngerdmau district (into Urdmau and Ngetbong), and Ngiual (into Ngerachechong and Ngeramecholuk). Ngeremlengui does not seem ever to have been divided into balanced subdistricts, although the archaic group of villages depending on Ngeremeskang was so divided (see chapter 6).

ever, when most districts became chartered "municipalities" under the Trust Territory government and then "states" under the national constitution, district councils have been created which have actually usurped most of the absolute authority of councils at capital villages.[11] Also, a unifying pan-Belauan council of chiefs, the Rubekul a Belau (Elders of Belau), representing all the district capitals, developed only under pressure from colonial administrations. Some of these village leaders were assembled in Ngerard by Spanish priests in order to agree to halt intervillage warfare. Before the German colonial period, no Reklai titleholder from Melekeok had ever stepped inside Meketii meetinghouse in Oreor, where these pan-Belauan sessions began to be held. And it was not until the Japanese administration that chiefs from both Beliliou and Ngeaur, generally considered to be low-ranking districts, were allowed to join the other chiefs in this council. A man from Beliliou composed a brief song to mark the occasion of this change in status of Odesangel, the poetic name for the district:

> *Ng dimlak a kingellel er a Meketii sel lemei a Rubekul a Belau.*
> *Ng dimlak lngar er a basech er a irechar a Odesangel le ng mechitechut*
> *   e chelecha el ng mesisichang me debesechii me longeleuid.*
> It did not have a seat at Meketii [meetinghouse] when the Elders of
>   Belau assembled.
> Odesangel was not on the list in ancient times because it was weak,
>   but now that it is growing stronger, let us list it as the seventh
>   [on Ibedul's side of heaven].

Federations, the final type of multivillage association to be noted, consist of networks of shifting alliances among villages from several districts. Although the same term, *renged,* "tied together," is used for federations and districts, the diachronic stability of districts is not matched in the case of federations, which were the product of military expansion of a powerful village, the temporary solidarity of villages allied against a common enemy, or the result of kinship and marriage ties shared by local representatives of high-ranking house affiliation networks. Membership in federations involved mutual assistance in war, pooled contributions to support the financial obligations of village chiefs, and reciprocal visiting to celebrate the taking of a head trophy or to perform elaborate dances. Since chapter 4 is devoted to a comprehensive investigation of the mythological foundations and political ramifications of multivillage federations, little more needs to be said at

11. For a contemporary case study see Parmentier 1986b.

this point. As will be shown, ties of confederations which were traditionally based on positive ideologies of identity or cooperation became
increasingly coercive in the nineteenth century, with the development
of two opposed alliances, one focused on Oreor village and the other on
Melekeok village, which channeled competition over access to Western
arms and goods.

HOUSES, TITLES, AND COUNCILS

In Belau political relations among villages are dominated by the actions
of chiefly titleholders residing in high-ranking houses (*blai*). As a brief
preface to a description of the title system, a few points concerning
marriage, descent, and residence may be relevant here.[12] The dyadic
relationship between husband and wife is only the intersection of more
important exchange relationships between the side of the husband and
his sisters, on the one hand, and the side of the wife and her brothers,
on the other hand. The essence of this wider affinal link is the asymmetrical presentation of food and services from the wife's side to the
husband's side, with the goal of receiving valuables in return. A man's
sisters are his ultimate source of financial strength, since they guarantee
a steady supply of incoming wealth which he can use in turn to take care
of his own affinal obligations. A high-ranking woman marries a man of
at least equally high rank, since her male child, as potential heir to her
house's title, will thereby enjoy the benefits of a considerable payment
at the death of his mother. From the husband's point of view, marriage
to a high-ranking woman may indeed be a "costly affair." Not only will
his reputation be elevated when he presents the required valuables to a
distinguished house, but he can take pride in the fact that one of his
sons will have a good chance of taking a high title some day.

Chiefly houses that intermarry can simultaneously perpetuate their
status and insure that alienated valuables eventually return to their origin. This appears to have been the case in Oreor, where the Idid and
Ikelau houses intermarried so that the child of chief Ibedul (of Idid
house) becomes Ngiraikelau (of Ikelau house), and the child of
Ngiraikelau becomes Ibedul. These financial considerations are among

---

12. The focus of this book is on village and intervillage political relations, so topics such
as kinship, exchange, land tenure, and the title system as it relates to household affairs, rites
concerning ancestral spirits, succession competition, and multivillage house affiliation
systems are reserved for a subsequent publication. The literature on Belauan kinship is
extensive; see Barnett 1949; Force and Force 1961, 1972; Parmentier 1981:107–130,
429–527; Parmentier 1984; Smith 1981, 1983.

the principal reasons for the prevalence of rank-endogamous marriages, both within a district and across districts. Such marriage could also be used to solidify peace after a period of intervillage hostility; the marriage of chief Reklai of Melekeok to Bilung, the highest female title in Oreor, in the mid-nineteenth century is a famous example.

Because Belauans conceptualize the "children of women" (*ochell*) of a house to be stronger members than "children of men" (*ulechell*), there is a matrilineal bias, which creates a systemic disharmony when coupled with the fact that women go to live in their husband's villages. In other words, a "strong" female member of house located in one village does not live there, and her eldest male child will return to this homeland (*kotel*, "the back of his heel") only in old age when he takes the local title. Similarly, a senior woman who either divorces or outlives her husband can always return to her home, where she plays an important role in decision making concerning title inheritance, the expenditure of financial resources, and the distribution of land. But because of the prohibition on her sharing a house with her brother, she will live in a small house adjacent to the main "house of the title." And since a prominent man knows that he cannot pass his title or the house of the title to his son, he will strive to present him with other signs of wealth, such as the coveted dugong bone bracelet.

This combination of matrilineal priority in title inheritance and patrivirilocal residence means that, for all except those destined to return home to take the house's title, village loyalty is disjoined from kinship affiliation. A consequence of this is the high mobility well documented in folklore, including both the migration of families and whole villages and the wandering of single individuals seeking fame and fortune. Increasingly, however, violent warfare in the early nineteenth century and massive depopulation toward the end of that century drastically limited this mobility, and titles began to be held by local males with weaker ties to the core matriline.

The village's foreign policy (*kelulau*) is the total responsibility of between four and ten officeholders who sit together as the decision-making council (*klobak*). The title system is the most important point of articulation between the sphere of domestic activity (*tekoi er a blai*) and the sphere of public activity (*tekoi er a buai*), since titleholders are simultaneously heads of houses and members of village councils. Each principal house in a village has belonging to it a male title symbolized in certain ritual contexts by a coconut frond (*dui*) metaphorically carried by the house's senior matrilineally related man. Each title is a named office which exists independently from the person holding the position at any one time, and it is a serious violation for anyone other than a wife to continue to use a person's personal or house name after he has acquired a title. Belauan titleholders resemble Tikopia chiefs more than Solomon Island big men, in that the sacredness (*meang*) and power (*klisiich*) surrounding them derive from their carrying a title which occupies a permanent position in the village's social hierarchy rather than merely from the skill, achievements, and personal charisma of individual incumbents. And in Belau, genealogical closeness to the matrilineal core (*ochell*) of a house is always a significant factor in title succession. There are titleholders tracing only patrilateral affiliation (*ulechell*), but a man chosen without matrilineal credentials can never exercise his office with full confidence. He will be especially vulnerable to usurpation by individuals with stronger *ochell* ties (particularly the brothers of the former titleholder) and will need to rely heavily on the residual authority of the senior women of the house.

The person who holds the title is called *rubak*, a term derived from the human plural marker *re-* and the word *obak*, "male elder"—found in *obekul*, "older brother," and in several important titles, such as Obakeraibedechal, Obakeramechuu, Obakeraulechetong. Since houses claiming titles are themselves ranked in each village, the *rubak* of the highest-ranking house is also the leader (*merredel*) or "head of the village." This position is symbolized by his assigned seat in the village meetinghouse, by his claim of precedence in ceremonial food distribution, and by expressions of respect and deference by villagers. The chief's head, the most tabooed part of his body, must never be touched; his food is served in specially covered containers; his seat in the meetinghouse must not be occupied by anyone other than his children at play; villagers must detour off the path when the chief passes; and at his death the chief receives a more elaborate funeral rite than lesser titleholders. Above all, the chief "carries the voice of the village," in that his speech has the force of law.

As the focal point of village political life, the leader functions as provider and protector for visitors who have no other local affiliation. In chants, the chief is called the "cave" in which homeless wanderers, like driftwood, are anchored in security:

> The *rubak* of Ngemis is so helpful in taking care of the poor and
>   homeless; we use him as our sheltering cave, we who are poor as
>   we travel around, for the rough sea took away my anchor line,
>   and I grew very worried.
> The *rubak* of Ngimis is so helpful as he lets down his line to
>   become the anchor line for my canoe, and I fall asleep until
>   daylight. (Yamaguchi 1967:33; my translation)

My informants pointed out a metaphorical link between the word *rubak* and the words *oak*, "anchor," and *omak*, "to anchor": the *rubak* anchors the village polity so that it does not capsize when disturbed by high wind or waves. Not only people but also things coming from outside into the village are the property and responsibility of the leader; this prerogative is clearly evident in the way chiefs manipulated foreign commercial trade and claimed rights to be the first to benefit from any new entity or practice introduced into the environment (formerly, cloth, iron, weapons; more recently, motorboats, electricity, freezers, imported clothing). Correlatively, the leader is also the village's representative in dealings with the outside world, and as the repository of its stories and upholder of its customs he is the only legitimate source of discourse about the village, although the role of messenger or spokesman is frequently relegated to the fifth or tenth-ranking titleholder.

Traditionally, title succession went from older brother to younger brother, or from mother's brother to sister's son. Some powerful houses were divided into balanced moieties, or side-leg segments, which alternated or competed for succession to a single title. In more recent times, however, succession by patrifiliated individuals from other houses has become common, and many titles are held by distantly related individuals whose connection with the local house is based on ancient migration traditions or stories about former cooperation or service (see Parmentier 1984).

At the death of an important titleholder, the coconut frond which symbolizes the sacredness of the title is removed from the head of the deceased, combined with a leaf from an especially vigorous taro variety named *dudek el bisech*, and then either transferred directly to the heir or held for a period of time by the senior women of the house. In either case, this *teliakl el dui*, "wrapped coconut frond," is subsequently hung up on the rafters of the house, since the newly chosen titleholder cannot assume his responsibilities or exercise his authority in the village until three procedures are accomplished. First, he must undergo a period of confinement (*chelsimer*) in a small walled structure near the main house. This seclusion insures that villages cannot look upon the face of the man who is thereby accumulating the "sacredness" (*meang*) and "taboo" (*mekull*) of the title; it also gives his senior female relatives a chance to instruct him in matters concerning the house's traditions and finances. A person being installed as village chief will also receive instruction in political skills from an older colleague from an allied village. Second, during this period the women of the house prepare special foods for ceremonial distribution to local and visiting dignitaries. Details and nomenclatures differ from village to village, but generally these meals are labeled "entrance to the title" (*olsisebel a dui*). A particularly large food portion called *odekuil* is presented to the titleholder on the opposite side of the meetinghouse; this creates an imbalance in the reciprocal relations prescribed between these two *rubak,* which will be reversed when the other partner in turn dies. These feasts culminate in the preparation of an extremely costly delicacy consisting of pounded tropical almond candy formed into the triangular shape of a dugong. This mound of candy is referred to as the "bridge of the titleholder," since it constitutes a final requirement before the new titleholder can walk from his house to the meetinghouse.[13] The third requirement, pertaining only to individuals taking the chiefly title in Melekeok, Oreor, and Imeiong villages, is for the new titleholder to legitimize his link to the house's past by retracing the ancestral migration route and to receive at the village where this journey began the woven pandanus head covering (*dekedekel a btelul*) symbolic of the previous sea journey, as well as valuables (*tichiau*) representing the continued support and allegiance of these now-distant relatives. The man about to become Ibedul of Oreor travels south to Mengelang village (near Ngesias) in Beliliou, and the man to become Reklai of Melekeok travels north to Ngerdimes village in Ngcheangel. Having completed these three preparatory actions, the new titleholder is permitted to take his assigned seat in the chiefly meetinghouse, to claim the food portion prescribed for his position in the ranked council, and to be addressed by his title rather than by his personal name.

Partly as a result of the sharp depopulation of the latter part of the nineteenth century and partly in accordance with norms concerning service to the senior women of a house, it is possible for an energetic man to carry more than one title at the same time. Since prominent houses maintain strong ties of affiliation (*kebliil*) with equally high-ranking houses in other districts, the matrilineally strong members of a house will certainly consider awarding a vacant title to a nonresident member of the *kebliil* network who has demonstrated service to the house or who can trace a kinship connection stronger than that of any

---

13. There are two additional details of this practice that suggest the mediating role of the female category in the process of title acquisition. First, the candy's name, *mesekiu el miich,* "almond candy dugong," is an allusion to the story about the female Dugong of Ngerieleb; second, the word *miich* is a metaphor for female genitals (as used in the expression *techel a miich,* "meat of the almond," which refers to the matrilineal core of a house). The feminine mediation of chiefly power has been shown to be a widespread pattern in Oceanic societies. Cf. the role of bark cloth called "the path of the god" in Fijian installation ceremonies (Sahlins 1985b:85–86); in Belau the accession to the chiefship in Beluusung (in Irrai) is said to require the spreading of a woven pandanus mat (*telutau*) for the new titleholder.

locally available males. The most well known example of the extent to which this practice of accumulating titles can go is the case of Blas, a man from Irrai who held a proverbial "ten titles."

Story of Blas

Ngiraibuuch grew old and weak and was confined to the floor, so he depended on Blas for everything. Blas would go fishing all by himself and then come back and scale the fish and prepare food for Ngiraibuuch, and then he would go back to his own house. And the very same thing happened when Ngiraibuuch died, for when they started to look for someone to be the new Ngiraibuuch all the people said, "No, the new *rubak* will be Ngirachoang Blas." And so in this way he became the titleholder. All these contributions he made to the house of Choang worked to bring the people of the house close together and made other people very desirous of entering the *kebliil* of Ikelau, as well as the other houses which were affiliated with Ikelau in Ngeremlengui, Ngetbang, Irrai, Ngeremid, Ngerechemai, Ngerekebesang, and Beliliou. These places are far away from each other and yet they are still *kebliil* houses with respect to Ikelau. All this was because [Blas] had taken heed of what Ibedul had instructed him as the way to win his fortune [i.e., serving senior women]. So he was able to carry all these titles at that time, and it was permitted for him to do so since the powerful men, senior women, and the other *rubak* of Ikelau all agreed to this and followed the principles of the *kebliil*. And so Blas became the only man to have ten titles. (Kesolei 1975:6; my translation)

This story is informative additionally because it demonstrates that the selection of titleholders from the *kebliil* network is a relatively presupposing matter; that is, the houses where Blas took a title did not thereby become *kebliil* to each other for the first time. Rather, Blas carried titles in houses which were bilaterally related to Ikelau, the second-ranking house in Oreor village.[14]

Titleholders representing their local houses meet regularly in the village meetinghouse to discuss matters of public interest: strategies for warfare, arrangements for entertaining visiting parties, debates over the level of fines, imposition of regulations for exploiting the village's agricultural and fishing resources, adjudication of disputes over land

---

14. A song text I recorded give a list of Blas's titles as follows: Irokl in Ngetbang, Ngiramengiau in Ngeremengiau, Ngiraikelau in Oreor, Rechuld in Irrai, Berebor in Irrai, Rechiungl in Ngeremid, Ucherochoar in Ngerechemai, Ngiraibuuch in Ngerebeched, Chesbangel in Ngerekebesang, Ngirakidel in Beliliou, and Ngirturong in Imeiong.

ownership, collection of money to pay for concubine groups, decisions to repair or construct a new meetinghouse, instruction in village history and traditions, and the acceptance of new members to the council. An informant summarized these various activities under the categories "inventing laws" (*melibech a llach*), "conducting foreign affairs" (*oltobed er a kelulau*), and "keeping the village in order" (*mengetmokl er a beluu*).

The council is called *klobak*, a term derived from the abstracting prefix *kl-* and the word *obak*, "male elders"; the best translation might be "set of elders." Another expression referring less to the body of titleholders as a group than to the sum of individual titleholders in a village is *rubekul a beluu*, "elders of the village." The council is known by its official name usually formed by adding the locative prefix *ngar*, to the name of the central square or the name of the village. Thus the council of Imeiong is Ngaraimeiong; in Melekeok it is Ngaramelekeong, and in Oreor it is Ngarameketii, named after Meketii meetinghouse. The meetinghouse itself is usually located in the central square of the village; very large villages might also have a public meetinghouse next door, used to house visiting concubines and other guests (see photograph 3). Each titleholder sits at a specifically designated place on the floor, with the four high-ranking titleholders taking their assigned positions at the four corners. Confined to their seats, these men transact business by using messengers who scurry back and forth communicating opinions and questions through whispering. This style of discourse is the reason why chiefly politics is called the "way of whispers" (*rolel a kelulau*) and why the meetinghouse is referred to as the "building of whispers" (*olbiil er a kelulau*).

Equally important, though, is the influence of this discourse style on the nature of political relations in the village: subtle maneuvering along preestablished paths of affiliation among titleholders is more successful than powerful oratory and obvious arm-twisting. These paths involve, first, the focalization of political affiliation of lower-ranking titleholders upon the four cornerposts of the meetinghouse and, second, the balanced opposition between two factions or sides of the meetinghouse led by the two highest-ranking titleholders.[15] In other words, a lower-ranking member of the council could communicate with his cornerpost representative, who would then convey the message to the leader of their side. Whispering isolates all but the more important *rubak* from any awareness of the degree of dissension, collusion, and falsification in these discussions. As a proverbial expression puts it: *ko er a osechel a*

---

15. Barnett (1949:175) describes an atypical pattern in Ngebuked village, where council members allied to Mad and Krai, the two most important chiefs, actually sat in different buildings standing side by side in the village square.

mengur el merael er a milkolk e mo er a milkolk, "like the milk of the coconut, which flows from darkness into darkness." That is, the style of political discourse is like drinking a coconut, since the milk never sees daylight as it passes from nut to mouth. By keeping discourse so closely restricted, the two leading titleholders can carry out strategems that would anger or insult the local population if they knew what was being said. One *rubak,* for example, can pretend that another has paid an outstanding fine, while actually accepting no money at all in return for a future favor. Or these leaders can quietly pay fines on behalf of young men from their houses without these misdeeds becoming embarrassing general knowledge.

In addition to the four cornerposts and six or more affiliated titleholders, several capital villages, such as Oreor, Melekeok, and Imeiong, have a secondary council of up-to-ten minor titleholders representing houses from other villages or hamlets closely associated with the capital. In Imeiong the secondary council is known as Ngaracheritem, while the secondary council in Melekeok is called Ngaruchob. Although these lesser titleholders do not have a strong voice in council deliberations, they do hear final decisions and plans which they are entrusted to carry back to their homes. These men are also required to make financial contributions when a new meetinghouse is purchased or repaired. These contributions are distributed by seating position, with each *rubak* and his affiliated titleholders purchasing the roof portion directly over his seat, except for the cornerpost titleholders, who have heavier obligations, and for the fifth-ranking titleholder, who pays for the central ridgepole.

In some villages there is a distinction in responsibility for the first and second titleholders, who in addition to being in a cooperative relationship of "mutual friendship" also function in different spheres of activity. In Imeiong, Ngebuked, and Melekeok, for example, the second-ranking titleholders (Ngiraklang, Krai, and Rechebong, respectively) are said to be in charge of local village affairs, while the first-ranking titleholders (Ngirturong, Mad, and Reklai) take responsibility for foreign affairs, especially warfare. This correlation is interesting in light of traditions which explain that Ngirturong, Mad, and Reklai are all usurping chiefs who seized power from earlier leaders.[16] In other words, the Belauan evidence apparently contradicts the general Aus-

16. Semper (1982), however, notes that in Ngebuked village it is Mad who takes charge of local religious activities and the ancestor cult, while Krai functions as the leader of warfare and as director of public works. Without challenging Semper's intimate knowledge of the situation in Ngerard in the nineteenth century, it should be noted that in 1783 it was Krai rather than Mad who took charge of the village's foreign policy (Keate 1788:178); Krämer (1917–29, 1:104) mentions that Krai was the former "head chief" of

tronesian pattern of a relatively "female," sacred, and locally-oriented
first leader and a relatively "male," profane, and externally-oriented second leader. But this is so only if the details of political history are ignored. While there is little evidence that the titled houses of a village are
normally viewed as ranked segmentary lines, Aoyagi (1982:17) presents a fascinating counterinstance when he notes that in Ngcheangel the
political division between Ngerdilong and Ngerdimes subdistricts corresponds to the opposition between two brothers, the older Obakeru-
song and the younger Rdechor:

> In spite of the fact that Obakerusong was older than Rdechor, the
> latter has been regarded as the head of Ngcheangel, on the whole.
> Obakerusong just sat down issuing orders because he was older,
> while Rdechor was obliged to go on errands, but this task placed
> on him a substantial responsibility for the islanders. At formal
> parties, Obakerusong was entitled to receive fish and pigs' heads as
> proof of his higher status.

So village leadership was never a static affair, as numerous accounts
of internal rivalry, conflict between political and religious leaders, and
shifts in title rank make clear. The position of chiefs was never as secure
in precontact times as it was during the colonial regimes, and a study of
the traditions of many districts shows a common pattern in which the
first and second, or first and fifth, titles switched positions. Title reversals and usurpations mark the history of villages such as Imeiong,
Melekeok, Ngebuked, Oreor, Ngerdmau, Ngersuul, Ngetbang, Irrai,
Ngeredelolk, Ngimis, and Ngeredebotar[17] and in several of these places
the usurping agent is called a god (*chelid*) rather than a *rubak*.[18] The
local priest (*kerrong*) or spokesperson of a god could be a powerful
political agent, since these religious functionaries control the system of
prophecy (*omengelil*) and tribute (*tenget*) offered to the god. Representatives of the gods in Ngerechelong were particularly powerful, as
Cheyne discovered:

> There are two *chelid* at Ngerechelong, both women. They are wives
> to the god of Ngerechelong; one lives in Ngebiul [i.e., Ngebei],

---

the village; and Barnett (1949:174) writes that Krai's house Ngeredok is given first place in
"nominal or traditional orderings."

17. In Irrai the reversal was between Obakeratkar and Ngiraked; in Ngeredelolk
between Obakeramengelang and Obakerangeredelolk; in Ngimis between Rebulkuul and
Rekemesik; and in Ngeredebotar between Bechars and Mechab (see story below).

18. Villages where a "god" is the leader include Ngebiul, Ngiual, Ollei, Ngersuul,
Ngesias, Ngeredelolk, Ngerechol, Irrai, Ngerdmau, and Chol.

the other at Olekel [i.e., Ollei]. It is astonishing the power they have over the natives; even the chiefs are afraid to offend them. The prophetess of Ngebiul said this morning that the god of Ngerechelong—who is named Ngiraidemai—told her last night that he had killed Tet [the village chief of Olekel] yesterday, because he had not given her presents. (Cheyne 1863–66: 20 July 1864; cf. Barnard 1980:19, 29; Kubary 1969:21)

This is a reference to the famous trickster figure Medechiibelau, who under the guise of various names such as Ngiraidemai, Ngiraiulong. and Sechaltbuich is said to have usurped the first title from half a dozen villages. In Irrai village, for example, Medechiibelau seized the title Ngirikiklang, deposed the earlier chief Obakeratkar, and instituted a fellow traveler Ngiraked in a high position (PCAA, Irrai File).

A chief rules in respectful recognition of the council of which he is the leader and in the knowledge that ultimately the support of the populace contributes to his own status. The Story of Bechars of Ngeredebotar expresses the relationship between chief and people and also illustrates the potential for title reversal in the council:

Story of Bechars of Ngeredebotar

This is the story about Bechars and Meruk from the village of Ngeredebotar in Imeliik district. Ngeredebotar is a village in Imeliik district and is situated in the northern part of Imeliik.. In ancient times of Belau this village still had a full population, which lived very comfortably because its taro complex and hillside area were extensive and its fishing area was teeming with catch. Its river was large, and even in a state of drought its waters did not dry up. There was nothing at all which might cause difficult living conditions in the village, and the people living there were completely content. There was nothing which burdened the village other than village work projects. Whenever there was a public work project, Bechars, the chief of Ngeredebotar, took charge. This chief held his position on the basis of being very high-ranking, and as the chief of Ngeredebotar he was greatly feared in the village. When he directed work or any village affair he showed no consideration for low-ranking people; he treated them as if they were children from his own house. And so in all of Ngeredebotar there was not a single person who was happy with how he treated the people of the village. Meruk, the second in rank to Bechars, was a modest and soft-spoken man. He and his wife were just the same in their behavior, and their house always had plenty of food and betelnut to chew, and the whole village of Ngeredebotar came to relax there and eat breakfast, lunch, and dinner every day. He, his wife, and their children were alike in their generosity and kindness toward the villagers who came to gather at Meruk's house night and day. In contrast, practially no one went to Bechars's house except his own relatives.

And so when he pronounced the time for village work, Bechars would go out all by himself, but whenever Meruk walked in the village the people would greet him, and they would proceed together to the work project. When work was finished, they would depart and go together to Meruk's house; and if Meruk was not with them they would go get him and depart together. The people continued to do this, and after a while Bechars grew ashamed of his own behavior, since he was losing the capacity to govern because his harsh words and stern appearance could do nothing to unify the people of the village. And the villagers avoided his house whenever they walked by.

One day Bechars went over to Meruk's house and asked, "My friend, Ngeredebotar is turning around, so I beg you that we join together to lead the village and that we strengthen our relationship, as it was in ancient times." After he said this Bechars called the village to a meeting, but the village ignored his words and went fishing instead. So Bechars went back to Meruk, whose messenger was the only person who had gone to the meeting, for Meruk was the only one who obeyed Bechars's summons, since all the people of Ngeredebotar did not follow him and so did not attend. At this point Bechars realized that the people of the village despised him and his behavior and that his high rank applied within his own house and not to the public at large. And so he pleaded with Meruk, "Friend, I give you charge over the village, and you will carry the responsibility for the village. You are still the second person in rank, but you will take control of the village. I will still carry the [chiefly] title, but you will eat the first food portion. I will go lower down and eat the second food portion." So Bechars decided to give up his food portion, but not his title.

This was the way things were from ancient times until the present day, and there is a proverb which goes, "You are like Bechars of Ngeredebotar, growing pale."[19] And so if we are high-

---

19. The Belauan is: *ke ko er a Bechars er a Ngeredebotar e di mo becheleleu*. McKnight (1968:12) cites this proverb, but bases his interpretation on the "cockroach [*bechars*] of Ngeredebotar," rather than on the story given here. One of my informants said that *becheleleu* means "ashamed," not simply "pale."

ranking, we should not say, "I am high-ranking," for then we will be the only ones to respect us. But if we are high-ranking and our appearance is good and our voice humble, then people will respect us. (Kesolei 1971:49–50; my translation)

A chief who attracts to his establishment only his own "children," who fails to function as a source of food and hospitality, and who constantly calls attention to his own rank will, according to the moral of this story, earn the fear, but not the respect, of his village (cf. the story of Irakl, translated in Parmentier 1981:695).

In political intrigue, trickery often gives way to overt violence, as several narratives about assassination attest. The usual situation in these stories is the murder of the older brother by younger brothers who won the support of the senior women of the house, or else the murder of the first-ranking titleholder by the second-ranking titleholder, who then assumes the position of village leader (see chapter 7 for such an account). Perhaps the most detailed record of such political upheaval is Kubary's (1885) account of the changes of leadership in Ngetelngal district, where the latecomer Reklai of Uudes house usurped the title from Tmekei. Kubary himself was an eyewitness to the usurpation of the Ibedul title at Oreor in 1872; a rival faction led by the second-ranking titleholder Ngiraikelau forced Ibedul to leave the village to live in low-ranking Ngeremid hamlet and then installed a puppet chief too timid to assert the power of his office. And because each of these acts of usurpation results in a reordering of title rank rather than the abolition of the defeated title, the list of titles in a village at any one time becomes a complex synchronic sign of the dynamics of district history.

The principal means by which titleholders exercise and perpetuate their authority in both domestic and public spheres is the manipulation of valuables or money, the essential medium of Belauan social life. While it is true that having high rank (*ilteet*) is in principle distinct from being rich (*merau*), as stories about foolish chiefs who have squandered their financial resources prove, the combination of these two factors is the main source of chiefly power. Valuables acquired by members of the house are controlled by the joint deliberations of the male titleholder and senior women, who may decide to use them to discharge social obligations at various customary events, to exchange them for valuables of other types of combinations, to pay fines incurred by young people affiliated with the house, and to pass them to deserving children. Other pieces belong directly to the title itself, and it is the *rubak*'s responsibility to protect these for the future. Often it is these inalienable valuables which wives of titleholders wear on necklaces, thus publicly demonstrating the financial status of their husbands' families. A third category of valuables is *chelebucheb,* black and white impressed beads of several grades, which are the medium of chiefly politics. Alliances, treaties, bargains, reconciliations, silencings, and fines, for example, are handled by presentation of these *chelebucheb,* and an important *rubak* will usually travel with one or more of these pieces hidden in his handbag to meet any situation that might arise. Although passing these *chelebucheb* back and forth was the norm, clever titleholders in collusion could conceal their lack of ready financial resources by following a ploy called the "strategy of the withered betelnut leaf." According to this technique, the first man sends his (empty) handbag across the meetinghouse with this leaf carefully covering the opening. The opposite man peers privately into the bag and exclaims, "My friend, what a large valuable!" A titleholder who is also the head of a village is additionally responsible for managing the public treasury (*udoudbeluu*), consisting of valuables entering the village during various ceremonial presentations and reserved for delayed intervillage reciprocity.

One way titleholders as a class maintain their social position is by making sure that nontitled persons (*remeau,* "naked") do not acquire valuables, or if they do acquire valuables, to scheme to relieve them of their wealth. Since fines (*blals*) imposed by the village council are not negotiable, chiefs can either trump up imaginary charges or else watch carefully to catch the slightest infraction and then impose a serious penalty. Another technique is to hoard knowledge of the names and histories of particular valuables. Since the value of a piece depends in part on the story told about its previous "work," commoners without this esoteric knowledge are likely either to fail to realize the full potential of their money or to be fooled into falsely judging the value of the money of others. In addition to excluding nontitleholders from participating in financial transactions, high-ranking chiefs can actively increase their own supply of valuables by various earning techniques (*kerruul*). Chiefs lose status by working with their hands (e.g., fishing, carpentry, farming), so they resort to manipulating financial transactions in contexts such as intervillage money collections, concubine exchanges, dancing trips after headhunting raids, presentation of tribute by dependent villages, and selling dugong bracelets, and they resort to outright deception in making change (see below). Skill in acquiring money is so important to their status that one titleholder told me that his grandfather, an extremely wealthy and powerful man from Ngerard, washed his grandson's feet in water which had first been rinsed over valuables, so that the young boy would learn to attract money (cf. Kruijt 1914:240).

Little has been said up to this point about specific institutionalized mechanisms that serve to connect villages of a district and to link villages from different districts. The next sections will focus on four such institutions: warfare, money collection, concubinage, and village friendship. None of these continues in unchanged form in modern Belau, but the specific patterns of village relationships established by these mechanisms prior to this century still dominate contemporary political and social life.

WARFARE, HEADHUNTING, AND RECIPROCAL HOSTILITY

Given the absence of interdistrict political councils in the precolonial period, it is not surprising that intervillage hostility functioned as a primary means of political integration. Warfare, as described in early ethnographic accounts and as revealed in lengthy war chants and narratives, took two principal forms: swiftly executed raids (*ururt,* "dashes," or *mekemad,* "killings") carried out by a small party of warriors seeking to capture a single head, and all-out sieges (*benged el mekemad,* "held-against battle") aimed at the total destruction of the village under attack (Kubary 1885:127–41; Krämer 1917–29, 3:298–307). The political motivations for sending out a raiding party and for waging a pitched battle were very different (cf. McKinley 1976:124). In the case of raids, the goal was not the destruction of a village, the acquisition of new territory, or the establishment of a slave relationship with a defeated population. Rather, seizure of a single head (*blebaol,* "present, offering") enabled the successful village to gain *chelebucheb* valuables, the currency of chiefly politics. A chief in need of an *chelebucheb* piece to meet personal or political obligations encouraged the strongest men's club of his village to attack a village in another district. The war party planned its strategy in utmost secrecy for fear that inmarried women might betray the plan to their home village. If omens were favorable, the men decorated themselves, painted their bodies with strength-inducing turmeric (cf. Sopher 1964:119), and traveled secretly to a staging camp near the proposed attack site. The raid itself frequently took place at night or just before dawn.

Having cut off the head of an unsuspecting woman or feeble old man, the party returned home in glory displaying the *cheleotl* standard signalling victory. The warriors were then treated to specially prepared food and drink, while details of their adventures were related with formulaic exaggeration. Next, the head was taken on a sequence of visits to neighboring, friendly, or allied villages, where at each stop a group of

warriors performed a ceremonial dance, and the local titleholders purchased the head with a *chelebucheb* valuable. Should a village refuse to
participate in this custom, this would be taken as a repudiation of the
alliance, as when Ngerard decided not to accept a head trophy brought
by Ngirturong of Imeiong on behalf of Oreor (Semper 1982:174). At
the end of this series of visits, the head was either unceremoniously
discarded on the barren hills behind the village or left to rot on a large
offering stone (*omeroel*) dedicated to the village god.

Warfare was thus an important instrument of chiefly political econo-
my, since it brought in necessary *chelebucheb* pieces and since the subsequent dancing trip dramatized the current state of intervillage alliance.
Kubary describes this in terms of the opposition between Oreor and
Melekeok:

> Since these lands pay no taxes, however, these expenses have to be
> covered in some other way, and this is the purpose of the war-
> dance. The supreme chief tours the districts with which he is on
> friendly terms with a head which has been captured by his warriors,
> performs the war-dance, and receives in exchange a sum of money
> corresponding to the size of the land. In this way, Oreor, for
> example, receives a large amount of money from all the villages, but
> they would not permit Oreor to perform another war-dance soon
> after. Oreor, therefore, has to wait until other districts also get a
> head and make the war-dance, by which means the money given to
> Oreor comes back to them. All the governments in turn have the
> same advantage, and Oreor, together with its allies Ngeremlengui
> and Imeliik, looks for a head on the Ngetelngal side, while
> Melekeok seeks its victim in Oreor, Imeliik, and Ngeremlengui.
> (Kubary 1873:197)

Although Kubary (1895a:154–55) claims that the widespread use of
Western firearms in the nineteenth century did not change this basic
pattern of taking a single head, my informants mentioned that there
was a significant increase in headhunting when imported knives and
axes replaced wooden clubs (*brotech*) and a further intensification of
destructive warfare after the introduction of firearms.

These raids were not carried out in a random fashion. It was advantageous for chiefs of hostile villages to maintain a structured relationship of reciprocal hostility (*kaucheraro*), in which a raid in one
direction was answered after a space of a year or more by a raid in the
other direction (cf. Downs 1955). This formalized relationship was labeled by the name of the footpath or sea route which linked the capital
villages of the two warring districts. Thus, for example, the relationship
between Melekeok and Oreor was called Klai, and the relationship be-

tween Oreor and Imeliik was called Keanges. When active hostility flared up between these pairs of villages, the paths were said to be severed (*lloched*), and when the ratio of heads taken was temporarily in balance the paths were said to be peaceful (*budech*, literally "bound together like coconut leaves in a sheath"). Often raids carried out along these prescribed paths did not attack the capital village but rather an outlying, unprotected hamlet, where the war party would meet little resistance and did not risk loss of life.

But warfare was more than an instrument of chiefly politics; it was also the focus of much of the daily life of the men's clubs. The untitled men of a village functioned as a standing militia entrusted with the protection of the village from outside attack, and they were always eager to win personal renown for skill and bravery. Successful warriors were known as the "pride of the village" (*chedesiil er a beluu*), and their victories brought honor to the village as a whole and especially to the chiefly council's reputation for political acumen. For individual warriors, raiding provided an opportunity to become initiated into the club organization, to advance in positions of club leadership, and to impress female admirers with their physical prowess. The following short song about Ngiratumerang also illustrates some of the nonpolitical aspects of headhunting. This Ngiratumerang was a young man from the highest-ranking house in Imeliik. An unusually handsome man, he spent most of his time in the company of visiting concubines, whose constant attention prevented him from mastering the manly art of war. After being mistreated at the hands of Ngarametal club of Oreor, however, Ngiratumerang decided to study spear throwing from a recognized master living in Ngersuul. And it was there that he was finally able to demonstrate that his newly acquired powers equalled his good looks. In his honor the women sang:

Song of Ngiratumerang

We watch the battle at Ibangelei and at Okerduul. I clutch the medicinal potion in my hand and marvel at your body glistening in the sun's rays, Ngiratumerang. And you hold the club and the kingfisher spear and dash through the shallow water, with left hand swinging that way and right hand this way. What a wonderful sight to behold!

We watch the battle at Ibangelei and at Okerduul. I clutch the medicinal potion in my hand and marvel at your body glistening in the sun's rays, Ngiratumerang. It was just like coconut oil spilling over from the center of your back as they blockaded the mangrove channel. War cries and shouts and your leaping—oh, my young man, you are so wonderfully powerful!

We watch the battle at Ibangelei and at Okerduul. I clutch the
   medicinal potion in my hand and marvel at your body glistening
   in the sun's rays, Ngiratumerang. It was just like a god had
   arrived and, chewing betelnut, had stepped down to you right in
   the middle of the shallow water. The war cries and shouts and
   your leaping—oh, my young man, you are so valiant.
We watch the battle at Ibangelei and at Okerduul. I clutch the
   medicinal potion in my hand and marvel at your body glistening
   in the sun's rays, Ngiratumerang. The spears of the men from
   Ngeremid were like jumping mullet fish, and so I called out to
   you, "Stand up and take care to dodge and deflect the spears of
   the men of Ngaramengai club. Come and take this drink."
   (Kesolei 1975:43; my translation)

The admiration of these women was well deserved, for Ngiratumerang
was fighting to revenge his home village of Imul (in Imeliik), whose
men's club had been the victim of a surprise attack by warriors from
Ngarametal (Sharks) club of Oreor, and to regain his personal honor,
which had been tarnished during a long period of idle hesitation in the
company of flattering concubines. As the story which accompanies the
song relates, Ngiratumerang was able to repulse the warriors from
Oreor by several well-aimed spear tosses, each of which struck one of
the leaders of the raiding party.

Intermittent raids are only the first type of traditional warfare. The
second type, called "sieges" or "pitched battles," aimed at the wholesale
destruction of a village by burning down residential houses and public
buildings, slaughtering inhabitants in great numbers, and uprooting
gardens and taro patches. Faced with such an attack, villagers were
forced to flee their homes and take up temporary residence with friends
and relatives in other villages. A survey of stories of these extended
battles reveals several closely related political motives for waging this
type of warfare. First, the position of capital village within a given district was evidently not a matter of permanence, but rather was subject
to alteration through warfare. According to many accounts, the capital
villages of Imeiong in Ngeremlengui district, Melekeok in Ngetelngal
district, and Oreor in Ngerekldeu district all attained their present precedence after overthrowing warlike neighbors in all-out sieges which
left no houses standing. Imeiong's victory over Uluang, for example,
not only marked its ascendency within Ngeremlengui, but also founded
a set of friendly alliances with villages such as Ngeiungl, Ngellau, and
Ngeremetengel, which assisted in the assault (see the story in chapter
7). The defeated people of Uluang fled in several directions. Some

headed northwards and, after stopping briefly in Ngeremeskang, traveled to the house of Umerang in Melekeok; another group escaped by sea and sailed around the island to the chiefly house of Uudes in Melekeok. This linkage between Uluang in Ngeremlengui and Melekeok is expressed in the similarity between the names of these two important houses and the names of two prominent terraced hills in Uluang, namely, Uudes and Umerang.

Second, the destruction of a village could be a means to acquire valuables according to two principal techniques. The pattern of Oreor's repeated attacks on Ngerdmau during the eighteenth and nineteenth centuries illustrates the first strategy, called "rebuilding a village" (*osumech beluu*). Reputed to be rich in valuables, which their people took from their former home at Oliuch (near Melekeok), Ngerdmau was devastated a proverbial seven times by war parties sailing from Oreor. Each time its residents fled to a friendly village on the eastern side of the island, and each time the village was rebuilt and the people reestablished in their homes by the assistance of men's clubs from Melekeok, Oreor's primary rival in other contexts. Part of the money used to repay Melekeok for its aid was then handed over to the leaders of Oreor, and then this cycle was repeated. The final instance of this took place in mid-nineteenth century, as described in the famous War Chant of Urdmau, a section of which is translated below.

War Chant of Urdmau

There were only young men from Oreor, who ate fiery food and drank Western liquor, which enraged their spirits.

Stop the boat so we can disembark at Nglas dock and scatter our gunfire at Beketii rock.

We climb up on hands and feet at Delolk landing and then descend to the base of the coconut trees, and fire upon the chests of the young men and children of Urdmau who scatter, crossing over in the direction of Ngerechetang.

Then the young men [of Ngerechetang] arrive and carry away their leaders who were killed by spears. The wounded writhe like jumping mullet fish. And they run away helter-skelter across these large hills and through the ferns as far as Ngiual.

Upon [the young men's] arrival there the people of Ngerebokuu await them in front of the meetinghouse at Ibtaches. They all laugh as they get up all at once to greet Ngiraiuet, saying, "So Arebedul is about to arrive, but where is he to go? Is he going to prepare a taro patch near a meetinghouse so far away that it is out of range of human hearing?"

Expelled from their village by the rifle-carrying men of Oreor, the people of Ngerdmau fled across central Babeldaob. Upon arrival at Ngiual, their leaders Ngiraiuet and Arebedul faced the insulting prospect of finding living space beyond earshot of the center of Ngiual.

The second technique for obtaining money was to demand valuables as a condition for calling off an impending assault. In contrast to the situation of headhunting raids, where *chelebucheb* pieces were frequently acquired from allied villages that entertained dancing parties, this strategy of appeasement required face-to-face negotiations between chiefs of opposing villages and involved the ceremonial presentation of a large *bachel* valuable. Only a foolish or stingy chief would sacrifice his village by being slow to produce the required money—and this is precisely the point of the stinging criticism directed against Arurang in the War Chant of Urdmau:

> Those who made the path paid a *bachel* valuable to Idid [house of
> Ibedul]. Are you stupid enough, Arurang, to chart a different
> course now?
> And you, Arurang, are still stingy with those valuables collected
> from Ngarabeouch, while we are about to be expelled by the
> fighting force assembled in front of Urar channel.
> Are you going to chart a different course?

Arurang, one of the leaders of Ngerdmau, risked the safety of his village on the eve of attack by refusing to contribute to the pool of money collected by the village's titleholders (Ngarabeouch, named after the high chief Beouch). Many times in the past this strategy or path had successfully staved off destruction, and yet Arurang still dared to "chart a new course."

Several informative details concerning this technique as employed between Oreor and Melekeok are provided by Lieutenant Wedgeborough, who witnessed one such negotiation between Ibedul and Reklai in 1791. The display of English firearms and canons so amazed the warriors of besieged Melekeok that Reklai decided to come to terms without bloodshed.

> The chief [Reklai] gave into the hands of a *rubak* a bead, which he
> very carefully inclosed in his hands, and then moved slowly toward
> Ibedul, with his body bent, as is usual on approaching the King; he
> said something in a low tone of voice, that seemed to meet the
> approbation of the assembly; he then appeared to be in the act of
> presenting this bead, and Ibedul on the point of receiving it, when
> he suddenly drew back his hand, and asked, if so rich a present did
> not entitle the bearer to some reward; the King immediately gave

him a China bead of the second size;[20] as soon as the *rubak* had
received it, and not till then, he, with great solemnity, resigned the
rich present to the hands of Ibedul, who made a motion to
retire. . . . Lieutenant Wedgeborough was naturally anxious to
know what it was that had put an end to so much dissension and
bloodshed; the King kindly indulged him in his request, at the
same time enjoining him to be extremely careful, lest he should let
it fall to the ground; for if such an accident happened, it would
never be taken up. This precious token of peace and amity was a
bead or stone of a yellow colour, in length about two inches, in
depth or thickness one inch or more, formed like a wedge [*bachel*],
with two holes at the base, for the purpose of putting a line to
suspend it on. (Hockin 1803:43–44)

This description illustrates an additional subtle pattern of chiefly exchange according to which the giving of an extremely famous *bachel*
piece, handled with reverential care by the chief's messenger, requires a
smaller substitute or counterpayment (called the "body" [*bedengel*] of
the first piece) to be given in return. Ibedul, clearly in a position to set
the terms of this peace agreement, consents to hand over this money
because the implication of this mode of exchange is that the first *bachel*
is so large that, out of respect to it, a smaller substitute needs to be
awarded to partially fill the void created by its alienation. Thus, Ibedul's
newly received *bachel* increases in value in proportion to the generosity
of his own counterprestation. Detailed stories still recalled in Ngeremlengui describe a similar peace conference held at Olouch forest in the
late nineteenth century in which chiefs Reklai of Melekeok and Ngirturong of Imeiong reciprocally exchanged *chelebucheb* pieces.

A third motive for carrying out sieges was to initiate or reinforce a
relationship of "enslavement" (*ouker*) between conquering and con-
qured villages. The enslavement of villages and the extraction of tribute
(*tenget*) existed both within a single district and between districts. In
several parallel cases, in fact, the consolidation of district polities was
the result of the overthrow of the oppressing village (*outingaol el beluu*)
through the collaboration of several enslaved villages (*ker el beluu*).
Within Ngerechelong district at the northern end of Babeldaob island,
for example, the hamlets of Ngeiungl, Ngerekeam, and Ngesud are said
to have formerly been slaves of Melekei village. And within Ngetelngal

20. It is not clear if this "China bead" was one of the "several China beads" distributed
earlier by Wedgeborough, or a Belauan piece which looked like those beads; see McCluer
1790–92:119.

district on the east coast of the island, the central villages of Melekeok, Ngerames, and Ngerubesang were enslaved by a group of villages to the south, including Oliuch, Ngeburech, and Ngeruikl. This situation lasted until the yoke of servitude was thrown off by an attack supported by the god Uchelchelid of Ngerebeched. This left Tmekei of Melekeok as the overall head of the district and reversed the tribute relationship, so that now Ngeburech had to deliver concubines to Melekeok (Krämer 1917–29, 2:115; Hockin 1803:33).

Similarly, Ngchesar, the district just south of Melekeok, became recognized as an independent political entity only after a long period of slave status during which it was demeaningly called the "channel of Ngetbang." Since Ngetbang, located deep within the recesses of Ngeremeduu bay, traditionally had no fishing area of its own, its fishermen used the eastern shore at Ngchesar as a landing place. Villagers from Ngchesar were forced to carry fish as tribute to the Ngetbang chiefs at Ngeredubech village. This tributary relationship originated when Ngchesar petitioned the leaders of Ngetbang for a place to reside. Originally from Delbochel, a village in southern Beliliou, the people of Ngchesar migrated first to Ngerechelong and lived there at a place they called Delbong (the name being a sign of their homeland), until the combined forces of Mengellang and Ngriil villages drove them southward to coastal land controlled by Ngetbang.

Story of the Founding of Ngchesar

These people who fled to Ngchesar spoke to the *rubak* of Ngetbang, asking, "Can we live here?" The reply was negative, but they persisted saying, "Let us live here, and when we go fishing we will carry our catch to Ngetbang." So this was agreed on, and they took up residence there. They would travel across the hillside and come to Ngetbang. [The fish they brought] was called tribute. A man from Ngetbang stood guard at the bridges. There are so many small rivers and if people from Ngetbang walking toward Ngchesar came upon a bridge with the trunk end pointing toward Ngetbang, then the people of Ngchesar would be subject to a fine. The young people of Ngchesar were warned not to build their bridges in the wrong direction. But when they got angry at this rule, they would build a bridge in the wrong direction and then get fined.

Ngetbang then had control over Ngersuul and Ngchesar and even commanded respect in Melekeok. When Lbai, one of the leaders of Ngetbang, traveled to Melekeok, they would carry a lot of firewood to the meetinghouse to be sure the fire would not go out during his visit. And if Lbai was on his way to Ngchesar, news of his arrival spread quickly. And so they would prepare fine foods and carry firewood to the meetinghouse.

But after a while Ngchesar grew stronger and became tired of carrying fish to Ngetbang. So one time they went fishing and caught a rayfish and said to the young men, "Go into the hillside and make many spears, and then stick them into the rayfish. Carry it that way to Ngetbang." So they carried the rayfish with spears sticking out of it, and when the leaders of Ngetbang saw it they thought, "This situation has become dangerous." So they sent word to Ngchesar, saying, "This is the end. Do not send any more fish here." The rayfish with spears was the *olangch* that a war was impending.

Lbai and his associates realized that enforcing tribute payments and gestures of respect was possible only while Ngchesar was small and powerless. Rather than risk defeat at the hands of their slaves, they decided to accept the *olangch* and cancelled Ngchesar's obligation to bring fish. In doing so, however, they set in motion the gradual decline of landlocked Ngetbang as a viable political force on Babeldaob.

According to a story recorded by Krämer (1917–29, 3:29), tribute payment demanded by powerful Ngerekebesang included young boys destined for human sacrifice (*teltul*). Obak, the chief residing at Ulechetong house, sent war canoes to Ngeriab village in Beliliou to announce the beginning of a series of feasts, culminating in the slaying, stuffing, and roasting of human captives from Ngeriab. With the help of the trickster figure Boi, the people of Ngeriab finally challenged this oppression and convinced Ngerekebesang to substitute a pig in the sacrificial ritual.

The disgrace of being compelled to pay tribute stimulated heroic fighters to pledge themselves to the task of ridding their villages of this oppressive restriction. Although Ngiual was itself subjugated by both Melekeok and Oreor during the nineteenth century, according to folklore it oppressed the residents of several villages on the east coast of Ngerard district, at least until the hero Tuchuleaur (Carries Ngeaur) came to their rescue, as the following story describes.

Story of Hostility between Ngiual and Ngerard
The people from Ngerard killed all the male children in Ngiual. Every month they would come to visit Ngiual, and if there was a woman who had given birth to a son they would kill him. This continued for a very long time, until Ngiual was full of women. Then one woman gave birth to a child named Ngirangemelas, and as he grew older she concealed his maleness by having him wear a

grass skirt like a woman. Even when he was older he wore a grass
skirt. One day when he was bathing he looked at the girls and then
looked at himself, and noticed that his body was different. He
asked his mother, "Mother, when I went to bathe with my friends
I noticed that I have this thing which stands out, but the girls do
not." His mother cautioned him, "Don't even speak; don't notify
anyone of this." But when he grew to adulthood he learned that
the reason there were so few people in Ngiual is that Ngerard was
causing this destruction [of male children]. "Very well," he
thought, "I am going to do something about that."

So he began to study the behavior of fish. He would go down
to the beach when no one was there and watch *kelat* fish jumping
in the water. He made a net out of coconut fronds, and as the fish
jumped up he caught them in his net. When his net was full he
took the catch back to the village and said to his mother, "Here is
your protein food." He continued to do this, and then she thought,
"He has become a man." And so he went on to study the art of
making spears and clubs. And so the next time the people of
Ngerard came back to Ngiual he went down to the beach to a spot
near the northern border with Ngerard. He stood there and
watched the boats come down the coast, and he took his spear,
speared one of the men, and then fled from the beach. Then he ran
down the beach and from another spot speared another man, and
then ran again and speared a third man. From three spots he
speared three men from Ngerard. So the people of Ngerard now
knew that there was indeed a man in this village. And so when a
war party came again he was there to defend the village
singlehandedly. And so Ngiual became strong once again. Even
today people from Ngiual and people from Ngerard are still
arguing about the boundary on that beach.

But there was a reason for this hostility between Ngiual and
Ngerard. Ngiual used to be a powerful village and often made war
on Ngerard. In fact, in ancient times it was Ngiual which was the
stronger village. They said to the people of Ngerard, "If a piece of
driftwood floats in, bring it to Ngiual as tribute. But do not haul it
straight; you must haul it sideways in the water." So they were
forced to bring driftwood to Ngerard, and this took many days
since it was such a difficult task. This happened again and again.
The man Tuchuleaur [from Ngesang village in Ngerard] learned of
this treatment and decided to destroy Ngiual. And eventually
Tuchuleaur proved to be stronger, and in this he used the services
of the warrior Ucherulsiang.

But now I remember that there is an even more basic reason for

the hostility [between these two districts]. In ancient times the
people of Ngiual were people from Ngeremeskang; the name of
their village was Ibars. And so the people of this village
[Ngeremlengui] carried rayfish to feed them, since this village of
Ibars did not have access to fish, being so far from the sea. This
food is called *odingel*, "visiting food," rather than *tenget*, "tribute."
And so the people from Imeiong village brought them rayfish and
clams. In turn the people of Ibars came to Imeiong, bringing
pigeons and birds' eggs. But Ibars was a very difficult place to live
in, so after a while they decided to move to Ngiual. They simply
climbed up the hillside and descended to Ngiual [on the other side
of the island], which is really quite near. In Ngiual they went to a
village named Ibuuch, on the Ngerard side of the district. They
asked permission from the leaders [of Ngiual] and settled there.
But there was a man prone to gossiping who visited them there,
and when he returned home to Ngiual he reported, "The people of
Ibuuch are kicking Ngiual," since they slept with their legs
pointing toward Ngiual. The chief of Ngiual was furious, and he
scolded the people of Ibuuch, "Why when you sleep do you kick
Ngiual?" But the people of Ibuuch said, "We promise not to do it
again." So they began to sleep with their head in the direction of
Ngiual. And then someone reported, "The people of Ibuuch are
carrying Ngiual," since their heads were pointed in that direction.

A long time later a man named Tuchur [from Ngerard] was
killed; he was the older relative of Tuchuleaur. They fled and went
to Ngerard. This was a war party from Ibuuch which killed
Tuchur, a titleholder in Ngerard. A long time passed, and this man
Tuchuleaur (the one who killed his own son) married a woman
from Ngiual. And he traveled there and sat down on the stone
backrest in front of the chiefs' meetinghouse. A concubine in the
meetinghouse looked out at him and winked at him. She did this a
second and then a third time. He went up to the door of the
meetinghouse and said, "Woman, come here. I have something to
say to you. What is the reason that you were winking at me, while
I was sitting there?" She replied, "The head of your older relative
(*okdemelem*) is buried right here. The side of his legs are pointing in
the direction of the god house." (This means that he was like an
offering to the god.) Tuchuleaur said, "Enough. Now I know." He
took a piece of money, a *delobech kesuk*, and said, "This is your
payment. Thank you very much."

After this he began to do a lot of things to express his anger
against Ngiual. When he went fishing with men from Ngiual he
said, "Let's look for some raw fish to eat." He looked in particular

for the scorpion fish, which had a very harsh taste. "Bring me that to eat." His thought was, "Unless I can eat this fish without blistering my mouth, Ngiual will never be destroyed." So when his mouth became inflamed he remained silent. When he went back to the village he nursed it with warm water until it healed. The next time he went fishing they were out in a rather old canoe, and when fish appeared he called out, "I will bail us out." And he struck the canoe so hard that it broke in half. They struggled and struggled and just managed to get their canoe back to Belod landing place. He thought, "Yes, I can destroy Ngiual." He did many other things like this. Once he cut down a large *ukall* tree, one with the most branches on it. And he tried up all the branches so that there were none left on the entire tree.

The hero Tuchuleaur endured this and other tests of his resolve to destroy oppressing Ngiual, including the willful murder of his own son, whom he presented to his Ngiual wife in a basket. Finally with the assistance of chief Tmekei of Melekeok (but without the aid of Ngira-klang of Imeiong), Tuchuleaur defeated Ngiual and terminated the tribute payments which had humiliated the villages of Ngerard for generations. As a sign of his triumph he asked to be buried in a sitting position, so that he could keep a perpetual eye on the despised village of Ngiual to the south.

Although the subject of warfare dominates historical traditions as recorded in stories, chants, songs, proverbial expressions, and pictorial carvings, it should not be concluded that headhunting raids and destructive sieges were the only mechanisms of intervillage relations. Additional institutions which served to tie together villages from different districts included periodic money-collection ceremonies, institutionalized concubinage, and formalized village friendship. Only the last of these continues to be effective in the postcolonial era.

Money Collection, Concubinage, and Village Friendship

To a large degree the financial status of a district was determined by the ability of its capital village to stage elaborate ceremonial feasts, called *mur* or *mulbekl*, attended by dignitaries from allied villages.[21] The

21. *Mur* is the general term for "feast." The two categories of feasts are *mulbeluu*, "village feast," which is an affair involving a single household held, e.g., to honor a wife or to exorcize the sickness affecting a family member; and *mulbekl*, which is a village affair involving visiting parties from other villages. More commonly though, the latter type of ceremony is called *ruk*, after the name of the male dance which is the focal point of the first day's activities.

mulbekl can be viewed as the inverse of warfare, since the financial transactions take place between friendly villages. From the perspective of
untitled villagers the high point of these festivals was the "letting out of
the dancers," a highly trained, lavishly costumed group of men from the
host village who performed a variety of stylized, militaristic routines.
Captain Edward Barnard gives an excellent description of one such
dance he witnessed in Ngerechelong in 1832.

> I attended one grand dance at a neighboring town of all the young
> men of Ngerechelong. It was in rehearsal (for they sing and dance
> together) more than a month at length. The all-important day
> arrived. No national jubilee was ever celebrated in a civilized
> country with greater satisfaction than was the dance at Inreese
> [Ngriil?]. A platform or stage eighty or ninety feet long was erected
> on a spot of clear ground near the middle of the village. The
> dancers were divided into three classes of about fifty in each. When
> all was ready, one man brought out three spears and lay them in
> front of the stage at about forty yards distance. The dancers that
> came out of a hut, marching with a solemn step, ascended the
> stage, formed a line in front of the audience, all as nature formed
> them with the addition of only a little red paint. In a few moments
> they began the song and dance. They never change places with each
> other, but jump back and forth a few feet, stomping with all their
> might, at the same time giving what may well be called a wild
> Indian yell. If the quantity of enjoyment is to be judged by the wild
> sounds of laughter that accompanied their exhibition, they must
> have had it in no small degree. After occupying the stage for about
> half an hour, they retired in the same solemn manner as they
> ascended it. After the stage was clear, one man took a stand in the
> middle to prepare for another class. Before they ascended the stage
> a person stepped from the crowd to where the spears lay and threw
> them at the one on the stage. As fast as he could take them up, the
> other caught them as they flew past him, then turned and threw
> them into the woods just behind him. The other classes were
> similar. (Barnard 1980:26–28; spelling and punctuation
> modernized)

From the historical context of this performance it is clear that it celebrated the fact that Ngerechelong district had managed to obtain a
valuable symbol of political prestige, namely, the American survivors of
the wrecked *Mentor*.

But from the point of view of the titled chiefs, the focal point of the
ceremony was the money collection (*boketudoud*), at which time leading

titleholders from each invited village paid valuables, a *kluk*, a *delobech*, or an *chelebucheb*, depending on their relative rank and current wealth. In addition, outmarried women from the host village returned home to present financial contributions from their husbands to their titleholding brothers and mothers' brothers. The formal presentation of valuables by these visitors in order of the rank of their local titles was more than a simple payment for food and entertainment enjoyed during the days of the feast—even though expectation of financial gain did spur the host village to create an atmosphere conducive to generosity. As is the case with most ceremonial exchange in Belau where food and money pass in opposite directions, the presentation of valuables was both a sign of the strength and continuity of existing alliances and an investment destined to yield profitable return with the passage of time. Invitations to attend the *ruk* dance at the *mur* feast of a wealthy, high-ranking village were a jealously guarded privilege. And more specifically, the bestowal of rights to perform certain ceremonial functions, such as opening the feast by blowing the conch-shell trumpet, letting out the dancers, and setting up the ritually efficacious *mesang* stick, was used to commemorate previous acts of intervillage cooperation, common migration histories, and mutual friendship.

In short, the current status and past history of political alliances and district organization were symbolically and literally played out during the *mur* feast. For example, the privilege of letting out the dancers was held by Ulimang village for the feast at Melekeok, by Ngeraus and Melekeok for the feast at Ngerubesang, by Oreor for the feast at Irrai, and by Imeiong for the feast at Oreor. In this last case, Kubary (1885:111) notes that Oreor's feast was restricted so that, of all the chiefs who came to present money, only chiefs from Imeiong and Ngerard were permitted to witness the dances—a privilege storytellers explained in terms of the Milad myth: Imeiong is the senior sibling and Ngerard is the spoiled sister's son of Oreor (see chapter 4).

Elaborate feasting lasting in some cases up to seven days (with three days being the norm) only characterized the *mur* feasts of high-ranking villages such as Imeiong, Oreor, and Melekeok. But in Irrai and Ngerard slightly less extended ceremonies were marked by distinctive local variations. During the *mur* feast in Irrai, that is, in Ngerechumelbai district, villagers from the two subdistricts, Ngerikedam (including villages in the southern half of the district) and Desbedall (including villages on the northern shore), converged on the capital village carrying raw taro wrapped in bamboo bundles. Then a ceremony in honor of the local god Medechiibelau involved a brief but spectacular bout of sham warfare between the two subdistricts, intended to impress the god and to represent what, in Kubary's (1885:110) words, "might be the result if the government of the chief land did not intervene in a conciliatory role." Among the privileged visitors were people from Ngetbang, another village dedicated to Medechiibelau, who claimed for themselves the *meas* fish caught during the festivities. Also, pieces of carved wooden statuary set up during the dancing were subsequently removed to the protection of caves on rock islands adjacent to the coast. In Ngerard all the villages within the district joined together at the capital Ngebuked for a feast known in chants by the special name Kikeruau (after Ruau, the name of the meetinghouse). The celebration was attended only by Ngerard people and was not geared to the collection of money from visiting chiefs (Kesolei 1975:7).

Both Belauan and Western historical sources indicate that the elaboration and frequency of *mur* feasts featuring *ruk* dancing fell off sharply during the nineteenth century. Rapid depopulation made it difficult to organize large-scale club activities, and then the consolidation of political alliances around the two dominant villages of Melekeok and Oreor made it less feasible to stage money-collection ceremonies outside these two centers. By the time Krämer was in Belau in the first decade of this century, these customs existed only in informants' memories, and his account (1917–1919, 3:312–16) relies heavily on earlier eyewitness ethnographic reports of Semper and Kubary, both of whom attended modified versions of *ruk* dances. The German colonial administration was effective in supressing *ruk* dancing as well as other forms of feasting, intervillage visiting, and exchange, in which large expenditures of energy diverted villagers from agriculture and fishing.

In addition to warfare and money-collection ceremonies, a system of institutionalized concubinage created both symmetrical and asymmetrical political ties among villages.[22] This exchange of concubines took three general forms in traditional Belau. The most highly structured and politically important practice was called "lined up in a row" (*blolobel*), in which a party of ten women representing a village's ten ranked houses and titleholders lived in the chiefly meetinghouse of another village for approximately three months.[23] The concubines were each assigned to local titleholders in strict order of rank rather than by personal preference, with the representative (*rual*) of the first house

22. Important ethnographic sources dealing with concubinage include Barnett 1949:121–23; Krämer 1917–29, 2:92 and 3:274–76; Kubary 1885:51–53 and 91–98; Ritzenthaler 1954:24–25.

23. Alternatively, McManus (1977:24–25) derives the term *blolobel* from *bolobel*, "mullet (jumping fish)," which leap in unison out of the water.

taking as her lover the highest-ranking titleholder of the host village. For the duration of her stay, a concubine performed menial tasks such as tending the fire in the meetinghouse, carrying loads of harvested taro from the gardens, and keeping the meetinghouse floor and yard clean. But more importantly, she entertained her consort with sexual and artistic charm. Once a month the concubine's sponsor—her father, mother's brother, or other relative—sent food to the host village to feed her (understandably, poor relations between concubines and wives of local chiefs made this necessary). And on an irregular basis she prepared wrapped bunches of betelnut and pepper leaf (*deluus*) as a token of affection for her lover.

The visit of a concubine party came to a close in a ceremony named *ketkad*, in which the hosts paid for the services of the women with valuables; the value of these payments was proportional to the relative position of the host in the chiefly council hierarchy (see the Story of Cherechar and Rungiil in chapter 5). Each sponsor received financial payment (*oredem*) directly from one of the titleholders, and in addition a large piece of money called *olsechekiil* (normally of the *bachel* type) went to the chief of the concubines' village. This *olsechekiil* money was held by the highest-ranking titleholder in trust for the village and was used to pay for the services of *blolobel* parties which might visit the village in the future. If two villages exchanged parties of women, that is, participated in what is termed "mutual concubinage" (*kaumengol*), then the *olsechekiil* payment traveled a "restricted" path back and forth between the corresponding chiefly houses. But if the relationship between villages was asymmetrical, with women coming from only one of the villages, then this valuable passed along a "generalized" path to a series of chiefly houses in different villages.

The second form of concubinage involved groups of women who traveled to another village to earn money through sexual services to the local men's club. In contrast to the more formalized *blolobel* arrangement, in which women were the instruments of chiefly moneymaking, and in which sexual relationships formed during the visit were prescribed by strict rank order, these "concubines of the men's club" (*mengol er a cheldebechel*) decided on their own to visit a certain club, and the individual payments they received were not matched by a comprehensive *olsechekiil* payment from the host village's chief. As a general rule, the political consequences of this type of concubinage were not important, except in a few unusual instances in which the hosting men's club committed acts of violence against one or all of the visiting women. Then, this tragedy often became the cause for revenge warfare. More normally, however, the relationships established remained at the club level, with a particular women's club becoming the favorite partner of a particular men's club. In some cases, a women's club heard about a brave or handsome man who had recently acquired a particularly valuable piece of money, so they set out with the expressed purpose of winning that valuable for themselves and for the honor of their village.

Another variation involved a woman called "sail rope concubine" (*klemat el mengol*), who on her own initiative traveled to another village to become the lover of a particularly high-ranking or wealthy man. While the ten-woman *blolobel* group followed an important political path between villages, a sail-rope concubine pursued a path that was "crosswise" or "askew," that is, one not necessarily prescribed by formal intervillage ties. And it is this feature that informants note when explaining the meaning of the term *klemat,* the name of the rope used to rig sails on a sailing canoe, since these ropes are tied crosswise in relation to the direction of the sail.[24] An ambitious woman who approached a chief from another village as a sail-rope concubine, with the single purpose of acquiring money, was known as a woman who "carries away the money" (*mengol er a udoud*). The money earned through this practice did not, however, remain her personal property; when she returned home it went to the chief as part of the "village money" (*udoudbeluu*) reserved for later use in paying off fines incurred by local people. Although they were relieved of the money they had earned, these women did benefit individually in that their authority or "voice" within the household and village increased in proportion to the number and value of the money pieces they obtained in this way.

A third type of concubinage, involving the involuntary detention of women captured in warfare, differed considerably from the first two types, in that no money was exchanged between chiefs and villages in return for services, and in that no reciprocal political alliances were established or strengthened. Kubary speculates that the existence of this category of captured or slave women (*uulech,* literally, "discarded grass skirt used as a doormat") is evidence that the entire institutionalized concubinage system as found on Belau and Yap is the result of the decline in warfare and the consequent shortage of nonlocal women. Without subscribing to this hypothesis based on the nineteenth-century doctrine of survivals, I think it is possible to agree with Kubary's linkage of slaves and warfare and to see in the institution of captured women an important political instrument functioning instead of and also along with the payment of valuables.

The women referred to by the derogatory label of "doormats" were

---

24. McManus (1977:120) gives the phrase "concubines brought as hostages" for the term *klemat el mengol;* this definition is at variance with the information I recorded in the field and with Belauan texts I have studied.

brought to a conquering village by the victorious raiding party and installed in one of the clubhouses, where they were treated contemptuously by the women of the village. Because their connection with their older brothers, fathers, and mothers' brothers had been severed, these women were not in a position to arrange a politically advantageous marriage, since there was little chance of the peaceful reciprocity of food and money required between affines. From the perspective of their male captors, however, this offered an opportunity for them to marry disconnected women and have children and still avoid the normal situation in which a man's children had stronger matrilineal ties to their mother's village. Not only were offspring of doormat concubines not likely to cause serious drainage of financial resources, but they were also not likely to desert their fathers to take matrilineal titles elsewhere.

The political significance of these captives centered on three possibilities. First, women could be voluntarily or coercively given up by one village to another in order to avoid imminent destruction. Oreor's massive assault on Beliliou in 1783, for example, ended without bloodshed when, as a sign of their submission, the chiefs of Beliliou handed over a group of women to Ibedul of Oreor (Keate 1788:204–5). Second, women from a conquered village figured in the terms of peace settlements demanded by the conquering village, either in place of or in addition to financial payment (see, e.g., Delano 1817:62–63). Third, the existence of captives subject to disrespect and severe hardship was a powerful incentive for their home village to plan a revenge raid or even to plot a massive counterattack with the help of allied villages.

Setting up these three forms of concubinage—lined-up-in-a-row, sail-rope, and doormat—does not imply that there was always a clearcut boundary between the types. A party of three women traveling together to another village could function, for example, as a small *blolobel* group, especially if they represented the three high-ranking houses of their home village; or else they could consider themselves independent *klemat el mengol*. Or to cite another example from a story involving Melekeok and Ngkeklau villages (Krämer 1917–29, 3:275), if a village which regularly sent *blolobel* parties to an allied community should refuse to continue to do so, they were open to attack by their former partner, whose raiding party then tried to take as doormats what they once received as *blolobel*. And finally, it is not always possible to tell, on the basis of stories, chants, and songs, whether concubinage relations were symmetrical or asymmetrical. With reciprocal visits often three or four years apart and with alliances between major villages frequently unstable and shifting, a given visit by a group of women created temporary financial imbalance as much as it affirmed reciprocal relations.

A final dimension of intervillage relations that needs to be noted briefly is the mutual friendship that tied villages together and that provided motivation for both formal and informal mutual assistance, good will, and respect. A village that maintained institutionalized friendship with a village in another district refrained from participating in warfare when the path between the two districts became severed, sent visiting parties to be entertained with dancing and feasting in their partner village, and came to the aid of its friends in village work projects and to its defense in wartime. This form of intervillage relationship could originate in several ways. The villages of Ngkeklau (in Ngerechelong district) and Ngeburech (in Ngetelngal district) were friends because their villages were founded by people from the same ancient migration led by Uchelkeklau from Ngeredelolk in Beliliou (Kubary 1885:116). Ngeruikl (in Ngetelngal) and Ngerechol (in Beliliou) were friends because they shared the same local god. And Ngeremlengui, Oreor, and Ngesias (in Beliliou) were "related through ancestral spirits," in that reciprocal visiting parties carried the *kleangel,* a wooden box holding the ancestral spirits of the three villages.[25] Ngerebeched (in Ngerekldeu) and Ngeremetengel (in Ngeremlengui) became friends when their respective chiefs, Obechebachelsekerel and Ngiradilubech, traveled together around Belau.

In addition to relations grounded in common origins, shared gods, and the personal activities of chiefs, another source of mutual friendship was when a village rendered assistance in warfare to a village outside its immediate district or beyond the network of alliances existing between the capital villages of two districts. When warriors from Imeiong in Ngeremlengui, to cite one example, attempted to attack a small village in Ngerechelong, their war canoes ran aground at low tide. Men from nearby Ngeiungl village rescued the canoes, and this began a pattern of association which later was called upon when Imeiong recruited allies in its campaign against oppressing Uluang village (story text given in Parmentier 1981:190–91). In each of these examples, the connection between villages does not pass through the capital village of the districts involved and therefore does not form part of the official foreign policy of the chiefly council at the capitals. (In the same way, personal friendship can operate outside the more regimented, formalized relationships grounded in affinal obligations, house affiliations, and title linkages.) Because village relationships of all types are often based on particular

25. An informant said that he had heard two explanations for this connection: first, that these three village are called "children of the cormorant (*deroech*) bird"; and second, that Ngesias began the relationship when it sent large quantities of goods to Oreor and Ngeremlengui after receiving a high-ranking child who drifted ashore.

(real or postulated) events—a migration, a war, a visit from a god, or
an act of assistance—the specific reason/origin (*uchul*) of the tie is recalled when the concerned villages interact. But since these relationships prescribe only a general attitude of cooperation, solidarity,
and amity, the two villages are not linked by any permanent su-
pravillage political institutions such as having resident ambassadors,
participating in a council composed of representatives from both villages, or enjoying rights to succeed to each other's chiefly titles.

Village friendships can be commemorated in songs (*boid*) performed
during festivities involving men's clubs from the two places. During the
Japanese period many people from Beliliou were forced to move to
Ngerard, where some were buried during the war. When the war ended
those who returned home to Beliliou composed the following song in
honor of Kerradel, the poetic name for Ngerard:

Song of Kerradel

Kerradel, our villages are so far apart.
I came by night to Oreor and I slept at Kemais landing.
In the morning I sailed around Ngerengel point and caught sight
    of Imiungs, and I recalled their efforts on my behalf.
I remained silent and sailed on until I reached Ongedechuul [i.e.,
    Ngerdmau] and recalled their efforts on my behalf.
I remained silent and sailed on until I caught sight of Ngeuel point
    and arrived at Ebilmaiang rock, where I broke into tears.
Kerradel, I have been away for such a long time that this path of
    ours at the shoreline of Ngeskii, at Ngeskeras, and at Ngetelual
    has become overgrown.
Now these places are filled with [the graves] of those whose fate
    concerns us all.
Would that I could just say: you that are sleeping, arise! Let us
    greet each other, I and they, and together travel down to
    Beliliou.

The bond between Beliliou and Ngerard is conceived of as an overgrown path, and the motivation for the friendship lies in the continuing
presence of graves of ancestors in Ngerard.[26]

26. This is undoubtedly the same village friendship referred to by Barnett (1970:20),
who witnessed a "visiting party" dance in 1948.

1. Malsol Ngiraibuuch Ngiraklang (1980)

2. Iechadrachuoluu

3. Belau Museum bai

4. NGEROACH

5. Imiungselbad (Lucking 1984, fig. 69)

6. Terraces near Imeiong

7. Ngartemellang

CHAPTER

3

Diagrammatic Icons and
Historical Processes

This chapter forms a theoretical bridge between the introductory contextual and ethnographic material presented in the first two chapters
and the more detailed case studies in the following four chapters. At
issue here is the relationship between two kinds of culturally constituted semiotic entities: classes of materially embodied signs of/in history, what Belauans call *olangch,* and various schemes or models
according to which these signs are deployed in action and interpreted in
ideological reconstruction. Briefly, the argument is that a full understanding of embodied signs in any culture requires careful investigation
into the broader semiotic networks in which these signs play their
meaningful roles. But more particularly, these models of sign organization are themselves subject to culturally specific normative valuation
and semantic labeling and thus have a degree of meaningfulness independent of the signs they structure. The semiotic models discussed ab-
stractly in this chapter will reappear in the analysis in chapter 4 of their
ideological employment in myths of pan-Belauan political origination,
in the sketch in chapter 5 of the synchronic overlapping of these models
in Ngeremlengui district's spatial organization, in the comparison in
chapter 6 of high- and low-ranking historical perspectives on the district's internal hierarchical polity, and in the account in chapter 7 of the
story of Ngeremlengui's interdistrict relationships.

In his classic discussion of semiotic relations, the philosopher Peirce
notes a connection between three types of signs and three modes of
temporality. Signs he calls "icons," in which the relationship between
expressive sign vehicle and represented object is grounded in some formal resemblance, are inherently oriented toward the past, since these
signs function meaningfully without the actual spatiotemporal existence of the represented object. In contrast, signs he calls "indexes"

require some relationship of contiguity between expression and object and are thus necessarily anchored to present experience, discourse, or action. Finally, signs Peirce calls "symbols" bring a formal representation into relation with an object represented only on the basis of some further interpreting representation's action of imputing or endowing that relation with a conventional linkage (see Parmentier 1985b). As such, symbols always point to the future, in that this semiotic relation is essentially a processual regularity. As Peirce concludes: "Thus the mode of being of a symbol is different from that of the icon and from that of the index. An icon has such being as belongs to past experience. It exists only as an image in the mind. An index has the being of present experience. The being of a symbol consists in the real fact that something surely will be experienced if certain conditions be satisfied" (Peirce 1931–35, 4:447).

This chapter takes up this Peircean insight into the functional potential of certain types of sign relations and establishes the cultural valuation of these signs as they organize patterns of social relations in Belau. At issue are certain signs within a subclass of icons Peirce calls "diagrams," which represent the relations among parts of some represented object by analogous relations among component parts of the sign vehicle. Cultural diagrams are well documented in ethnographic literature. The elaborate temple organization of Bali (Geertz 1980) represents the hierarchical relations among social units and cosmic categories. And the residential organization of Tiv hamlets (Bohannan 1958) is a concrete diagram of the segmentary genealogical relations among patrilineages. In the Belauan case, however, multiple or complex diagrammatic icons need to be analyzed in order to understand how each is differentially engaged in channeling social activity and in directing the course of social change in the face of exogenous factors such as colonial domination, induced political modernization, and sudden shifts in population.

Four Diagrams of Social Relations

In order to properly analyze the role of diagrammatic icons in Belau, a more complex theoretical apparatus is required than these over-simplified illustrations might suggest. In Belau there are four principal diagrams which organize the composition and interrelations among persons, roles, and sociopolitical units, and whose lexical labels are used frequently in discourse about the nature of social action: "path" (*rael*), "side" (*bitang*), "cornerpost" (*saus*), and "larger"/"smaller" (*klou*/*kekere*). (Although the discussion will use these English glosses rather than indigenous terms, only Belauan meanings are implied.) Each of these expressions is associated with a particular schematic or compositional arrangement of elements, as well as a range of semantic meanings derived principally from reflection on a physical prototype or exemplar conceived of as the basis for metaphorical analogy. The argument will proceed in terms of these four dimensions, displayed in figure 1: lexical labels, schemata, physical prototypes, and semantic fields.

To begin with the first diagram, the word "path" refers primarily to numerous trails running across hillsides and through forests which connect villages. The word can also be used to refer to social action in two related senses. A path is a method, technique, patterns, or strategy—in short, a way of doing something. Warfare strategies, fishing techniques, oratorical skills, and patterns of exchange are also called "paths." But paths are also established linkages, relationships, and associations among persons, groups, and political units which were created by some precedent-setting action in the past, and which imply the possibility, as well as the obligation, for following the path in exchange, marriage, cooperation, and competition. The corresponding schema of paths involves a series of homologous elements tied together in a linear thread, beginning at a spatiotemporal origin point and concluding at a terminal point.[1]

The associated semantic field of paths includes three general features which derive from reflection on journeys or migrations along trails. First, points linked together by a clear path have achieved a degree of structural homology and hence positive cultural identity. This set of elements functions as a unit vis-à-vis other sets of elements and shares a sense of commonality signalled in myths and stories by the depositing of identical symbolic markers—sacred stones, trees, valuables, place names, and titles—at each location where a god or ancestor stopped on the journey which began the path. Second, the linked elements can be viewed in terms of sequential precedence, with the origin point outranking all other points, according to a logic which stipulates that priority in time implies seniority in ceremonial precedence. Third, underlying all the examples mentioned above is the notion of a culturally created regularity which imposes upon inchoate experience a degree of linear order. A path implies the possibility for repeated action within prescribed confines, whether it be retracing a footpath through the forest, pursuing well-attested methods of fishing, or following established social linkages. In semiotic terms, paths in Belau function as "sign types," that is, general regularities which impose their template or pat-

---

1. The metaphor of the path is common in Oceania and Indonesia; see, for example, Bateson 1958:237; Cunningham 1965:374; Koskinen 1963:58–70; Sayes 1984.

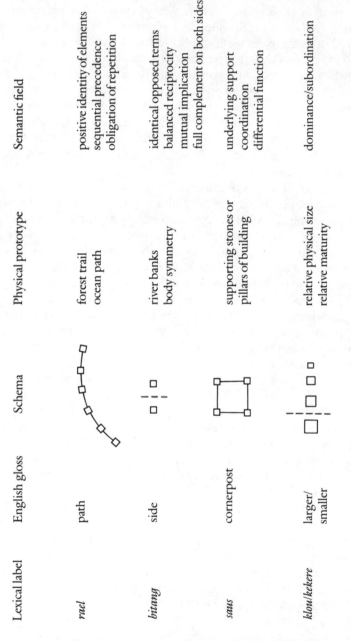

Lexical label	English gloss	Schema	Physical prototype	Semantic field
rael	path		forest trail ocean path	positive identity of elements sequential precedence obligation of repetition
bitang	side		river banks body symmetry	identical opposed terms balanced reciprocity mutual implication full complement on both sides
saus	cornerpost		supporting stones or pillars of building	underlying support coordination differential function
klou/kekere	larger/ smaller		relative physical size relative maturity	dominance/subordination

FIG. 1. DIAGRAMMATIC ICONS OF SOCIAL RELATIONS

tern on "sign tokens," so that these individual occurrences are meaningfully categorizable as instances or "replicas" (to use Peirce's terms)
of the general rule. Much more needs to be said about paths, but the
purpose of this initial overview is to clarify by one example the relationship among analytic categories of label, schema, prototype. and semantic field.

If linear linkage is the organizing principle of paths, then pure opposition is the essential feature of the second diagram, "sides." A
Belauan side is not like our notion of a side of a house or side of a
mountain, but rather is one-half of an oppositional pair in which both
halves are identical, yet inverse. A common expression for sets of pairs
in many contexts is "one side and other other side," the implication
being that the relevant universe of elements is exhausted by the combination of two halves and, further, that there is pressure keeping the
two sides from converging, overlapping, or collapsing. Even the use of
the single term "side" implies that a matched partner exists: to walk to
the side of the village implies that one is presently standing on the other
side of the same village. Obvious physical prototypes for the diagram of
sides include riverbanks, especially when the water divides a village into
two symmetrical parts, and bilateral body parts, especially eyes, legs,
and breasts. As these natural embodiments suggest, the value of identical, yet opposed, terms is matched by the sense that each member is
substantively and functionally complete, and that each member exists at
the same ontological level. The side of a riverbank can only be another
riverbank. Finally, the semantic field of sides carries the meaning that
the two elements are related by balanced reciprocity, either peaceful or
hostile. Exchange goods, feast foods, and head trophies moving from
one village, house, or club to another require that return or revenge be
made after a time delay proper to the custom in question. It is this
aspect of sides that leads to the apparent paradox that opposed social
units can be said to be simultaneously mutual friends and mutual enemies, since aggressive competition between units presupposes the per-
petuity of the structure as a balanced whole.

The next diagram, "four cornerposts," combines features of paths
and sides to express the relationship between four coordinated elements
supporting a total structure: individual cornerposts are said to be linked
by paths, and the set can be divided into opposed groups of two sides.
Used primarily to refer to four stone or wooden pillars supporting the
roofs of various buildings, the term "cornerpost" is also used in talking
about the coordinated system of political relations among the four
chiefly titleholders in a village (the "cornerposts of the village") and

among the four principal villages of the archipelago (the "cornerposts of Belau"). In both these examples, the four chiefs and four villages are hierarchically graded and functionally differentiated. Often the highest-ranking element represents the set in relation to other sets, while the second-ranking element takes responsibility for the internal workings of the structure. More generally, however, the diagram of "cornerpost" is a quintessentially cultural sign. There do not appear to be any naturally occurring objects in the Belauan universe that exhibit this particular property of coordinated integration of four elements supporting an encompassing structure. In fact the prototype for the cornerpost diagram is the chiefly meetinghouse where the four high-ranking titleholders take their prescribed seats at the four corners. The meetinghouse, in turn, stands metonymically for the order of Belauan culture as a whole.

The final diagrammatic icon which figures prominently in categorizations of social relations does not have a single lexical label. The pattern of larger/smaller is a continuum of elements in a series which are ranked according to the degree or strength of a single feature. Any two elements can be compared as larger and smaller on the basis of features such as worth (for pieces of money), social rank (for persons and houses), power (for chiefs), and sacredness (for gods and chiefly titles). While these various referents are typically associated with these features, it is also possible for more than one feature to be used in reference to a single, graded object: a high chief simultaneously possesses social rank, sacredness, and power. Given a single dimension of contrast, however, a ranked series of elements can be constructed, and individuals are fond of drawing up cognitive as well as written lists of graded titles, houses, clubs, villages, valuables, and land parcels.

Thus the model of larger/smaller expresses the Belauan image of hierarchy, seen as a syntagmatic chain of co-occurring elements that asymmetrically imply each other (see Valeri 1985:93). The most obvious prototype for this diagram of graded series is the biological fact of relative maturity, ripeness, or size. Relations among men, especially brothers, are carefully graded by age, with a distinct term of address used for males senior to and junior to speaker. (Interestingly, female siblings, not implicated to the same extent in the manipulation of power and status, exchange a single term of address). As a class, older people are distinguished from younger people, and implied in this differentiation is a gradation from dominance to subordination. Similarly, the political authority of a chief possessing an important title both surpasses and encompasses that of a lesser chief with a minor title.

These four diagrams, then, provide cognitive templates with corresponding lexical labels, prototypical embodiments, and semantic fields.

Each of the diagrams also has institutional instantiations in social and political contexts, which are structured according to the iconic features represented in the schema and which are labeled with the same term used in reference to the prototype. And these prototypes are the most obvious explanatory referents for the cultural meanings of each institutional pattern. Informants who reflect on the connection between social institutions and existing prototypes frequently give a causal argument: that, for example, balanced sides of a village exist because the river happens to divide the land into symmetrical sections, or that houses in different villages are linked by paths of mutual houses because an ancestral migrating group cut an actual trail through the forest or across the lagoon. In other words, the iconism of the prototype is interpreted by causal contiguity (what Peirce calls "indexicality"). This is much like the argument that a photograph resembles the depicted object since it was produced in contiguity with it. That is, from the Belauan point of view, prototypes are not merely convenient objects for metaphorical or analogical reasoning, but are in fact presupposed causal models which generate patterned social reality.

One consequence of this is that understanding of social relations and institutions tends to focus on these diagrams as internally coherent, distinct patterns, rather than as systematically or transformationally related complexes. Furthermore, the selection of lexical labels in discourse about social relations is never trivial, since each diagram is associated with a core semantic meaning: sequential linkage, balanced opposition, differential support, and graded dominance. If a group of titleholders, for example, could be alternatively referred to as having a path in common, or as sitting on opposite sides of the meetinghouse, or as being sacred cornerposts of the village, the choice of vocabulary will automatically carry with it the particular cultural valuation of the associated diagram. Because of this fact, the four diagrams cannot be analyzed as if they were merely abstract geometrical patterns related by transformational rules or were mutually reducible without change in meaning.

The analytical problem is that, while awareness focuses on simple or transparent cases of the diagrams, ethnographic evidence suggests that the social instantiations of these patterns occur in complexes, either the multiplication of one diagram (intersecting paths, overlaid cornerposts) or the interpenetration of different models. Given this inversion between awareness and reality, the task becomes to show that there are certain potentials inherent in diagrammatic complexes which are not subject to high levels of awareness and manipulation and yet which do have vital consequences for the historical and processual realities of social relations and institutions.

TYPIFICATION AND NODALITY OF PATHS

If paths function as sign types by allowing for repeated action along or within narrowly defined ranges of variation, then in principle it would seem that all paths, whether followed or not, and whether clear or obscure, would be equally immune to change by real social action and historical contingency. This is, however, far from the truth, for several reasons. First, paths are commonly categorized along the dimension strong/weak and less frequently differentiated along the dimension ancient/recent. Like the real paths through tropical forests, social paths can become overgrown and indistinct without constant activity in the prescribed direction. A neglected social tie can, however, be rejuvenated by actors who take advantage of the fact that even the dimmest paths never really die; they merely sleep, awaiting future recognition. A strong path, correlatively, exercises a compelling force on social action. Such linkages convey obligations that cannot be regarded as optional, since they are often constitutive rather than accidental features of the social units in question.

There is a built-in conflict here between the degree to which a given use of a path in exchange, cooperation, or warfare can be contextually marked by some feature of the path itself (so that this particular event stands out against the accumulated weight of all previous events) and the clarity and strength of the path. The most creative action is the one which invents the social relationship in the first place, while subsequent action within the established constraints is relatively presupposing of this invention. In other words, a traveler choosing the "path less traveled by" succeeds in marking this individual journey only at the expense of avoiding main arteries of social relations.

So repeated actions that ultimately guarantee the clarity and power of a path do not themselves index a particular journey as distinct. An initial journey blazing a new trail will not, on the other hand, achieve recognition as a legitimate path until a second traveler decides to retrace the new trail. This accounts for the way in which a visitor arriving at some customary event such as a funeral, money collection, or feast can be quickly integrated into the prescribed order of exchange and service if a recognized path is announced. Only a high-ranking or wealthy person is daring enough to "invent a path" or "plant a relationship" not followed before—in fact, rank can be seen as the culturally constituted capacity to create "types" of relations. Such action is normally thought to be more the domain of gods or heroic ancestors. If creating new paths is the job of these powerful characters, violating prescribed routes is characteristic of mythological tricksters such as Medechiibelau and Uchulsung.

The second dimension, of ancient/recent, insures that not all paths are equal. An ancient path is one which was instituted by a god or ancestor, while a recent path is of historical or contemporary origin, and its permanent institutionalization is not yet assured. Expert knowledge of these ancient paths is an essential part of the responsibility of chiefs, and great rhetorical power can be harnessed by a learned elder who, upon hearing of the creative postulation of a new path, can narrate a story accounting for some even earlier pattern of which the proposed action is merely a presupposing replica. Such rhetorical oneupsmanship carries the additional implication that the visitor who claimed creativity does not know the real reason/origin for the path and so in a real sense does not know what he is doing at all.

Thus, Belauan paths have the potential for what I call cultural typification, that is, the power to categorize or denominate token actions as being significant instances of an instituted regularity (see Parmentier 1981:49–54). And furthermore, the criteria of strength and temporal priority make it possible to express progressive states of the transformation from creative origination to presupposed regularity.

A second potential inherent in paths is the capacity of path complexes to specify the differential nodality and directionality of social relations. The term nodality here refers to ways in which social linkages cross each other at a shared point, by merging two separate lines into a single unified path, or by joining minor elements at a central point. Nodality is best illustrated ethnographically by the system of house affiliation, which organizes networks of houses in intravillage and intervillage contexts. Briefly, within a village, houses of cornerpost titleholders function as foci of networks of dependent, satellite houses. Satellite houses enter into social relations with houses in other villages only by passing through or following along the more direct relations established by nodal chiefly houses. In addition, chiefly houses enter into paths of affiliation with houses in other villages according to ancient migration traditions and stories of former cooperation and allegiance to common gods. Since each important house in any one intervillage network is also a member of other crosscutting networks, bonds of mutual house affiliation are both directional and nontransitive. In either intravillage or intervillage cases, it would be a breach of protocol for an individual from a satellite house or from an indirect path to contribute money or service outside the prescribed lines of nodality or to jump over the nodal house to claim a direct linkage (Parmentier 1984 and chapter 5).

Typification and nodality, then, are two inherent potentials of social relations and practices modeled according to the diagram of paths. Both result from the fact that, contrary to the simple perception of an isolated prototype, social relations occur in interlocking, intersecting complexes and are evaluated according to criteria such as strength and temporal priority. Ethnographic and historical records reveal the most important processual consequence of path complexes: that once established, paths and the nodal articulation of elements tend to be self-perpetuating. The continuity of house-affiliation links, for instance, is maintained despite on-the-ground trends in demography, ecology, and history. This is because a house in a network that becomes abandoned, destroyed, or encompassed is perpetuated both conceptually and practically by means of a cultural fiction. The existence of a sequentially continuous path is inconsistent with the disappearance of any one of its intermediate points, since a broken or interrupted line forfeits the priority residing in the temporal depth of its origin point. That is, a given element is strong relative to its position from the point of origin. And more importantly, the overall depth or lateral extent of a path contributes to the rank of the linked elements taken as a set: chiefly houses display numerous gravestones of ancestors and engage in widely dispersed exchange relations during customary events.

As a result, even abandoned houses are still formally invited to attend social events, and titles are still awarded to men who rule over nonexistent social units. Satellite houses also work to perpetuate the fiction of continuity, since they will contribute money in the name of the extinct nodal house in the hope that future benefits and prestige destined for the fictional category will accrue, albeit mediately, to them. Also, in order for a satellite house to assert its direct nodal status, it must arrange for some even-lower-ranking house to pass through it in exchanges. Thus the power to create cultural fictions operates in harmony with the status-maintenance potential in paths to enable the house-affiliation system to resist attempts by a sequence of colonial governments to dismantle allegedly wasteful ceremonial exchanges. Even in the face of the forced breakup of extended households, the construction of privately owned residential houses, and the imposition of patrilineal inheritance against the traditional matrilineal pattern, this system has become rigidified or frozen in both conceptualization and practice.

RECONTEXTUALIZATION AND REVALUATION OF SIDES

The second diagram of opposed sides is socially realized in several dimensions: (1) in the division of a village into two "sides of the mangrove channel" (*bita el taoch*), which splits the men's and women's clubs into competitive halves; (2) in the balanced organization of titleholders of a village into two "sides of the meetinghouse" (*bita el bai*); (3) in the competitive, but reciprocal, relations between the two leading houses (*bita el blai*) of large villages; (4) in the "two side legs" (*bita el oach*), which are segments (either through fissioning of the offspring of sisters or alternative migration traditions) of high-ranking houses; and (5) in the political opposition between two warring "side heavens" (*bita el eanged*) confederations focused on the powerful villages of Oreor and Melekeok. In each of these expressions the term "side" is modified or specified by a noun referring not to the opposed elements themselves but to the inclusive contextual domain (channel, meetinghouse, heaven) of the pair. This contrasts with the normal pattern of larger/smaller expressions, where the adjective modifies the object referred to (e.g., *klou el udoud,* "large valuable"), leaving the determining feature (here, "worth") formally unspecified.[2] The point to note is that in side expressions, neither the typical object referred to nor the relevant encompassing domain of opposition specifies a positive evaluative feature in respect to which the two elements differ.

A second general observation is that, in the five examples given above, each side contains a set of member elements, not just a single term. Traditionally a large village contained six meetinghouses for men, divided into two sets of three according to the position of the two highest-ranking chiefly houses. The clubs on each side were additionally graded into junior clubs (for young unmarried men skilled in fishing and warfare), middle clubs (for heads of independent households who had not received chiefly titles), and senior clubs (for "retired" elders too weak to participate actively in village affairs). The physical arrangement of these clubhouses often reflected the division of the village by a mangrove channel, with the junior clubhouses located near the landing, the middle clubhouses set back along the main road, and the senior clubhouses located near the central village square. In other words, the actual instantiation of sides here involves the diagram

2. Blust (1980b:226) suggests that the dual division of village settlements into two sides of a river is a feature of Proto-Austronesian social organization. His argument that the symbolic valuation of this division is generally right/upper bank/masculine and left/lower bank/feminine does not, however, fit the case of Belau (cf. Biersack 1982; Fox 1979:166–67; Lancy and Strathern 1981; Onvlee 1983). Furthermore, Blust's (1981:68) theory that Austronesian dual organization correlates with a system of four marriage classes conceals the important point that dual and quadripartite models in Belau imply distinct cultural meanings.

of larger/smaller as well. Contrary to the simple meaning of pure opposition or twinned inverses, the on-the-ground realization of sides can be described as the opposition of a set of graded elements—but not the graded opposition of sets of elements. A similar combination of diagrams is evident in the arrangement of seating positions of titleholders in the meetinghouse. While the cornerpost chiefs sit at the four corners of the building, all other titleholders sit along the two long sides. The opposed sides of the meetinghouse are oriented to the first- and second-ranking chiefs, who sit facing each other at the "face" of the building. This illustrates the principle of focalization of sides, for exchange, discourse, and alliance between titleholders on each side is possible only through the first two chiefs. Thus sets of elements grouped together as sides become articulated by the dominant term in a larger/smaller series.[3]

These two aspects of sides, independence from a differentiating feature and focalization of graded sets on the dominant term, help account for some of this diagram's processual consequences as revealed in the indigenous and Western historical record. The first consequence is that social categories or institutions organized by cornerpost relations tend to become reduced to sides in the face of imposed social changes. The functional differentiation of four coordinated elements required for cornerpost institutions is difficult to maintain, given factors such as depopulation, abandonment of houses and villages, linearization of lines of authority transmitting colonial rather than local commands, and intensification of status competition due to the importation of Western guns, goods, and money. For example, a village council without the manpower to maintain the functional differentiation of four-cornerpost titleholders can salvage some of its dignity by replacing the four-part organization by a two-leveled opposition between titleholders as a group and commoners as a group. Or the efforts by colonial powers to locate the reigning chiefs of a village undermined the delicate balance among political roles and encouraged head-to-head competition between the two leading chiefs on opposed sies. The number of title reversals and violent usurpations involving these two offices is a striking aspect of nineteenth-century Belauan history. Finally, there has been a general collapse of the quadripartite polity established according to

3. In his study of competition in Belau, McKnight (1960:149) observes an aspect of this focalization in the context of the shifting locus of competition among side-leg segments of houses in post-war Belau: "Interclan competition continues to focus upon the attainment of the title of clan [i.e., house] chief, but it has lost many of its other, especially its horizontal, dimensions."

myth by the goddess Milad into a competitive hostility between side heavens focused on Oreor and Melekeok. While this intensification is directly linked to the importation of firearms, the resulting political opposition is structured by indigenous patterns of social relations.

A second consequence, one which seems to run counter to this notion of sides as the reduction of cornerposts, is that pure side oppositions in several contexts have become progressively recontextualized and revalued with positive differential features. In traditional village political life, for example, the opposition between two sides of the meetinghouse is symbolized by reciprocal giving of valuables and foods by an incumbent chief to his newly appointed counterpart. This form of delayed reciprocity has largely vanished in the contemporary scene, partly because a new form of two-levelled government consisting of a body of titled chiefs and an elected municipal council has displaced the axis of political competition and responsibility. In Ngeremlengui district, chiefs and elected officials meet independently (although in the same building), take responsibility for different aspects of village life (roughly, customary vs. acculturated), and operate according to radically different procedural styles (deference vs. voting). Thus the graded opposition between inherited and elected office has replaced the symmetrical balance between sides of the meetinghouse (cf. Feinberg 1980:371; 1982:3–5). One elder noted that the modern council was the "new sails," in contrast to the "old sails" of traditional chiefs— making an allusion to the distinction between recent and ancient lines in a village. This is an excellent example of the reinterpretation of one diagram by another—sides by paths—for rhetorical effect.

Similar recontextualization is evident in the development of club organization during the colonial period. The German administration encouraged the merger of men's clubs, not merely across age grades but also across sides of the mangrove channel, on the grounds that severely reduced population made interclub competition a waste of manpower. This organizational collapse was artificially halted during the Japanese administration, when all Belauan men were again divided into three club grades, but this time ignoring the side pairing of identical clubs. Today in Ngeremlengui, club organization reflects the complete abandonment of side channels, along with a recontextualization of clubs along lines of village rank. That is, the men's club from high-ranking Imeiong village now encompasses all the other clubs, whose men enter into it in order to participate in districtwide activities. There has also been a revaluation of club structure along gender lines, with unified men's clubs and unified women's clubs taking responsibility for specific duties and competing with each other to increase the reputation of the village.

STRUCTURAL COMPLEXITY AND
HISTORICAL VULNERABILITY

At this point in the argument, with processual consequences of corner-posts and larger/smaller diagrams remaining to be discussed, it should be apparent that it is misleading to artificially isolate the four diagrams for the purpose of orderly exposition. As long as abstract awareness of their structure and meaning is at issue, the four diagrams could be treated independently, but when actual ethnographic instantiations are under consideration, complex implicational relations and rhetorical effects become the rule rather than the exception. To put it simply, ethnographic realities and actors' awareness are inversely correlated, since complex structures involving different diagrams (historical condensation of cornerposts to sides, articulation of sides by large elements of a series, or alternative codings of cornerpost and side title affiliations) have properties not subject to overt manipulation and simple lexical labeling. Opacity to consciousness, however, far from being a protection against the impingement of real historical forces, in fact can be seen as contributing to the immediacy and unavoidability that characterize the interaction between colonial policy, demographic variation, and ecological limitations and the Belauan social institutions instantiating these diagrammatic icons.

Quadripartition in Belau shares with similar iconic forms found through the Austronesian world an intrinsic potential for coding historical transformation. This potential operates along two related dimensions. First, cornerpost organizations, such as the four powerful villages of the group, the four chiefly houses within a large village, the four ranking titles in a council, and the four satellite houses surrounding a principal house, all mark the cultural accomplishment of order and maturity out of chaotic lawlessness and structural immaturity. Scattered villages connected by overlapping ties of alliance and hostility become a total Belauan polity only when these linkages are organized by the unifying figure of quadripartition. Similarly, unconnected migrating groups can establish houses in a given locality, but the achievement of their political integration as a coherent village is coded by the quadripartite coordination of ranking houses.

Second, cornerpost patterns also function as historical signs of stages of institutional development. The fact that quadripartite diagrams form overlying complexes, each layer mirroring and thereby reinforcing each other layer, might lead to the premature conclusion that this diagram is essentially static. But cornerposts have the additional potential for coding social process in terms of "episodic sedimentation," to borrow a phrase from geology. This potential is clearly illustrated by the example of the development of four-part household networks within a village. Each principal house (that is, each house with an important chiefly title) is conceived of as one of the cornerposts supporting the village as a whole. At this village expands (due to general population increase or relocation of abandoned inland sites) additional houses are established on land controlled by these principal houses. In time, the newer satellites themselves become organized by a quadripartite ideology according to which they are the cornerposts of the house affiliation network. A chiefly house is thus a cornerpost member of the village, and, at a lower level, the organizing principle of house affiliation for lower-ranking houses. Thus the reduplication of cornerposts within cornerposts serves as a sign of historical depth: social units subdivided into iconically similar nested structures are regarded as having temporal priority over internally undifferentiated units. Not only is structural complexity a sign of historical precedence, but processual development is registered in stages, since the gradual ramification of houses acquires political significance only when four elements are joined together (cf. Van Ossenbruggen 1983:45–46).

The recent debate over the theoretical status of Tikopia's four clans is particularly instructive when seen in light of the Belauan evidence for explicit quadripartite orders. Firth rejects the structuralist reinterpretations of both Leach and Hooper on the grounds of a cautious historical empiricism: "I think that the number of any particular kind of social unit can quite well be a development of historical circumstances, and need not be predicated from a theory of symbolic expression of deep structural thought" (Firth, in Hooper 1981:49). But the options need not be symbolism or history, since Belauan quadripartition is precisely a "symbolic expression," in that it manifests the four characteristics of diagrammatic icons discussed above (lexical label, schematic shape, physical prototype, and semantic field), *and* functions as a means of coding the "development of historical circumstances."

To these positive potentials for layered reinforcement and staged reduplication must be added two additional features contributing to the vulnerability of cornerpost institutions. The first, noted above, is that the coordinated, differential functioning of cornerposts is difficult to maintain given the linearization imposed by colonial powers. The decision to base colonial governmental and commercial institutions in Oreor village automatically undermined the coordinated political relations characteristic of the traditional cornerposts of Belau. Oreor in fact became a district center, a notion completely alien to Belauan political ideology. Also, the use of appointed "acting chiefs" to substitute for traditionally selected leaders also repudiates quadripartite principles, since the second-ranking chief's function is bypassed. In fact, the concept of political representation is incompatible with the ideology of coordinated, differential support among cornerpost chiefs.

A second source of historical vulnerability is the requirement that cornerpost structure be contextually anchored by the first-ranking element in the set. Like the directional orientation of Christian cathedrals, a north/south calculus governs the placement of the "face" of chiefly meetinghouses; this orientation then determines the pattern of roof-beam construction, which in turn points to the seating position of the first-ranking chief. In the ideal case, a village's four principal houses, four chiefly land parcels, and four high titles all form a vast homologous system of overlying iconic levels. But the potential for reinforcement is countered by the need to anchor the structure, since a change in the anchoring element can upset the entire system. A reversed title, a usurped seat, an abandoned residence, or an alienated land parcel can create a skewing of the entire cornerpost structure. More generally, however, the failure of one overlaid iconic structure tends to lead to the disruption of its mirror images. The collapse of the chiefly meetinghouse in Imeiong was quickly followed by the abandonment of all four cornerpost houses in that villages. To paraphrase a local interpretation, once one pillar of the system is withdrawn, the roof can no longer be supported. This combination of orderly stability and inherent fragility is found on Ponape (Caroline Islands), where the polity is described in an indigenous account as supported by four cornerstones: "Now, for all these corners, if one of these collapses, a time of trouble will occur in the state which made it" (Bernart 1977:30).

The processual consequences of cultural elements graded in terms of larger/smaller series follow from the fact that this diagram, unlike the other three, is not constituted by entirely formal relations. Elements can be linked in a line, opposed as paired inverses, or set in quadripartition without specifying any positive feature that would link the elements to some aspect of the social life. That is, paths and sides are elementary formal relations, and cornerposts are more complex cultural structures; but the diagram of graded series always implies some positive feature which elements possess differentially, such as physical size, biological maturity, monetary wealth, political authority, sacredness, or social rank. A chiefly title is important relative to another title with respect to political power; a bead valuable is large relative to another piece with respect to its worth. All graded series in Belau require the distribution of a feature value *in* the elements referred to.

This quality implies that larger/smaller series function to implicate elements in each of the other diagrams into the pragmatic realities of social action and historical experience, as well as to integrate a given diagram with replications of itself. Several illustrations of these principle have already been given: (1) the principal house (*klou el blai*) in an affiliation network provides the institutionalized paths between satellite houses and the extravillage world; (2) the corner of the highest-ranking chief (*klou el rubak*) is the point of orientation for the seating positions of all other cornerpost titles; and (3) the men's club from the dominant village (*klou el beluu*) of Imeiong becomes the encompassing club for districtwide activities.

Identifying this integrating potential as an inherent feature of the larger element in a graded series is actually to restate the processual truth that an element which acquires integrative, constitutive, or nodal position in social life becomes thereby the larger term. And furthermore, because larger elements perform these three systematic functions, they acquire the additional capacity of being the repository of cultural history. History is constructed in the sense that these dominant elements structure the impact of events and record the impact in their own complex institutional shapes. Belauan history is told about and by capital villages, ranking houses, and high chiefs. Whereas the constructed image of the past is, as Peirce argues, largely iconic in character, the actual process of historical creation requires contextual or indexical signs—precisely the domain of larger/smaller series.

And because of this engagement in historical processes, the diagram of graded series, more than the other diagrams, is subject to erosion in the face of imposed change. This erosion can be seen as a result of two policies: first, the attack by colonial authorities on elements labeled "larger," and second, the repudiation and replacement of the cultural principles underlying the differential values of these series. Inculcation of democratic egalitarianism in politics challenges the principle of inherited social rank and thus the grounds for the grading between high-ranking and low-ranking houses and persons. Introduction of quantitatively graded Western money implies a homogenization of the qualitative, functionally specific system of Belauan money. Legislation dealing with joint tenancy and patrilineal land inheritance removes one of the important supports of the strict grading of male siblings. And representation of villages in national legislative bodies according to relative population renders the traditionally sanctioned status of dominant villages inoperative.

Belauan responses to these developments are especially interesting, given the focus of the arguments presented thus far. The collapse of graded series of titles, land parcels, money, houses, and villages has led to a situation in which these elements as a group are lumped together as "traditional," in contrast to acculturated, Western, or recent institutions. Leaders selected by traditional procedures are opposed to elected officials; Belauan money joins with American cash to give customary exchanges twin sources of value; and the populous, Western-oriented capital at Oreor has become politically and ideologically opposed to villages on Babeldaob island.

A second response to the collapse of graded series is to remove or isolate from action, discourse, and experience the actual signs embodying the highest-ranking terms of the set. Ethnographic examples to be analyzed in subsequent chapters include the following: (1) at the moment when Imeiong village was victorious over enslaving Uluang village, the Imiungs Stone emblematic of the village's sacred rank was removed to the distant village of Ngellau on the other side of the island; (2) the valuable Bederiich piece of money which cemented the final peace between Imeiong and rival Melekeok is today on display in a German museum; (3) in the nineteenth century, chief Ngirturong of Imeiong abandoned his residence and built a new house at neighboring Ngeremetengel, and from that time the graves of Ngirturong titleholders were placed there rather than at the ancestral burial platform in Imeiong; and (4) during the American period many district chiefs moved to Oreor, thereby removing the sacredness of their high titles from the local village context.

Unseen, unoccupied, unused, and unspoken, these signs continue to perform their integrative and constitutive functions even though and because they are removed from the exigencies of ongoing social activity. This paradoxical combination of immunity from contextual impingement and continued cultural functioning characterizes the top, sacred, or transcendent position in hierarchies found in other Austronesian and Southeast Asian societies. In semiotic terms, these larger elements, isolated in practice from contact with other elements in a ranked series, take on the function of a sign type; but as a sign type without meaningfully existing instantiation, its continuity is maintained only at the cost of vacuity. Chiefly meetinghouses no longer stand at the central square of large villages but are rather preserved as museum specimens, on emblematic flags, and on picture postcards. Sacred stones representing village gods are left hidden under forest cover. Money pieces, taken out of customary circulation, are stored in private safe-deposit boxes.[4] And ranking village sites, long abandoned for more convenient coastal locations, are visited by school children as archaic remnants suitable only for photography.

The ethnographic analysis of cultural diagrams is, of course, only one facet of a total understanding of the link between social relations and historical process. The discussion here has focused on the function of these diagrams as instruments of limited self-representation, that is, as meaningful constructs in which the structure and processual regularities of Belauan society are recorded, imagined, and interpreted. The ethnographic particulars demonstrate that the diagrammatic representation of social institutions and relationships seizes as its semiotic means the very organizational structures of society itself, as Fortes realized in his classic analysis of Tallensi shrines. The significance of this seemingly trivial claim is the implied criticism of the notion, formulated with clarity by Durkheim and Mauss (1963), that the formal relations among social groups are the natural source of concepts of space and time. In their view, collective representations are universally about social relations and consequently—if unintentionally—those relations are themselves rendered meaningless or noncultural (Sahlins 1976:115). The argument here, in contrast, is that patterns of social relations are valid vehicles of expression as well as denoted objects.

In this chapter I have also attempted to counter a theoretical practice in the other direction, namely, the technique found frequently in structuralist writings of manipulating cultural symbols according to transformational rules in such a way that the underlying structure remains constant. This practice makes the unwarranted assumption that structure consists entirely of "patterning of internally organized relations" (Leach 1973:41). To be sure, relational patternings are widespread in social representation, but they exist as cultural rather than purely logical constructs. As has been demonstrated, while there is a syntax of the four Belauan diagrams that governs their compositionality and contributes to their relative historical vulnerability, each of these diagrams is endowed with semantic meanings derived from the prototypical referents

---

4. Cf. Rossel Island, where the highest-valued pieces of money no longer circulate (Liep 1983:125) and may not even physically exist, due to their supernaturally endowed rank (Berde 1973:190).

that are not reducible to properties of geometrical relations. That is, Belauan diagrams are not just icons; they are *iconic symbols,* and consequently their instantiations are meaningful, not only as formal resemblances between expression and object (that is, as icons), but also because of the culturally specific valuation imposed on each pattern (that is, as symbols).[5]

5. Despite the use of the phrase "quadripartite structures" in the title of his book, Mosko (1985) offers little ethnographic evidence for the presence of quadripartition as a culturally valorized diagrammatic model, as this type is well documented in other parts of the Austronesian world. The parallel sets of inverted homologies which he deduces are artifacts of an analytical formalism which is clearly inappropriate for a society which does not, as the reader is informed, recognize the normative existence of four clans and which apparently does not utilize a semantically articulated and semiotically instantiated notion of four corners, four posts, or four parts (cf. Firth 1979:64).

CHAPTER

4

Models of Transformation of
Belauan Polity

A series of recent publications by Sahlins (1981, 1985b) illuminates the relationship between history and structure in the Oceanic context by charting a dialectical course between two constrasting approaches. The first approach, popular with historians, holds that the organizational categories of a culture in place at any one moment are the cumulative outcome of the actions and interests of individuals; in this view, structure is statistical history. The second approach, more common among anthropologists, assumes that cultural categories are rigid, synchronic impositions upon individual experience and contextual action; thus history is the inevitable instantiation of some immutable "culture-as-constituted." The solution Sahlins proposes is an elegant one: by combining these two analytical concepts into a unified notion of "structural history," he points to the diachronic interplay of cultural categories and particular events. As categories become functionally revalued in the process of social life, structure emerges precisely as the pattern of this transformation. So culture, in this way of thinking, is profoundly historical—constituted by real powers and their concrete interests. It is also structural—revealed in the systematicity of diachronic processes.

This processual definition of structure as "a dynamic development of the cultural categories and their relationships, amounting to a world system of generation and regeneration" (Sahlins 1985b:77) sheds new light on two aspects of Belauan culture, the linkage between which seems at first glance puzzling. The first aspect is the set of diagrams or models pervasively instantiated in traditional sociopolitical organization, namely, linearity, or paths; quadripartition, or cornerposts; and dual opposition, or sides (discussed in chapter 3). The second aspect of the culture Sahlins's analysis sheds light on is a set of myths narrating a progressive sequence of cultural eras, each expressed as a distinctly shaped order of villages and chiefs. A single term, *renged* (found in the verb *merrenged,* "bind together, tie up in a bundle"), combines the temporal and spatial meanings of the English glosses "era" and "polity." The political organization of villages within a district is a *renged,* or "federation," and the earliest period referred to in mythical narratives is the *mechut el renged,* "ancient times." These myths first describe the foundation of the Belauan cultural order in the "era of Chuab" as a loosely knit string of eight villages located along the eastern side of the archipelago. Their political affiliation stems from the south-to-north path of the journey of the mythological figure Chuab, who instituted chiefly titles and councils at each village. After the destruction of this archaic order by a great flood ordered by the high god as punishment for lawless behavior, a second cultural period called the "era of Milad" emerged. The dominant villages of this second polity were aligned in a quadripartite pattern which the myth explains as the result of the birth of four stone children to the goddess Milad, the only survivor of the flood. This order in turn became condensed in the postcontact period into two rival alliances focused on the militarily powerful villages of Oreor and Melekeok. Political chants and historical narratives speak of this arrangement as two opposed side heavens, referring roughly to the eastern and western sides of the archipelago.

Thus this narrative sequence of cultural eras is coded in terms of the progression of spatial models, from paths, to cornerposts, and finally to sides, with each model originating and coming into prominence in a particular period. These three models are, then, both "diagrammatic icons" instantiated in various sociopolitical institutions found in traditional villages and also members of a transformational set which organizes indigenous understanding of the islands' political development. They are, in sum, "epistemological eras," to use McKinley's (1979:322) excellent phrase (recalling perhaps Foucault's notion of "episteme"). Now, in light of Sahlins's concept of structural history, the question which immediately arises is why these three models should be selected in mythical discourse, and why in this particular sequence. One could possibly view these models simply as reflections of independent social realities: that the first settled villages were in fact linked by genealogical and political paths tracing actual migration histories, and that the subsequent quadripartite and dualistic political orders developed as Belau grew into an increasingly hierarchical and stratified society. According to this naive Durkheimian argument, Belauans were able to conceptualize things generally in quarters only after reflection on their quadripartite sociopolitical organization. At the other extreme, one could claim that this progression of models is an entirely rhetorical, poetic, or ideological device constructed after the fact and bearing little relationship to concrete factors such as interisland migrations, resettlement patterns, shifting political alliances, and contact with Western colonial forces.

The solution proposed here mediates these extreme responses by arguing that the narrative sequence of political orders demonstrates a coherent logic once the cultural significance of the underlying models is grasped, and that these meanings are in turn shaped by the contextual application of the three metaphors to particular political circumstances. This chapter focuses on the task of discovering the narrative motivation for the application of these models to particular kinds of mythical and historical contexts. In harmony with the previous chapter's conclusions, it will be shown that in mythological narratives the model of the path expresses Belauan conceptions of origination and cultural typification; the model of four cornerposts expresses the ideas of structural maturity, coordinated support, and organizational transformation summarizing temporally layered contingencies; and the model of side heavens codes notions of totalized focalization and contextual revaluation. The precise meaning of these generalizations will emerge in the following discussion of the three political eras.

LATMIKAIK AND THE ORIGIN OF PATHS

Soon after my arrival in Ngeremlengui in 1978, my village hosts learned that I was anxious to begin the study of Belauan culture without the aid of interpreters and without the use of English. One of the village's outstanding storytellers, the man who eventually became my closest friend, "father," and main informant, decided that I should get my first exposure to the language and style of traditional narratives (*cheldecheduch*) by taping several stories for later transcription practice. When I asked where we should begin, he smiled knowingly and said that the only place to begin is "at the beginning," that is, with the story of the origin of Belau. The sequence of stories I recorded that night became the foundation not only for my language learning but also for my understanding of traditional Belau. Following my teacher's lead, I begin this discussion of the development of political order with this same story, which I now realize is about the origin of culturally defined relationships in general. For convenience of exposition I divide the myth into four sections, the Story of Latmikaik, the Story of Chuab, the Story of the Cursed Children of Chuab, and the Story of the Feast of Secheseball.

Story of Latmikaik

So you want to hear the story of Latmikaik. Belau was totally empty and had no people dwelling in it. Uchelianged (Foremost of Heaven) looked out upon it and saw the expanse of the sea, which was completely empty. Uchelianged's voice then said, "Let a land arise. Let a land arise." So a piece of land rose up to the surface of the sea at a place called Lukes, between Ngeaur and Beliliou today.

And then there was a clam which came into being there. This clam grew larger and larger, and then there came into being the insides of the clam. And, like a human being, the insides of the clam grew larger and larger and became pregnant, with its belly swelling to a large size. Its belly was very large. But it was not able to give birth. Uchelianged observed this condition and said, "Let there be a strong sea. Let there be a strong, running sea to shake it up so that it can give birth." When it gave birth there were many, many fish.

And then these fish in turn gave birth and gave birth, until the sea was crowded. When the sea became crowded, Uchelianged said to Latmikaik, "Tell your children to gather together rocks and coral and pile them up to the surface of the sea." So they cleared away the rubble beside Ngeaur and built it up until it reached the surface of the sea. Uchelianged then said, "Build it so that you will be able to travel to the heavens." So Latmikaik said to her children, "Build it even taller so that we can come near to the heavens. And then we will ask for earth from the heavens and put it all together so we can travel to the heavens." The meaning of this expression is that this Babeldaob is the heavens, and these creatures are creatures beneath the sea.

And so when they had built it very tall it became slightly tilted. They informed Latmikaik that they could not travel to the heavens, since it had become tilted. Latmikaik then said to them, "Bring me a measuring instrument so I can take a look at the situation." They brought a measuring instrument, and when the measurement was made, if the [stones] fell over the end would reach Oikull (Measured) village. Latmikaik then said to them, "Go ahead and kick it over." They kicked it over, and when it fell, Beliliou and all the rock islands all the way to Oikull were created. And now the children of Latmikaik could travel to Babeldaob. As they traveled, the land of Belau became more and more crowded. Villages became crowded with people. These children of Latmikaik could live on land or in the sea.

In this version of the Story of Latmikaik, the origination of the islands and people of Belau is the result of two commands uttered by the high god Uchelianged, the foremost deity in the mythological pantheon.[1] By the first command Uchelianged causes the first piece of land to emerge from beneath the empty sea at a place called Lukes (other variants give the name Mekaeb) between the islands of Ngeaur and Beliliou. At this stable point of intersection between the void of the sea (*daob*) and the heavens (*eanged*, PAN *langit*), the first creature, a giant clam named Latmikaik, gave birth to myriad fish, the "children of Latmikaik."[2] Uchelianged made this spawning possible by creating rough seas and winds to shake the clamshell so that its swollen insides could burst out into the primordial waters. Still today fishermen link heavy fish spawning to rough seas, saying that fish are smart enough to give birth under the cover of murky waters (Johannes 1981:183; Klee 1976:234; Krämer 1917–29, 3:341).

In later discussions the storyteller explained to me the significance of the clam as a symbol of fertility by connecting the reference in the myth to the "insides of the clam" to the childbirth practice in which the father of the child brings a large clam from the sea to the house of his wife's mother. The clam remains there for the duration of the pregnancy; when rotten, the insides are discarded, but the shell remains as an *olangch* of the important role both parents play in the continuing nurturance of the child.[3] Two aspects of this mythological reference and cultural practice are associated with maleness: the sea as a masculine realm contrasts with feminine land; and the rigidity and permanence of the shell represents the male contribution to the child's form and character, in contrast to the female contribution of substance and social identity.

Uchelianged's second creative utterance causes these fish children to pile up coral rubble from the sea bottom to form a stone bridge enabling them to climb up from the realm beneath the sea to the heavens.

---

1. *Uchel,* "first, foremost," is the common prefix for chiefly titles, as in Ucherbelau, Uchelchol, and Ucherringal. For a summary of the traditional pantheon see Kubary 1969 and Krämer 1917–29, 3:334–37.

2. Cf. Walsh and Liñi 1981:360, which gives the text of a parallel origin myth from Vanuatu in which a clam emerges from beneath the sea and maintains a stable position on top of a rock in the face of winds and waves.

3. Semper (1982:123) mentions a buried clamshell which serves as a marker of land ownership; cf. McKnight 1961:21. The version of the Story of Orachel which I collected in the field also mentions the "insides of the clam" (*dmengel a kim*), as does the text of the same story in PCAA, Ngeremlengui File.

But when this bridge becomes unstable and topples over, it is trans-
formed into a series of stepping-stones across which the original creatures of the sea can migrate from the southern region of the archipelago, through the central rock islands, to the large northern island of
Babeldaob. In this event, the vertical cosmological axis constituted by
the unmediated differentiation between "beneath the sea" and the
"heavens" rotates to a horizontal axis along the surface of the sea
formed by a linked or bridged differentiation between southern "lower
sea" and northern "upper sea."[4] And in terms of the movement of the
children of Latmikaik, the aspiration to climb to the heavens becomes
the quest for a land-based cultural existence as distinct from the amor-
phous precultural life beneath the sea.

   But both these transformations are grounded in a more fundamental
theme of this myth. The account of the origin of Belau (*uchul a Belau*)
in both geographical and cultural senses is phrased in terms of the construction of a path (*rael*) along which motion takes place from a beginning point (*uchul*) at Lukes or Mekaeb to an ending point (*rsel*) at
Oikull. The key word which appears in the phrases "origin of Belau"
and "beginning of a path" is *uchul,* which means not only "origin" and
"beginning point" but also more generally "source," "basis," "cause,"
and "reason." The basis for these extended meanings appears to be the
meaning "tree trunk," so *uchul* is simultaneously the physical support
for upper limbs and the point at which growth originates.[5] And since
bridges are frequently made from tree trunks, the bottom of the trunk
becomes the *uchul* of the bridged path, while the top of the trunk becomes the *rsel* of the path. These intertwined meanings provide the
semantic motivation for Uchelianged's actions in creating the Belauan

   4. Various explanations have been offered for the terms "upper sea" and "lower sea."
Kubary (1885:57–58) notes that the distinction is based on prevailing wind direction;
Kusakabe (1979:1) suggests that it is related to the direction of sea currents. Another
obvious solution is simply that the northern island of Babeldaob is higher in elevation
than the islands of the lower sea. The explanation offered in the text under study here is
that the upper reaches on the stone bridge which emerged out of the sea toppled over to
the north, so there is a resulting correlation of "up" and "north." Krämer (1908:184)
defines the place name Babeldaob as the "northern side of the high island divided by the
Ngiual-Ngerdmau line"; this is based on a confusion of the name Babeldaob, which refers
to the high island as a whole, and the relative directional expression *bab el daob,* "upper
sea," that is, to the north of the speaker.
   5. The same semantic range is found in related terms such as PAN **puhun,* "tree
trunk, base, origin" (Dempwolff 1934–38, 3:120); Proto-Philippine **pu:gun,* "tree
trunk" (Zorc 1978:111); Fijian *vu,* "bottom, basis, root" (Capell 1941:315); Tami *pu,*
"ground, reason, source"; *kai-pu,* "base of tree" (Bamler 1900:237); Busama *hu,* "trunk
of tree, foundation, cause" (Hogbin 1963:14); Kédang *pue,* "trunk" (Barnes 1979:28);
and Rotinese *huk,* "trunk, stem, cause, origin" (Fox 1971:221; Fox 1980a:14).

archipelago by providing at the same time a path leading from the starting point near Ngeaur to the measured terminus at Oikull (Measured) village at the southeastern tip of Babeldaob. In other words, the act of creation makes possible the paradigmatic action of movement along a path. In fact, origination and movement are reduced to a single moment by this logic which takes literally the notion that etiological explanation requires description of how things "came" to be. Thus myths and narratives set in the archaic world of the children of Latmikaik repeatedly involve the creation or invention of cultural institutions and social groups in the southern islands and their subsequent movement northward to sites on the high islands such as Babeldaob and Oreor.

So in describing the origin of the first path across the islands of the archipelago, the Story of Latmikaik is a necessary presupposition of all other stories set in this archaic world. These stories tell, for example, of the discovery of fire in an *oseked* tree at Ngeriab on Beliliou by the brothers of Kerengokl and of the spread of this miraculous phenomenon to northern villages. The art of carpentry (*kldachelbai*) and customs associated with the purchase of meetinghouses originated beneath the sea between Beliliou and Ngeaur, where the culture hero Orachel, overhearing the noise of a divine underwater construction project, stopped to study the techniques of measurement and carving. Political organization, too, is said to have started in the area of the lower sea. The first chiefly council was instituted by Chuab at Rois village on Ngeaur and then introduced to eight other northern villages, which thereby formed the "polity of Chuab" (see below). The dual division which splits villages into opposed sides of the mangrove channel is said to have begun at Ngeredelolk village on Beliliou and from there was imitated by northern villages. And the totemic clans found throughout the islands started when the god Tellames visited his fish-lovers at Mekaeb near Beliliou. It is almost formulaic for migration narratives to begin with the phrase: "the origin [of the group] is at Ngeaur." Expelled from their southern homelands because of warfare, ecological pressure, or political strife, villagers from Ngeremasech, Ngchemliangel, Oikull, Medorem, and Ngetmedei—to mention only a few—relocated on Babeldaob in villages bearing the same names and often with identical lists of titles.

The importance of citing these examples of the pervasive cultural drift from south to north lies not in any correlation, probable though it may be, with what the archaeological record may ultimately reveal about the settlement sequence of the archipelago, but rather in making a more general point about the role of the model of the path in narrative structure and conceptual organization. Rather than having separate schemes for space and time, traditional Belauan culture unites these two Western categories through the notion of a journey (*omerael,* from the verb *merael,* "to walk, to travel," itself derived from the noun *rael,* "path, road, way" [PAN **dalan*]). The journey of a god, person, group, or mythological creature provides a basic space-time continuum for conceptualization and discourse (cf. Goody 1978:293).

Certain deictic and verbal forms indicate this role of movement along a path in linking temporal and spatial categories. The spatial opposition between "in front of, before" and "in back of, after" is based on the model of motion of elements along a linear path. Anything ahead (*uchei*) on the path will arrive at a given location before (*uchei*) anything traveling behind (*uriul*). Thus, the expression *er a uchei er a mekemad* means "before the war," and the expression *er a uriul er a mekemad* means "after the war." And especially peculiar to Americans learning the language is the usage in which a river is divided into *uchei er a omoachel,* "upstream," and *uriul er a omoachel,* "downstream." In the Belauan view, the water or an object floating on the water passes a point upstream and then arrives later (*uriul*) at a point downstream; that is, water does not flow to a spot "in front" (*uchei*) of where it is at a given moment.

Similarly, the verbal opposition between *mong,* "going, motion away from speaker," and *mei,* "coming, motion toward speaker," is employed to make relative temporal distinctions. The spatial model in this case is center/periphery, where motion toward the speaker at the center is *mei* and motion away from the center is *mong.* Thus anything which is *ngar er a mei,* (literally) "located at the coming toward," contrasts with what is *ngar er a mong,* (literally) "located at the going away." This is not simply the opposition between "future" and "past." Rather, the distinction is the relative one between "nearer to here and now" (*ngar er a mei*) and "farther from here and now" (*ngar er a mong*). The period of German colonial administration is *ngar er a mo el tekoi,* "a relatively distant affair," in comparison with the period of the American administration, which is *ngar er a me el tekoi,* "a relatively recent affair." Furthermore, *mong* is used as an auxiliary verb to form the future tense: *ng mo mesuub,* "he will study"; and the past tense form of *mei* is used as the auxiliary *mle* with stative verbs, as in *ak mle smecher,* "I was sick."[6]

Traditional time reckoning, depending on the correlation of relative motion of stars, sun, and moon with periodic regularities of fish spawning, growing seasons, tidal fluctuations, and climatic variation, is an-

---

6. It is not completely agreed upon among linguists, however, that the past tense auxiliary, *mle,* is related to the past tense form of the verb *mei,* "come."

other example of the way movement links space and time. One of the more esoteric areas of knowledge concerns the correlation between lunar cycles and biannual shifts in wind direction which marks the six-month "year" (*rak*). This linkage is described in the story of the journey of the god Rak, who was given responsibility by the high god Uchelianged to oversee the monthly movement of the moon (*buil*). Starting from his house in Ngetmel, a now-extinct village at the extreme northern tip of Babeldaob, Rak moves with the moon in a southerly course down the east side of the island.[7] At each month Rak resides at a different village, while the moon rests atop a rocky promontory or hillcrest nearby. Six villages north of Melekeok are visited during the "year of the east wind," and Melekeok and five other villages to the south are visited during the "year of the west wind." At the end of his journey Rak arrives at the southern tip of Ngeaur and then travels rapidly along the line of the western reef back to Ngetmel to begin his journey again.

Thus lunar cycles (counted by "darknesses" between new moons) and wind shifts are coded in terms of Rak's twelve-month (and twelve-stop) journey encircling the archipelago. Note, however, that the journey of Rak is not a narrative version of the observed motion of any celestial body. The oscillation of the vertical path of the moon and the variation in its setting point in the western sea—from north to south and then from south to north—does not correspond to the linear journey of Rak, although it does account for the names of individual months and for the fact that these six names are repeated in each of the two "years."[8] It is rather the twelve-stop journey of Rak which links temporal units such as months and years to specific locations. Additional points could be added from astronomical and calendrical lore to support the general claim that the journey or migration is an important narrative device by which temporal and spatial categories are correlated.

The notion of a journey not only presupposes the model of the path but also frequently involves the general historical mechanism, *olangch*, to anchor these mythological narratives in perceived experience. The *olangch* referred to include various categories of objects such as stones, trees, pottery fragments, names, and practices which are left behind at

7. For a full account of the cycle of months and the corresponding patterns of spawning, winds, and growing seasons see PCAA, Irrai File, "Palauan Months." See also Klee 1976 for the journey of Rak and for a list of the villages where the moon rests on its southerly path.

8. When the path of the moon is directly overhead, for example, the month is named *chelid*, "middle, center," and this marks the middle of the six-month year; see also Krämer 1917–29, 3:325; McManus 1977:42.

successive points by persons or groups traveling along a path. In order
to see how these signs function in connection with paths, a brief
thought experiment is helpful. Consider the following imaginary journey: one sets out to visit a distant place, and beginning from a starting
point one has the option of following a path made by previous travelers, whose repeated footsteps have worn a clear strip across the grassy
hillside, or of setting out on a new course over untraveled terrain. The
decision to follow the well-trodden path means a relatively presupposing journey, since the path is well marked, and the act of following an
established way does not indexically distinguish this particular journey
from previous ones (since one traveler's footsteps only minutely increase the definition of the path). But the decision to chart a new course
means a relatively creative journey, not only because a new trail is established, but also because this new trail, indistinct though it may be at
first, points to the particular journey which first passed that way.

There is thus an inverse relationship between the strength, clarity,
and size of the *typical* path and the indexical "creativity" (Silverstein
1976) or any one *token* journey along it. Imagine, further, that our
traveler does not proceed directly from the starting point to the destination but passes through six intermediate locations. At each of these
eight locations he deposits an identical white stone to mark the visit.
Consider now the significance of the white stones from the perspective
of the completed journey. The stones can be interpreted dynamically, as
marking the successive steps on a journey, or statically, as determining a
set of structurally homologous points on a line, each possessing an
identical white stone.

As this thought experiment suggests, the model of the path, combined with the functioning of *olangch,* is capable of transforming temporal sequence into spatial organization, because once established, the
points of connection continue to exist as a stable, structural linkage
which transcends the particular founding act. A journey along a path is
thus the paradigmatic cultural act, since it is the simplest form of presupposition; spatiotemporal linkages once established can become the
template or semiotic type for future actions and relationships. And
more importantly, the fact of static, structural homology among linked
points in the system, marked by the equivalent of white stones in each
location, can be read as evidence for temporal sequence by simply pos-
tulating the prior existence of a journey. In this fashion, villages possessing identical elements such as names, houses, stones, titles, or
distinctive practices can be put into a structurally defined set (the villages having X), and then this structure points to a prior movement
which originally distributed the tokens shared by members of the set.

Objects mentioned in other myths which play the role of white stones in our hypothetical example include trees of a particular species, exchange valuables of the same class, parts of a single house, identical names and titles, and similarly shaped stones.

So the myth of the origin of Belau does indeed "begin at the beginning." In describing the emergence of the first creatures and the construction of the stone bridge, the first section of the myth establishes the model of the path as a presupposition for all cultural action and relationship. The "in the beginning" of Belauan mythology is not the divine act of differentiation of light from dark, heaven from earth, or male from female, but rather the ordered mediation of lower sea and upper sea by motion along a path from an origin point to a measured terminus. The children of Latmikaik migrate to Babeldaob, but they are not exactly foreigners, since they originated within the archipelago. Similarly, they came from the sea, but crossed a bridge which initially stretched to the heavens.

CHUAB AND THE FIRST POLITICAL FEDERATION

With this understanding of the general importance of interrelating spatial and temporal dimensions by a journey along a path, we are prepared to grasp the significance of the next portion of the myth of the origin of Belau, which tells the story of Chuab, one of the many children of Latmikaik. Chuab travels from the southern village of Rois on Ngeaur to eight other villages in the archipelago and at each village "plants" or installs a chief to carry the highest title and a council of titleholders to take charge of the behavior of villagers. These titles and councils, as the *olangch* of Chuab's journey, play the role of white stones in the hypothetical example discussed above. According to many stories set in this "archaic world," Belau was populated by creatures who were half fish and half human. These creatures lived on land during the day and then returned to the sea at night; also, all sexual reproduction took place in the style of fish spawning.

Story of Chuab (Variant 1)

Uchelianged then said, "Now one of your [Latmikaik's] children will come up out of the sea to Ngeaur. Her name is Chuab. Her task is to create chiefly councils." And another of the children of Latmikaik was Uchererak. Uchelianged said to Uchererak, "You are to travel to Babeldaob, to Ngetmel, where there is a house which will be your residence. You will take responsibility for the spawning cycles of fish." Uchelianged then said to Chuab, "People

today are very lawless, and without chiefly councils they will never
become law-abiding. You will have the responsibility for creating
councils."

So Chuab created a council at Rois, a village on Ngeaur. The
first chief was Ucherkemur el Reked. The second chief was
Ucherkemur el Bebael. The third chief was Ucherkemur el Chai.
The fourth chief was Ucherkemur el Chedeng. The fifth chief was
Ucherkemur el Lilebangel. They entered the meetinghouse of
Ngcheed, which is the meetinghouse in this village, and served
there as chiefs. They instructed the people of Ngeaur. But this was
not possible to do.

Chuab then traveled northward and came to Beliliou, to
Ngerechol village, where she created a council at Ngerechol and
said, "You will be Uchelchol." And then she instituted a council
there. Then she traveled and came to Belau [i.e., Babeldaob] and
came to Imeliik at Imul village, where she created another council.
She then went to Ngeremid and created another council. She then
came to Ngerusar and created another council. She went to
Ngersuul and created another council. She went to Ulimang and
created another council. She went to Mengellang and created
another council. She summoned the chief of Mengellang and said,
"You will be Bdelulabeluu (Head of the Villages)." The name of
this village Mengellang comes from saying that this chief will hold
steady (*mengellakl*) the other chiefs.

A second recitation of the same story differs from the text above in
providing more explicit information about the role of Uchererak in
controlling the spawning cycles of fish, in linking Chuab to another
character, the Woman of Ngetelkou, who moved from Ngeaur to Beliliou, where she bore several children, and in listing the names of
Chuab's children. The portion of this second variant given below expands on the basic theme of the first variant, the creation of chiefly
councils at a series of villages visited by Chuab.

Story of Chuab (Variant 2)

So Chuab and the Woman of Ngetelkou lived there [at Ngeaur].
And the Woman of Ngetelkou bore a child and called her Tellebuu.
This Tellebuu in turn gave birth and bore her first child Kebliil,
and then bore her second child Seked, a boy. She bore her third
child, a girl, Dedaes. They all crossed over to Beliliou, and they
went to Liull house at Beliliou. They lived there, and people started
giving birth. They were fish-people who could live in the sea and
could also live on land.

Chuab also gave birth and bore her first child, a girl,

Chitaueiuei. She then bore her second child, Labek, and then bore another male child, Boid, and bore another male child, Mengelechelauchach, and then bore another male [child], Omuutaidnger. They traveled, circling around Belau. Chuab lived there, and more and more people were born, and those who lived in the sea came up on land. There was no marriage, but they just mated in the sea and gave birth there.

The lawlessness of these people grew very great, and so Uchelianged said to Chuab, "Create chiefly councils which will be the reason (*uchul*) for lawfulness at Ngeaur." So Chuab appointed Ucherkemur el Reked and these other chiefs who were also named Ucherkemur, and they carried the responsibility for Ngeaur. When Ucherkemur came up from the sea he rapidly became out of breath in sitting [on land], so they searched near Mekaeb and brought the shell of the giant clam [Latmikaik] and placed it in front of the meetinghouse at the village of Rois, named Bairebech. And the waterspout at Bkulengeluul shot up into the air and filled this clamshell with water, and so the shell became the drinking vessel of Ucherkemur. There were Ucherkemur el Reked, and Ucherkemur el Bebael, and Ucherkemur el Chedeng, and Ucherkemur el Chai, and Ucherkemur el Lilibangel. These became the chiefs, and they were the only ones at that time.

Uchelianged then said, "Now travel to Belau and create chiefly councils there." So Chuab traveled northward to Ngerechol and appointed Uchelchol to be the chief at Beliliou. Chuab traveled northward to Belau and established Secharaimul, and established Tucheremel at Ngerusar, and established Rechiungl at Ngeremid. Chuab then traveled to Ngersuul and created a council at Ngersuul, and then came to Ngeruikl and created a council at Ngeruikl. Chuab traveled northward to Ulimang and created a council at Ulimang and then established Bdelulabeluu as the chief of Mengellang. These chiefs were the eight chiefs [of Belau].

As these two variants of the same story detail, Uchelianged (Foremost of Heaven) continues to supervise the development of the social order by commanding two of the children of Latmikaik, Chuab and Uchererak, to set out on journeys to the northern islands. As the *olangch* of his authority and power, Uchelianged gives his name Uchel (Foremost) to the god Rak (Year), who then becomes Uchererak. This god, whose yearly journey from Ngetmel to Ngeaur was discussed above, carries in his name what the storyteller called the "signature" of Uchelianged and takes responsibility for the movement of the moon and the corresponding spawning cycles of fish. Chuab is given the cor-

relative regulatory authority for controlling the behavior of land creatures, and she creates the first political institutions to enforce the law of
Uchelianged. First at Ngeaur and then in eight villages in a line arranged from south to north along the eastern coast of Babeldaob,
Chuab "plants" chiefly councils, bodies of titleholders which govern the
internal and external affairs of villages.

The most important aspect of the Story of Chuab for our attention
is the way in which path, journey, and historical sign (respectively, *rael*,
omerael, and *olangch*) combine to constitute the "polity of Chuab." By
planting chiefs with parallel titles at Rois (the Ucherkemur series) and
by creating parallel councils at eight additional villages, Chuab in-
stitutes the earliest political order of the archaic world of Belau. The
sequence of these two acts of political institution reveals an important
feature of Belauan narrative: the first act is the template or prototype
for the second. First Chuab forms a council of five fish-chiefs at
Bairebech meetinghouse in Rois village. The first word of each of these
names is the same title, Ucherkemur (Fish Tail), while the second
words are five extensions of this title: Reked (Orange Spinefoot),
Bebael (Gold Spinefoot), Chedeng (Shark), Chai (Barracuda),
Lilebangel (type of fish) (cf. Krämer 1917–29, 4:3).[9] Having thus established the principle of *olangch* in a transparent way (here, the similar
Ucherkemur titles for all five positions) at a single location, Chuab then
plants a second series of chiefly titles and councils at eight spatially
separated locations. But in this second creation, not only the places but
also the titles are different, so these eight villages form a homologous
set or polity (*renged*) only mediately, on the basis of Chuab's journey. If
the Story of Latmikaik introduces the operative principle of paths, the
Story of Chuab presents the principle of *olangch* as the material embodiments semiotically arranged in a linear fashion. The villages, titles, and
locations of the polity of Chuab are listed in table 2 (some storytellers
do not include Rois as one of the official villages in the group).

This mythical account of the villages of Chuab is reinforced by several ethnographic references to this archaic federation. Kubary mentions
five villages as the "children of Chuab" in his discussion of various
nineteenth-century political alliances.

> In a similar way, there exists an original relationship between the
> communities of Mengellakl [Mengellang], Ulimaol [Ulimang],
> Chelab, Ngchesar, and Irrai, who all call themselves *ngelekel a lild*

---

9. Another version of this story gives a sixth chief, Ucherkemur el Chad (Human
Being).

TABLE 2. POLITY OF CHUAB

Village	Title	Location
[Rois	Ucherkemur	Ngeaur]
Ngerechol	Uchelchol	Beliliou
Imul	Secharaimul	Imeliik
Ngerusar	Tucheremel	Irrai
Ngeremid	Rechiungl	Oreor
Ngersuul	Obakeramechuu	Ngchesar
Ngeruikl	Ngirnguloalech	Melekeok
Ulimang	Ngirairung	Ngerard
Mengellang	Bdelulabeluu	Ngerechelong

"children of the spear (bamboo reed)," and so between Chol, Ngerusar, Ngeremid, Imul, and Ngersuul, who are the children of Chuab, a woman from Ngerdmau, this letter having arrived by air on the back of the *kedam* (Dysporus [frigate bird]). The origin of these lands, which goes far back in the prehistoric period of Palau, can be recognized even today, for no *remengol* [concubines] exchange takes place between them and no direct war is waged. (Kubary 1885:120–23)

My informants in Ngeremlengui insisted that Kubary is confused when he reports that Chuab was a woman from Ngerdmau, and that he mistakenly conflates the Story of Kedam (see Obak and McKnight 1969) which narrates the founding of Ngerdmau district with the Story of Chuab. And yet, with the exception of Chol, all the villages noted by Kubary as "children of Chuab" are listed in the versions of the story I collected in the field. Krämer (1917–29, 4:2) mentions the following villages as "children of Chuab": Ngersuul, Ngerebkei (located near Ulimang), Ngerusar, Imul, and Ngeremid. Aoyagi's Ngerard informants give a slightly different list of the eight villages of Chuab, including Ngerechol, Imul, Ngerusar, Ngeremid, Bungelkelau, Ngeruikl, Ngellau, and Ngerebkei. But in trying to explain the eight villages of Chuab as a doubling of the four cornerposts which organize the distinct polity of Milad (see below), he concludes, "I have no clue how to interpret this number at present" (1979:2). And finally, a contemporary titleholder from Ngeaur lists the villages of Chuab as Ngerechol, Imul, Ngerusar, Ngersuul, Ulimang, and Mengellakl—differing from the text given above only in the omission of Ngeruikl (PCAA, Ngeaur File).

Beyond the evidence internal to these stories themselves, there is little in the records of tradition and archaeology to support the claim implied in the texts that these eight villages formed an actual political federation at some early point. In fact, much of the possible corroborating evidence runs counter to such a claim. The key myths set in this archaic world takes place in villages other than those listed as members of the federation of Chuab. These stories trace the branching out of the children of the Woman of Ngetelkou and other ancestral women from Ngeaur and Beliliou in several interrelated births (*cheroll*) located, for example, in Beluusung in Irrai (Story of Turang), Roisibong in Imeliik (Story of Obechad), Ngetmel in Ngerechelong (Story of Dirracheleos), and Ngibtal off the coast of Ngiual (Story of Dirrachedebsungel). Also, the twelve villages visited by Chuab's brother Uchererak (i.e., Ngetmel, Ollei, Mengellang, Chol, Ulimang, Ngiual, Melekeok, Ngchesar, Ngerduais, Ngeremid, Ngemelis, and Ngeaur) have in common with the federation of Chuab only the fact that most of the villages in the two sets are located on the eastern side of the archipelago. Archaeological evidence suggests, however, that ancient population centers were located on the west coast of Babeldaob, especially in areas surrounding Ngeremeduu bay. The great stone faces and megalithic structures at Bairulchau between Ollei and Ngerebau in Ngerechelong and at Ngereklngong in Ngeremlengui both point to ancient centers in areas other than the villages of Chuab. And a comparison of the titles of chiefs of the eight villages in the federation with lists of ranked titles for these villages of Chuab compiled in 1910, 1952, and 1974 reveals that, while four of the titles (Secharaimul, Tucheremel, Rechiungl, and Obakeramechuuu) are consistently given as the first titles of their respective villages, none of these villages is regarded as the capital of a historically attested district. In other words, villages and chiefs other than those associated with Chuab have in the modern era taken over leadership of local districts—assuming, of course, that the villages of Chuab formed such a federation. This lack of correlation should not obscure the point that this mythological era of the archaic world of Chuab represents a state in which villages are linked by migration paths and marked by sets of parallel cultural features. The Story of Chuab is important because it narrates the beginning of this mode of political interconnection, a pattern which will be repeated in less explicit forms in many myths and stories set in later eras.

The myth of the origin of Belau, the first two segments of which, concerning Latmikaik and Chuab, were presented above, continues in two more segments, the Story of the Cursed Children of Chuab and the Story of the Feast of Secheseball. The third segment describes the northward migration of Chuab's five children after their mother's death at Ngeaur. In spite of being the source of the original eight chiefly councils and the vehicle for conveying Uchelianged's laws, Chuab eventually hinders the development of cultural habits, especially the practice of eating cooked food. Clinging to her old habits of consuming vast quantities of raw food and grown to gigantic proportion, Chuab threatens the food supply of her local village and is burned to death by her worried children (other variants say angry neighbors). This mode of death motivates her name, which the storyteller linked to the word *chab*, "ashes."[10] Ashamed of their mother's fatal habit, Chuab's five children flee from Ngeaur and migrate to the north, only to meet a parallel fate due to similar eating habits.

Story of the Cursed Children of Chuab

Now Chuab had five children. Her first daughter was named Chitaueiuei, and then she bore a son named Labek (Ocean Swell). And she bore another son named Boid (Traveling Song) and then another son named Mengelechelauchach (Reminds the Coral). And then she bore another son named Omuutaidnger (Piles Up the Reef). And by this time fire had been discovered in Belau. Dilidechuu (Hen Woman) had found fire and sent it over to Ngeaur. Then Uchelianged pronounced the law, saying, "No one may eat raw fish, and particularly no one may eat another person." People at this time were like fish, so one person could eat another person. But Chuab continued to eat food which was raw, including fish and any kind of food growing on trees. Her children became very ashamed of her, so when she was sleeping they carried firewood to the cookhouse, made a fire, and lit the wood. Chuab perished in the fire, and then Uchelianged said to her children, "You have slain your mother, so you are cursed and you are to be known as the Cursed Children (Ngalekdmeoang). You are cursed and you will just wander at sea."

They traveled away and they went to the sea passage in front of this village [Ngeremetengel] at Ngeremlengui. They came to live in this village. But they continued to eat fruit from trees, for the eating habits of their mother had come now to them. They ate so much that there were no more fruits and leaves on the trees, and the residents of the village became worried, saying, "With these people here we are all going to go hungry." So they took the

---

10. Kubary (1969:39) points to the similarity between the names Chuab and Yap as evidence of an early cultural association between the two island groups. He fails to note, however, that in Belauan the name for Yap is Belulechab (Land of Ashes).

[poisonous] gallbladder from the blowfish and fed it to them, and
the two sons who drank this poison died. They were buried here,
and their grave is up on the hillside behind Ngeremetengel. The
name of the grave there is Grave of the Cursed Children. The other
three escaped and descended to Ngchesar, and the very same thing
happened there. They still practiced their eating habits there, and as
a result there was a scarcity of food in Ngchesar. The people of
Ngchesar got very worried, and they also took the fish poison and
fed it to them, and two of the sons died. They are buried at
Ngchesar, and the grave site is located behind Ngerengesang on the
hillside. The grave site there is also called Grave of the Cursed
Children. So there is the grave here and one in Ngchesar.

The woman [Chuab's daugher] fled and jumped into the sea, for
she could be like a fish. She entered the fish trap of a man from
Ngeruikl named Bekeu (Brave), who had put his trap at Idimes.
When Bekeu came back to inspect his trap he saw what he thought
was a fish in the trap, a grouper. But when he took out his spear,
the fish said to him, "No! No! You will injure me!" He took the
fish out and put it in the boat, and then took it to his house at
Ngeruikl. They lived there, but when she dined she ate not only the
food but the pots and the fiber trivets (*iluodel*) as well, so they
called her Mengailuodel (Eats Trivets). So then Ngirakebou [chief
of Ngchesar] sent word to Melekeok, saying, "This woman who is
living here is going to destroy this village." Reklai [chief of
Melekeok] said, "Have her come here, for there is plenty of food in
Melekeok." So she went there, but after a short while Reklai sent
word to Ngerard, "Madrangebuked [chief of Ngerard], this
woman here is going to destroy this village. No one has anything
to eat any more." Mad (Madrangebuked) sent word back, saying,
"Send her here, for you know very well that Ngerard is full of
things to eat." She went there, and they fed her until there was
nothing more to eat, and the villagers then prepared the gallbladder
of the blowfish and gave it to her. She drank it and died, and they
buried her at the gravestones in front of Tublai [Madrangebuked's
house]. If we go there today the grave is still there. This is the end
of the story of Chuab. Chuab did not fall over and form the land.
She was a person.

The opening portion of this third section of the origin myth is well
known in contemporary Belau due to the popular "storyboard" carving
representing the giantess Chuab falling to her death (Krämer 1917–29,
5:1). Less widely known, however, is the subsequent part describing

the migration of Chuab's children to Babeldaob. The names of the four male children all connote some kind of motion connected with the sea. According to sea lore, each year large sea swells (*labek*) pass from south to north. The coming of the swells is signaled by the journeys of Mengelechelauchach, whose task is to "remind the coral" that the appropriate time has come, and Omuutaidnger, whose job is to "pile up coral rubble" at shallow places along the reef. What is most important to note is the overall narrative logic of the story, in which the cursed children migrate from village to village and meet their deaths at three places, Ngeremetengel, Ngchesar, and Ngerard. At the first two villages the graves of the four male children bear the same name, Debellelangalek-dmeoang, while the grave of the daughter Chitaueiuei (renamed Mengailuodel) is marked by stones in front of the house of chief Mad of Ngebuked village in Ngerard. The grave site in Ngeremetengel is still visible today as an elevated hill just behind the village. These graves are the historical markers (*olangch*) which anchor the spatial/temporal co-ordinates of the journey around Babeldaob island in a set of homologous places.

But these three places, together with Melekeok, the fourth village mentioned in the text, are not part of the "polity of Chuab" as listed in table 2. In fact, the three chiefs who compete to see if their respective villages are capable of feeding the children of Chuab all carry titles belonging to an entirely different political era (*renged*), the origin and structure of which will be analyzed in the next section. In other words, the death of the children of Chuab is accomplished by reading back into the archaic world a cast of characters from the subsequent "new world" of Belau. This interpenetration of two successive polities within the same story is efficiently accomplished by locating the graves of Chuab's children at sites whose political importance emerges only in stories set in the following era. This technique of linking successive portions of a long narrative by means of a unifying *olangch* (here, the grave sites) can also be seen in the first two segments of the origin myth, where the clamshell from which sprang the first sea creatures returns in the second segment as the drinking vessel of Ucherkemur at Bairebech meeting-house.

This technique of interpenetration of political eras through the mediation of an *olangch* is clearly demonstrated in the related Story of Madraklai recorded by Krämer (1917–29, 4:114–16). Here the villages associated as "children of Chuab" are seen as a cooperative group whose political independence is being threatened by their geographical proximity to a second set of villages. Functioning as the *olangch* in the story is a valuable of the *mengungau* type. Madraklai lived in Ngerdmau and had a sexual liaison with a woman from Ngerebkei in Ngerard district. This unfortunate fellow tried to signal to his concubine while she was sitting in the meetinghouse by tossing a wax apple in her direction. But the fruit struck her in the navel and killed her. When chiefs from her home village Ngerebkei learned the tragic news, they decided to rally all the children of Chuab to descend upon Ngerdmau in fully armed war canoes in order to demand reparations. Terrified of an impending attack, the leaders of Ngerdmau commanded the deceased woman's lover to pay for his act with his life so that the village could avoid destruction. But Madraklai chanced upon a valuable piece of money in the mangrove channel of Ngerioulbai and managed to save himself by offering this money in place of his life.

The titleholders representing the villages of Chuab, including Obakeramechuu of Ngersuul, Tucheremel of Ngerusar, Secharaimul from Imul, and Rechiungl from Ngeremid, then met to decide who would take the single piece of money.

> They took the piece of money from him [Madraklai] and returned to Ngerebkei. There they discussed who should receive the money. The two high chiefs [Secharaimul and Obakeramechuu] decided that Rechiungl should take it, but he did not want it, because he was considering the proximity of Oreor [to Ngeremid].
> Tucheremel was likewise afraid to take it on account of Irrai, just as Secharaimul feared the leader of Ngerekeai [i.e., Rengulbai of Imeliik]. Finally, Obakeramechuu, who in those days was female, for a woman carried both the male and the female titles, took the *mengungau* piece, since the village of Ngersuul was not dependent on any other village. (Krämer 1919–29, 4:115; my translation)

So the consolidated action of these five villages under the banner of children of Chuab was instantly thwarted by threats imposed on several of these villages by powerful neighbors, namely, Oreor, Irrai, and Imeliik. Only Obakeramechuu of Ngersuul dared to claim this valuable piece of money, because she alone did not live in fear of being invaded. The political environment presupposed by this story is one in which the villages of Chuab exist as a powerless reminder of the archaic world of Belau in the midst of a different polity in which the quest for valuables motivates political relations. Taken together with the villages visited by the children of Chuab (that is, Ngeremetengel, Ngchesar, Melekeok, and Ngebuked), the villages mentioned in the Story of Madraklai in fact constitute what is known as the "new world" founded by the goddess Milad.

The Termination of the Polity of Chuab

Having hinted at a radically different future political order, the myth of the origin of Belau concludes in a fourth and final segment which describes circumstances leading to the breakup of the polity of Chuab. This segment, the Story of the Feast of Secheseball, tells about the fateful feast held at Beluusung village in Irrai in honor of the eight titleholders installed by Chuab. This proved to be their final get-together, since after the theft of a valuable named Medatumloket by the food server to chief Bdelulabeluu of Mengellang, the high god Ucheli-anged disperses the federation of Chuab and commissions another group of messenger gods called collectively the Ruchel (Foremost) to travel throughout Belau to impose new chiefs and new councils.

Story of the Feast of Secheseball

And then after a period of time one of the senior men from Ngerusar, not the chief Tucheremel but just a man from the village, prepared a feast in honor of this body of chiefs (*klobak*). The men's club Ngaracheremrumk went out on a fishing expedition for this feast. They cast their nets off the coast of Oikull and fished in the direction of Dngerdukl. But when they pulled in their net there was just one triggerfish (*dukl*). So they cast the net out again, and they pulled it in and came up to Ikrelngkesiil. When they inspected the net, two fish had been caught, Medatumloket and Ngerengellecheluu (Echo). The leader of the fishing party said, "Let's quit. These fish will be for the feast of Secheseball. But let's go over to the rock island Dmengedib and broil the triggerfish and dine, and then let's unload our catch at Beluusung."

So they docked at the rock island and collected firewood and started a fire. They told the young men, "Bring the triggerfish up, for we are famished. Then we will return home in the morning." But when they opened the net Ngerengellecheluu escaped. They chased after it in every direction in the vicinity of the island. They called out, "It's over by you!" and the fish called back, "It's over by you!" The fish just repeated whatever they called. If they said, "Over there!" it called back, "Over there!" And even though they chased after it for a long while, it eventually got away, so they just broiled the triggerfish and ate it.

They then took Medatumloket back to Beluusung, prepared it, and put it in the pot. They summoned the village chiefs of Belau (*rubekul a Belau*). At this time there was no fire in Belau and they were going to eat the fish head in the pot uncooked.[11] When the eight chiefs of Belau arrived, the first person to serve food was the food server from Ngerechol. They told him, "Go see to our food, for the chiefs are hungry." But when he looked in the pot, the fish's eye blinked at him. The food server replaced the lid and returned to tell Uchelchol, "There is something strange about that fish." So the chiefs conferred and selected a man from Imul, but when he went to look into the pot the very same thing happened. The chiefs conferred again and selected a man from Ngeremid. But all the food servers were used up, and the last was Madraikelau. They sent him and he went to look in the pot, and when he saw the fish he told it, "Get yourself ready because these chiefs are hungry." The fish said to him, "First pluck out my eye." He plucked out the eye and put it in his mouth and then returned to distribute the food portions.

After the feast was over, the chiefs found out that the food server to Bdelulabeluu had stolen the eye of Medatumloket. This council of chiefs which came to dine together at this feast then dispersed, and this marked the end of the archaic world of Belau. After they dispersed the Ruchel [messenger gods] began their journey.

The feast mentioned in this story is one of a variety of feasts (*mur*) held in honor of chiefs, wives of chiefs, titleholders from other villages, or clubs visiting from friendly villages. The sponsor of the feast engages one or more men's clubs to supply fish on the appointed day and arranges for taro to be harvested by women of his own or allied villages. As the story relates, Ngaracheremrumk club of Ngerusar contracted by Secheseball caught one triggerfish at Dngerdukl, and then on a second pass with their nets they caught two additional fish, Medatumloket and Ngerengellecheluu. The name Ngerengellecheluu contains a reduplicated form of the word *ngor*, "voice, noise," and in the story this fish escapes its pursuers by repeating or reduplicating their calls (*ngor*), causing deictic confusion. (Today the word *ngerengellecheluu* means "echo," a phenomenon common in the rock islands area where steep-sided islands are found in clusters.) The second name Medatumloket is composed of three words: *mad*, "eye"; *te*, "they"; and *miloket*, "pay out (money)." So this name means (roughly) "the eye they paid out." And a contemporary informant who was once in possession of this particular

---

11. There is a contradiction between this sentence and the statement in the next scene of the story, in which fire is present.

piece from the *chelebucheb* class commented that this valuable is particularly "dangerous" (*kengaol*) because it resembles a human eye (see Ritzenthaler 1954:45). The name of the sponsor of the feast, Secheseball, is also motived by the action of the story. Secheseball means "is to be ladled out" (from the verb *melcheseb*, "to ladle"); the ladling here refers to the distribution of portions of boiled fish to the assembled chiefs of Belau.[12] In Krämer's text, the chief from Mengellang acquires the privilege of cutting up ceremonial food portions and of receiving the head, but there is no mention of the theft of the eye or of the relevance of the federation of Chuab.

Although this story does not involve the migration or journey along a path, it does share in common with the first three segments of the origin myth the interlocking of narrative repetition and geographical homology. In the story the strange fish is successively investigated by food servers assigned to the chiefs of Ngerechol in Beliliou, Imul in Imeliik, Ngeremid in Oreor, and Mengellang in Ngerechelong—four of the villages belonging to the polity of Chuab. The symbolism here depends on the custom of prescribed food distribution when chiefs assemble for feasts. Put simply, the order of service and the size of food portions mirror the ranked hierarchy of titles and villages. Failure to distribute the proper food portions (*deliukes*) and violation of the prescribed order of service are serious affronts to the dignity and respect of these ranked positions and can even signal the seizure or usurpation of precedence by a lower-ranking chief or village.[13]

12. The two fish names are also found in a text collected by Krämer (1917–29, 4:162–63), in which Tucheremel captures the turtle god "Madatumloget" (Medatumloket) and a creature called *ngerengel'le golu* (*ngerengellecheluu*, "echo"). Citing Bishop Walleser's (1913) dictionary as his authority, Krämer links the word *golu* (Walleser's *chelu*) with Samoan *volu*, "sea turtle." If Krämer's etymology is correct, this story about Secheseball takes on added comparative interest in terms of the widespread connection between turtles and chieftainship in Oceania (Kubary 1885:111; Lessa 1980; Milner 1952:369; Ushijima 1982:55). Kubary notes, for instance, that when the chiefs of Ngeremlengui come in war canoes to "open the *ruk*-dance" at Oreor, a turtle is eaten at Meketii meetinghouse.

13. A clear example of the seizure of ceremonial food portions is found in the Story of Melamitoi (Kesolei 1975:34–36). As the child of a woman from the house of Iretech on Beliliou, Melamitoi had a strong claim to the chiefly title Itbik. But since his ancestors migrated from Beliliou to Babeldaob, he was not present to take this title. Later in life, however, he did return to Beliliou. And when he learned that the title was held by a man who was only a child of a man of the house, he decided to stake his claim. One day when the chiefs were assembled in their meetinghouse, Melamitoi seized Itbik's prescribed portion of the tropical almond candy (pressed into the shape of a dugong) which was being distributed. The other chiefs were astonished at this display of aggressiveness, but none hesitated in accepting his claim to the honor when they learned his true descent.

This section of the myth resembles the other sections in the role *olangch* play in anchoring the story to some extranarrative values. The stolen *chelebucheb* piece clearly functions as such a sign, parallel to the clamshell of Latmikaik and the councils instituted by Chuab found in earlier story segments. This valuable is an appropriate sign in this section depicting the termination of the archaic world, since not only are these *chelebucheb* valuables the financial instruments of chiefly politics, but also the particular one mentioned is associated with the eye of the fish. Thus the seizure of this valuable can be seen as equivalent to eating the head of the fish, the most highly valued food portion assigned to chiefs. It was Mengellang village in northern Babeldaob to which Chuab assigned the task of stabilizing the other villages in the federation, and this responsibility is the motivation for the name of the village, "holds steady." The violation of protocol takes place at precisely the point in the hierarchy of villages where its destabilizing consequences are most apparent.

Contemporary informants recall very little about the villages of Chuab or about the archaic world in general. In the course of their fieldwork in Ngerechelong in the 1950s the Forces recorded a passing reference to an anomaly in food distribution order which possibly points to this political arrangement.

> The northern and southern confederations which existed at the time of Wilson's arrival [i.e., the side heavens to be discussed below] were described in the 1950s by an elderly informant as a "new thing." He noted that Palauans recalled a more ancient power distribution which was different. He commented further, by way of example, that evidence of this earlier power structure could be seen in the discrepant status behavior in recent times when all the chiefs of the different municipalities [i.e., districts] came together for some event—even an event of modern origin. At such time, the ranking chief of one of the northern municipalities (Ngerechelong) was given the prestige serving of feast food—the head of a turtle or pig. Other chiefs received portions deemed less prestigeful. By right of seniority in the "newer" political confederations, the chiefs of Oreor and Melekeok should have received such portions. Instead, the ancient custom in which the head of the turtle goes to the man who bears the ranking hereditary title from the ranking village in Ngerechelong was honored. In 1971 even younger informants were well aware of this seemingly aberrant pattern of food distribution. (Force and Force 1972:11)

The Forces do not reveal the name of the village in Ngerechelong or the name of the highest title which received the head of the turtle. But in light of the texts given above, the comment by Krämer about Meda-tumloket, and the description of this village as the "ranking village of Ngerechelong," it is safe to conclude that it is in fact Mengellang. An informant from Ngeremlengui explained to me this honorific survival in terms of the opposition between the archaic world and the new world of Belau.

> This is indeed true. When the elders of Belau meet together, the head of the pig or fish does not go to Reklai [chief of Melekeok] and does not go to Ibedul [chief of Oreor]. Rather, it goes to the chief of Mengellang. But this has to do with the archaic polity, that is, the polity before Milad existed. Mengellang is one of the villages of Chuab. (But is this still the case today?) No, this is no longer the case, for the titles in existence today are the children of Milad. If the chiefs of Belau have a meeting which takes place in Ngeremlengui, then the head of the pig goes to Reklai; but if the meeting is held in Oreor, the head comes here [to Ngirturong of Ngeremlengui]. This practice about the leader of Mengellang is over with. The leader of Mengellang today is Chuong, that is, Chuoretei. But in the old times he was called Bdelulabeluu, which is the title from the time of Chuab and Latmikaik.

Before we can make the transition from the archaic world of Chuab to the new world of Milad, a slightly different version of the Story of Chuab needs to be discussed briefly. Variants of this version differ from, the story analyzed above in that they state, by a rhetorical conden-sation, that the fallen body of the giantess formed the geographical features of the archipelago.[14] Some of these variants assign specific places to particular body parts on the basis of an iconic association: her head formed the detached island Ngerechur located just off the north-ern tip of Babeldaob; her breasts are visible as two hills situated in Melekeok; her legs bent in pain became the twisted coast of Imeliik; and her stomach formed Ngiual, where villagers have large appetites.

Story of Chuab

Long ago there were no Palau islands. There were just two islands, Ngeaur and Beliliou. In the Palau islands there once was a woman from Ngeaur. Her name was Latmikaik. She bore a baby girl,

---

14. Texts of this version of the Story of Chuab are found in Aoyagi 1979:20; Krämer 1917–29, 4:2; Kubary 1969:66; Miyatake, in Pätzold 1968:172–73; PCAA, Ngeaur File; and Semper 1982:151–52.

whose name was Chuab. The next morning when Latmikaik got up she found that the baby could crawl. Then after she got up the following morning she found the baby could walk. Chuab continued to grow very rapidly, and on the fifth day she had grown still larger. She could consume the amount of food ordinarily sufficient for four men. Her height would increase so rapidly that in order to feed her, her food was tied to the end of a long bamboo pole and lifted up to her mouth. She grew so tall that it was now impossible to get food to her. So she now had to obtain food and water for herself. So at times she would reach in somebody's pig pen and grab one of the hogs and eat it. Sometimes even young children were just snatched and eaten to satisfy her hunger. In order to stop this the village people gathered and went to her mother to tell her about it. Her mother couldn't face the village people, much disgraced, so she told them it was all right if they killed Chuab. The people decided to gather a lot of wood to start a fire. Chuab thought this was rather unusual, so she inquired of her mother why the village people were gathering so much wood. The answer was that since she, Chuab, wasn't having anything to eat everyday, the wood was gathered to start a fire to cook food for her. Now that enough wood was gathered they, the village people, went to look for coconut leaves. After the wood and the coconut leaves were gathered it was all placed at the foot of Chuab and a fire was started. Then Chuab fell and died and her body became the Palau islands as follows:

> Ngerechelong village: head
> Arrenged village: neck
> Imeliik village: vagina
> *desbedall,* east coast: back
> *kiukl,* west coast: stomach
> Oreor
> Ngmelachel islands: burned legs
> Ngerekebesang
> Ngeruktabel

After Chuab fell her mother asked the village people to cover her with a mat. There weren't sufficient mats to cover the entire body since it was so enormous so branches had to be used. Even the branches and mats couldn't cover but half her body. So the Palau islands are half forest and half plains. And the people of the Palaus are the worms which were born from her rotted body. So the names of these islands should really be Blelau (meaning fairy tale) instead of Palau.[15] (Palau Museum n.d.)

This well-known version of the story certainly has as much ethnographic legitimacy as the version presented before it. Semper, Kubary, and Krämer all heard that the body of Chuab formed the islands, and Krämer reproduces a beam carving made around 1870 which depicts her falling over. The storyteller who told me the lengthy myth of the origin of Belau insisted, however, that the notion of Chuab's body forming the islands was incorrect and indeed foolish, since the chiefly councils created by Chuab existed before her death, which could thus not have been the time when the land was first formed. Our task is not to select the "true version" (*mera el tekoi*) of the myth, but rather to try to see how all the versions are related. The clue to this relationship is provided by an additional short text given by Krämer (1917–29, 4:2), according to which the stone tower created by the fish creatures at Ngeaur takes on human form and is named Chuab. When this tower collapses the broken stones form the islands of Belau. The reason that this text is important is that it represents the ultimate step in rhetorical condensation. That is, in the lengthy version I collected the story of the stone bridge constructed by the children of Latmikaik and the story of Chuab's death are distinct, though sequential, segments of the origin myth. Then in the variants mentioned above, the giantess Chuab, a woman from Ngeaur, falls over to form various geographical features of Babeldaob. And, finally, in Krämer's text the narrative logic of these two versions is conflated, with the stone tower explicitly identified with Chuab herself. All three versions involve a transformation of vertical and horizontal spatial axes and all three associate Chuab in some way with the geographical differentiation of villages. But the Ngeremlengui version I recorded seems to place explicit focus on the model of the path which characterizes so many stories set in the archaic world. That Ngeremlengui should accentuate the path

15. A fuller sequence of names for the islands is given in a short variant recorded by a Belauan storyteller Ngiraked (in Miyatake 1933:67): "The first people sprang up at Ngeaur, at the house of Ngetelkou. One old woman lived there, and her name was Obechad. This old woman did not have a husband, and she became pregnant and gave birth to a child named Chuab. This child grew larger and ate constantly and became so tall that [Chuab] projected out the roof. [Chuab's] mother was terrified, so she collected coconut fronds and burned down the house. By the seventh day Chuab began to shake and fell over in the northern and eastern direction. Then there was no place (*beluu*) named Belao; the first name of Belao was Chuab; the second Blelao, and the third Balao" (my translation).

model is understandable as an effort to maximally differentiate this archaic world from the succeeding cultural period, the "era of Milad,"
defined by a quadripartite polity in which Ngeremlengui itself becomes
politically prominent.

THE DESTRUCTION OF BELAU
AND THE REBIRTH OF MILAD

In the formation and structure of this new political order of Milad, the
model of cornerposts becomes operative as the pervasive cultural logic
of the era. If the model of the path created in the era of Latmikaik
signals the origination of presupposable, cultural relationships, the
model of four cornerposts implies a degree of structural stability and
coordinated interrelationship among elements. As we will see, these
cornerposts are also conceptualized as four siblings, the children of
Milad, so part of the task at hand is to chart the implications of this
ideology of kin-based coordination for intervillage political relationships. As in the preceding section, this analysis attempts to identify
a quadripartite logic not only in narrative organization and political
relations but also in its embodiment in *olangch* which function to anchor this abstract pattern in perceptible, relatively permanent markers.

But before the Story of Milad can be presented, we must consider
the Ruchel gods, whose journeys occupy a transitional phase in the
development of Belauan polity. While explaining the Ruchel (Foremost) to a group of villagers, an elderly storyteller noted that this set of
gods functioned in much the same way as colonial agents: of foreign
origin and possessing powers beyond those found locally, they came to
Belau with the declared intention of increasing proper behavior by imposing new laws. But no sooner were they established than they began
to manipulate the local political situation, to engage in economic exploitation, and to usurp positions of village leadership. Then, unable to
manage their newly acquired authority, they fell into the same wicked
ways they had originally preached against. As a result, they were replaced by a second and then a third wave of immigrant groups, who
then repeated the same cycle. The succession of waves of English,
Spanish, German, Japanese, and American powers was, by this account, only a continuation of a pattern well established in the mythology of the Ruchel gods (cf. Goodenough 1986:559).[16] And the

16. Kubary (1885:221–22) notes that when the Ruchel gods migrated to Belau, they
brought with them the system of titles and knowledge of sailing, and working their way
from north to south they gradually replaced indigenous leaders. The emblem of these
Ruchel is the image of a sailing canoe (Kubary 1969:19).

receptiveness to Western goods and practices that characterizes Belau throughout the colonial period is traced directly to the tradition of the Ruchel, since as a category, foreigners bringing money, firearms, and new religions are "next to the gods" (*bita er a chelid*).[17] What this storyteller did not mention is that stories about these gods also continue the basic pattern of *olangch* and journeys that is often found in stories set in the world of Chuab. The first Ruchel group includes eight gods whose names correspond to the villages where they eventually settled. Setting out from Ngeaur, these gods took over village leadership as follows: Uchelkldeu at Ngerekldeu (Oreor), Uchelbungs at Ngerbungs (Imeliik), Uchelsung at Beluusung (Irrai), Ucherchemliangel at Ngchemliangel (Beliliou), Ucherutechei at Ngerutechei (Ngeremlengui), Ucherringall in Ngerringall (Ngerard), Ucheltmel in Ngetmel (Ngerechelong), and Uchelkeklau in Ngkeklau (Ngerechelong).

The many stories which describe the activities of these characters do not concern us here; what needs to be pointed out is simply that this list of villages and gods forms a coherent set because of the fact that each leader's name begins with the title Uchel (Foremost). The second group of Ruchel gods arrived at Beliliou as part of a migration party under the overall direction of Chuodel (Ancient), also called Ngirabeliliou. The boat (*diall*) which is said to have brought them to Belau remains in the form of a large rock named Ngerungor off the coast of Ngeredelolk village on Beliliou. In addition to Chuodel, who took the fifth title at Beliliou, this group included Uchererak, who became the local god at Ngeremlengui (the fifth house at Imeiong had his seat), Oreor (at Ikelau house), and Ngerard; Sechaltbuich, the god of Ngerdmau; Tunglbai at Imeliik; Medechiibelau (whose name changes several times) at Irrai, Ngetbang, and Ngerechelong; and Uchelkebesadel at Ngerekebesang (near Oreor). In two cases members of this second group seized leadership directly from members of the first group (Uchelkebesadel from Uchelkldeu, and Medechiibelau from Uchelsung); and in two other cases Ruchel from the first group continued to hold power after the second migration (Ucherutechei and Ucherchemliangel). Thus it is only after three unsuccessful attempts (the chiefs of Chuab and the two groups of Ruchel gods) at establish-

---

17. This link between the Ruchel of mythology and the colonial powers was concretized in the religious vision of Rdiall, a man from Ngkeklau who during the Spanish period prophesied the arrival of steamships. Rdiall surrounded his house with paintings of various kinds of ships, some shown with sails and some with smokestacks. When asked by his associates in Ngkeklau how he learned of this new method of sailing, he insisted that he had been visited at night by the Ruchel in person, who wore Western-style hats, shoes, and clothing.

ing a stable political order that the high god Uchelianged chose to destroy the existing race and then to reconstitute it, not on the basis of the immigration of externally derived, miraculously powerful usurping male gods linked only by marriage to local territories, but rather on the basis of four indigenously generated children of the goddess Milad, whose life-giving action took place in the mountains of central Babeldaob.

Milad is one of the principal characters in a lengthy cycle of stories which straddles the archaic world and the new world of Belauan narrative. Like many stories, the Story of Milad begins on the southern island of Ngeaur at the house of Ngetelkou. The senior woman of Ngetelkou has a daughter, who lives at the house of Teliko in Ngeredubech village, the ancient capital of Ngetbang district on the island of Babeldaob. This woman has two children, a son Ochaieu (Long-winged Sea Bird) and a daughter Dilmalk (Chicken Woman). When Ochaieu is accused of eating several village children that were playing at the bathing pool Diosechbong, these three characters are all forced to flee from Ngeredubech. So they travel to the east coast, where Ochaieu proceeds on to Ngchesar, while the mother and daughter pass through Irrai on their way back to the lower sea, that is, to their ancestral home on Ngeaur. At Irrai they are befriended by Renguul of Ngetechong, who convinces them to remain at his house, since the woman of Teliko has become ill. Dilmalk's mother dies in Irrai and is buried on the hillside Omsangel (Carrying Basket) by Renguul, who then adopts young Dilmalk as his daughter. Dilmalk, the character whose name will eventually change to Milad, then leaves Irrai to return to Ngeaur so that she can be with her grandmother, the old woman of Ngetelkou. There she marries Olungiis, one of the Ruchel gods renowned for his giant penis. Olungiis and Dilmalk, whose name now changes to Dilidechuu (Hen Woman), have five children: Kerengokl, Belebalech, Techedueau, Keruaolbukl, and Kumer. This family splits up when Olungiis departs to join his fellow Ruchel gods on their journey to Belau, that is, to Babeldaob, to instruct the villagers in the law of Uchelianged.

Dilidechuu with her children then moves to Ngeriab on Beliliou, where she takes the name Obechaderiab. Dilidechuu continues to reside at Ngeriab, and another son Mengidabrutkoel (Spider) marries a woman from Ngiual. For the first time in Belau, this couple conceives a child in the manner of human sexuality rather than in the manner of fish spawning. And when Mengidabrutkoel's wife Turang is about to give birth, her mother-in-law Obechaderiab travels north to Ngiual to supervise the delivery. Later she takes up residence at the house of Chedebsungel on Ngibtal, a reef island located off the coast between

Ngiual and Melekeok, where she takes on the house name Dirrachedebsungel.

At this point we pick up the story line in the version I recorded in
Ngeremelengui.

Story of Milad

The Ruchel traveled around Belau and observed the great
lawlessness of the people, and there was nothing that could be
done about it. So they went to Ngeraod and there notified
Uchelianged, who said, "We should plan to wipe out the entire
human race (*klechad*), so that a different race of people can rise up
who will obey the law." And so this was the plan decided upon by
those who went to Ngeraod.

There was a road leading to this village of Ngeraod, and the
Ruchel appointed Temdokl to stand guard in order to prevent
anyone who came there from entering the village. So Temdokl
stood there and guarded the road from the young men of nearby
Ngerechebukl and Irrai villages. But Ngiselacheos (Eggs of the
Sun) went there—this Ngiselacheos was the child of
Dirrachedebsungel, one of the people from the village of Ngiual
who had gone to live at the house of Chedebsungel on Ngibtal.
This island of Ngibtal was destroyed by the sea, and she
[Dirrachedebsungel] was carried to Ngerechebukl. One day when
she was out collecting firewood, she found an egg in the hollow of
the *blacheos* tree and she brought it back to be her food. She forgot
all about it, and when she went to inspect it later the egg had
hatched, and there was a person. She took the child and raised
him, and called him Ngiselacheos. When Ngiselacheos grew older
he was out playing, and with his friends he went to Ngeraod,
where Temdokl was guarding the entrance to the road. He
[Temdokl] shouted at them to send them away, but they noticed
that he had only one eye. Ngiselacheos said to his friends, "Let's go
back there, because I have come up with a plan to get past." When
they returned he shouted at them and sent them away, but this
time they plucked out his eye. They went into Ngeraod where they
committed lawless acts, like dragging off women.

So the Ruchel met together and said, "What happened to
Temdokl?" When they went to visit him, they saw that his one eye
had been stolen. So they decided to call in the Tekilmelab [seven
gods who go fishing for human catch], who then became their
messengers. When they arrived the Ruchel took a coconut which

had been roasted and gave it to the Tekilmelab, saying, "Take this coconut and go down the west coast and circle around the island, and when you come to a village where the coconut bursts open, that is where you will find the eye of Temdokl." So they sailed down the west coast and circled around until they arrived at the far side of Ngesechang—the side of Ngesechang toward Irrai—at a place called Ulechong. That was where they were when the roasted coconut burst open. They then knew, "It must be right here." They proceeded to the edge of a rocky point and hung up the roasted coconut and called the place Ngeremelecharakl (Place of Hanging Up). They went on and came upon some men fishing with hand nets from the village of Ngerechebukl, and they asked for seven fish. They took these fish and said, "Let's go into the village, for there is smoke coming from there, and where there is smoke there is fire."

When they entered the village of Ngerechebukl there was an old woman living at a house named Uchulabkau (Trunk of the *Bkau* Tree). So she was named Dirrauchulabkau. They approached and said, "Mother, what are you doing?" She replied, "I am boiling taro." "We will leave our fish here with you while we go in search of this thing [Temdokl's eye] we are looking for, and we will pick them up when we return." When they left to go into the village she took their fish, which were hanging up, and then she took her taro and sliced them down the middle and put the raw rabbit fish inside, tied them all up in a bundle, and set them aside. Those who had come to the village in search of the eye of Temdokl returned without success, and they asked her, "Where are our fish?" "Right here," she said, and she gave them the taro she had stuffed with the fish.

They departed and as they went they complained bitterly about this old woman, saying, "That old woman was so starving for food and without a husband [to fish for her] that she took our fish. Well, we will get something to eat when we get nearer to Ngeraod." But by the time they stopped and unwrapped the taro, the rabbit fish on the inside had become cooked, and the leader of the group said, "That old woman was very helpful." They returned and warned her to have her son Ngiselacheos make a bamboo raft with a very long anchor rope, because a flood was going to come at the next full moon. This was the end, and after this the people who are alive today appeared. That other world was finished.

They [Dirrauchulabkau and her son] prepared pieces of bamboo for the raft and lashed them together, and fixed a long anchor rope to a rock. So when the sea rose up Dirrauchulabkau climbed aboard, and the tide rose up, broke the anchor rope, and carried her to the top of Ngeroach (At the Leg) mountain. When the flood waters receded, the Ruchel said to Uchelianged, "We are going to look for that old woman who was so helpful." Uchelianged said, "Yes, go ahead. Take some ashes and place them on her nose, and she will rise from the dead." They took ashes, but before they could do what Uchelianged said, the ashes blew away and disappeared. They went back to Uchelianged, who told them, "This time blow into her nose." So when they went back, they blew in her nose, and she rose from the dead, and when she woke up they called her Milad (Was Dead). Her name was Milad because she rose from death.

Milad lived at a large rock formation like a cave [at Ngerebesek forest], and there she gave birth to people. She gave birth to Imiungs, Melekeok, Imeliik, and Oreor. At this time Ngeremlengui became named Imiungs; Ngetelngal became named Melekeok; Cherenguul became named Oreor. These were the four children of Milad: Imiungs, Melekeok, Imeliik, and Oreor. Imiungs is the leader (*merredel*) because it was the oldest, and Melekeok was also a leader because it was second oldest. Imeliik is a leader because it is a woman. Oreor is the youngest and has no food in its own villages and must get food from Babeldaob. The meaning of Oreor is "overactive" (*sureor*); and the meaning of Melekeok is "stubborn" (*tekeok*), which is like the word *tekangel*, that is, it just stands upright and does not budge. Imiungs just sits in one place, like an old person. Imiungs just sits and nothing can disturb it, and it does not laugh. Imeliik before Milad was named Ngerekeai—no, in ancient times it was Imeliik and at the time of Milad it became Ngerekeai. This was the only daughter of Milad. The meaning of Ngerekeai is that a newborn child is placed in swaddling fiber (*keai*).

Krämer's (1917–29, 4:65–66) text of this same story follows much the same narrative line as does this contemporary version, except that, first, his informant does not link Dirrauchulabkau (Dirrabkau in his text) with earlier manifestations of the same character under the names Dilmalk, Dilidechuu, and Obechaderiab. Second, his text identifies Ngiselacheos with another character, Terkelel, who marries the daughter of the chief of Ngcheangel. And third, Milad gives birth to five rather than four stone children, the additional offspring being Ngebiul. A third version, recorded earlier but in a much simpler form by Semper, agrees with Krämer's version that Milad had five children from whom the present population is descended. But unlike either the story I collected in Ngeremlengui or Krämer's text, Semper's story mentions that Milad's children were fathered by the male inhabitants of the heavens, the Ruchel gods discussed above.

> One day, as the story goes, one of the chiefs went up to heaven, from where the gods looked down every night with their twinkling eyes, the stars. He stole the eye of one of these celestial residents. When he brought it back to Palau, they made their money from it. This is the same money we use today. Because it comes from the gods, we revere it so much. That's why you people from the West can't imitate it, though you've often tried to do so. We can easily see how it differs from the real money of the gods.
>
> The robbery enraged the gods. They decided to get revenge and descended to earth. They immediately went to the village where the stolen eye was hidden. Here, they assumed the form of ordinary men and asked for hospitality at the huts. But the people there were most inhospitable. They refused to give them food and drink. Only a woman living by herself in a small house treated them well and served them the best she had, taro and fish. Before the gods left, they told her to build a bamboo raft before the next full moon. And on the night of the full moon, she was to sleep on it. She obeyed them. A frightful storm and rain came on that night; the ocean rose ever higher, flooded the islands, washed away the hills, and destroyed the people's houses. They were at a loss as to how to save themselves, and they all died in the constantly rising waters. But the kindly old woman was raised up on the raft on which she slept and drifted for quite a distance until her hair was caught in the branches of a tree high atop the hill at Ngeremlengui. Here she lay, as the water ebbed. The celestial dwellers then came and looked for their ward. But they found her dead. They summoned one of their women from heaven. She entered the dead body and revived it. Those men begat five children upon her. Then they ascended to heaven and the real god inside the woman's body also left in order to return home. These five children populated the islands anew. All of us who live here now are descended from them.[18] (Semper 1982:152–53)

18. Semper (1982:152n) also cites another version of the Milad story which is con-flated with the Chuab story: "[Milad] descended from heaven and created the individual districts as separate islands, namely, Oreor, Ngeremlengui, Ngerechelong, Melekeok, and Irrai. Only Ngebuked arose by itself from the flood. The selection of the places, all featuring peculiar hills or mountains, is important. The ones near Melekeok are especially striking for that rounded shape which the Spanish have always indicated as *tetas* on their

The final version of the Story of Milad to be cited was recorded by Kubary and places the site of the goddess's rebirth at Roisbeluu, an elevated village in Ngeremlengui near Ngeroach mountain. In Kubary's text the Obechad, a group of gods, rather than the Ruchel are named as the agents of her resurrection.

In olden times, before present-day men existed, the inhabitants of the Palau Islands were probably all *chelid* [gods], for they were strong and performed marvels, and the *chelid* went around on earth like other men. One of these *chelid* by the name of Temdokl, who was one of the Obechad, came to Ngerechebukl in what is today Irrai and was killed by the inhabitants there. The rest of the seven allied gods went to look for him and came to the same place; the inhabitants of this region were known to be generally proud and spiteful. The gods were received ungraciously everywhere with a single exception—an old woman by the name of Milad received them in her house and informed them of the death of Temdokl. Full of grief and anger, the gods decided to avenge him, but in order to reward the friendliness of the old woman, they decided to save her. They advised her, therefore, to prepare a raft and to fasten it to a tree with a rope made from vines of the forest. About the time of the full moon, a monstrous flood set in and covered the whole of Palau, but the good Milad cruised around on her raft until finally even her rope was too short and she met her death in the deluge. Her body drifted around and finally became entangled by the hair in a thicket of the Roismlengui. When later the gods came to earth to visit Milad and found her dead, they regretted her fate so deeply that the oldest Obechad determined to call her back to life. This he did by blowing his breath into her chest, but he also wanted to make her immortal, and for that he needed a water of immortality which one of his comrades was supposed to get for him. But one of the gods, Terriid [White-browed Rail], whose totem is the Railus pectoralis, was malicious and did not wish to have men be immortal. So he persuaded the *cheremal* tree (hibiscus) to perforate the taro leaf in which the water was carried; this the tree did by means of a withered, unpretentiously protruding branch tip. Thus, Milad lost her immortality and the *cheremal* received such a lasting life that the smallest piece of it,

---

charts. Of them, it is said that Milad tore off one of her breasts and threw it into the ocean; from it came the hills near Melekeok." The special place assigned to Ngebuked might be explained by the fact that this village is where Semper's principal informant lived.

when laid in the ground, germinates and grows into a tree. But the
enraged Obechad punished Terriid, and even today he bears the
traces of it in the broad red streak which he has on his head. Since
then, the *terriid* [bird] is considered the symbol of malice and envy.
Milad remained in Ngeremlengui and became the mother of
modern men. (Kubary 1969:32–33; cf. Kubary 1873:222)

An important idea contained in this version of the story is that human
mortality is the price of cultural rebirth through Milad.

The following discussion and analysis of the Story of Milad as exemplified in these versions is divided into five general headings. First,
fragmentary references to the basic story found in additional Western
sources will be cited. Second, the names of Milad's children will be
examined in terms of their folk etymologies, which provide the key to
understanding the symbolic relationship among the villages. Third, a
survey of other stone remains associated with Milad and her children
will illustrate the degree to which these physical signs have been used to
legitimate and explicate the political structure created at the end of the
myth. Fourth, through the combination of Belauan and Western
sources, political relations among dominant villages will be shown be
coded by an ideology of siblingship among Milad's children in which
the fundamental cornerpost order is augmented by a fifth term, the
"sister's son" of the male offspring of the goddess. And fifth, two chants
will be cited which demonstrate the relevance of the story for chiefly
political rhetoric. In other words, the central focus in this chapter is the
story's political dimensions rather than its other symbolic and structural
features or its relationship to other stories set in the same cultural era.

Semper was not the only nineteenth-century visitor to hear that a
great flood destroyed an earlier race of people who inhabited the islands, and that the present race sprang from a single woman Milad.
Captain Barnard, whose whaler *Mentor* wrecked at Belau in 1832,
learned from the people of Ngerechelong that "like the most of the
human race they have a tradition of a universal deluge."

> Their tradition is that on a time the sea rose very high, the low
> ground was overflown. All retreated to the hills. The sea continued
> to rise till all but the highest hills were covered. At length came on
> a mountainous wave and swept all away. One woman was caught
> by her hair in the top of a tree and saved; from her the present race
> sprang. They say the tree still stands. (Barnard 1980:29; spelling
> and punctuation modernized)

Thirty years later Captain Cheyne was told the following fragment by
chief Ngirturong of Imeiong.

Ngirturong tells me that the Palau Islanders have a tradition of a flood; that one woman with child escaped by getting on the Peaked hill in Ngeremlengui, and that the islands were again peopled from the offspring of this woman. (Cheyne 1863–66: 29 June 1864)

That Ngirturong told this to Cheyne is itself significant, for in doing so this chief affirmed the high status of his own district, an especially important claim given the context of Oreor's political ambitions in the mid-nineteenth century.[19]

Kubary, who heard the story less than ten years later, grasped more fully its political implications.

The differences in rank of the lands [i.e., districts] is based on a tradition which runs as follows: "A woman named Milad bore four children, three sons and a daughter. This woman was the *chelid* [god] who created Palau, and the children were in order Imiungs in Ngeremlengui, Melekeok in Ngetelngal, Oreor in Ngerekldeu, and Imeliik." These are the four largest lands in Belau. (Kubary 1873:211)

In citing the names of the "four largest lands" together with the names of their districts, Kubary alludes to the differentiation between these capital villages and the lesser villages within the districts; but he does not code this differentiation in terms of the renaming of the four districts, as in the Ngeremlengui version of the story. Kubary felt that the supremacy of these four capital villages constituted a pan-Belauan polity in which "the communities of Ngeremlengui, Melekeok, Imeliik, and Oreor observe the rank conferred upon them by birth, and regard each other as equals" (1873:221). In another passage Kubary adds the important observation that this political system is determined not only by the birth order of Milad's children but also by their gender differences.

The five lands of Ngeremlengui, Imeliik, Oreor, Ngebiul and Melekeok trace their descent from this Milad. Imeliik was the daughter and Ngeremlengui the *kwod* (the first-born);[20] the Roisbeluu land in Ngeremlengui, the highest elevated village in the archipelago, is likewise the oldest, and has an oblong stone on the

19. The same motive might have been present for Barnard's source in Ngerechelong as well, for at that time their political relations with Oreor were extremely strained.

20. The spelling *kwod* here is confusing. Kubary could mean *kot*, "first child," or perhaps *chuodel*, "oldest, ancient."

spot where Milad is said to have been found dead. (Kubary
1969:33)

In the previous discussion of Chuab it was pointed out that very
little evidence is to be found in indigenous, archival, ethnographic, and
archaeological sources which would indicate that the eight villages of
Chuab formed an actual archaic political regime. In the present case of
the federation of Milad, the situation is quite different, for many
sources abound in references to Milad, the four sacred stones, and the
political relations among the four corresponding principal villages of
Imiungs, Melekeok, Imeliik, and Oreor. And whereas the model of the
path and the various forms of *olangch* linking Chuab's villages had to be
teased out of the various stories in the origin myth cycle, the model and
signs in the Story of Milad are entirely explicit, both in the extant texts
and in the attested realities of political relations. While the federation of
Chuab was regarded in the colonial and modern periods as a vague,
archaic background standing in opposition to the "new thing" (*beches el
tekoi*) or "new world" (*beches el belulechad*) of Milad, the quadripartite
order of four villages labeled children of Milad played a powerful, typifying role throughout these periods by coding political action and social rank in terms of the coordinated yet differential interaction among
the four cornerposts.

NAMES AND STONES OF MILAD'S CHILDREN

The first version of the Story of Milad presented above expresses most
clearly the notion that Milad's act of giving birth is simultaneously the
act of giving new names to four important villages on Babeldaob.
Ngeremlengui district is given the new name Imiungs; Ngetelngal is
named Melekeok; Imeliik is named Ngerekeai; and Cherenguul, a poetic name for Ngerekldeu district, is renamed Oreor. As should be apparent from the discussion of village, district, and federation typology in
chapter 2, each of these cases of renaming corresponds to the specifica-
tion of the capital village of each of the four districts. Just as in giving
personal names and in awarding titles, where the bearer epitomizes the
social group which is the custodian of the name or title, here too the
four named villages come to stand metonymically for the political districts they control.

Folk etymologies explaining the meaning of these four names in
terms of human behavioral characteristics are fairly uniform across
sources. The oldest child, Imiungs, remains close to his mother at
Ngeroach mountain (photograph 4), and this motionless superiority is

expressed in the word *imiungs,* found in phrases such as *imiungs el mad* and *mad el imiungs,* "the Imiungs face," which describe the haughty or severe countenance (*imings*) said to characterize the people of Imiungs village. This facial expression was translated by a Belauan into English by the phrase, "to shun other people and disregard others as human beings" (PCAA, Ngeremlengui File). A man from Imeiong told me that *imiungs* implies that "we are very slow to speak up, and in meetings with other people we do not laugh or joke around."[21] As the oldest child of Milad, Imiungs village is proud to the point of being contemptuous of lower-ranking villages, whose geographical removal from their "mother" at Ngeroach mountain symbolizes their subordinate positions.

The name of the second child, Melekeok, is derived from the word *tekeok,* which means "openly boastful," "stubborn," or "self-congratulatory." In contrast to Imiungs's high rank derived from the unchangeable fact of birth precedence, Melekeok's second position among Milad's children correlates with its aggressive self-praise. Sources differ concerning the name of the third child and only daughter, Ngerekeai in Imeliik district. If strict parallelism is to be maintained, the name of this child would be Ngerekeai (the name of the capital village of the district), but several sources give Imeliik as the name of Milad's third child. In folk etymologies Ngerekeai is derived from the word *keai,* a thick betelnut tree fiber used for rain hats, basket coverings, and swaddling for babies. One source gives the name Imeliik an etymology based on the word *omeliik,* "to pick (coconuts)."

> [Milad] began to have children. The first born was Ngeremlengui, second was Melekeok, third was Ngerekeai (female) and the fourth was Oreor. Melekeok was competitive and bully, so it was placed far away. Oreor was active, so it was also placed far to the south. Ngerekeai and Ngeremlengui stayed with their mother. Imeliik was responsible for picking (*omeliik*) coconuts for Ngerekeai; that is why they are called Imeliik. (PCAA, Melekeok File)

Oreor, the youngest child, was so hyperactive that Milad placed him farthest away on a separate island. The name Oreor shows the stem *-reor,* which is also found in *oureor,* "to work," *ureor,* "labor, work," and *sureor,* "energetic, active" (cf. Ehrlich 1984:6). Contemporary informants point out that Oreor has in fact been energetic as the center of

---

21. Aoyagi (1979:21) notes that "The eldest stone-son was named Imiungselbad who was always sitting down without talking. His mother pitied him and kept him under her care in Ngeremlengui."

Western commercial activity and the site of the national government, and that it was recently boyishly rash in its selection of a youthful man to hold its chiefly title Ibedul.

Hidikata recorded several of these folk etymologies in the course of his research on sacred stones, oral traditions, and ancient villages in the 1930s.

> On Palau, any baby who is so irritable by nature as to bite his mother's nipples is called *tekeok el ngalek* (*ngalek* means child). As a baby, Olekeok used to bite his mother's nipples, so goddess Milad named him Olekeok. Likewise, a baby so nervous that he keeps looking left, right and all around is called *sureor el ngalek*. That is the reason why the goddess named another child Oreor. Any baby so calm and quiet as to sleep helplessly is called *bechisngull el ngalek*. The name of another child, Imiungs, was a corrupted form of this word. Imeliik was another of the goddess' children, and the child-pouch was located at Ngebiul, a settlement of Ngerechelong. (Hidikata 1973b:70)

The qualitative gradation evident among the children of Milad corresponds to the antithetical forces of *celeritas*, "swiftness, rashness," and *gravitas*, "heaviness, seriousness," which Sahlins (1985b) (followed Dumézil) correlates with the dualism of the active, conquering, warlike aspect and the peaceful, ceremonial, priestly aspect of Fijian chieftainship. The boyish rashness of Oreor, Milad's youngest son, contrasts sharply with the dignity and passivity of Imiungs, the oldest child. The two middle terms of the series, the boastful, stubborn Melekeok and the fruitful, nurturant female Imeliik or Ngerekeai, can be viewed in terms of the inherent instability of the two extreme terms of the set. Structurally, the existence of Melekeok gives the energetic Oreor an additional term upon which to exercise its active power, which derives from military strength, externally acquired influence, and achieved political alliance. Such activity directed toward Imiungs would be futile or counterproductive, since the "sacredness" of all the children of Milad is said to remain with Imiungs near the "mother" of the entire polity (see chapter 6). And the existence of the female Ngerekeai gives the system the potential to generate a fifth term, an offspring of Ngerekeai, which stands in the privileged relation of sister's son to the three brothers.[22]

But before this fifth term can be described, note must be taken of

---

22. Useem (1949:113), in a subjective but remarkably penetrating passage, contrasts these villages by comparing them with cities in the United States: Oreor is the Manhattan of Belau, Melekeok is Boston, and Ngeremlengui is Philadelphia.

another village, Ngebiul or Ngebei, which is labeled a "child of Milad" in several accounts. In addition to the four children/stones/villages of Milad, several sources mention that Ngebiul, a small east coast hamlet in Ngerechelong district, is the fifth child of the goddess (Hidikata 1973b:70; Krämer 1917–29, 4:66; Kubary 1885:122–23). The name Ngebiul (the village is known more commonly today as Ngebei) is said to be derived from the word *biull,* "to be wrapped up" (from *bail,* "wrapping, clothing"). As my informant explained:

> When Milad gave birth to the four children, she took the afterbirth (*rached*) to the edge of the stone pavement in Ngerutechei [an ancient village at the base of Ngeroach mountain] and wrapped it up and placed it in a coconut shell and set it out to draft at sea. This afterbirth floated outside the reef and circled around Belau until it entered the lagoon at Toachelbiull in Ngerechelong and came to rest at a village called Ngebiul. And so the people of Ngebei have a path following this afterbirth, although today this path has become weak through neglect. But in olden times, they had a very important path to Melekeok, Oreor, and Imeliik. When they go to Imeliik they enter strongly into the principal house of Uchelkiukl, in the role of the woman, and they can also become Rengulbai [chief of Imeliik]. And at Uchelkiukl they can also carry the title Ngirachorraol. When the people of Ngebei come to this village in a visiting party, they are given the finest food, and they also bring presents when they arrive.

According to this information, Ngebiul is most closely linked to Ngerekeai (Imeliik), Milad's only daughter, but should not be considered as the fifth child of Milad at the same level of importance as the other cornerpost villages. In contrast, Semper, Kubary, and Krämer all do mention a fifth child of Milad—Semper does not specify that this child is Ngebiul, and both Kubary and Krämer give conflicting testimony in other passages that Milad had only four children. These contradictions in the sources—at least in the Western sources, for Belauan language sources uniformly mention only four children—point to the fact that there are alternative ways of coding the political implications of the events described in the Story of Milad. As we will see, these codings can stress, on the one hand, the identical parentage of the villages as children of Milad or, on the other hand, the siblingship relations among the villages.

These folk etymologies are at the same time explanations for the names of sacred stones and other objects which stood in the named villages as the *olangch* of the political order created by Milad. The spot

in Ngerebesek forest at the foot of Ngeroach mountain where Milad
gave birth is marked by a huge volcanic plug approximately fifty feet
high, called by contemporary villagers the "house of Milad" or the
"cave of Milad." At this site can be seen the stone table (*toluk*) Milad
used, and the black ash on the ceiling of the cave is pointed to as evidence that she cooked taro there—the taro she cultivated at nearby
Ngeruuchel swamp.[23] Her stone cooking pots (*olekang*) were removed
from Ngerebesek to Orukei square in Imeiong; today some of these
stones remain there beside the stone pillar Ngartemellang.[24] Between
Ngerebesek and Imeiong lies the sacred village (*meang el beluu*) of
Ngerutechei, where an enormous anthropomorphic stone named
Tmud guards the entrance to the village at the corner of Ibungellchang
pavement. An informant explained the connection between Tmud and
Milad as follows:

> The reason the stone is called Tmud is that this is related to the
> word *tut,* "nipple, breast." When Milad gave birth to her four
> children, she took out the afterbirth. So when she took the
> afterbirth to the edge of the stone pavement and put it out to drift
> at sea she said, "I nursed (*tmuut*) my children which were stones,
> but you people will nurse real children at the breast."

The most important lithic sign associated with Milad found in the
general Ngeroach area is Imiungselbad (Imiungs Stone), the representation of Imiungs as the oldest child of the goddess (photograph 5).
This sign is actually two stones, a circular mortarlike stone with a hol-
lowed-out center and a smaller spherical companion stone called Imiungseldui (Imiungs Title) resting on the rim. Both of these stones
stood in Orukei square until they were both transported to Ngellau
village (north of Ngiual) as repayment for military assistance during
Imeiong's war against Uluang (see chapter 7). Krämer (1917–29,

---

23. This stone table is probably what Kubary (1969:33) is referring to when he
mentions an "oblong stone" marking the spot of Milad's death; his location of this stone
in Roisbeluu, however, is not supported by any other evidence. Hidikata (1973b:20)
states that Milad herself was represented in a stone carving which stood at the foot of
Ngeroach mountain; I found no physical evidence for this, and none of my informants
had even heard of such a sacred stone. Hidikata apparently did not learn about the "house
of Milad," nor about the "cooking pots of Milad," since these objects were at that time
held in secrecy especially by followers of Modekngei religion. Kubary (1873:222) also
mentions that Milad's body turned into a stone "which may still be seen today."

24. The guide who (reluctantly) took me into Ngerebesek forest noted that other pots
from the same location, distinguished by tightly fitting lids, were taken to the Modekngei
center at Ibobang.

4:140) and Hidikata (1973b:69, fig. 88A) both saw these stones and briefly mention the story of their movement from Imiungs to Ngellau. People from Ngeremlengui say that before this battle Imiungselbad, then resting at Orukei square in Imeiong, received "nourishment" from the food contained in the adjacent cooking pots of Milad and was protected from evil forces by the upright pillar Ngartemellang.[25] Informants also note that the function of the smaller stone is to "respect" the larger stone, implying that the sacredness of Imiungselbad, and thus the village of Imiungs, depends in part on there being something or someone to hold it as sacred. Although there is no direct native exegesis to support the claim, it is certainly possible to speculate in light of Austronesian parallels about the connection between this circular mortar stone and the "feminine" quality of Imiungs as the oldest child of Milad.[26] To be sure, Imiungs is the oldest son, but the qualities of stability, centrality, passivity, fertility, and sacredness which characterize Imiungs are also female symbolic qualities found additionally to belong to the first chief of a village, who can be in certain contexts the "mother of the village."

Embodiments of the other children of Milad stood in the remaining villages as well, as Krämer describes.

> Futher details about these sons [of Milad] are found in the legendary stones; we learn for instance that the son Sureor [Oreor] was born on Ngeroach mountain, but that he was so unruly [*sureor*] that his mother could not keep him. He was lying on the mat that she used as a protection against the sun (*rengerengel a Milad*) and when she threw it, the child and the mat fell in Oreor, where they were both preserved as stones in the Irachel *blai*. The son Olekeok [Melekeok] was also troublesome, and so she sent him to Melekeok, where his stone is still standing. The placenta [*rached*] of Milad drifted on a coconut shell to Ngebiul creek, where it

25. Imiungselbad is one of several mortarlike stones reported in Belau; similar stones are widespread in Indonesia and Melanesia; see especially Kaudern 1938:8, fig. 3, and 25, fig. 16; Fox 1924:223. Riesenfeld (1950:246) cites a stone from Maevo village in the New Hebrides which resembles Imiungselbad in that a second stone, corresponding to Imiungseldui, sits on top of the larger mortar stone. Also, the symbolic unity of the female Imiungselbad and the male vertical pillar Ngartemellang, both located traditionally at Orukei square, is echoed in a similar pair of stones found in Bali described by F. A. Liefrinck (in Swellengrebel 1960:28), and a pair found in an Ifugao village in northern Luzon (Christie 1961: plate 12).

26. Schulte Nordholt 1971:200, 371, and 414l See also Nooy-Palm 1979:69, who notes that the first house in Pantilang village (Sa'dan Toraja, Indonesia) has the claim to the title Great Rice Mortar.

turned to stone. The boy Imiungs was well-behaved, and so he was permitted to live with his mother. But the stone came to Ngellau. A shark (*chedeng*) and a ray (*rrull*) remained on Badelchedeng [Shark Stone] hill after the flood. (Krämer 1917–29, 4:66–67)

Kubary (1885:131) saw the Melekeok stone or Olekeok in the late nineteenth century and notes that it was associated with the practice of taking head trophies.

> In Melekeok the Ngemoroel is surrounded by a pretty little grove of *kesuk* [croton] and *gorden* [?] trees, this being looked on as the house of the god Olekeok, who consumes the *blebaol* [head trophy]. This divinity, who belongs to the older gods, is symbolized by a small stone resembling a human face that is hidden in the middle of the grove.

This stone remained near the chiefly meetinghouse in Melekeok and was there in 1909 when Krämer's wife sketched it; her sketch is comparable with one Hidikata made twenty years later (Krämer 1917–29, 2:90; Hidikata 1973b:71). Unable to locate the stone in 1980, I was informed that some time after World War II it was taken from Melekeok by followers of Modekngei religion, who were then assembling sacred stones from all over Belau at the seat of their movement in Chol, and that following a court suit the stone was returned to its rightful place but has since disappeared. Another possibility, though, is that the stone was destroyed when the Japanese extensively rebuilt the stone platforms at this location to make military fortifications.

The Oreor stone, or Sureorelbad, was seen by Krämer at Irachel house next to a large flat stone, the "protecting mat of Milad," but both were apparently missing from that location during Hidikata's visit (1973b:76). Aoyagi (1982:11) was told that this stone was given to Mengellang (in Ngerechelong) in return for military assistance. This is curious, since this gift must have been given after 1910, but by then interdistrict warfare had been over for several decades. And finally the sacred stone representing Ngerekeai was not found by Krämer or by Hidikata. Krämer (1917–29, 4:66n) mentions only that it was in the form of a pot which rested near the meetinghouse at the ancient site of Ngerekeai village. Table 3 summarizes the information presented thus far about the children of Milad.

POLITICAL RELATIONS AMONG MILAD'S CHILDREN

In turning our attention from these folk etymologies and sacred stones associated with the Story of Milad to the political implications of the

TABLE 3. CHILDREN OF MILAD

Village	Etymology	Birth Position	Stone
Imiungs	haughty	oldest son	Imiungselbad
Melekeok	stubborn	second son	Olekeokelbad
Ngerekeai	swaddling fiber	only daughter	Olekang
Oreor	energetic	youngest son	Sureorelbad
Ngebiul	wrapped	afterbirth	

new world which emerged after the great flood, the most important point to begin with is that the villages of Milad treated each other as siblings (*ruchad*). That is, not only does the story give grounds for an ideology of overall precedence for these four capital villages as the cornerposts of Belau, but it also dictates a pattern of interaction modeled after the relations between brothers and sisters. That the villages of Milad are called the cornerposts or Belau and are also conceptualized as siblings is entirely consistent, since the cornerpost model is itself based on the idea of differentiated, yet coordinated, support, the same norms which govern cross-sex siblingship.

Without going too deeply into the complexities of the kinship system, it is necessary only to point out several key features of siblingship (see Smith 1981). Siblingship is one of three fundamental interpersonal relationships, the others being parent-child (*klaungalek*) and husband-wife (*klaubuch*). An argument could be made, in fact, that siblingship is the most important of these three, as evidenced by the close relationship between the term *ruchad*, "siblings" (*re*, "plural marker," + *ochad*, "cross-sex sibling") and the general term *kauchad*, "to be in a kinship relationship" (*kau*, "reciprocal prefix," + *chad*, "human being"). A sibling group's solidarity derives from the identical parentage and corresponding house affiliations of its members, while its internal differentiation derives from the complementary social roles assigned to brothers (*rudam*) and sisters (*rudos*). In the ideal case, a sister's primary loyalty lies with her brothers rather than with her husband, and her life is spent helping her brothers by contributing financially to their customary obligations. Due to their different matrimonial destinies, cross-sex siblings are rarely resident in the same village, indeed, any form of close, physical contact is carefully avoided. But this does not in the least undermine the bond of mutual sympathy (*klaubetikerreng*), like-mindedness (*kltarreng*), and cooperation (*klaingeseu*) which characterize siblings. Within the sibling group the relationship among brothers is fundamentally hierarchial and competitive in its stress on relative age, while sisterhood (*klodos*) is considered to imply almost mystical singleness of personhood and identity of interest.[27] And finally, brothers and sisters operate in contrasting social realms: whereas the world of sisters is that of the house, the family, and the taro path, the world of brothers is that of the clubhouse, village political affairs, and activities associated with earning money.

That the principal villages were related by an ideology of siblingship was not grasped by early visitors to Belau, who categorized political roles and affairs in familiar Western terms such as "king," "sovereign," "federation," "governor," and "alliance."[28] Kubary was perhaps the first to see beyond the simplistic picture described in eighteenth-century sources, in which Ibedul of Oreor and Reklai of Melekeok are seen as competing "kings" of Belau.

> Imiungs, Melekeok, Imeliik, Oreor, and Ngebiul trace their descent back to Milad, the woman who was excluded by the gods from the general destruction of the Palau islanders. Although she, belonging to Ngerechebukl, was driven by the waters to Ngeremlengui, she was resurrected there and became the clan ancestress of today's big states. The relationships between these communities, which arose more recently, have not been preserved in such purity as among the older states; they became the leaders of larger groups and the interests they represented had taken on an extended significance. The relationship, though admitted, morally, yields to political considerations and, as a result of the influence that has been obtained over other communities, to individual feelings of ambition and greed. On this account they sometimes make war on each other, and Imiungs takes *remengol* [concubines] from Melekeok and exchanges wives with Ngerekeai, with the sisterly Imeliik. (Kubary 1885:123)

27. It is interesting to note that the opposition between sisterhood and brotherhood is not reflected in a symmetry of roots for "female" and "male." The basic root for "female" is *dil* (PAN *ina*), found in *delal*, "his mother," *ouchedil*, "to have (someone) as mother," and *uadil*, "old woman." The basic root for "male" is *dam* (PAN *ama*), found in parallel forms *demal*, "his father," *ouchedam*, "to have (someone) as father," and *uadam*, "old man." But observe that, while *dam* is also found in *rudam* (*re* + *odam*), "brothers," the word for sisters, *rudos* (*re* + *odos*), is not related to the root *dil*. Rather, the root for *rudos* is *dos*, a word meaning "similar, resembling, massed together," found principally in archaic songs and chants.

28. In the "Constitution of Pellow" ratified by the chiefs of Oreor for the benefit of the trader Cheyne, terms such as "absolute sovereign," "throne," "order of succession," "nobles," "king," "governor," and "government" are employed by the translator John Davey (Semper 1982:195–97).

In this passage Kubary highlights three important modes of intervillage relation, namely, mutual hostility, concubine exchange, and intermarriage. This third mode, according to Kubary, involves Imiungs's exchanging wives with "sisterly" Imeliik. While it is apparent from Krämer's genealogies of chiefly families of Oreor, Melekeok, Ngebuked, and Imeliik and from genealogies I collected in Ngeremlengui that male and female titleholders from high-ranking houses from these villages did intermarry extensively, the available evidence does not indicate that these rank-endogamous marriages were part of a regular set of prescribed affinal alliances, either symmetrical or asymmetrical. This is not to say that marriage cannot be a powerful political instrument. The financial obligations of the husband's house to pay a large *bachel* valuable to the wife's house at the termination of marriage necessitates that high-ranking women (*meteet*) avoid marriage into money-poor houses. Indeed, such a financially disastrous marriage, termed "falling" (*tmorech*), was subject to a severe fine imposed on the women's financial sponsor. But it would be a mistake to use evidence of actual eighteenth- and nineteenth-century political marriages to judge the validity of the ideology of "founding" relations among these villages of Milad (Sahlins 1983b:84 n. 15), or, inversely, to deny completely that the mythological charter expressed in the Story of Milad was never realized or implicated in particular exchanges, marriages, or wars. Events do not simply generate ideological formations as reflections of their own logic, nor do mythological relations mechanically compel events according to a rigid template. The historical or mythological records may note, for example, an incident that inverts the prescribed relations among the villages of Milad, but the contextual significance of such an event lies precisely in its being perceived by contemporaries as a violation of an authoritative, normative model.

Contrary to Kubary's statement that Imiungs regularly took women from Imeliik, that is, that the high-ranking houses such as Klang and Ngerturong married women from Uchelkiukl house, Krämer places these brother and sister villages in a different light.

> The woman Ngerekeai [Imeliik] was placed in the middle between her two brothers, in order that she could give them money and good counsel. This is today the obligation of sisters in Palau. While the brothers stood as stones in the above-mentioned villages [Imiungs, Melekeok, and Oreor], the sister remains as a pot (*olekang*) near the *rubakbai* [chiefly meetinghouse] in Old Ngerekeai. (Krämer 1917–29, 4:66n)

As the sister, Imeliik is devoted to the financial support of her brothers, most especially of her youngest brother, Oreor. Should a large or famous valuable enter Imeliik through the customary channels of marriage payment or fines, the three brother villages could scheme to acquire it, either peacefully through the inherent right of the brother to take control of his sister's earnings or forcibly through threat of attack. In the story of Rungiil and Cherechar (see chapter 7), for example, the Uluang leader stops off to visit his sister at Imeliik in order to acquire money to meet his own obligations.

Other narrative evidence suggests, however, that Imeliik was not consistently supportive of her three brothers, and that she even took advantage of her symbolic status as a woman to wage war without risk of counterattack. After its own attack on Oreor prior to 1783 (the so-called War of Ngirakederang) was repulsed, Imeliik began to cooperate with Ibedul's efforts against Beliliou. This support was, it seems, both insufficient and unreliable. When the Englishman McCluer presented a few beads to a delegation of Imeliik leaders in 1791, Ibedul complained that Oreor's sister village did not deserve such valuable presents. As McCluer understood Ibedul's feelings, "for when we [the English] were not here they [people of Imeliik] never came near him [Ibedul] but assisted his enemies with men and canoes" (McCluer 1790–92: 5 February 1791; cf. Hockin 1803:26). Not only did Imeliik fail to "come near" Ibedul, but other chiefs tended to avoid coming too near Imeliik. In a gesture that perplexed his English allies, Ibedul refused to come ashore at Ngerekeai, the capital of Imeliik, when his party landed there in 1783. An informant explicated this behavior in terms of the prescribed physical avoidance between brother and sister.

This avoidance also implied that Imeliik could function as a place of refuge and protection. A story about a man named Beludes concludes with his flight from pursuing warriors. Stopping successively at Ngerard, Ngerdmau, and Ngeremlengui, Beludes is refused protection by the chiefs of these villages. Finally at Imeliik, chief Rengulbai welcomes him with the words, "Imeliik is the deep channel of Belau (*mechesengelel a Belau*)." This expression means that, as a woman, Imeliik is like a deep sea channel that one enters only at risk of great danger. This symbolism of Imeliik as female applies to its high chief Rengulbai as well; at his death women carrying taro stalks come to participate in the mourning rituals (Kubary 1900a:49).

Not only can brothers demand money from sisters (ultimately, of course, from their sisters' husbands), but older brothers can take charge of financial dealings of their younger brothers. Imiungs played this role of older brother (*obekul*), for example, when Oreor and Melekeok became embroiled in political intrigue in the late nineteenth century. Oreor jealously guarded its favored position with respect to Western commercial and military influence and resisted attempts by several merchants to set up trading operations in Melekeok and Ngerard for fear that these villages would receive arms in return for fish, trepang, and agricultural produce. When Kubary finally managed to visit Melekeok in 1871, he was given a valuable by chief Reklai. Learning that Melekok had given such favored treatment to their foreign visitor, the leaders of Ngeremlengui demanded that the titleholders from Oreor purchase Kubary's money back and have it returned promptly to Melekeok. And if Oreor did not have the necessary money on hand, chief Ngirturong of Imiungs offered to contribute an *chelebucheb* piece to aid his "younger brother."

> This was another proof of the importance which the natives of Palau attach to their money. Furthermore, it showed that Ngeremlengui [i.e., Imiungs] was claiming its right to play the *obekuk* [my older brother], the elder, in relation to Oreor, and thereby humiliated and angered it. (Kubary 1873:205)

Imeiong's privilege deriving from its position as firstborn is evident in a story about people from Ngcheangel who used to carry tobacco and bananas to Oreor as tribute for Ibedul. Once when these canoes were sailing down the west coast toward Oreor they passed directly in front of Imeiong. Fishermen from this village called out, "Where is your tobacco?" But they replied defensively, "We have no tobacco, only Ibedul's tobacco." But the fishermen replied, "Forget Ibedul. Ngirturong is in the village!" So they took the tobacco and special foods from the canoes and sent them on their way empty-handed. When Ibedul learned that his tribute had been waylaid by people from Imeiong he said, "Never mind, but next time sail outside the reef past Imeiong." As the storyteller commented, "The reason Ibedul said 'Never mind' is that the older person had taken the tribute, and Ibedul is respecting Ngeremlengui as the older brother."

To these illustrations of the potential for financial exploitation of Imeliik by her brother villages and of the intervention of Ngeremlengui in the sibling rivalry between Oreor and Melekeok can be added an example of the political solidarity of the villages of Milad, taken as a sibling set and referred to as the "cornerposts of Belau." In politics and in kinship, disputes within a sibling group are set aside when the group needs to present a unified public image. At the death of Rengulbai Oukalsol, the chief of Imeliik, a funeral chant was composed which expressed the common parentage of the villages of Milad and the contrasting roles of Imeliik and Oreor in the general political discourse of

Belau.[29] In particular, this chant states the need of these villages to overcome geographical distance instituted when Milad physically separated her four stone children.

Funeral Chant of Rengulbai Oukalsol

Hail, Oreor, most fortunate of those born of Milad. When we go there we respectfully greet it and duck down to ignore any of its faults, which I continue to bear, so that Imeliik continues to exist as a village.

Hail, Imeliik, which is like a canoe which we strengthen by putting up sails and distributing ropes. Ibedul is her mast so that Imeliik can set sail.

The first expression of the *kelulau* enters at Rudelokl and the female titleholders collect medicinal plants, which after being boiled stand ready. And they then say, "Rechucher, raise up the coconut drink, for we are related through common ancestral spirits."

The *kelulau* is a unified word which we receive fully and which we take into careful consideration, whether we be young people or old enough to carry a chiefly title. And so they said, "Rengulbai, when we go to Oreor and return home again, our spirits travel together, so that we will no longer be at odds with each other."

And so when we are no longer scattered apart, chiefs, I will hold Oreor in my hand and lift it up high, for I do not want it to drop down, so that its body will be irritated on the sleeping mat.

This *kelulau* comprises my own reputation, chiefs, which crosses over the sea swells and comes up the hillside. And when they land at Delui and proceed to Meketii, the chiefs in the meetinghouse will carry it and say, "The lamp is extinguished, the lamp of Imeliik."

With this lamp extinguished, who is there in the village who will go down to Rudelokl to welcome the boat, which is the boat of Meketii and Imiungs as they travel?

In political chants of this type, the relationship among villages is frequently spoken of in terms of the movement of "whispers," that is,

---

29. Krämer (1917–29, 2:168) mentions that Oukalsol lived around 1800; this chant was composed at the time of his death when the "lamp" of the village was extinguished. The word *kelulau* is left untranslated here; it literally means "whispers," but stands here for the entire language of chiefly politics, protocol, and strategy. Rudelokl is the mangrove channel leading to Imeliik; Delui is the landing place of Oreor; Meketii is the meetinghouse of the chiefs of Oreor.

political discourse reified as bundles of words transported by sailing canoe from one village's landing place (here, Rudelokl in Imeliik) to the meetinghouse of another village (here, Meketii in Oreor). The chant for Rengulbai Oukalsol is composed from the point of view of the elders of Imeliik, who have just lost their guiding "lamp." Since representatives of all the principal villages attend the funeral of the chief, these elders take special pains to flatter the visiting dignitaries from Oreor: this village is the most fortunate of those born of the goddess Milad, since it is not only the recipient of respectful obeisance from other villages, but its faults and excesses due to aggressive youthfulness will be quietly overlooked, so that in return its sister Imeliik's perpetual existence is secured. Imeliik can only set sail and prosper when outfitted by her brother Oreor with upright mast, strong sails, and trimmed ropes. The separation of Oreor and Imeliik caused by Milad's original placement of the two villages, with her youngest son farthest away on a separate island across the channel from her daughter Imeliik, will be ended. And, finally, Imeliik will take care that Oreor never falls from its high position and that no irritation disturbs its tender young body.

In explicating the interrelationship between the cornerpost model and the ideology of siblingship of the villages of Milad, my informants said that Ngebuked, the present capital of Ngerard district, was regarded as the child of Imeliik, Milad's only daughter. As was noted above, small dependent hamlets are called "children of the mother village," but here the two villages concerned are in different districts and are, in fact, at opposite ends of Babeldaob island. As these informants explained, the position of Ngebuked can be understood in terms of the "offshoot of the turmeric plant" (*chebedel a kesol*) calculus which specifies the linkage between a man and his sister's children (Hidikata 1973a:12; Barnett 1949:26; Force and Force 1961:1204). This metaphor derives from the fact that the root of the turmeric plant develops projections or buds on its sides, some of which in turn produce additional offshoots. This system of multiple projections from the same "mother" root is a metaphor for the way in which female children of a house generate offspring who are in a strong matrilineal line (*ochell*), in contrast to offspring of males who become increasingly removed from this line with each passing generation. When I asked about Kubary's observation that Ngerard in the nineteenth century shifted its alliances between its two mother's brothers, Oreor and Melekeok, an informant clarified this by means of the turmeric metaphor.

Kubary is correct in saying that Ngerard was allied with Melekeok. Do not forget, though, that Kubary was himself a Melekeok man [he held the fifth title during his residence there]. Ngerard is like the child of the sister of both Melekeok and Ngeremlengui, so Ngerard can be allied on both sides. So this is the reason: it all depends on which side you are speaking from. Should a fine be imposed on Ngerard from one side, Reklai [of Melekeok] will pay it off. Ngerard is like the offshoot of the turmeric root of Ngeremlengui, and it is also the offshoot of the turmeric root of Melekeok. If a person from Ngerard is fined while staying in Ngeremlengui, Ngirturong will pay it off.

As the sister's son, Ngebuked is granted special protection and privilege by its mother's brothers and is lovingly spoiled by its mother Imeliik. This privilege accounts for information given to Aoyagi in Ngerard in 1977.

> An informant told me that Ngebuked had been higher in rank than those two principal villages [Ngeremlengui and Oreor]. Because Ngebuked had a lot of money, men of Ngebuked used to go to Oreor to enjoy *mengol* [concubines]. During their stay in Oreor, they were given every possible privilege by Ibedul; to use a special water place for taking a bath, which only Ngebuked men and Oreor women were permitted to use, to visit married women in Oreor freely without being refused by their husbands, who would be punished by Ibedul if they refused. . . . Ngebuked men were treated like kings by Ibedul and his villagers until they had spent all their money on Oreor *mengol*. (Aoyagi 1979:36)

This royal treatment, which Aoyagi interprets in terms of the acquisition of valuables, was said by people from Ngeremlengui to be rather an indication of Ngebuked's status as the spoiled sister's son of Oreor. People from Ngerard also claim that Ngebuked belongs among the four cornerposts of Belau, since Ngerekeai is a woman and cannot therefore assume this position, even though it is a legitimate offspring of Milad (Aoyagi 1982:13).

Imeliik, too, would come to the defense of Ngebuked, its child, when that village was in danger, as the following story shows.

Story of Dirrengulbai Who Defended Ngerard
The chiefs were all assembled in Oreor, when this chief from Ngerard named Skeras touched the buttocks of Ngirturong Dildenguich as she tended the fire in the meetinghouse.[30] She

---

30. Dirrengulbai is the female title corresponding to the male title Rengulbai. This brief story is part of a lengthy narrative about Dildenguich, a woman who held the male title Ngirturong in Imeiong.

exclaimed, "What is this? We are both chiefs and we are fondling each other?" So this Skeras fled from the meetinghouse. Now after this, people said that surely men from Ngeremlengui would destroy Ngerard, since this chief from Ngerard had fondled the buttocks of this woman, who then held the title Ngirturong. Dirrengulbai from Imeliik then said to the assembled men's and women's clubs, "We are going to go to Ngerard." So they got into their war canoes and sailed to Ngebuked in Ngerard and came to the meetinghouse which stood right across from the channel entrance. This old woman remained in the meetinghouse making baskets, and she instructed the club members to build a large protecting wall from the mangrove channel all the way up the hillside on the other side. So they built this up with stones, and this stone fortification still stands in Ngerard today. They remained there, and so the war party [from Ngeremlengui] never did attack Ngerard. Finally, they returned home to Imeliik.

The storyteller then offered the following commentary on the political relations presupposed by the story.

The reason these people from Imeliik came to protect Ngerard is that Ngebuked is the child of Imeliik. Ngeremlengui and Melekeok also treat Ngebuked as a child, since Ngebuked is the offspring of the turmeric plant, being the child of the sister. For this reason Ngebuked was a very spoiled village; Ngeremlengui on the west side and Melekeok on the east side would take care of it. If Ngebuked committed a crime, Melekeok could pay its fine, or if the crime was committed near Ngeremlengui, then Ngirturong could pay the fine. It was indeed a spoiled village.[31]

Western historical accounts bear this out, for Ngerard constantly played Ngeremlengui off against Melekeok and refused to join Oreor's fight against the Ngetelngal federation headed by Melekeok (see below). In 1783, for example, Ibedul tried to convince Madrangebuked, the head of Ngerard, to join with him alongside the miraculous foreign power of Captain Wilson's English troups. But even the gift of an English scarlet coat was not enough to impress Madrangebuked, who was

---

31. Ngeremlengui's protection of Ngebuked can also be seen in the proverbial expression applied to Ngerard: *ngiull e ngedall,* "picked up and taken home." As the village of Ngerdmau, located on the west coast of Babeldaob between Ngeremlengui and Ngerard, rose in power, people from Ngerard began to be afraid to sail down the coast to visit Oreor. So war canoes would depart from Ngeremlengui, proceed to Ngerard, and then escort the visiting party safely past Ngerdmau. Cf. McKnight 1968:28.

clearly attempting to coax Wilson to travel to Ngerard for his own purposes.

> After they had got to the outlet of the creek [of Imeiong], one of the *rubak,* who was going to the northward [to Ngerard], where he lived, parted company, carrying away in his suite eight or nine canoes. This *rubak,* whose name was Mad [Madrangebuked], had two bones [dugong bracelets] on his arm. Captain Wilson had given Ibedul the spaniel dog, which the King had with him at this time. When they were out of the creek, and Mad was taking leave, Ibedul delivered to him the dog, and also the scarlet coat; but they were afterwards returned to him, as our people saw him wear the coat when he went against Beliliou, and saw the dog frequently afterwards at Pelew [that is, Oreor]; which satisfied them that they were only lent to Mad to take to his island, that he might shew them to his own people,[32] Captain Wilson having declined going to visit them, though strongly solicited, excusing himself on account of the long time it would occasion his being absent from Ulong. (Keate 1788:178)

This impasse continued until the 1860s, when Oreor and Ngebuked finally came to blows. In the role of the senior brother, Ngirturong of Imeiong tried to arbitrate the dispute, as Cheyne reports in his journal: "Ngirturong came on board in the morning. He goes back to Ngeremlengui tomorrow as arbitrator between Oreor and Ngebuked. The Oreor men killed a Ngebuked man at Ngcheangel on the 15th instant, made prisoners of the other four and brought them with their canoes, 3 muskets and a woman to Oreor" (1863–66: 25 June 1865). A decade later Ngerard once again established peaceful relations with Oreor, but continued to court the alliance with powerful Ngetelngal district on the east coast (Kubary 1885:189).

CHANTS OF MILAD

In trying to understand the relationship between political ideology and historical events coded in terms of the Story of Milad, two chants about Milad are particularly useful. These chants, along with commentary provided by my informants, provide a Belauan point of view on the interrelationships among Milad's children and illustrate the allusive character of political rhetoric. The first text is the Chant of Milad (*cheselsel a Milad*), which would be sung at the funeral of a high-ranking

---

32. Wilson thought that Ngerard was a separate island.

chief from one of Milad's villages; the second text is the Chant of the Elders of Belau (*cheselsel a rubekul a Belau*), which I taped in Ngeremlengui in 1979 during a meeting of Belauan leaders.

Chant of Milad

We who have been born were living at the mountain, and we proceeded single file toward Ngeroach and there distributed the villages, and you went to the lower sea.

Woman Milad, you are the origins of those who were born and of children and of sisterhood, and now they gather us together as before a mother hen.

Woman Milad, you are our origin, we who were born, and you quiet the squalls and the calm stretches all the way to beyond the reef. And now perhaps those poling are also calmed.

And these, *rubak,* are the coconut fibers which you take to tie up the *kelulau.* I wish for peace, *rubak,* and so if you tie it up I will be calm as I travel.

And so the coconut fibers will be the cords you use to repair it and bind it tightly, and we can ignore whatever those who pass by have to say.

The words of passersby are various but we are of one birth, and having shaped the villages you journey toward the lower sea.

As you go toward the lower sea, Imeliik is the woman who prepares the food, which is the food of Meketii and Imiungs when they travel.

Recognizing the extreme difficulty I was having understanding the hidden meanings of this chant, an informant provided a detailed phrase-by-phrase exegesis, making explicit the connection between the Story of Milad and the political order represented by Milad's children. These comments will be summarized verse by verse.

1. Milad and her four children born at the foot of Ngeroach mountain live together in Ngeremlengui. From the base of the mountain they walk single file toward the peak, and there these four are distributed to different parts of Belau as the villages of Milad. Milad and her oldest child, Imiungs, stay put, while Oreor and Imeliik proceed toward the lower sea to the south.

2. Milad, as the mother of these four children, is also the source/origin (*mechud,* from *uchul*) of sets of children (*klengelakl*) and especially of sets of sisters (*klodos*) who in turn gave birth to the Belauan race. Milad gathers all these people together and protects them as a mother hen shelters her chicks.

3. The stabilizing effect Milad has on Belau is like the power to quiet

squalls at sea, so that fishermen returning from outside the reef can glide their canoes over waters so still that they can see clamshells on the bottom. Here the fishermen stand for all Belauans, who enjoy the stability and calm of Milad's political regime.

4. In this verse Milad addresses all the titleholders of Belau and declares that the political strategy of the chiefs of the principal villages has been established once and for all. This *kelulau*, symbolically carried from chief to chief in a handbag, is tied up tightly so that Milad's wish for peace will be guaranteed. Although her children have departed to the four corners of the island, this unified *kelulau* is so tightly bound together than Milad can travel without worry.

5. Milad's *kelulau* is bound up with coconut fiber like the cord used to fasten the outrigger of the canoe. Those who carry this secure and stable *kelulau* can safely ignore all negative comments by passersby. As this first chant makes apparent, the ideology of birth precedence of the villages of Milad is realized in a particular style of political discourse, the *kelulau* which passes secretly among these villages. In place of smoke-filled rooms, Belauan political strategy is metaphorically concealed in tightly-wrapped-up betelnut handbags.

6. This is to remind the children of Milad that, in spite of the idle gossip of passersby, they are born of the same mother. Here the chant alludes specifically to chiefs Ngirturong and Reklai, who have the same mother. It is the villages of Oreor and Imeliik that are said to be shaped by Milad.

7. When the chiefs of Imiungs and Oreor travel, they do not take along traveling food (*okau*), but rather they detour to Imeliik where their food is prepared.

The second chant continues this theme by describing the operation of the siblingship polity in terms of bilateral path between the meetinghouses standing in Milad's villages.

Chant of the Elders of Belau (portion)

The council meetinghouse [lit. house of whispers] is at Meketii [in
 Oreor] and the *kelulau* flows straight along the rain gutter to
 Orukei square and then to Ngaruau meetinghouse [in Ngerard].
 The brothers of the village assemble to assent to it, as if it were
 straight as a returning arrow.
The council meetinghouse is at Meketii and the ancestral spirits are
 at Idid. The *kelulau* journeys along the rain gutter to the
 meetinghouse at Ngerekeai and then follows the bridge to
 Orukei square [in Imeiong] and then goes to Ngaruau

meetinghouse of Madrangebuked. The chiefs assemble and
assent to it, as if it were a drenching downpour.

These words were chanted in 1979, when members of the Rubekul a
Belau, the body of high chiefs representing Belau's districts, visited
Ngeremlengui to discuss the draft national constitution with local villagers. The chant suggests a connection between the four-cornerpost
model of district polity and the model of the path which was so important in the stories set in the era of Chuab. The secret discussions, or
whispers, formulated by the chiefs at Meketii meetinghouse in Oreor
are communicated to other major villages by a messenger (formerly, the
mediating, fifth-ranking titleholder) entrusted with this "weighty mission" (*obereod el tekoi*). The messenger, said to carry the whispers tightly
wrapped up in his handbag, goes to the meetinghouse at Ngerekeai (in
Imeliik) and returns to Oreor with the reply of Rengulbai's colleagues
in the council there. The movement of the *kelulau,* the chanter explained to me later, among the four villages associated with Milad on
the west coast of Babeldaob follows a series of bilateral paths, so that
Meketii's messenger goes only as far as Ngerekeai. From there Rengulbai's messenger carries the message north to Orukei meetinghouse in
Imeiong, and finally Ngirturong's messenger travels the last leg to confer with Madrangebuked at Ngaruau meetinghouse in Ngerard. The
two verses of the chant given here (there are probably many more
verses) employ two different similes for the reception of the *kelulau* in
Ngerard. First, the "brothers" (*odam*), or untitled men of the village,
meet together and consent to the decision, which appears to them as
straight as an arrow; next, the titleholders (*obak,* that is, the *rubekul a
beluu*) assemble and agree to this *kelulau* as if it were an encompassing
rain shower leaving no place untouched. Part of the reason, I think, that
the chanter selected these verses in 1979 was that he was attempting to
point out in an indirect way what he felt was the political folly of these
high chiefs traveling around the islands as a "visiting party."

> This practice of a visiting party of the Rubekul a Belau traveling
> around is a very recent thing. In former times only the appointed
> messenger would journey, carrying the message [of the chiefs]. But
> the messenger from Oreor goes only as far as the meetinghouse of
> Keai in Imeliik and then returns to Oreor; and then the messenger
> from Keai travels to Orukei [in Imeiong].

Exposed to the sight and free interrogation of titleless villagers, including women and young people, these sacred chiefs were in violation of
the very principles of the *kelulau* they came to discuss.

SIDES OF HEAVEN OF BELAU

Readers familiar with the classic ethnographies of Belau are no doubt puzzled by the fact that up to this point little mention has been made of the notion of sides of heaven (*bita el eanged*) which, according to many published accounts, organizes the archipelago's districts into two balanced halves (Barnett 1949:177–78; Force 1960:34–36; McKnight 1960:78; Useem 1949:98–99). What many standard ethnographies take as an immutable dualistic political order I would rather regard as a third stage in a complex picture of political development which became codified only after substantial Western contact. As warfare intensified throughout the nineteenth century, conflicts between villages increasingly became focused around two hostile political federations. My use of the term "focused" here is intended to avoid engaging the debate over whether or not interdistrict or interisland political federations existed in many Pacific societies before the advent of European influence (see, e.g., Sayes 1984:4). My argument is that the presence of foreign commercial interests and imported firearms stimulated the rigidification of local alliances, and that this favored the selection of the sides-of-heaven model as the dominant conceptual metaphor. Roughly, villages on Babeldaob's east coast (*desbedall*) were allied to Melekeok's chief, Reklai, and villages on the west coast (*kiukl*), as well as villages on the southern islands of Ngeaur and Beliliou, were allied to Oreor's chief, Ibedul (see table 4). While it is undoubtedly true that the steady influx of imported firearms and the competition over access to foreign trade significantly raised the stakes of intervillage struggles in this period, the conceptualization of the lines of opposition drew on the traditional geographical division of Babeldaob into two sides of heaven. The heaven referred to in this expression is not the celestial realm, but rather Babeldaob island itself, which, as was noted in the previous discussion of the Story of Latmikaik, was the destination of the original creatures who migrated from beneath the sea.

Babeldaob island is symbolically split into two sides of heaven by a north-to-south line called Raelkedam (Path of the Kite) following a mountainous ridge running from the northern shore of Ngerdmau through the center of Irrai in the south. The name of this dividing line comes from the story about the founding of Ngerdmau, in which people from Ngerekedam village in Irrai pursue their lost kite (*kedam*) along this central ridge until they arrive at Ngerdmau. Some informants mention a more ancient term, Raelbalech (Path of Shooting Arrows), the route along which the mythological character Belebalech habitually walked while pigeon hunting. A crosscutting division is men-

TABLE 4. SIDES OF HEAVEN OF BELAU

Side of Heaven of Ibedul	Side of Heaven of Reklai
Oreor	Melekeok
Ngerdmau	Ngcheangel
Ngeremlengui	Ngerechelong
Ngetbang	Ngerard
Imeliik	Ngiual
Irrai	Ngchesar
Beliliou	
Ngeaur	

tioned in some traditions according to which the trickster god Medechiibelau (Breaks Belau into Pieces) bisected Babeldaob by tossing out two small islands, Ngemolei and Ngerutoi. The line formed by these two islands runs across the center of the island, roughly from Ngeremlengui to Melekeok, and marks the "center of Belau" (*chedul a Belau*). It is important to note, however, that the resulting four quadrants are never referred to as equivalent to the four cornerposts of Belau. Also the sides-of-heaven opposition is not parallel to the relative opposition between lower sea and upper sea (cf. Force 1960:34–35; Krämer 1908:184). As an informant explained:

> The reason for the expression "upper sea" is that the first Belauans were the children of Latmikaik, who lived beneath the sea and then came up to the surface and said, "This is the upper sea." The islands of Belau were the "upper sea." The division between side of heaven and side of heaven also splits Belau in half, but on the two sides of the islands, east coast (*desbedall*) and west coast (*kiukl*). Oreor is on the side of the west coast, and so are Ngerard and Ngeremlengui. Melekeok is on the other side. Beliliou and Ngeaur are also on the side of Oreor. The meaning of this division is that the sides are enemies. But you should not say that the villages on one side are necessarily mutual friends (*kausechelei*); they are just a side of heaven. Irrai is on the side of Oreor; spatially, of course, it is on the other side, but politically it is on the side of Oreor—just like the confusion within Ngeremlengui where Ngirturong's house is on the north side of the village.[33] We say: Irrai is the right hand

33. That is, although chief Ngirturong's residence is north of the central square of Imeiong, his geographical responsibility lies to the south in the direction of Oreor (see figure 3).

or Oreor, while Beliliou and Ngeaur are the left hand of Oreor. In other words, Irrai guards Oreor from Melekeok, its enemy. The expression "upper sea" means *honto* [Japanese "big island"] for the people of Beliliou, and yet it means "toward Ngerdmau" for the people of Imeiong. So this expression does not have the important significance that the expression "side of heaven" has, since it does not designate villages which are in a relationship of mutual hostility. The people of the west coast are one side of heaven and the people on the east coast are the other side of heaven.

Evidence of endemic warfare and intervillage alliances contained in early Western sources and in many narrative traditions does not support the claim that an established political opposition between villages on eastern and western sides of heaven characterized Belau in precontact times. When the *Santo Domingo* sailed through the southern zone of the archipelago in 1712, for instance, Belauan captives taken on board indicated by signs that inhabitants of "some small islands" (probably Oreor and Ngerekebesang) were then at war with inhabitants of the "large island" (i.e., Babeldaob), and that people from the smaller islands were on friendly terms with other islands to the south (Beliliou and Ngeaur) (Krämer 1917–29, 1:83). The political tensions reflected in these comments resemble the famous War of Ngirakederang, which pitted Oreor against Imeliik. A young man named Ngirakederang, who was heir apparent to the chiefly title Rengulbai at Ngerekeai village in Imeliik, was captured by fishermen from Oreor. When they brought him back to their clubhouse they arranged for concubines to tattoo an image of a triggerfish on his thigh. After his family paid the required ransom, Ngirakederang returned home and, citing the tattoo as a *olangch* of his anger, vowed to take revenge. The opportunity finally arose when he received the title Rengulbai. He recruited villages on both coasts of Babeldaob, including Melekeok, Ngchesar, Ngerechau, Ngiual, Ngerdmau, and Ngebei; to defend itself from attack, Oreor in return recruited allies from Ngerekebesang, Ngerebeched, Ngeruktabel (in the rock islands), Nglabang (in Ngeremlengui), and Mengellang (in Ngerechelong). Note that this conflict put into opposition Ngebei and Mengellang, two villages from the same district.[34] Oreor's combined forces succeeded in deceiving their enemy by parading at night with lit torches up and down the village's paths and channels, giving the impression of great troupe strength. The two sides in this conflict were

34. This list of participating villages is taken from my recording of the War Chant of Ngirakederang.

obviously not clearly divided by the east coast—west coast split, and the abortive battle itself bore little resemblance to the wars of destruction waged in the subsequent centuries.

In the late eighteenth century, Oreor, with the help of Captain Wilson's men, embarked on a series of campaigns to extend the range of its political influence. First chief Ibedul convinced his foreign guests to accompany him on a brief excursion to Melekeok (21 August 1783). The 125 war canoes involved in the expedition terrified the local inhab- itants, but more importantly the warriors impressed the Englishmen with their military might and bravery. Almost before the postbattle cel- ebrations were over, Ibedul formally requested more substantial as- sistance for a second assault against Melekeok. When asked the reason for this hostility, Ibedul explained, "That some time back, at a festival at Ngetelngal [i.e., Melekeok], one of his brothers, and two of his Chiefs, had been killed, and that the two islands had been at war ever since; the people of Ngetelngal, so far from making any satisfaction, had pro- tected the murderers" (Keate 1788:115). Ibedul's hopes greatly in- creased after witnessing a demonstration of the *Antelope*'s swivel gun. A second assault on Melekeok began on 10 August 1783, this time with over two hundred war canoes (and ten Englishmen) led by Ibedul him- self, decked out in the scarlet cloak given to him by Captain Wilson. The besieged warriors from Melekeok were amazed at the power of English muskets.

> The spears were mutually directed with much animosity, and the English kept up a continual fire, which not only did great execution, but puzzled and bewildered the enemy in the extreme, to comprehend how or why their people dropped, without receiving any apparent blow. They perceived they had holes in their bodies, yet saw no spear sticking in them, nor could they devise by what means they had thus in a moment become deprived of motion and life. . . . No sooner therefore did the firing of the musquets spread dismay amongst the people of Ngetelngal, than a different effect was produced in those of Pelew [Oreor]. The moment the report was made, they all rose up in their canoes, and set up such hallooing and shouting, that the whole air was filled with their noise, which greatly added to the terror of the enemy, who finding themselves unequal to so powerful an attack, betook themselves to flight. (Keate 1788:139–40)

Ibedul's forces celebrated victory by presenting the slain bodies of their enemies at several allied villages, where dancing and feasting distributed the political impact of the triumph. In the third and final campaign against Melekeok during Wilson's stay in the islands, constant bombardment by the swivel canon destroyed residences and put the inhabitants to flight. But still refusing to negotiate a truce, Melekeok's chief, Reklai, suffered the insult of having his sacred backrest stone carried off from the council square (Keate 1788:170).

The overall political picture which emerges from the battles of 1783 does not, however, support the image self-consciously projected by the people of Oreor that Ibedul was "King" of Belau, and that all other districts were either supportive vassals or treacherous rebels. Rather it seems that the leaders of Ngetelngal, Ngebuked, Oreor, Imeliik, Imiungs, and Beliliou possessed full sovereignty over their lands and that Ibedul's aggressiveness was encouraged by his accurate perception of the military advantage provided by Captain Wilson. Several years later Captain Proctor summarized his understanding of Belauan polity:

> Ngetelngal and Imeliik are on the same island, the largest of the group which is called Babeldaob; this island is divided into several districts, or governments, Ngetelngal being the largest; the capital of which district is called Melekeok, where their King resides, whom they style Reklai, and who is constantly in hostility with Ibedul. The next district is Ngerard, the chief of which has the title Krai, and is friendly to Oreor, as is Imeliik; these are the principal, and also the largest districts of the island of Babeldaob, which is about sixty miles in circumference. There are several other small districts, some friendly and some hostile to Ibedul, who being an independent prince, was generally at war with the King of Ngetelngal to preserve that independence. (Hockin 1803:32)

Other foreign visitors were more easily fooled by Ibedul's posturing:

> [Ibedul] was considered when he was young as the greatest warrior ever bred in the Pelew Islands; and yet as eminent for his justice and humanity. His subjects were in general strongly attached to him; but some of them, who lived in the distant islands, notwithstanding his great and good qualities, were ungrateful and unwise enough to revolt from him. While we were there [1791], some of the people were in a state of rebellion. As Captain Wilson had done before us, we joined the king, and went against the inhabitants of Ngetelngal, one of the islands under his dominion. (Delano 1817:59–60)

Or as the missionary James Wilson reported, "Babeldaob [is] divided into several districts, each of which is governed by a separate chief, acknowledging the supreme authority of Ibedul" (1799:305).

But it is also true that Ibedul's campaigns against Ngetelngal and Beliliou between 1783 and 1791 brought into play an emerging coalition that in time would be identified as the western side of heaven. Oreor's assault on Beliliou was supported by canoes from Ngeremlengui, Imeliik, and Ngerekebesang (Keate 1788:206). That the solidification of sides of heaven was concurrent with the intensification of hostility between Ibedul and Reklai is further demonstrated by events of 1791, when the East India Company ships *Panther* (Captain McCluer) and *Endeavour* (Captain Proctor) arrived at Belau. As soon as Reklai learned that these vessels had landed, he sent emisaries to Oreor to present a conciliatory bead to Ibedul, who received it "with great apparent coolness."[35] This valuable did not deter Ibedul's hostility, however, since four months later (16 June 1791) two hundred war canoes from Oreor, accompanied by Lieutenant Wedgeborough and a party of Englishmen, set out one more time for Melekeok. Having refused an initial presentation of valuables from Reklai's representatives, Ibedul demanded more stringent terms, pointing to the forty muskets poised for action just offshore. Negotiations continued until evening, when Ibedul further frightened his enemy by having "rockets and fireworks" discharged over the heads of the astonished villagers. Melekeok finally came to terms the next morning, and Ibedul was carried triumphantly into the central square of the village.

> The litter, which looked much like a bier to carry the dead, was brought. . . . The king [Ibedul] was taken out of his canoe by the arms of his returning subjects, was set upon the litter, and eight men of Ngetelngal carried it in their hands off the pier, and then on their shoulders up a paved way to the place of state. They enthroned him on a high seat, made of wood, and covered with mats. My fellow officer, the surgeon, and myself followed, and stood by the throne. The two first chiefs approached him, half bent, holding the jewels suspended by strings, and presented them to his majesty. He received them with dignity and grace, and afterward bade them stand erect. He put such questions to them as he thought proper, and as the occasion required, all of which were answered to his satisfaction. The under chiefs were then called, twenty five in number. They also approached half bent, kneeled, brought their breasts to the ground, and kissed the king's feet. He

---

35. McCluer (Hockin 1803:26) refers to this valuable as a "large bead, or coarse emerald." If his observation as to the color of the bead can be trusted, this would be an inferior prestation, given the seriousness of its intended task.

then bade them rise, and questioned them as he had done the others. After this ceremony was over, the women were brought according to the treaty. . . . I was curious to know whether any of the women would be unwilling to go with those by whom they were chosen; but I discovered in their countenances only cheerfulness and pleasure. (Delano 1817:64–65; cf. Hockin 1803:42–44)

Although the English visitors interpreted the acts of submission in this ceremony as acknowledgement of Ibedul's position as the "superior *rubak* of all the Pelew islands" (Hockin 1803:44), a more accurate assessment is that Ibedul and Reklai had formalized a reciprocal relationship of mutual hostility (*kaucheraro*), according to which disputes would henceforth be handled through political mechanisms such as presentation of valuables, taking hostages, exchanging concubines, and paying tribute in food, rather than through destructive assaults.[36]

Oreor could surely have conquered Melekeok at any time during this period, but the political strategy adopted in 1791 indicates that the focalization of conflict through the two capital villages of Oreor and Melekeok served to allow the chiefs of these places to make rapid progress in lining up allies on their respective sides of heaven. In the following decades, for example, Oreor waged war against Ngeredelolk in Beliliou, Ngertuloech in Ngetbang, Oikull in Irrai, Ngerechelong (19832), Ngiual (ca. 1840), Ngerdmau (ca. 1850), Melekeok (1850), Ngebuked (1860) and Chelab in Ngerard, Ngcheangel (1872), and Ngersuul (1875).[37] Through these wars of subjugation Oreor assured the subordination of villages in the western and southern side of heaven and further exacerbated its traditional hostility with Melekeok.[38] In response Melekeok succeeded in solidifying its rule over villages on the eastern coast of Babeldaob, including Ngiual, Ngchesar and Ngersuul, and mounted an unsuccessful effort to attract Western commercial operations (curing sea cucumber, in particular) to its member villages.

36. Ibedul's success at achieving a political settlement greatly impressed his foreign supporters, who took his actions as a sign of elevated morality; see, for example, Delano 1817:60.

37. This list contradicts the claim of Vidich (1949) that warfare took place primarily within, rather than between, confederations. The extensive raiding between Ngeremlengui and Melekeok (discussed in chapter 7) also argues against his point.

38. There is some evidence that in the middle of the nineteenth century Reklai and Ibedul assisted each other in wars within their respective confederations: Reklai helped Ibedul defeat Urdmau in 1850, and Ibedul aided Reklai in his effort to subdue Ngiual in 1840. Such collusion between high-ranking individuals who are officially opposed to each other is typical of Belauan political strategy.

Melekeok's early acceptance of Catholic missionaries may have been motivated by this same rivalry.

Though Oreor's monopolization of Western military and commercial interests stimulated its aggressiveness at the close of the eighteenth century, these same external forces ironically made it difficult for Ibedul to obtain complete control over the archipelago in the next century. That is, the same forces which enabled Ibedul to call himself "King George" (Paullin 1910:733; cf. Sahlins 1985b:140 for Hawaii) also led to the codification of sides-of-heaven opposition, an arrangement requiring two competitive factions. The merchant Andrew Cheyne, for example, refused (at cost of his life) to accept the restrictions imposed on him by his jealous Oreor hosts. In return for trading privileges and land rights, he even distributed firearms to many other villages, thereby upsetting Oreor's monopoly on this vital source of power.

> Rengulbai, king of Imeliik, told me in his house in Imeliik on the 6th instant that the Oreor chiefs told them to knock off fishing for beche de mer about the middle of July, and that being afraid of offending Oreor they were obliged to do so, against their will. The Oreor people has been acting towards me in this way for years, deceiving me, by telling lies, and preventing the other tribes from fishing. The only way to put a stop to this villainy is to arm the other tribes, so as to make them independent of Oreor. (Cheyne 1863–66: 27 September 1865)

A rival commercial establishment in Ngerard district under the direction of Edward Woodin also challenged the terms of competition between Oreor and Melekeok, since chief Mad of Ngebuked could play off the two warring factions. Ngerard in fact managed to spurn an attack by Oreor in 1860, after which the naturalist Semper, then visiting Babeldaob, reported that the important political rivals in Belau were Ngebuked and Oreor, rather than Melekeok and Oreor.

> I have already indicated how the districts on Babeldaob separated into two groups because of the presence of Cheyne and Woodin and how they acknowledged the leadership of Oreor and Ngebuked; with that state the smaller states of Beliliou and Ngeremlengui and Imeliik on the southwest coast and Ngerechelong at the northern end of Babeldaob were allied, whereas Ngetelngal and Irrai were allied to Ngebuked. At the northern end of the group, cut off by a broad deep-water channel, Ngcheangel—a true atoll—remained neutral. The assimilating power of these two momentarily most powerful states had already

grown so large that a number of other villages, which had earlier
played a not insignificant role, had entered a directly dependent
relationship to them. (Semper 1982:30–31)

The point to note in this passage is that Ngerard's elevated status is
immediately channeled into a dual set of political alliances. The imbalance caused by Woodin's presence in Ngerard prompted Ibedul to
request Captain Brown of the *Sphinx* to sail there "not to make an
attack on the place, but on a humane and peaceful mission, to try and
remedy the mischief that Captain Woodin of the schooner *Lady Leigh*
had been doing for some time, namely, making a revolution in the
group by supplying the Ngebuked people with arms and ammunition
to resist Ibedul's government" (Cheyne 1862: 9 September 1862). A
clear signal of Ngerard's rising sense of self-importance occurred in the
1860s, when a group of men from Imeiong visited a string of allied
villages on the western side of heaven to perform war dances with a
head trophy taken from the opposed side of heaven at Blissang, a
hamlet near Melekeok. Warmly received at Oreor, Imeliik, and Irrai,
the dancers were refused entrance to Ngerard on the grounds that Imeiong was functioning as an instrument of Ibedul and that accepting the
dancers would be an insult to Ngerard's friendship with Melekeok. A
still-cited story mentions an ancient fraternal bond between the chiefs
Mad of Ngebuked and Reklai of Melekeok (cf. Semper 1982:217–18).

Throughout the nineteenth century, successive Ibedul titleholders
tried to convince Western traders, voyagers, and colonial officials that
they were the legitimate King of Belau, while at the same time these
foreign personnel attempted to stabilize the polity for their own purposes (Kubary 1873:183). Two contrasting ducuments which illustrate
this state of affairs are the "Constitution of Pellow," drafted by Cheyne
and signed by the leaders at Oreor in 1860, and a "Treaty between the
King of Korror and the King of Melegoyok in the Pelew Islands,"
signed in 1883 at the insistence of Commander Bridge of the British
man-of-war *Espiegle*. The first document represents an effort by Cheyne
to exchange official legitimation of Ibedul as "absolute sovereign of the
whole Pelew islands" for a guaranteed trade monopoly. After stipulat-
ing the rule of succession for the Ibedul title, the text proceeds to grant
Cheyne exclusive trading privileges, to be protected by installing loyal
Oreor chiefs in as many districts as possible:

> 3. Ngirturong, a Noble of high rank who is now Governor of
> Ngeremlengui District, shall hold that appointment during his
> lifetime.
> 4. A Oreor Noble or Chief shall be appointed Governor of Irrai,

Ngerechumelbai District, to prevent the people obtaining arms from passing ships and for the protection of trade.

5. Should the present Governor of the Ngerard District (Ngebuked), and who is a Oreor chief, fail in making his people carry out the provisions of the Treaty of Commerce made by us with Capt. Cheyne, or allow his people to obtain arms or ammunitions he shall be succeeded by a more competent person.

6. A Oreor Chief shall be appointed Governor of the Ngerechelong District, to prevent the people obtaining arms from passing ships and for the protection of Trade. (Semper 1982:196–97)

The murder of Cheyne in 1866 not only rendered this artificial document inoperative but also created a power struggle among various factions within Oreor. And this in turn encouraged east coast villages to act more aggressively toward foreigners.[39] Several times during the century these villages had benefited from the political manipulation of shipwrecks along their coastline, and in 1880, when the merchant O'Keefe's vessel *Lilla* wrecked off Ngerechelong, people from Ngchesar and Melekeok joined in the plunder.[40] The treaty of 1883 was the direct result of British military intervention after these east coast villages proved unable to pay the imposed fines. The English translation of the treaty made on the spot reads in part (PCAA 1976–78, 2: after 172):

> We the undersigned Chief of the Pellew Islands on this eleventh day of August A.D. 1883 do hereby solemnly agree to give up our old standing quarrels, to make peace with one another and to preserve it for the future. We also undertake to use every effort to prevent our people from committing murders or other acts of aggression either on each other or on foreigners.
> King Ibedul X
> King Reklai X

My own translation from the printed Belauan version is only slightly different:

> We the elders of Belau . . . are resolved to throw away that which

39. Apparently Cheyne tried simultaneously to exploit his close relationship with Ibedul of Oreor and to expand his commercial influence in the other side of heaven by selling guns to Melekeok. As Stevens (1867) writes, "The reason for murdering him was that Captain Cheyne had and was about to supply arms and ammunition to the King and Chiefs of Ngetelngal."

40. The district of Ngerdmau is also named in the table titled "Quantity and Description of Fines Obtained," attached to Captain East's (1882) official report.

was the cause of ill will among us, to become unified, and to pursue the well-being of Belau before the eyes of the elders from the West.

The marks of Ibedul and Reklai on this treaty represent an additional step in the codification of sides of heaven as the frozen structure of Belauan polity.

Especially in the late nineteenth century, realities of military and economic power made the application of the cornerpost model to Belauan polity the distinctive, if self-consciously archaic, claim of Imeiong. Although generally supportive of Oreor's confederation, Imeiong continued to express its autonomy by engaging in reciprocal headhunting raids on Melekeok, thereby bypassing Ibedul's own strategies. And yet by the time Western missionary and colonial interests put an end to intervillage raiding at the end of the century, the sides-of-heaven model had achieved ideological dominance. And during the successive Spanish, German, Japanese, and American colonial administrations, Ibedul and Reklai became recognized as twin "paramount chiefs" of the islands. And at the intervillage level, pooled labor, sporting competition, and fishing cooperatives all organized activities around this dualistic model. An elderly man reminiscing about the Japanese period phrased pan-Belauan club activity in terms of the model of sides:

> We began work at 7:00 in the morning and worked until 5:00; we worked ten hours each day, except for Sunday, when we rested. This labor was not "village work" (*cherrakl*), which refers only to work within the village; rather, this was work for the [Japanese] government. We worked at several different sites, and every night we returned to stay in the clubhouses in Oreor. Men from Ngeremlengui, Ngerard, and Ngerdmau stayed in one clubhouse which was very large, and the men from Melekeok, Ngiual, and Ngchesar stayed in another clubhouse. The significance of this is that this was one side of heaven and the other side of heaven. We worked together as a club, and stayed at Sechemus clubhouse, while the others stayed at Kerongel clubhouse.

And in 1974 the model was endowed with codified status in a Belauan document (PCAA 1974), reproduced in figure 2, depicting the seating arrangement for the leaders of all the districts in the two sides of heaven. According to this scheme, on the side of heaven under Reklai of Melekeok, the second place of honor is given to Madrangebuked of Ngebuked; and on the side of heaven under Ibedul of Oreor, the second place of honor goes to Ngirturong, the chief of Imeiong. Rengul-

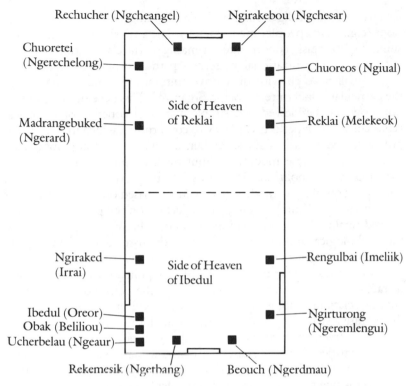

Rechucher (Ngcheangel)   Ngirakebou (Ngchesar)

Chuoretei
(Ngerechelong)   Chuoreos (Ngiual)

Side of Heaven
of Reklai

Madrangebuked   Reklai (Melekeok)
(Ngerard)

Side of Heaven
of Ibedul

Ngiraked   Rengulbai (Imeliik)
(Irrai)

Ibedul (Oreor)   Ngirturong
Obak (Beliliou)   (Ngeremlengui)
Ucherbelau (Ngeaur)

Rekemesik (Ngerbang)   Beouch (Ngerdmau)

FIG. 2. SEATING PATTERN OF RUBEKUL A BELAU (1974)

bai of Imeliik, representing what in the era of Milad had been one of the four cornerposts of Belau, is relegated to a minor position next to Ngirturong.

MODELS OF POLITICAL DEVELOPMENT

Does this account of the progressive unfolding of models of political development constitute no more than comparative support for Sahlins's thesis? In fact, I think the Belauan case shows clearly that "structural history" must consider not only the revaluation of cultural categories but also the recategorization of cultural values. Focusing on the former task, Sahlins's work on the conjunction of myth and history in Hawaiian, Fijian, and Maori cultures stresses the realignment of terms of binary and privative (i.e., marked/unmarked) oppositions concerning cosmological values (male/female, military power/agricultural

fertility, foreign/indigenous), and the recoding of proportional relations (e.g., chiefs:people::men:women). The analysis offered here, pursuing the latter task, concentrates primarily on the clarification of different kinds of organizational patterns—paths, cornerposts, sides, and
larger/smaller—each with distinctive cultural implications apart from
the particular values or terms being organized. This development should
not, however, be viewed as a simple matter of concrete or rhetorical
replacement, with paths giving way to cornerposts, which in turn disappear with the advent of sides. Rather, as abundant ethnographic data
reveal, each of these models is simultaneously present in a range of
overlapping sociopolitical institutions. The point, then, is that narrative
appropriation of these models in sequence is based on the projection of
corresponding cultural meanings in reflection on the past.

And finally, this appropriation does not exhaust the significance of
the mythological and historical narratives discussed above. On the surface it would seem that, in the use of the cornerpost logic to tell the
story of Milad's reconstitution of the islands' polity, quadripartition is a
metaphor for a historical process, namely, the consolidation of hierarchical relations among high-ranking villages. But, in a sense at least,
the narrative structures of the stories set in all three eras can be seen as
themselves metaphorical means for talking about more fundamental
matters. Stories about migration, for instance, are ways of discussing
the notion of typification, since movement along a path is the paradigmatic act which separates cultural from precultural existence.[41] The story of the flood and the birth of four stone children is a highly condensed
way to express basic ideas about internally generated stability, structural
maturity, and presupposed rank. And the labeling of political federations as sides of heaven suggests that totalizing opposition is one local
response to the impact of externally derived political regimes, whose
massive presence rendered impossible fragmented political action.

In order to explore further this analysis of cultural models of political
transformation, the next two chapters will investigate their relevance to
a single district, Ngeremlengui, where the distinction between paths
and cornerposts will be shown to correlate with a distinction in rank
between Imeiong, the capital village, and Ngeremetengel and Ngchemesed, two member villages.

41. Debate over the historical or religious significance of migration traditions often
overlooks the prior question of the cultural significance of basic notions of place, movement, and directionality; see, for example, Alkire 1984; Orbell 1975; Terrell and Irwin
1972.

CHAPTER

5

Kerngilianged:
The Political Organization
of Ngeremlengui

As anyone who has walked a mountain trail with a local guide or sat through a convoluted Land Commission hearing can attest, land is a central value in Belau. Not only is the landscape littered with named geographical features recalling the deeds of mythological and not-so-mythological characters, but individuals and groups conceptualize their social identity largely through relations with fixed parcels of land, whether house sites, villages, or districts. Of course land is more than a referent of symbolic geography and the mediator of social identity, since land—now including more generally taro patches, gardens, forests, fishing zones and residential areas—was for centuries the essential productive resource. The struggle for control over tracts of land and rich fishing areas, so evident in historical narratives referring to a period in the Belauan past prior to the massive depopulation of the nineteenth century, continues to dominate cultural discourse today, when taro and fish have to some extent been replaced by the government payroll as the source of wealth. This chapter approaches the subject of land from the perspective of the spatial arrangement of hierarchically differentiated social categories: capital villages and member villages, principal houses and affiliate houses, and senior men's clubs and junior men's clubs, for example. By reconstructing the complex "grammar of spaces" (Errington 1983:200) of Ngeremlengui in terms of the abstract cultural models detailed in chapter 3, I intend to illustrate concretely some of the status implications of patterns of geographical placement, such as bilateral directionality and hierarchical embedding.

FROM NGEREMESKANG TO NGEREMLENGUI

Ngeremlengui district lies between Ngerdmau and Ngetbang on the west side of Babeldaob island (see map 2); to the east, Ngeremlengui

shares borders with Ngiual, Melekeok, and Ngchesar.[1] The total enclosed area of approximately 26 square miles constitutes 18.5 percent of
the total land of Babeldaob. In ancient times, inhabited villages were
located in every corner of Ngeremlengui district, from Ibars at the upper reaches of the Ngeremeskang river to Roisbeluu near the top of
Chetiruir mountain, and from Ngeremasech, close to the western
lagoon, to Ngereklngong at Usas cape (see map 3). Although only
three villages in the southwestern portion of the region are presently
inhabited, local traditions and stone remains suggest that at a point of
maximum population, perhaps over three hundred years ago, Ngeremlengui consisted of over forty villages spread throughout the district's
territory. In the poetic language of chants and songs, this archaic collection of villages is known as Kerngilianged, a name formed from the
verb *kiei,* "to live, to dwell," and the noun *eanged,* "heaven, sky."
Roughly, this name can be translated as "dwelling as if in heaven," and
the name carries the connotations of high rank, numerical strength, and
a degree of condescension. As one informant explained, "The meaning
[of Kerngilianged] is that Ngeremlengui dwells in the heavens. The rest
of Belau is down below, while Ngeremlengui is in the heavens." The
contemporary name Ngeremlengui is given a folk etymology based on
the story of Milad. Thus, Ngeremlengui (Place of Molting) is derived
from *ngar,* "to be at," and *mlengui,* "molting." The process in which
Milad instituted the new world by giving birth to four stones representing the four important villages of Imeiong, Melekeok, Ngerekeai, and
Oreor is likened to a snake's shedding of old skin and putting on a new
skin.

   This rather celestial position of Ngeremlengui or Kerngilianged does
not, however, derive only from the charter myth of Milad, according to
which Ngeremlengui's capital, Imiungs, is the oldest child of the goddess. The high rank and political strength implicit in the name Ker-

---

   1. Under the provision of the Ngeremlengui Municipal Charter, the official boundary
starts at a point on the western reef known as Klairamesech and runs in an easterly
direction to the mouth of the Kaud river, which splits the abandoned village of
Ngeremasech into a northern side belonging to Ngerdmau district and a southern side
belonging to Ngeremlengui. The boundary follows this river and turns northeast to the
peak of Ngerechelchuus mountain, which at 786 feet is the highest point on Babeldaob.
The boundary then runs across a series of lower peaks, including Ngel, Tebadelrael,
Omtochel, Ngerbusech, Ngerekebuu, and Ollumarieb, and then turns south to Ngere-
badellmangel (At the Weeping Stone). From this point the boundary follows the course
of Kebeduul river, which empties into Ngeremeduu (At the Penis) bay, and crosses the
bay past Usas cape to the western reef at Toachelmlengui, the main reef opening on the
western side of the island. From Toachelmlengui the boundary runs west to the end of
Belauan territorial waters in the Philippine Sea and then turns northerly back to the reef
at Klairemasech.

TABLE 5. NGEREMESKANG'S SIDE CHANNELS

Side Channel of Ngerechebuuch		Side Channel of Ngerecheauch
Ngerikrongel	[within Ngerdmau:]	Nguukl
Kemaitngurd	Ngeremechereuang	Oidesomel
Ibars	Ngereklabong	Ngereboketereng
Ngeremasech	Ngeredekuus	Ngkebeduul
Klekall	Irur	Olbed
Irisong	Ngerechedach	Ngerebechederenguul
Medeues	Kasiang	Ngerecheauch
Bailchelid	Ngereksong	Rrekong
Ngedesaker	Ngesebei	
	Ngeremidor	

ngilianged are said to reflect the position of Ngeremeskang, a powerful capital village which controlled a large group of villages in the northeastern portion of present-day Ngeremlengui prior to the founding of Imeiong as the modern district capital. That is, there are at least two distinct polities in the history of Kerngilianged, and narrative traditions about the transition from one to the other record the migration of leading families from Ngeremeskang to Roisbeluu, a small village located on a mountain ridge above Imeiong. At its greatest extent Ngeremeskang ruled over twenty-six villages divided into two sides of the channel by the Kloultaoch, the central river of Ngeremeskang drainage, which empties into Ngeremeduu bay (see table 5). Each side of the channel owes special allegiance to one of the two high-ranking houses and chiefs at Ngeremeskang: the northwestern side, named Ngerechebuuch, was controlled by Obak, chief of the first house, Ibedechal; the southeastern side, named Ngerecheauch, was headed by Ringuchel of the second house, Ngeremobang.

My informants indicated that eight of the eighteen villages grouped together as Ngerechebuuch lie within present-day Ngerdmau district, and that in former times, before the founding of Ngerdmau as an independent district, Kerngilianged stretched as far as Choang river.[2] Ac-

2. The people of Ngerdmau are said to have fled from Oliuch (near Melekeok) and settled on the west coast between Ngerard and Ngeremlengui. Caught between these established districts, the people of Ngerdmau were denied access to fishing areas adjacent to their shore and were forced to scavenge by night whatever food they could. This deprivation is the source of the proverbial insult: *mesuk melas*, "put in, toss out." The point is that only the next morning would the fishermen from Ngerdmau realize the quantity of inedible things they had hastily stuffed into their baskets.

cording to this view, Kerngilianged was one of three large districts in central Babeldaob, each headed by a capital village located in the interior of the island. The two others were Ngerringall (now Ngerard), headed by chief Remesechau at Ngerechobetang village, and Mengorrabilngelaolukl (Carries the Center of the Thatching Lath) (now Ngetbang), headed by chief Obakeratkedesau at Ngeredubech village.[3] Both Ngerringall and Mengorrabilngelaolukl stretched across the island and had member villages on both coasts—in contrast to the pattern of historically documented polity where several districts have only one coastline. Present-day Ngchesar is said to have been only the coastal channel for powerful Ngetbang district. At some more recent time, Ngerdmau and Ngchesar became established as independent districts, the former by action of the god Sechaltbuich and the latter by a collective refusal to continue paying tribute to the Ngetbang chief at Ngeredubech.[4]

At Ngeremeskang the high-ranking houses of Ibedechal and Ngeremobang were served by the surrounding villages of Irur, Nguukl, Ngereboketereng, Ngeremasech, Klekall, and Oidesomel, all of which brought tribute in fish, taro, and other supplies to the capital in return for military protection. An informant from Ngeremlengui described this situation as a relatively cooperative relationship.

> Ngeremeskang had many slaves. One of these villages was within
> Ngerdmau, that is, the village of Irur, which was a slave of
> Ngeremeskang. It prepared lime and carried it to Ngeremeskang.
> And the people of Nguukl also went fishing and carried fish there.
> People from Ngereboketereng also carried food there, as did the
> people from Oidesomel. Oidesomel, I know, is a very small village
> located next to Ngeremeskang. These things were like the tribute
> given to all the chiefs of Ngeremeskang together; they were
> delivered to the first chief and he would then redistribute them to
> the other titleholders. Ngeremeskang itself had no access to fishing
> areas, so the men from Ngeremasech went fishing and then carried
> their catch there. And the men from Medeues, which is a small
> village, also went fishing and then carried their catch there. And the
> men from Klekall, another small village, took their catch there. But
> it is not exactly correct to say that these villages were treated like
> slaves, for this tribute was to help the people of Ngeremeskang. All
> these villages, however, were under the authority of the council at
> Ngeremeskang.

3. Hidikata (1973b:14) mentions that Ngetbang was a powerful district before the rise of Oreor, Melekeok, Ngeremlengui, and Ngerard. An informant gave the following as the member villages of Ngerringall: Ngerechobetang, Chelab, Ulimang, Ngellau, Ngkeklau, Ngerebkei, Oleiuul, Ngerekesang, and Madesengong.

4. This story about Ngchesar is reported in chapter 2.

This informant made a distinction between tribute-paying villages like Irur and Nguukl, which brought produce on a regular basis to Ngeremeskang, and enslaved villages like Ngcheangel, which in the late nineteenth century was compelled to send concubine women (*uulech*, doormats) to be enjoyed without recompense by the leaders of Oreor.

It is impossible to know for sure when Ngeremeskang's powerful leadership collapsed and when this land came under the control of Imeiong's chiefly council. My informants were still able to list the houses and titles of Ngeremeskang, but no one in contemporary Ngeremlengui mentioned a direct ancestral connection to these houses. I have not found the name Ngeremeskang in any early Western documents, and the numerous stories which take place in this village make no reference to foreign elements such as firearms, traders, or imported goods. But Ngeremeskang is not without any connection to more recent political entities such as Imeiong and Melekeok villages. Several stories deal, for example, with the intermarriage between high-ranking houses of Ibedechal in Ngeremeskang and Ngerturong in Imeiong (Parmentier 1981:497–501); other narratives place Ngeremeskang in a relationship of mutual hostility with Melekeok, and several sources note the migration of Ngeremeskang's inhabitants to Roisbeluu. It is this last event which today links the ancient polity of Ngeremeskang to contemporary Ngeremlengui, since when the residents of Ngeremeskang finally abandoned their land they rebuilt their village with identically named house foundations at Roisbeluu.[5] And many individuals today trace descent from these more recent houses.

Kubary sensed that Roisbeluu was a key to understanding an important transition in Belauan history.

> Very interesting is the name of the deity of Roisbeluu in Ngeremlengui, who was replaced by the later Ngirabaulbei. The name was Chedam el Chelid [Father God], and the interest is well-founded because Roisbeluu (Rocky Land), the highest land of Palau on the mountain Ngeremlengui, may well be the oldest settlement on the archipelago. This is the point of departure of the most recent history of the Palau Islands.[6] (Kubary 1969:18)

Kubary's intuition is substantiated to some degree by information I

---

5. Krämer (1917–29, 2:156) gives a list of houses and titles of Ngeremeskang. My informants gave a similar list, except that the fourth title is Ngirakesurangel rather than Ngiraketurang, and the seventh house is Bedechong rather than Pedong. I was also able to map the corresponding locations of many of these houses at Roisbeluu with the aid of a man whose grandfather lived there.

6. An informant gave Ngirakerrok as the name of the god of Roisbeluu.

collected, which claims that Roisbeluu is the point of articulation between two distinct phases in the development of Kerngilianged's polity.
Kubary's statement that Roisbeluu is one of the oldest villages in Belau
is not, however, supported by any stories I heard.[7]

Various interpretations are given for Ngeremeskang's fall and the
subsequent establishment of Roisbeluu. Krämer (1917–29, 4:135)
gives a story in which the residents of Ngeremeskang abandon their
homes out of fear of military retaliation from Melekeok, after Reklai's
warriors are ambushed on their way to raid Imiungs. Two storytellers
from Ngeremlengui who are well informed about both Ngeremeskang
and Roisbeluu insisted, rather, that Ngeremeskang was abandoned
when Obak, the Snake-Chief of Ibedechal house, vanished with his
wife Tibetibekmiich after the gods stole ceremonial food during a feast
held at the village square.

Story of Obak of Ibedechall (portion)

Obak, the Snake-Chief of Ibedechal house, was the reason that the
people fled from Ngeremeskang. Obak was the chief for a long
period of time, and then there was to be a large feast (*mur*). But
the *rubak* of the village refused to enter the meetinghouse. They
kept saying, "Let's wait just a bit; let's wait just a bit," until
evening came. That night they heard the sound of dancing in the
meetinghouse of the *rubak,* and they said to one another, "Let's go
see the dance. Who is doing the dancing?" But when they lit
torches to light the way, the flames kept going out. So this
dancing kept up until morning. The dance was as if to bid farewell
to the people. When the *rubak* finally went to the meetinghouse in
the morning, there was no one there. Obak was gone; his wife was
gone; they had vanished. The leftovers from the food of the feast
remained in the form of stones. What was left over from the
drinking container (*ilumel*) remains today in the form of a stone.
This is the reason that the people fled. The *rubak* of Ngeremeskang
fled and came to Roisbeluu, since they were so frightened that their
chief, the snake, had vanished. And there was no one else who
could take over the leadership. Their leader had taken his wife and
vanished.

---

7. Krämer (1917–29, 2:155) is evidently incorrect when he states that
Ngeremeskang flourished during the reign of Reklai Temol of Melekeok, who lived
"about a hundred years ago," that is, in the early part of the nineteenth century. Temol
was actually born in the village of Roisbeluu and figures prominently in the history of
Ngeremlengui's political relations with Melekeok in the 1880s and 1890s. By this time
Negeremeskang had long been abandoned.

The stone markers mentioned in this account are most likely the two large stones near Illang meetinghouse which Krämer (1917–29, 2:154–55) saw in 1907. The first is a basaltic pillar said to have been split in half by drunken gods, and the second is a stone water vessel said to have contained the coconut syrup left over from the feast. (On two hikes to the spot I was able to locate Illang platform but not the two stones.)[8]

Whichever interpretation is followed—retreat in the face of threats from hostile Melekeok or abandonment after the sudden disappearance of the chief—the fact remains that these people symbolized the continuity between Ngeremeskang and Roisbeluu by constructing a strictly isomorphic village organization at their new home.[9] A nostalgic song was composed to commemorate this move:

Song of Ngeremskang
Ng mo belual a ngar a Tot el doreng er ngii.
Me demedurs a lmoais e derdi mekerengang a bo mmedengelii a ungil el beluu er a Techebouch.
E dokor el mo er a Meskang e dorurech a dechel.
Of what use is the village of Tot which we pine for?
Let us fall asleep at nightfall and arise to greet a fine village at Techebouch.
We must put away all thought of returning to Meskang and get busy clearing taro patches.

Not only did the new inhabitants of Roisbeluu select this inhospitable spot because it offered protection from attack, but they also chose it because from the top of Techebouch road they could look out to the north and see their beloved Tot, the poetic name for Ngeremeskang.

The importance of citing this migration from Ngeremeskang to Roisbeluu lies not merely in the stereotypic reproduction of house names and titles at the new site, but also in the observation that the position of leadership of Kerngilianged did not remain with the chief at Ibedechal after that house changed location. Transplanted from inland Ngeremeskang to lofty Roisbeluu, Ibedechal house and its partner Ngeremobang came under the control of Klang and Ngerturong houses, the seats of the leading titleholders in Imeiong. This is a vital

8. Ngeremeskang was the location of a large pineapple-canning factory during the Japanese period, and much of the ancient stonework has been destroyed (Ehrlich and Mekill 1984:59, fig. 37).

9. This practice of reproducing the order of houses and titles in a new location is also mentioned in a story about the migration of people from Oikull, a rock island site, to Irrai on Babeldaob, where a newly founded village of the same name exactly duplicated the earlier political order (PCAA, Irrai File).

point, since in the view of some informants this pattern has been repeated in the modern era, when the titleholders at Imeiong in turn moved
their residences to Ngeremetengel. The debate over the status of these
high-ranking chiefs and their authority outside their home village turns
on the interpretation of the movement of Ibedechal house: does a relocated chiefly house carry its rank and authority into its new situation,
and does it transfer its elevated status to a new village? (See chapter 6.)

And with this transition in leadership and the emergence of Imiungs
as the new capital village of the district came a new political organization encompassing twenty-five villages, listed in table 6. This table is
organized by an analytical typology which ignores geographical proximity, political dependency, and temporal sequence in order to focus on
types of villages within the district. The six categories (and one final
category of incomplete data) summarize narratives collected in the field
concerning the foundation, migration, relocation, destruction, and affiliation of Ngeremlengui's villages.[10] Imiungs, the capital village, is the
single member of the first category; it is the center of district political
life and the location of the meetinghouse of the chiefly council,
Ngaraimeiong. The second category includes three villages whose stories and stone remains point to an existence prior to the consolidation
of Ngeremlengui district under Imeiong. The third category lists six
villages whose residents are said to have migrated from other districts
or other islands to these sites. The fourth category includes three villages which are small satellites, or side villages, belonging to what I
have called village complexes. The eight villages in the fifth category form
a subdistrict known as Kleuidelngurd (Seven Ridges), comprising a
central village Ngesisech (located just below Roisbeluu) and a group of
affiliated villages on ridges fanning out from the slopes of Chetiruir
mountain. The sixth category includes three villages that are merely
relocated or rebuilt sites adjacent to former locations; in each of these
three cases there is considerable continuity in village names and in the
organization of houses and titles. A final village, Ngerutoed, forms a
seventh category; I simply recorded no information about its origin,
organization, or history other than that its residents moved down to
join Nglabang hamlet at some point.

It would be an enormous and tedious undertaking to systematically
report all the folklore, historical narratives, and house migration traditions I recorded for these villages of Ngeremlengui. So my rationale for

10. Without the aid of Krämer's (1917–29, 2:152–57) list of extinct villages collected in the course of several days in Ngeremlengui, I would not have been able to elicit
the stories I recorded over the course of two years.

TABLE 6. VILLAGES OF NGEREMLENGUI

(1) *Capital Village*:
Imiungs
(2) *Archaic Villages*:
Ngerutechei
Beluuraklngong
Ngetechum
(3) *Immigrant villages*:
Roisbeluu (from Ngeremeskang)
Ngedesiur (from Ngeaur)
Ngchemesed (from Ngemelis)
Beluurametengel (from Ngerecheu)
Uluang (from Ngeruangel)
Orull (from Ngetmadei)
(4) *Side Villages*:
Ulechetong (next to Imeiong)
Nglabang (next to Imeiong)
Bitalbeluu (next to Ngerutechei)
	(5) *Kleuidelngurd Villages*:
	Ngesisech
	Rrangchuong
	Cheloitelbeluu
	Ngekebai
	Idechor
	Imiich
	Ngeremariur
	Ngetmadei
	(6) *Relocated Village Sites*:
	Imeiong (from Imiungs)
	Ngereklngong (from
	  Beluuraklngong)
	Ngeremetengel (from
	  Beluurametengel)
	(7) *Village of Unknown Origin*:
	Ngerutoed (merged with Nglabang)

organizing table 6 according to typological criteria rather than according to geographical or chronological order is to point out that certain types of relations among villages recur in several cases, and that the processes of village foundation, affiliation, and demise are also repeated. In order to exemplify these relations and processes, the following discussion will focus on the three villages which are still inhabited, namely, Imiungs (or Imeiong), Ngeremetengel, and Ngchemesed. The last remnant of Kerngilianged district, these three villages are connected by physical, historical, and conceptual paths that reproduce on a much smaller scale the types of linkages found among the full set of Kerngilianged's villages.

SPATIAL ORGANIZATION OF NGEREMLENGUI

Map 3 illustrates the relative position of the three extant villages of Ngeremlengui.[11] From Ngeluong river mouth a long, twisting mangrove channel passes through the "gates" of Imeiong formed by two rocky promontories, Mederemel (the location of the sacred stone

11. The sketch map of Ngeremlengui printed in Hidikata 1973b:20 unfortunately misinterprets the more carefully drawn and labeled map printed in the Japanese original. In particular, the locations of Ngeremetengel and Ngereklngong are incorrect.

Iechadrachuolu [He Who Protects]) and Babelngas (Above the Iron-
wood Tree). Running southeasterly, the channel cuts through a dense
mangrove swamp for a quarter of a mile before it splits into a northern
arm leading to Imeiong and a southern arm leading to Uluang and
Ngerutechei. The northern arm winds through the mangrove swamp
until it emerges at the landing place of Ulechetong hamlet. From there
the channel broadens into a small lake—or mud flat, depending on the
state of the tide—with Nglabang hamlet on the northern side and Imeiong proper straddling the channel to the east and south.

Separating these two arms of the channel is an elevated terraced
hillside which begins at the edge of the mangrove swamp, ascends to the
modern graveyard Olekull, and then stretches southwesterly in a series of
carved "staircases" to the terraced hillcrest at the entrance to Ngesisech
village just below Chetiruir (Dizzy) mountain (see photograph 6). This
entire terraced area shows the same pattern of elongated levels, but the
compactness of the gradations increases sharply midway between the
present village of Imeiong and the site of Ngerutechei at a section of land
called Ingesachel (At the Ascent). This is the ancient location of Imiungs,
which occupied the crest of this terraced strip above and to the south of
the present village of Imeiong. In the absence of thorough archaeological
investigation it is impossible to determine the number and size of the
stone foundations, roads, and grave pavements of this archaic village, but
judging from the magnitude and elaboration of the terraces themselves,
it appears that Imiungs was a huge village complex located strategically
on the heights between two rivers, protected on the west by mangroves
and on the east by mountains.

Just as Mederemel and Babelngas rocks on the southern and northern sides of Ngeluong entrance guard the mangrove channel leading to
Imeiong, so the two small hamlets of Ulechetong and Nglabang guard
the approach to Imeiong's two landing places, Melengel and Chelsechei, where formerly canoe sheds and clubhouses stood. The dual
principle of "one side and the other side" (*bitang me a bitang*) extends
to the division of the village of Imeiong into two sides of the mangrove
channel. These two sides, however, are both located on the southern
side of the channel, so Ngerdong river does not actually split the village
into two halves. Rather, the obvious physical division of land into two
sides of a channel provides the grounds for a general conceptual model
which has here, as in many villages, been shifted at right angles, so that
the main stone roads leading from Melengel and Chelsechei landing
places to the central square Orukei (Food Basket) mark the division of
the village into the "side channel of Klang" and the "side channel of
Ngerturong," following the names of the two high-ranking houses.

This dual division, which will be examined in greater detail below, is linked to the opposition of the two rocky promontories at Ngeluong. The northern rock Babelngas belongs to the title Ngiraklang of Klang house, while the southern rock Mederemel belongs to the title Ngirturong of Ngerturong house.

Two sacred stones (*meang el bad*) add another dimension to this spatial organization. At Orukei square, located at the center of Imeiong and by that fact at the center of the district as a whole, stands the stone pillar Ngartemellang (About to Destroy) (see photograph 7), and at the entrance to the village on the western coastline stands the carved stone face Iechadrachuolu (He Who Protects) (see photograph 2).[12] These two stones are correlative foci of a single notion concerning the movement of news (*chais*) into and out of the village: the inner stone Ngartemellang is said to protect Imeiong from any unfortunate scandal, rumor, or report leaving the village, while the outer stone Iechadrachuolu is said to prevent any trouble, threat, or upsetting words from entering the village through the mangrove channel. Orukei square is the center of the village (*bilngel a beluu*), not just because it is the location of Ngartemellang stone and the mediating, or interstitial, point between the two sides of the channel, but also because the meetinghouse of the chiefs named Ngerekebesalbai (Meetinghouse Purchased from Ngerekebesang) and the meetinghouse of the village named Ngesisechelbai (Meetinghouse Purchased from Ngesisech) stood on this broad pavement (Krämer 1917–29, 2: after 144, pl. 1). These buildings are said to "house the politics" of the chiefs of Imeiong; and the name of the square, in its poetic form Orukiil, is used metonymically in chants to represent Ngeremlengui as a whole. The spatial organization of Imeiong's houses, stones, channels, landing places, and hamlets is presented schematically in figure 3.

Paths fanning out from Orukei square link Imeiong to the other villages in the cluster, that is, to Ulechetong and Nglabang hamlets, as well as to nearby Ngerutechei, Roisbeluu, Ngesisech, and Ngeremetengel villages. These footpaths across hillsides and along riverbanks are the source of conceptual paths linking the villages of Ngeremlengui to the capital at Imeiong. And the log bridges which span the rivers and mangrove channels separating various villages index the differential and directional ranking of these villages. As will be discussed in more detail in chapter 7, the direction of the trunk end of

---

12. Ngartemellang is from *tomellang*, the inchoative form of the verb *melemall*, "to destroy"; Iechadrachuolu is from the noun *chad*, "person," and the verb *mengeluolu*, "to protect."

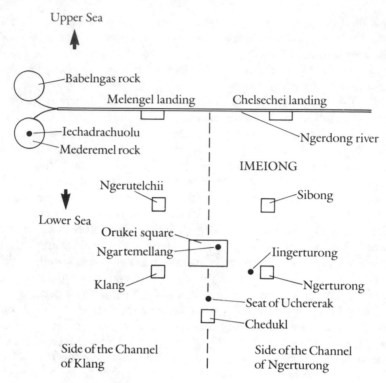

FIG. 3. SPATIAL ORGANIZATION OF IMEIONG

bridge-construction logs points to the origin or source of rank, that is, toward Imeiong. The difference in rank between Imeiong and the three southern villages of Ngeremetengel, Ngchemesed, and (abandoned) Ngereklngong is expressed in the name Edeuteliang (Three at the Other End).[13] These three villages together are known by this label because they are at the other end from Imeiong, both geographically and conceptually.

Of the more than forty villages included in the lists given above for Kerngilianged (including Ngeremeskang and Ngeremlengui), only three villages are recognized today as integral teritorial units. Ule-chetong and Nglabang hamlets have merged with Imeiong to form the first unit, which covers lands of former villages such as Ngedesiur, Buikbeluu, Roisbeluu, Ngesisech, Ngerutoed, Uluang, Ngerutechei,

13. To say that Ngereklngong is abandoned is correct, although there is at present an occupied house situated near the ancient stone remains of Beluurakngong.

and Bitalbeluu. The second unit, Ngeremetengel, encompasses the former villages of Ngetechum, Beluurametengel, Orull, and the small lands of Ngerechelngael, Ii, and Omisaolmlai—these later being more properly considered the residential sites of single extended families rather than as villages. Ngchemesed forms the third unit and includes within its territory the former lands of Beluurakngong, Ngereklngong, and the slopes at Ilild (Bamboo Spear) and Eoulbeluu (Lower Village). Thus these three villages, Imeiong, Ngeremetengel, and Ngchemesed, today comprehend lands which were never part of their traditional claims. Consequently the contemporary boundaries between these three date back twenty or thirty years rather than three hundred. In fact traditionally small villages like Ngeremetengel and Ngchemesed did not have well-established boundaries; the central house site area, corresponding taro patches, wooded areas, and coconut groves close to the village center were treated as village land (*chutem beluu*) under the overall responsibility of the chiefly council. Areas such as dense forests, terraces, hillsides, mountains and cliffs, and overgrown taro swamps reverted to the control of the chiefly council at the district's capital village. These undeveloped lands, called "public land" (*chutem buai*) or "public land of the village" (*chutem buai er a beluu*), could, however, be used by anyone from Ngeremlengui without prior permission—that is, until the Japanese administration claimed all public land on Babeldaob as "government land."

The remaining land outside the boundaries of these three villages is also classified as "public land," and today this includes the entire Ngeremasech area, as well as the drainage basin of the Ngeremeskang river as far as the district borders of Ngerdmau, Melekeok, Ngchesar, and Ngetbang. Differing accounts are given of the exact dividing line between this expanse of public land and the territory belonging directly to Imeiong. Some informants state that the boundary follows the course of the Ngeremeskang river from Tonget as far north as Bailchelid, a prominent hillcrest north of the ancient village of Ngeremeskang; from there the line runs directly north to the channel at Ngeremasech. Other informants suggest that all of the public land of Ngeremlengui should be considered as village land under the control of Ngaraimeiong council at Imeiong. Since there is no definite boundary limiting the extent of Imeiong's traditional responsibility, and since this chiefly council is also the ultimate legitimate authority for the district as a whole, the public land of Ngeremlengui is coterminous with the village land of Imeiong—or so these informants claim. In the context of recent Land Commission hearings to establish parcel boundaries and to issue permanent titles of ownership, these two interpretations of public land are readily understandable. An individual hoping to claim land in this area will have to prove the merits of his or her case before this council or before the national government's Land Commission, depending upon which body is deemed to have proper authority over the land parcel in question. A recent effort to avoid the inevitable clash between these two forms of authority through the establishment of a municipal land authority for the district was not eagerly received in Ngeremlengui. As a result, the exact nature of the boundary and jurisdiction of the district's public land remains a hotly debated issue.

From this overview of the spatial organization of the most recent stage in the formation of Ngeremlengui's polity, it should be clear that no single principle can be given to simplify the complex process by which twenty-five villages collapsed into the remaining three. Rather, various repeated processes can be identified: the unification of several smaller units into a single village; the final abandonment of a village site; the expansion of a capital to encompass neighboring hamlets; the relocation of a village on an adjacent piece of land; and the settlement of immigrant groups on land provided by an existing village. The political results of these various processes can be summarized, though, by recalling two general categories of intradistrict affiliation described in chapter 2: cooperative alliances based on a rank distinction between capital (*klou el beluu*) and member villages (*kekere el beluu*), and the enslavement of subjugated villages by oppressing villages. In the contemporary picture, there are no longer any villages in Belau which must pay tribute, tolerate mistreatment at the hands of powerful neighbors, or remain otherwise oppressed by traditionally based sanctions. But the first distinction, between high-ranking capitals and lower-ranking member villages, continues to be a significant force in many districts. In order to understand this we will need to investigate the specific differences between capital villages and member villages, in this case between Imeiong and Ngeremetengel.

SIDES, CORNERPOSTS, AND PATHS IN IMEIONG AND NGEREMETENGEL

In chapter 4 three general models were identified as fundamental organizing principles of narratives of Belau's political development: paths, cornerposts, and sides. There it was concluded that the developmental sequence of these models in folklore correlates with a meaningful logic according to which paths connote origination and cultural typification, cornerposts connote coordinated support and historical maturity, and sides connote focused opposition open to decontextualized replication. When these models, with the addition of the fourth model of large/small gradation in rank, are used to talk about the symbolic organization of houses, titles, and villages within Ngeremlengui district, the same cultural meanings are implied, even though the models are often overlaid on the same set of institutional terms. The most general spatial division of Imeiong into two sides of the channel corresponds to the political opposition of its two high titles, Ngirturong and Ngiraklang, who represent the houses of Ngerturong and Klang.[14] Prior to their abandonment after World war II, Ngerturong house stood on the eastern side of Orukei square, while Klang house stood on the western side. Each was linked to the central square by a raised stone walkway. A stone road named Ngerulebtuchel running from Orukei square to Chelsechei landing marks the boundary of the side of Ngerturong, while a stone road named Tengatl (Steep) leading from the western corner of Orukei to Cherob (Halt) road terminus and then to Melengel (Block Off) landing marks the side of Klang.

The most obvious correlation of this east/west dual division is the location and affiliation of the six meetinghouses of Imeiong's men's clubs and women's clubs. Although the clubs in Ngeremlengui as a whole have been consolidated, and their meetinghouses have fallen to ruin, at the time of its maximal strength Imeiong boasted six men's clubs, three belonging to each side. And each of these clubs occupied a separate building, as listed in table 7. The junior-grade club on Klang's side was housed at Melengel near the channel, and the corresponding club Ngaratemekai on Ngerturong's side occupied Ngerulechau clubhouse on the eastern side of the road from Orukei to Chelsechei. While these junior clubhouses located near the channel were relatively "outside" the village proper, the clubhouses of older men were located progressively toward the "inside" of the village. Blissang and Balang clubhouses on Klang's side and Bangaruau and Diberdii on Ngerturong's side all follow this spatial pattern of balanced sides and graded centrality. Although women's clubs are organized by the same dual logic, with three clubs affiliated with each side, this pattern is not made spatially explicit, since the women's clubs do not have their own meetinghouses.

These two axes of the spatial organization of clubhouses mirror their assigned public responsibilities and patterns of competition and coop-

14. Ngirturong, a chiefly title, is formed from the third-person emphatic pronoun *ngii* and means literally "the one of Turong"; Ngerturong, formed from the stative verb *ngar*, "to be located at," (with reduced vowel), is the name of the house of the title Ngirturong.

TABLE 7. IMEIONG CLUB ORGANIZATION

Men's Club Name	Grade	Meetinghouse
Side of the Village of Ngerturong:		
Ngaratemekai (Grouper)	I	Ngerulechau
Ngarachotilech (Hand Axe)	II	Bungaruau
Ngarabersoech (Snake)	III	Diberdii
Side of the Village of Klang:		
Ngaraius (Crocodile)	I	Melengel
Ngarabelod (At Belod)	II	Blissang
Ngaratebelik (Wild)	III	Balang

Women's Club Name	Grade
Side of the Village of Ngerturong:	
Ngaramalekaurad (Coconut Frond)	I
Ngarachemaiong (Dragonfly)	II
Ngaracholchesech (Stuffing Instrument)	III
Side of the Village of Klang:	
Ngarakorekerdii (?)	I
Ngaramecherur (Filled with Liquid)	II
Ngaraeabed (Clouds)	III

eration. The basic opposition between the two sides of the mangrove channel is reflected in practices such as competitive fishing expeditions, warfare raids, dancing, and feasting, in which an activity sponsored by the clubs on one side was reciprocated on a delayed basis by the clubs on the other side.

The fishing-expedition feast (*onged*) is held by the women from one side of the channel in the village. The food will be prepared by those on one side of the channel and the people on the other side will eat the food during the feast. When food is plentiful, it is carried over to the other side of the channel. The men from the clubs are the suppliers of fish and go out on a fishing expedition, and the women order food from them. When one club goes fishing, they catch fish which is then purchased by women on the other side of the channel. This is just like competition, for after a period of time the people on the other side will in turn prepare to go out on a fishing expedition to make a feast. One feast may last as long as two or three weeks, until the food runs out, and then even more food is taken over to the other side. When I was young there was a feast on the side of the channel of Klang in Imeiong, and all the food came from the side of Ngerturong. This was during the German period, but it was the very last one, since Winkler prohibited the holding of feasts. (cf. Kubary 1885:86–87; Krämer 1917–29, 2:142)

Also, day-to-day social relations of young men were regulated by this division, as the same elderly informant recalled.

If we were members of a club from one side of the channel, we certainly were not permitted to enter into a clubhouse on the other side. The leader of the club instructed us in this rule: never enter the clubhouse on the other side of the channel, for should you go in you would be fined. It is not a good idea to be in the company of members of clubs on the other side, since it would look like a person is a spy, trying to overhear decisions which he can then report back on.

This obvious dual division is, however, crosscut by the age gradation of clubs into junior, senior, and retired men. Junior club members are unmarried men still studying techniques of warfare, fishing, and dancing; senior members are men who have established independent houses but have not yet received titles; retired club members are elderly men who no longer play an active role in public life and who are not occupied with responsibilities of chiefly titles.[15] While senior men constitute the village's warriors, "retired" men spend their time mending fishing nets and traps, carving spears and cooking utensils, and exchanging stories about their days of glory. In Imeiong the pattern of recruitment into these clubs does not follow genealogical lines; that is, young men from Klang house do not necessarily join the junior club on the side of Klang. Rather, when a male child is born at an important house in the village, leaders of various clubs vie with each other to be first to place a small wristband on the baby's arm as a sign that he will join their club when he grows up. Although generally a man passes his life in clubs on the same side of the channel, it is possible to switch affiliation, especially if violation of club rules or insubordination toward club leaders leads to forcible ejection, or if an individual sees greater opportunity to display bravery or cleverness in some other club.

A second expression of this spatial dualism focused on the houses of

15. Mature men holding chiefly titles belong to Ngaraimeiong council and are thus not involved in club activities.

Klang and Ngerturong is the division of responsibility of their respective titleholders, Ngiraklang and Ngirturong, for the directions of upper sea (*bab el daob*) and lower sea (*eou el daob*) relative to Imeiong. For example, if a person from Ngeremlengui commits a crime in Ngerard (a district to the north) and the Ngarauau council there sends a messenger to Imeiong to collect a fine, Ngiraklang is required to pay the required valuable. If, on the other hand, a visiting delegation from Oreor (to the south) comes to Imeiong, their food and sleeping arrangements are the responsibility of Ngirturong. As noted above, the two rocky points in front of Imeiong also correspond to this directional division: Babelngas is owned by the title Ngiraklang and Mederemel is owned by the title Ngirturong.

Consistent with this directional opposition is the practice of taking the woven pandanus head covering as a prerequisite for installation of new holders of the Ngirturong and Ngiraklang titles. The man about to become Ngirturong retraces his house's ancestral migration route to the house of Kidel in Beliliou, while the man about to become Ngiraklang travels northward to the house of Ngedengcholl in Ngerdmau. At these sites a small meal is prepared. During the meal the new titleholder dons the woven hat to represent the sea journey which is the reason for the *kebliil* linkage among these houses. Since only a man with matrilineal affiliation dares to embark on this historically explicit journey, the practice also serves to differentiate powerful from weak titleholders, who have never worn the woven hat.

These first two houses of Klang and Ngerturong are distinguished from the other title-bearing houses in Imeiong by the presence of refuge stones located on the stone platforms in front of the houses. The more important site, called Iingerturong (Cave of Ngerturong), is a small curved stone which symbolizes the protection granted to anyone fleeing warfare who arrives in Imeiong. When warriors from Oreor burned down a village named Ngertuloech in Ngetbang, they carried off this curved stone and brought it to the pavement of Ngerturong as the *olangch* of their victory. Linking this refuge stone to Imeiong's status as the highest-ranking village in Belau, an informant said that Iingerturong was equivalent to the "cave of Belau."

> There is a very important story about this stone. It is a stone from Ngetbang. In ancient times men from Ngetbang were very strong, especially those from Ngertuloech village. When Oreor made war on them, they agreed that everyone would join the war party. While they were all fighting, other warriors from Oreor sneaked into the village and burned it down. And so people from Oreor

took these stones to Ngerturong as the *olangch*. This happened a very long time ago. The place were the battle took place is Ibetaut. They brought these stones to Ngeremlengui because it was the "older person," and the stones would be "reminders of the past." Today these stones have no other function than being *olangch*. There is a short song about them: "You, Ngirturong, you are the older brother of the side of heaven, and so didn't you think that the Cave of Ngerturong would be stood upon?" So if a person flees and comes to either Ngerturong or to Klang, no one can chase them. This is because both places are sacred.

According to this logic of sides, though not precisely consistent with its geographical specificity, Ngeremetengel is said to be "a village toward Ngerturong" and Ngchemesed is "a village toward Klang." This tie between these two lower-ranking villages and two principal houses in Imeiong stipulates that people from these villages provide taro and fish when these chiefly houses face ceremonial obligations, and that Ngirturong and Ngiraklang take responsibility for paying fines incurred by people from Ngeremetengel and Ngchemesed. When I asked how this linkage became established, I was told that a man named Rekemed from Ngchemesed came to Imeiong, where he eventually became Ngiraklang, and that Ngirturong Otobed built a house at Ongerool in Ngeremetengel in the mid-nineteenth century. On the basis of the movement of these specific individuals, the houses and villages were affiliated by paths that subsequently became prescriptive for later social activity. As will be seen in chapter 6, however, not all people in Ngeremlengui accept this way of thinking.

While the division of Imeiong into sides of the channel is obviously an important symbolic pattern, it is not considered by contemporary residents to be as essential as the quadripartition of the village's houses and titles. As figure 3 shows, four principal or high-ranking (*meteet*) houses (Klang, Ngerturong, Ngerutelchii, and Sibong) are located at the four corners of Orukei square. Each of these cornerposts includes an inalienable parcel of land, a chiefly title, and a taro patch (*lkul a dui*, "hat of the title") assigned to the titleholder. All other houses and titles in Imeiong become part of the village's political life through affiliation with these four foci of rank and power. Sets of principal houses with their affiliated satellite houses are known as *kebliil*, a term meaning "mutual houses"; and the names of these four *kebliil* derive from the names of the four cornerpost houses. Taken as a group, the titles housed at these four residences are distinguished from all other titles in the village by the label "four respected ones" (*teoa el chuong*), and the

TABLE 8. HOUSES AND TITLES IN IMEIONG

Houses	Male Titles	Female Titles
Ngerturong	Ngirturong	Dirrturong
Klang	Ngiraklang	Dirraklang
Ngerutelchii	Ngirtutelchii	Dirrutelchii
Sibong	Ngirasibong	Dirrasibong
Chedukl	Iechadrachedukl	Dirrachedukl
Iterong	Rechediterong	
Tbard	Ulebeduul	
Uchesbai	Mengesebuuch	
Ngerungelang	Okerdeu/Chelid	
(none)	Dingelius er a Klang	

wives of these titleholders are known by the corresponding label "wives of the respected ones" (*buch el chuong*).

Although each of these cornerposts is part of a different set of ranked houses and titles both within the village and across village boundaries, the ideology is that each has equal power (*klisiich*) and sacredness (*meang*) within Imeiong, so that village leadership could in principle be taken over temporarily by the second, third, or even fourth titleholder. Villagers contrast this cooperative rule to the situation in Melekeok, where, in their view, chief Reklai holds unchecked power, and in Oreor, where chief Ibedul is strongly confined by the consolidated voice of his chiefly council.[16] Traditionally and to some degree today, these four titleholders in Imeiong exercise coordinated, yet differential, responsibilities over village affairs. The first titleholder holds the position of overall leadership and represents the village in its political dealings with other villages; as such he is called "the person of whispers." The second titleholder takes charge of village activity such as work projects, fishing expeditions, and warfare; as such he is called "the person of the public" (*chad er a buai*). In a parallel to the Samoan distinction between chief and talking chief, the opposition between first and second titles corresponds to quietly exercised power and publicly verbalized authority. When Captain Wilson was in Imeiong in 1783, for example, Ngirturong (then the second-ranking title) expressed the "words of the village" and directed the ceremonial exchange, while

16. According to Kubary, Ibedul of Oreor "was only a puppet and the chiefs pulled all the strings" (1873:185).

both first chiefs, Ibedul of Oreor and Ngiraklang of Imeiong, remained relatively passive and in fact did not even speak to each other.

This division of responsibility and contrasting general orientation are reinforced by norms of formal reciprocity according to which the first and second titleholders mutually respect each other (*kakull*) and alternate in presenting special food portions (*odekuil*) at ceremonial feasts. These two titleholders also can demand payment of an *chelebucheb* valuable called "breaking the leg" (*oritech oach*) when one of them does. This payment clears the way for a new titleholder to assume his position in the village council and is returned when the other dies. The combination of close cooperation and formal rivalry which characterizes the relations between these two leaders helps explain the fact that they are referred to both as "mutual friends" and as "mutual adversaries." The third and fourth titleholders function as counterbalancing powers in the system of monetary fines that permeates village life. The third titleholder is "the person of fire," who argues for the severest possible penalty, while the fourth titleholder is "the person of water," who pleads for a lower fine.

In Imeiong, cornerposts and sides overlap in the way these four titleholders form two balanced political alliances, with Ngirturong and Ngirasibong constituting one side of the meetinghouse and Ngiraklang and Ngirutelchii forming the other side of the meetinghouse. These expressions refer to the meetinghouse floor, which is symbolically divided into two halves, with assigned seating positions for all titleholders arranged along the long side walls. These lines of alliance define division of responsibility for purchasing roof sections of a new meetinghouse, stipulate channels of communication in decision making concerning public matters, and determine patterns of loyalty in evaluating candidates to receive vacant titles. Depending on the rhetorical demands of a given situation, it is possible to speak of this dual division of all titleholders allied to either Ngirturong or Ngiraklang, or alternatively to refer to the four cornerposts of the meetinghouse as distinct from the remaining lower-ranking titles.

The rank order and patterns of alliance of the titles in Imeiong are complicated by the fact that, at some point in the nineteenth century, Ngirturong seized the position of leadership from Ngiraklang. It is extremely difficult to pinpoint the precise moment when Ngirturong's usurpation of the leadership of Imeiong was completed. Throughout the mid-nineteenth century Ngirturong's economic position became strengthened by his involvement with foreign traders, who established a curing station for bêche-de-mer in Ngeremlengui (Woodin 1851–52: 3 July 1852). The trader Cheyne relied on Ngirturong's kinship with

TABLE 9. CORNERPOSTS OF IMEIONG

Side of the Channel of Ngerturong		Side of the Channel of Klang	
Ngerturong	1 (2)	Klang	2 (1)
Sibong	4	Ngerulechii	3

Ngiraikelau (of Ikelau house) in Oreor to establish this station. But just because Ngirturong is referred to as "Governor" of the district in a document called the "Constitution of Pellow" drafted by Cheyne in 1861 (Semper 1982:194–97), this attribution cannot be taken as definitive evidence of the usurpation, since even in earlier times Ngirturong, as second-ranking titleholder, would correctly assume the role of managing this type of village economic activity and so could easily have appeared to an outsider as the head of the district.

When this process of usurpation was completed, the previously existing alliances on each side of the meetinghouse and the prescribed seating positions did not change. As a result, Imeiong violates the general rule for capital villages in Belau, that the first and third chiefs form one side, while the second and fourth form the other side. The affiliations of Imeiong's cornerpost houses and titles are given in table 9; the numbers in parentheses indicate traditional rank order, that is, rank order prior to the reversal of village leadership.

As in many Austronesian societies, the basic quadripartition of Imeiong's village organization is mediated by a fifth term, the house of Chedukl, which is the seat of the title Iechadrachedukl.[17] This fifth house, at least until the early decades of this century, was the site of the stone seat (*kingall*) of Imeiong's village god Uchererak; when Chedukl was abandoned this stone was carried to the related house of Ngerungelang, where the title Ngiramesungil holds the responsibility to "carry the god," that is, to be the spokesman for Uchererak.[18] Together,

17. Mediated quadripartition is a well-documented conceptual pattern; for Indonesia see Cunningham 1965:306; Hobart 1978:7; Jansen 1977:106; Schulte Nordholt 1971:319; van Wouden 1968:186; and Wessing 1979:117. For Polynesia see, for example, Firth 1967:285–87 (four clan-based chiefly backrests mediated by the post and slab of the god Atua i Kafika). For Southeast Asia see, for example, Heine-Geldern 1942; Tambiah 1976:102–11. But in the Belauan case the fifth term is not a transcendent central element surrounded by four quarters or a cosmic *axis mundi* or earth-navel (see Wheatley 1971:428–29).

18. I was also told that the seat of the god was intentionally carried from Chedukl to Ngerungelang by Ngarameaus club to protect it from destruction by the German authorities.

Chedukl and Ngerungelang are referred to as the *kebliil* of Babelobkal. This seat of Uchererak was where the god descended to speak through his chosen spokespersons. Titleholders at Imeiong could solicit the god by placing on the stone small offerings of money, flowers, or betelnut, and then by blowing on the conch-shell trumpet. On the sixth blast of the trumpet the spokesperson's hands began to tremble and on the seventh he would announce the god's arrival with the formula: "What's the news, *rubak?*" Issues taken up with the god included ridding the village of sickness (cf. Kubary 1873:187), securing a positive outcome in upcoming warfare, and insuring success in the village's financial dealings with its allies. In Imeiong communication with the god took the character of blunt manipulation rather than deferential reverence. The special character of Chedukl depends not only on its being the location of the seat of Uchererak but also on its political role as the mediator between Ngiraklang and Ngirturong. Although Chedukl is technically listed on Ngirturong's side of the village, in practice Iechadrachedukl is free to participate in customary activities on both sides of the village.

And like other fifth-ranking titleholders, such as Kloteraol in Oreor and Secharuleong in Melekeok, Iechadrachedukl has the duty to be the voice of the chiefly council when final decisions are to be communicated to men's clubs or to the village at large. According to Kubary (1885:65–66), Secharuleong's house Ngerungelang, located in the middle of Melekeok village, ruled that land long before the advent of chief Reklai and before the confederation of the principal houses into a unified political organization. In 1871 Secharuleong held the position of priest (*kerrong*) and was associated with the god Odalemelech (Planted at the Place of the Shooting Star), represented in a monumental stone face still standing near Ngeremelech. Similarly, traditions from Oreor state that Kloteraol was the head of the eastern sector of Oreor, Ngerusekluk, before Ibedul united the village (PCAA, Oreor File). Kloteraol served as the negotiator between Oreor and Imeliik in the political intrigue of the late nineteenth century. There are no corresponding stories in Imeiong which state that Iechadrachedukl was the leader of the village at some earlier time; but that Chedukl was the seat of the village god, that no migration traditions are recorded which trace the arrival of this house into Imeiong, and that the house itself is located between Ngerturong and Klang combine to suggest that Iechadrachedukl can be included with Secharuleong and Kloteraol in this special mediating category. But more importantly, Iechadrachedukl is entrusted with the heavy responsibility of carrying serious or secret messages between Ngaraimeiong council and other village councils. When Imeiong visits Oreor for a money collection ceremony, Iechadrachedukl supervises the removal from the rafters of the meetinghouse of the *kleangel,* a painted box bound with cord which is the dwelling place of the ancestral spirits of the former cornerpost titleholders of the village. And when the canoes reach Oreor, Kloteraol meets them at the channel and guides this precious cargo to Meketii meetinghouse, where the *kleangel* remains until the next ceremony. In line with his mediating position, he is also responsible for purchasing the central horizontal beam (*buadel*) section of a new meetinghouse and is charged with enforcing the ban on noise during funerals of high-ranking individuals. Finally, in apparent violation of strict rules of protocol and as an index of his interstitial position, Iechadrachedukl is permitted to cross the meetinghouse floor even while important titleholders are talking.

The internal political organization of Ngeremetengel differs in several important respects from that of Imeiong. First, the five houses in Ngeremetengel that control titles are not foci of local affiliative *kebliil* networks consisting of other titled houses. In other words, there are no village-internal alliances based on local *titles,* as was seen to be an essential feature of Imeiong's side-of-the-meetinghouse organization. Second, the principal houses in Ngeremetengel have female titles carried by senior women related consanguineally to the house (see table 10), in contrast to Imeiong's practice of assigning these complementary titles to wives of male titleholders. As is discussed more fully in the next chapter, Ngeremetengel resembles all other Belauan villages in this respect.

Third, this political structure reveals a complex process of historical layering not as self-evident in the Imeiong case. The location of the village has shifted twice, once in the mid-nineteenth century, from an archaic location named Beluurametengel above Ngerekebrong channel to a site at Oderderong channel, and again in the late 1940s to its present location on land reclaimed from the mangrove swamp. These and other historical factors account for the fact that the "autochthonous"

TABLE 10. HOUSES AND TITLES IN NGEREMETENGEL

Houses	Male Titles	Female Titles
Dilubech	Ngiradilubech	Uchelebil
Ngeremellomes	Iechadrametengel	Diltengrangr
Ngerungor	Bedul	Dilucheliou
Mechoang	Renguulramechoang	Dilnglodech
Ongerool	Ililau	Dililau

title Iechadrametengel (Man of Metengel) is given the second position, while the titles associated with the Ngerekebrong channel site (Ngiradilubech) and the Oderderong channel site, (Renguulramechoang) are assigned the first and fourth positions. Also, the fifth house, Ongerool, was built by people from Ngerturong house in Imeiong.[19] The frequent use of the expression "four clans" (*eoa el blai*) in English translations of contemporary municipal documents can be viewed, I contend, as a conscious analogy to the quadripartite order of Imeiong's cornerpost houses and titles—conscious, that is, on the part of Imeiong leaders who drafted the document. And finally, the village is not politically divided into two balanced sides of the mangrove channel, despite the fact that such a dualism is geographically available in the layout of houses with reference to the two mangrove channels.

AFFILIATE HOUSES AND TITLES

The four principal houses of Imeiong not only organize intravillage political relations and social activity but also belong to extensive affiliative networks called *kebliil*, "mutual houses," extending beyond the district's boundaries (Parmentier 1984). These ties of affiliation are primarily the result of ancient migration traditions which record the movement of groups and individuals which passed through Ngeremlengui. In the case of Imeiong, however, these stories uniformly presuppose the prior existence of the principal houses to which migrating groups attach themselves. Although the precise genealogical connections among houses linked by these paths of migration have usually been forgotten, each affiliated house considers itself permanently linked to the others, and as a result the networks function as mechanisms of political cooperation and solidarity. Men from these houses are considered strong candidates to take titles at any of the member houses, and the network channels financial contributions when a member incurs some obligation.

The same term *kebliil* also refers to networks of houses within a village which share ties of social solidarity, political alliance, and cooperation. In contrast to the permanence of the quadripartition of the four

19. Krämer's (1917–29:150) list of houses and titles in Ngeremetengel is a bit confusing without additional clarification. He lists Mordilong and Ngerabuil as second- and third-ranked houses, but these are actually the names of residences rebuilt in Ngeremetengel by people from Ngeremellomes and Ngerungor houses at Beluurametengel. The title given for Ongerool is Dingelius, which reflects the fact that a man with that Ngaraimeiong title happened to be living in the village when Krämer visited. And the annotation that Dilubech house is destroyed or abandoned conceals the more interesting fact that no such house ever stood at the Oderderong site of Ngeremetengel.

principal houses in Imeiong, lesser-ranking satellite houses are subject
to the ebb and flow of events. Founded, for example, by younger brothers of titleholders, widowed senior women, male offspring of members
of the principal houses, or strangers awarded land in return for labor
and loyalty, these smaller houses (*kekere el blai*) usually stand on land
near the principal house or close to the landing place associated with
the titleholder's side of the village. In some cases titleholders themselves
reside at an affiliate house, especially if they were established there prior
to assuming their titles, or if their claim to the title is subject to challenge. Repeated instances of the residence of titled chiefs at an affiliate
house can lead to the special recognition of this house as one which
"looks upon the title" (*melanges er a dui*), that is, which holds the privilege of providing candidates to carry the principal house's title in the
event of vacancy due to death, banishment, or political intrigue. A second special denomination is made for the affiliate house which is nor-
matively the residence of widowed senior women who return to their
matrilineal homes; restrictions on the physical proximity of brother and
sister compel these women to go to established dwellings, called
"houses of senior women" (*blil a ourrot*), independent from those of
male relatives holding titles.

The system of house and title affiliation within Imeiong can be illustrated by taking Klang as an example. Affiliated with the principal
house Klang are the houses Bailunged, Chaklsel, Klematelchang, Cheremang, Obekebong, Obeketang, and Tutang (all in Imeiong proper),
as well as the houses Taru, Duab, Melilt, Kamerir, and Telau (in adjacent hamlets). All these houses are known as "houses of Klang," or,
when their cooperation and unity are being stressed, as "mutual houses
with respect to Klang" (*kebliil er a Klang*). And, finally, while household heads at these houses of Klang may bear honorific house names
(such as Ngiraduab at Duab) or minor chiefly titles belonging to the
secondary village council Ngaracheritem (such as Otaor at Cheremang), none of these affiliate houses is recognized as a house of a title
belonging to the sacred council of ten titles, Ngaraimeiong. That is, a
titleholder may in fact reside at one of these affiliate houses, but the
house, or more properly the land upon which the house stands, does
not control a chiefly title of its own.

This general pattern of relatively permanent principal houses surrounded by relatively transient affiliate houses is further complicated by
an additional categorical distinction between (1) those satellite houses
whose alliance with a principal house has become institutionalized to
the degree that residents are automatically classified, by virtue of this
fact, as related to that principal house; and (2) those affiliate houses

which are allied to a principal house only on the basis of some personal contingency pertaining to the household head. Villagers express these two modes of relation with the phrases "paths of the house" (*rolel a blai*) and "paths of the person" (*rolel a bedengel*). This differentiation is not absolute, since in time small houses in the second category can pass into the first category if the personal factor becomes regularized through repetitive title inheritance, exchange, or cooperation. Affiliate houses in the first category are referred to as "cornerposts of the mutual house network" (*saus er a kebliil*), a phrase that replicates at a lower structural level the same quadripartite pattern found among principal houses within a village. Just as four principal houses arranged around the village square support the village as a coordinated unit, so these four (or more) cornerpost houses support the central, or nodal, principal house as a unified social category. In Imeiong, for example, the principal house Klang recognizes Cheremang, Obekebong, Taru, and Duab (as well as Klematelchang, by some accounts) as "cornerposts of the mutual house network of Klang." More common usage, however, refers to these houses simply as "houses of Klang" (*blai er a Klang*), where the linking particle *er* implies a stable, internal relationship, but not necessarily possession, as can be connoted by the English gloss "of."

The second category of houses affiliated with Klang included Melilt, Chaklsel, Tutang, and Bailunged. These houses are referred to as "houses [oriented] toward Klang" (*blai el mo er a Klang*), where the word *mo* implies motion or directionality from the first noun *blai* to the second noun Klang. This phrasing is also used to describe the relationship between Klang in Imeiong and Ngereburek house in adjacent Nglabang hamlet (see below). But since Ngereburek is itself the seat of a title, Ngiruburek, and has affiliated with it several satellite houses in the hamlet, the expression becomes: "Ngereburek is a mutual house network oriented toward Klang".

These ethnographic and linguistic observations suggest that two criteria are operative in distinguishing principal houses from affiliate houses: nodality and titles, that is, being the focal point for a network of local satellite houses and being the acknowledged seat of a chiefly title. The first criterion expresses whether residents of a house participate directly in social exchanges and political alliances with houses outside the village, or whether they must "pass through" or "go along with" principal houses in all external affairs. In the traditional village, affiliate houses contributed labor, food, and money in support of customary obligations of chiefly houses, and in return titleholders at these principal houses assumed responsibility for paying fines incurred by individuals at affiliate houses and for supplying valuables necessary at certain rites of passage.

The second criterion expresses whether or not the household head is entitled to an independent voice in the local chiefly council and to receive deference and respect accruing to the sacredness inherent in titles. In large capital villages such as Imeiong, Melekeok, and Oreor, the intersection of these two criteria yields an additional typological variation, namely, intermediate houses, which are seats of chiefly titles but are not nodal points of mutual house networks (*kebliil*). In Imeiong, for example, there are four principal, nodal houses and ten chiefly titles comprising Ngaraimeiong council. Obviously then, six of these titles reside at intermediate houses (in fact, only five do, since the tenth title Dingelius, the messenger for second-ranking Ngiraklang, does not have a house in Imeiong). These six titles are divided into two opposed groups by bonds of political alliance with either Ngirturong or Ngiraklang, the two highest-ranking members of Ngaraimeiong council. That is, the council of ten titles is split into two sides of the meetinghouse, with a total of five titleholders sitting along the side of Ngiraklang and five sitting along the side of Ngirturong. The important point to note is that the affiliation of these intermediate houses with principal houses is based on political alliance (expressed in the seating arrangement) and not on social subordination, kinship ties, or other dependency. Although there is no single term or regularity of expression which distinguishes the house in this third category, the corresponding titles are given the special label "lesser titles" (*kekere el dui*), in contrast to the four sacred titles at the cornerpost houses.

Imeiong village has four ranked principal houses (Ngerturong, Klang, Ngerutelchii, and Sibong), five ranked intermediate houses (Chedukl, Iterong, Tbard, Uchesbai, and Ngerungelang), and a large number of affiliate houses—not all of which were occupied at the same time. The ranked titles corresponding to these nine principal and intermediate houses, plus the tenth title Dingelius, make up Ngaraimeiong council. This council, in turn, is divided into "Ngirturong's side of the meetinghouse" and "Ngiraklang's side of the meetinghouse." Since the alignment of intermediate houses is in fact determined by political alliance of corresponding titles, these five houses are affiliated only with the first two principal houses, that is, Ngerturong and Klang. As a result, titleholders Ngirturong and Ngiraklang are supported in Ngaraimeiong council by three holders of lesser titles, namely, Iechadrachedukl, Mengesebuuch, and Okerdeu/Chelid on the Ngerturong side, and Rechediterong, Ulebeduul, and Dingelius er a Klang on the Klang side. The other two cornerpost titleholders, Ngirutelchii and Ngirasibong, do not enjoy this kind of embedded political support at

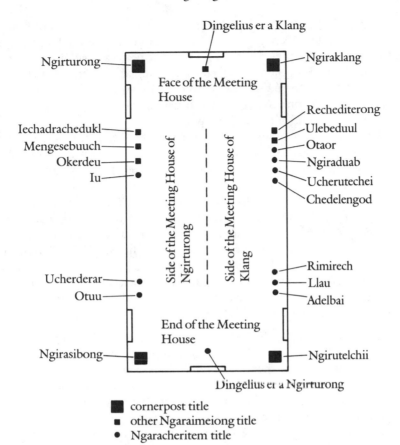

Dingelius er a Klang

Ngirturong — Ngiraklang

Face of the Meeting House

Rechediterong
Iechadrachedukl — Ulebeduul
Mengesebuuch — Otaor
Okerdeu — Ngiraduab
Iu — Ucherutechei
Chedelengod

Side of the Meeting House of Ngirturong
Side of the Meeting House of Klang

Rimirech
Ucherderar — Llau
Otuu — Adelbai

End of the Meeting House

Ngirasibong — Ngirutelchii

Dingelius er a Ngirturong

■ cornerpost title
■ other Ngaraimeiong title
● Ngaracheritem title

FIG. 4. SEATING PATTERN OF NGARAIMEIONG AND NGARACHERITEM

their respective corners, although they are joined by minor titleholders from a secondary council, Ngaracheritem, whose members are drawn not only from neighboring hamlets but also from Ngerutechei, Ngeremetengel, and Ngchemesed villages within the district of Ngeremlengui. Whereas the membership and order of Ngaraimeiong council are fixed, the membership of Ngaracheritem is subject to fluctuation, since these minor titleholders join the council on the basis of contingent ties to Imeiong's cornerpost houses. The seating pattern for Ngaraimeiong and Ngarcheritem councils is represented in figure 4.

CLUSTER HAMLETS: ULECHETONG AND NGLABANG

As noted in chapter 2, Imeiong is an example of a form of multivillage association labeled "village complex." The capital and its two flanking hamlets, Ulechetong and Nglabang, are linked by strong ties of house affiliation and cooperation. In fact, to a large degree satellite houses affiliated with the four principal houses of Imeiong have progressively become located in Ulechetong and Nglabang, as the traditional geographical distinction between Imeiong and its cluster hamlets has disappeared. This section investigates the organization, migration traditions, and political status of these two hamlets.

Ulechetong is a small hamlet located just west of Imeiong on the same side of Ngerdong river. Although it was governed by its own council, Ngaramengellang, the hamlet was in reality a "suburb" of Imeiong. The houses of Ulechetong do not have "real" titles, but rather just house names (*ngakl er a blai*), such as Ngiraduab at Duab house, Ngiralbong at Lbong, and Ngiraibut at Ibut. A man residing at Duab can be addressed by the name of his house in this fashion, just as Ngiraklang is called after the name of Klang house. The difference is that Ngiraklang is a title (*dui,* or more correctly, *klngiraklang,* "the title Ngiraklang") with authority, sacredness, and social existence apart from the titleholder, while a house name merely reflects a residential fact rather than a political role. McKnight explains this difference clearly:

> The birth-name (or the related pseudo-title) is used until the individual has married and acquired a house. By this time he is recognized as an authentic member of his clan and receives his first official change in name. The name he acquires at this time is a manor or lot-name and is "honorific" in that it suggests the capacity of the individual to maintain a family. . . . When a man and his wife acquire their lot-names, it is a discourtesy to call them by their birthnames. These may be used in private only within the nuclear family. . . . If a man, and his family move, it follows that the husband and wife acquire new lot-names and the new resident in their former lot acquires their former lot-names. (McKnight 1958:29–31)

The thirteen houses of Ulechetong recalled by informants are affiliated as mutual houses with all of the principal houses in Imeiong, according to the pattern shown in table 11. Although only Melilt, Kamerir, and Telau are occupied today, older informants recall that all the houses (with the exception of Kolebas and Dilekuu) were occupied when the informants were children. Analysis of genealogical histories of the men and women who lived in the hamlet reveals that these house affiliations reflect facts of title succession of household heads more than any other single factor. Bars house is a member of the *kebliil* of Ngerutelchii, since a former household head there became the titleholder

Table 11. House Affiliation in Imeiong, Ulechetong, and Nglabang

	In Imeiong	In Ulechetong	In Nglabang
To Ngerturong:	Ngerturong Chedukl Uchesbai Ngerungelang	Chetmur	
To Klang:	Klang Iterong Tbard Bailunged Chakelsel Klematelchang Cheremang Obeketang Obekebong Tutang	Melilt Duab Kamerir Telau	Ngeruburek Taru
To Ngerutelchii:	Ngerutelchi Chebechubel Itab Kokemerang Ngebei Lengleng Smaserui Ngeremau Smesei	Bars Rrekong	
To Sibong:	Sibong	Ibut Lbong Singdong Chetebong Kolebas Ngeremeketii Dilekuu	Tmeleu Ngersosol Mengerengei
To Chedukl:	Chedukl Ngeremesungil		

Ngirutelchii. Similarly, Chetebong is affiliated with Sibong house in Imeiong, since its former household head took the title Ngirasibong. Duab house, likewise, has produced no fewer than three Ngiraklang titleholders.

In addition to these particular house affiliations between Ulechetong and Imeiong, the land of the hamlet is said to be owned by Sibong house (*klalo er a Sibong*). The hamlet, accordingly, is said to be a "hamlet toward Sibong" (*beluu mo er a Sibong*), and its household heads are said to be "elders of Sibong" (*okdemaol er a Sibong*). This linkage of an entire village to one principal house is reminiscent of the district structure of Ngeremeskang, where each village owed primary allegiance to one of the principal houses at the capital. An informant related to Sibong gave the following account of the origin of this connection between Ulechetong and Sibong house.

Story of Odelomel of Ulechetong

The reason that I told this story to [personal name] yesterday is that the people from Sibong in ancient times came to Ngeremlengui from Ngerekebesang [an island near Oreor]. I think that they have heard this story, but they do not know the real explanation for it.

Dibech was a child from Ngerekebesang, and the reason she was called Dibech is that an old woman from Ngerekebesang, who was one of the senior women there, lived all by herself and did not have any children. She lived in the high-ranking house at Ngerekebesang, and she carried the female title of the house, where the male title is Obakeraulechetong. This is the first-ranked title in Ngerekebesang. This woman was the "female counterpart" (*kldorolel*) of this *rubak*. The *rubak*, however, lived in another section of Ngerekebesang at a place named Cheichol, which is the name of a village. He lived at Cheichol, and this old woman lived at another nearby village. A rock cliff divides the two sections; she lived on the side named Chiuong. She lived there on the other side and was childless, and this *rubak* lived on the other side. The two had nothing to do with each other.

One day this old woman went out to fetch water, and she returned to prepare her taro for boiling, so she went to the taro patch and came back. There is a small bathing pool named Dok where water flows up to the surface. She went to Dok to draw water for cooking her taro, and she found a little girl there. So she took the child home with her and said, "You are to be named Dibech, since you appeared (*dubech*) at the bathing pool." She raised the girl until she was older. And then she took this girl named Dibech and the name Ulechetong, which is the name of the house on the other side where the male elders lived, and the name Ibut, which is the name of the mangrove channel on the other side. And this old woman whose name is Odelomel came to Imeiong carrying with her this name Ulechetong, which is now the name of the hamlet next to Imeiong.

The first hamlet you come to as you travel up the channel is Ulechetong, and as you walk in the direction of Duab house, the house directly below that is named Ibut. All these names came originally from Ngerekebesang to Imeiong. This old woman and her child Dibech came here, and she deposited all these names at Sibong house. She left Ngerekebesang because she was angry with the *rubak* there, who did not help her out, and because she was childless. This is the reason. So she took the name of this *rubak*, Obakeraulechetong, and brought it along with the name of the channel, Ibut. She came to Imeiong and entered Sibong house. And so the man who is Ngiraibut can become Ngirasibong.

According to this account the woman Odelomel—not a personal name but a female title, Odelomeldil—abandoned her house at Ngerekebesang and moved to Imeiong, carrying with her a set of names as permanent reminders (*olangch*) of her home village. Because of her actions, Ibut house became specially recognized as the house that "looks upon the title" of Ngirasibong; that is, a man at Ibut could be considered a candidate to take the chiefly title at Sibong in the absence of stronger claimants from Imeiong proper. When I asked why there does not appear to be a contemporary path of social cooperation and exchange between Sibong and people in Ngerekebesang, the storyteller commented that, in abandoning her home, Odelomel cut off all connection with Ngerekebesang, and that this is the reason she took the various names with her. All of these names did not, however, end up at Ulechetong hamlet.

> This very same old woman who came to Imeiong continued to travel, and she went next to Ngetbang where she became the female counterpart of a very high-ranking man at Ngeredubech village. She took the name Ibut with her, and today this is the name of the road head in Ngetbang. She entered the house of this rich and high-ranking man, but he did not own a taro patch there. She carried the title Odelomeldil, which is a title from Ngerekebesang, so she did not deposit this title at Sibong house. So Odelomel became the female counterpart to Lbai. Odelomel went to Ngetbang, but she traveled further to Ngerechelong, so Odelomel became the ninth title in Ngerechelong, the one who carries the god. And from Ngerechelong she continued on to Oikull [in Irrai]—she is really a very famous woman—where she lived at the house of Etei.

While paths between Sibong and both Ngerechelong and Oikull are no longer important today, the path to Ngetbang, especially to Inglai house there, is still followed in contemporary exchange.

The relationship between Ulechetong hamlet and Sibong house is viewed from two contradictory perspectives by my informants. From the point of view of people of Imeiong, Ulechetong is a minor hamlet owned and controlled by the high-ranking house of Sibong, one of the cornerposts of Imeiong. The fact that people from Ulechetong who took the title Ngirasibong, rather than merely people from Sibong tend to reside in Ulechetong reflects the "suburban" nature of linkage. In need of room for expansion, Sibong families constructed houses there, and these houses are viewed as houses of Sibong located at Ulechetong (*blai er a Sibong el ngar er a Ulechetong*). But from the perspective of people of Ulechetong, the fact that houses such as Ibut, Singdong, Chetebong, Kolebas, and Ngeremeketii are mutual houses affiliated with Sibong (*kebliil er a Sibong*) reflects the tradition given above according to which Sibong itself was founded from Ngerekebesang through Ulechetong. The many Ngirasibong titleholders who lived at Ulechetong were people from Sibong who happened to be living at Ulechetong. In fact, however, neither of these perspectives seems likely to maintain validity, as migration traditions and institutional affiliations at the house level give way to personal linkages between Ulechetong residents and the other leading houses in Imeiong. In light of the abandonment of all these Sibong affiliate houses in Ulechetong, it would be reasonable to predict that in the near future the hamlet will be said to be a "hamlet toward Klang," since the three occupied houses (Melilt, Kamerir, and Telau) are all headed by men who follow personal paths to Klang—two in fact carry titles belonging to the side of the meetinghouse of Klang—rather than to Sibong.

The traditional relationship between Nglabang, a small hamlet across the river from Imeiong, and Klang house roughly parallels that between Ulechetong and Sibong. Nglabang is said to be the property of Klang, and all its houses are labeled "houses affiliated with Klang." One informant linked this dependence to the general responsibility, noted above, of Ngiraklang for things relating to the upper sea, that is, to the area north of Imeiong.

> Nglabang is the village across the channel from Imeiong. It is a low-ranking village, although it does have a separate council. Nglabang's houses are low-ranking and are oriented toward Klang, just as if they were mutual houses of Klang. The reason for this is that Ngiraklang has the distinct responsibility for everything on the other side of the channel facing Ngerdmau, while the side of the channel facing the lower sea is the responsibility of Ngirturong.

Evidence which emerges from narratives associated with this hamlet suggests, however, that its relationship to Imeiong is not entirely analogous to that of Ulechetong. One indication of Nglabang's more independent status is that it was internally subdivided into two sides of the village under the leadership of the household heads at Ngeruburek and Orraol. Ulechetong, in contrast, was an undivided entity under the leadership of Bedul at Melilt house. (How Ulechetong could be under Melilt, a house affiliated with Klang, and yet be considered a hamlet oriented toward Sibong remains an unanswered question.) This side division of Nglabang extends to a vast area north of the hamlet which was split into the property of Orraol (north to Ngedesiur) and the property of Ngeruburek (northwest to the coast). Informants explained, additionally, that when the nearby village of Ngerutoed gradually collapsed, its inhabitants came down to settle at various houses in Nglabang. Other indications of the relative independence of Nglabang are the huge size of the house pavement at Ngeruburek and the location of a sacred stone, the Btangch er a Chilong, in a small wooded grove behind Ngeruburek. Both the house platform and the stone figure in important stories of Ngeremlengui. The stone is said to have been the spot where Rdiall, a man from Ngkeklau whose religious visions and prophetic teaching stimulated the development of the Modekngei movement, buried the war spears of Ngeremlengui to symbolize the termination of hostility and to mark the start of a new era of peace and brotherhood.[20]

During the period of interdistrict warfare, Nglabang functioned as a spy for Imeiong in nearby Ngerdmau and would notify Ngiraklang if a raid against Imeiong was being planned. Also, people from Nglabang kept watch at the mountain pass Klailchutem northwest of the village for war parties coming overland from Melekeok.[21] Such cooperation between Nglabang and Imeiong is labeled "taking care of each other" (*kaukerreu*).

By the first decade of this century the meetinghouses in both Ulechetong and Nglabang had collapsed, and the two political councils, Ngaramengellang and Ngaratumul, were no longer functional. As these two hamlets lost population and local integrity, the degree of mutual relatedness (*kaudeleongel*) to the principal houses of Imeiong increased. As more families related to Imeiong's principal houses settled in these hamlets, titleholders in Ngaraimeiong were more frequently recruited

20. Today only an upright monolith and several small surrounding stones remain at Chilong; but in 1954 Osborne (1966:144, figs. 47C and D) photographed a smaller andesite stone face, which has since disappeared. This same photograph is reproduced in Bellwood 1979:287, fig. 10.6.

21. Similarly, Kubary (1873:185) notes that Ngmelachel, an island next to Oreor, functioned as a stopping point for all canoes on their way toward the capital; canoes that failed to stop would be attacked as enemies.

from affiliate houses there. Another pattern is that vacant titles in Ngaraimeiong and Ngaracheritem councils were filled by outsiders who, following either ancient paths (*mechut el rael*), distant links (*ngamekechui el rael*), or newly created connections (*beches el rael*), relocated their residences in "suburban" Ulechetong and Nglabang, where space was plentiful and house affiliations already recognized. For example, under the direction of Ubai Krai, the last inhabitant of Roisbeluu (whose people came originally from Ngeremeskang), people from Teuid house established a new residence at Rrekong. Since this man Ubai was awarded the high title Ngirutelchii, people from Ngerutelchii house also came over to Rrekong to join their kin. Also, Taru in Nglabang developed such strong relations with Klang house in Imeiong that its household head stood in line to be considered as a candidate for the title Ngiraklang. Informants could remember only one man, Samua, who eventually became Ngiraklang; more recently, Duab house has replaced Taru in the special status of "looks upon the title."

As a result of these developments at the same time that Ulechetong and Nglabang became a "hamlet toward Sibong" and a "hamlet toward Klang", respectively, the political boundaries between these hamlets and Imeiong proper began to disappear. Without independent councils and separate men's clubs, and with many household heads more directly tied to the four principal houses in Imeiong than to the local ranking houses (such as Melilt and Ngeruburek), Ulechetong and Nglabang, like more than a dozen other villages from Kerngilianged, collapsed into Imeiong. Today no distinction is drawn between these three entities, and residents of Ulechetong and Nglabang proudly call themselves "people of Imeiong," asserting thereby a claim to have higher status than either the people of Ngeremetengel or the people of Ngchemesed. Their claim is ironic in that, while people from the four principal houses of Imeiong have moved to Ngeremetengel, the residents of Ulechetong and Nglabang remain behind to fill in the vacuum left by these departures. In other words, there has emerged a subtle but important distinction between these current "residents of Imeiong" and the "real people of Imeiong," referring now to those related to the high-ranking houses which formerly surrounded Orukei square. The irony, then, is that in the current situation, low-ranking people reside in high-ranking Imeiong, while high-ranking people live in low-ranking Ngeremetengel. The implications of this asymmetry will become clearer in the next chapter when we discuss in more detail Imeiong's relations with Ngeremetengel and Ngchemesed.

CHAPTER
6

The Rhetoric of Intradistrict
Historical Narratives

This chapter explores the political implications of two rhetorical models underlying alternative oral traditions about the founding of villages in Ngeremlengui district. Rather than "attempting to arrive at the historical truth behind a number of conflicting versions" (Latukefu 1968:139), I will demonstrate the importance of specifying systematic differences between variants, in this case, differences skewed by the rank of the tellers' villages. In this regard, Miller's (1980:20) programmatic statement applies to the anthropologist as well as to the historian: "Differences, not agreement, allow the historian to decipher the ways in which narrators have composed their traditions, and in analyzing variation the historian locates where the history may lie. . . . Variation that once seemed a weakness in traditions emerges as one of their greatest strengths for the elucidation of their historical content." While multiple descriptions of the "same" event constitute proof for some historians that oral narratives are unreliable, they can also provide a perfect opportunity to uncover cultural principles behind narrative genres. That is, oral traditions express an implicit theory—or theories—of historical process which should not be dismissed as mere ideological bias or contextual skewing (see Spear 1981:175–76; Cohn 1961).

STATIC AND DYNAMIC PERSPECTIVES

Buried in the details of the two classic Western narratives about Belau, Keate's *Account of the Pelew Islands* (based on Captain Wilson's 1783 journal) and Semper's *Die Palau-Inseln im Stillen Ozean* (based on his visit in 1862–1863), lies evidence of a major shift in the political conditions of Ngeremlengui district. When Wilson accompanied a group of important chiefs to the district in 1783, their party entered a narrow

mangrove channel and poled up to the landing place of Imiungs village
(the old name for Imeiong). There Wilson observed the village chief, an
old man carried on a board, distribute valuables to the visiting dignitaries. To Wilson's eyes the village appeared to have been recently rebuilt after a destructive fire.

> This rivulet was both narrow and shallow, its sides full of
> mangrove trees, which in several places were cut away to make a
> free passage for the canoes to pass up and down. . . . After
> advancing near a mile up this creek (through part of which, it
> being low-water, the boatmen were obliged to get out and track
> the canoe) they came in sight of some houses; the conch-shell was
> again sounded, when three or four young men appeared, but
> returned back immediately, as if surprised; Rechucher [a titleholder
> from Oreor], on seeing this, ordered two of his men to go up to
> the houses, who returned with a piece of board, on which they
> seated Captain Wilson, and four of the men took him on shore,
> Rechucher walking by his side, the canoe being aground. The bank
> of the river was by this time crowded with the natives; through this
> throng they were conducted to a large house, there the novelty of
> seeing men of different colour to themselves had drawn together a
> fresh concourse of people, whose curiosity was still more raised by
> what they had heard of them in the late different expeditions. The
> Captain and his companions stayed at this place about half an hour,
> to rest themselves, and gratify the natives, who appeared
> exceedingly desirous to touch them; they then walked about a
> quarter of a mile further, where Ibedul with the *rubak* were
> expecting their arrival. They found the King [Ibedul] and the
> Chiefs in a large house or public building; the former made signs
> to Captain Wilson to sit down. They remained there about two
> hours, and then went to visit the *rubak* of the town, who was a
> very old man and unable to walk [i.e., Ngiraklang Chelungel]—
> being accompanied by Rechucher, who introduced them. A kind of
> stool or low table covered with boiled yams [taro], a tub of sweet
> drink, and a fish were set before them. They tasted them, and
> remained about half an hour with the old *rubak,* and returned to
> the great house, whither the provisions were sent after
> them. . . . This affair [a raid on the village depicted in a dance]
> appeared not to have happened very long before, as the materials of
> the houses which had been destroyed looked still rather fresh, nor
> were overgrown with weeds at that time. . . . The morning was
> ushered in with new dances. After breakfast there was much heavy

rain, with thunder and lightning; in the afternoon the weather clearing, the old *rubak* of the place [Ngiraklang] came down to the raised stone pavement, which was at one end of the great house where our people were; he was brought on a board slung with a rope at each end, and carried by four men. (Keate 1788;171–75)

But when Semper and a group of Ngerard chiefs stopped at Ngeremlengui on their way to Oreor eighty years later, their canoes passed through an artificial mangrove channel and emerged at Ngeremetengel village, one of the member villages of the district just south of Imeiong (see map 3). Whereas Wilson had been entertained by chief Ngiraklang at his house not far from Imeiong's central square, Semper visited the newly built residence of a man bearing the title Ngirturong, traditionally the second-ranking title in Imeiong's council. In contrast to the war-ravaged appearance of Imeiong that struck Wilson, Ngeremetengel seemed to Semper to be a well-kept, populous village, showing evidence of prosperous trading relations with foreign merchants.[1]

We were at the entrance to the channel reaching due east, which had been cut artificially into the mangrove thicket here as always. But the forest rising from the ocean was only of a slight extent here. The mangroves quickly disappeared from the southern side. A bare wall over one hundred feet high rose entirely perpendicularly; it appeared to consist of porphyry-like rock.[2] Soon thereafter, we reached the landing place. There was still enough space for our canoe inside the canoe shed. After it was well stored, we went on our way. The friend from Oreor had sent out a request beforehand to announce us at Ngirturong's house. . . . Following a turn in the rather sharply ascending path across the field, we suddenly came upon the paved main street of the village. This one was broader than the northern ones seemed to be as a rule and kept entirely free of weeds. On both sides were rows of low planted bushes touching upon the underbrush that proliferated under the palm and breadfruit trees with their large, scalloped leaves. Before the path reached the summit, above which the roof of a massive many-colored clubhouse rose with artistic beauty against the blue background of sky and the green foreground of trees, it turned to the right and formed a considerable open area. Half shadowed by

---

1. Stations for collecting trepang were established at Imeiong in 1844 (Cheyne 1971:338); in 1852, however, a station was established at Ngeremetengel (Woodin 1851–52: 3 July 1852; cf. Cheyne 1863–66: 17 June 1864)

2. This distinctive feature identifies the place as Ngeremetengel.

trees, but still warmed by the last rays of the setting sun, lay
Ngirturong's ancestors beneath large stones, only a few steps away
from his family's house. No grass or weeds grew here. . . . The
main house itself seemed to have just been built because it all
appeared so completely and carefully preserved. . . . Wherever I
looked, I saw greater abundance and comfort than I had seen in
Palau before. The influence that the busy trade with the trading
people from the West had worked upon the life of the villagers was
easily recognizable. (Semper 1982:181–82)

These successive glimpses of Ngeremlengui raise several questions
about the changing political relations among its constituent villages:
Why did Wilson's party of 1783 go to Imeiong, while Semper's party
of 1862 visited Ngeremetengel? What happened between 1783, when
village leadership was held by Ngiraklang, and 1862, when Ngirturong
represented the district in its dealings with Western traders? And what
was a high-ranking person like Ngirturong doing living and burying his
ancestors in Ngeremetengel, rather than in Imeiong, the seat of this
title? Answers to these questions do not lie in Western documents but
rather in the myths, chants, and narratives of Ngeremlengui, some of
which I was able to study during my fieldwork over a century after
Semper's visit. And the fact that I studied these traditions from men
holding the titles Ngirturong and Ngiraklang while they were both
living in Ngeremetengel is a signal that the shift in political weight from
the high-ranking capital Imeiong to low-ranking Ngeremetengel witnessed by Semper continues in the contemporary period.

Understanding Imeiong's relationship to Ngeremetengel, furthermore, turns on alternative interpretations of earlier stories about the
political relations between Imeiong and a now-extinct village named
Ngeremeskang, which at one time controlled a vast territory on the
western side of central Babeldaob (see chapter 5). The rise of Imeiong
as the capital of Ngeremlengui followed the decline of Ngeremeskang,
whose houses and titles were relocated at a small village Roisbeluu
(near Imeiong), without maintaining their high rank at this new site.
On the one hand, then, there are traditions telling about the fall of
powerful Ngeremeskang and the victory of Imeiong over its oppressive
neighbor Uluang (see chapter 7); on the other hand, there is the Story
of Milad (see chapter 4), which describes Imeiong's preeminent, firstborn position as an unchangeable mythic fact. The historical and contemporary relationship between Imeiong and Ngeremetengel is represented in stories in two ways: according to a *dynamic model* of Ngeremeskang's fall and Imeiong's rise of according to a *static model* of

Milad's cornerpost polity. So this and the next chapter constitute a unified case study of alternative historical perspectives on intradistrict village rank. The present chapter focuses on Imeiong's position as the capital of Ngeremlengui and presents a contemporary narrative that justifies the village's permanent role as the place where "the sacred remains." This perspective contrasts with that of lower-ranking Ngeremetengel, where storytellers adopt the dynamic model according to which village rank—their own and Imeiong's especially—is subject to change. The following chapter tells the story of Ngeremlengui district's political relations with other districts from the time of its victory over Uluang up to the final usurpation of the chieftainship by Ngirturong at the close of the nineteenth century. In the end, I will argue that village rank depends not just on coercive force and inherent privilege but also on historicizing power, that is, the power to construct the "official" record of the past.

UCHULADEBONG: WHERE SACREDNESS REMAINS

Given that the model of four cornerposts as an ideology of institutional arrangement involves coordinated support (as the four corner pillars of a building support the roof structure) and historical completeness (that a four-part structure has reached its full maturity and integrity), it should not be surprising to hear that the quadripartite order of Imeiong's "respected" titleholders is explicitly said to parallel that of Milad's four village-children. In contrast to stories set in the era of Chuab, the story of Milad depicts the formation of a new polity as a unified, internally generated constitution in which four villages, Imiungs, Melekeok, Imeliik, and Oreor, are affiliated according to norms of siblingship derived from their birth order and sex. Political transformation is viewed as an instantaneous rebirth of a coherent order rather than as a layered sequence of events, as in the migrations or journeys characteristic of the previous cultural era and the stories about the founding of low-ranking villages such as Ngeremetengel and Ngchemesed. The narrative of the institution of Imeiong's quadripartite political order similarly involves the simultaneous distribution of male and female titles by the gods at a stone pavement in Ngerutechei village, located just behind Imeiong in the shadow of Ngeroach mountain (where Milad landed after the flood). Again, historical transformation, that is, the "molting" of Ngeremlengui (Place of Molting), in which Imeiong is recognized as the district capital and in which the village's high-ranking titles are instituted, is coded in terms of a single, coordinated act taking place within Babeldaob, rather than in terms of sequential migrations and external sources of power. And as if to make this formal parallelism between the interdistrict Belauan context and the intravillage Imeiong context even more explicit, the two acts of political constitution take place at approximately the same place: Ngerutechei is the location of both Tmud, the stone face associated with the Milad story, and Uchuladebong, the stone pavement where the titles of Imeiong were distributed. In other words, the two quadripartite orders are both lithically anchored at Ngerutechei, so their formal similarity is reinforced by this indexical linkage.

The text presented below, which I recorded in 1980, is an account of the connection between the Milad polity and the distribution of titles at Ngerutechei. The narrator is himself a holder of one of the four corner-post titles of Imeiong and was formally instructing villages in the traditions of Ngeremlengui. The stone pavement Uchuladebong mentioned in the opening lines still stands in the center of the now-abandoned village of Ngerutechei. Of the many important points made in the text, the most important for the issue at hand is the linkage between the notion that the sacredness of all Belau remains in Imeiong, the first child of Milad (thus the political order of Imeiong was confirmed at the same moment that the polity of Belau as a whole was established), and the peculiarity of Imeiong's title system, namely, that wives rather than matrilineally related women bear female titles.

Story of Uchuladebong

The first lesson in the history of Ngeremlengui concerns Uchuladebong (Origin Point From Which We Go Forth) stone pavement. It all began when the Ruchel gods came to secure the actions of Milad at this place. They came here first and started what led to a lot of other things. We call this [stone pavement] Uchuladebong because this place marks where we began to obey the law, where we first instituted chiefly councils. And this place is the reason (*uchul*) that today we [Ngeremlengui] still hold the position of leadership [in Belau]. These are among the many "firsts" that started there. So it is said that this place is the "origin/cause of our going forth," and that the Ruchel came and began to list off that Imiungs is the first child of Milad, that Melekeok is the second, that Imeliik is the third, and that Oreor is the fourth. Imeliik is the third child and the only female.

This stone pavement Uchuladebong is at Ngerutechei village, and it is constructed out of basaltic rocks. When the Ruchel came and listed off these children of Milad, this is when they became the leaders of Belau. A single word/deed (*tekoi*) spoken on this one day became the reason for everything. The Ruchel came here to confirm the actions of Milad because the archaic world [of Chuab] had come to an end. The eight councils of the archaic world were over, and Milad gave birth anew to the human race, the people who are still alive today. So this means that these four children of Milad are to be respected and to be listened to. These four confer together and we listen to them. But then the sacredness of Melekeok was taken up and left here; and also the sacredness of Oreor was left here. The sacredness of this village [Imeiong] just stayed put and did not go anywhere. The sacredness of Imeliik, too, remained here. Melekeok respects this sacredness; it does not, however, respect this village itself. It is the sacredness of Melekeok which remains here which Melekeok respects; and the sacredness of Oreor remains here, so Oreor respects it. These villages respect neither the people nor the Ngaraimeiong council [of Imeiong].

And so the Ruchel said, "You *rubak* here [in Imeiong] are the four respected ones." The fact that there are four is because it follows the example of the four children of Milad. And so we respect them. Melekeok has its [chief] Reklai and the order of titleholders, but this village has the four respected ones, all of whom have identical authority. Today we use their names: Ngiraklang, Ngirturong, Ngirutelchii, and Ngirasibong. But in earlier times we just said, "the four respected ones are in the meetinghouse, so don't make any noise." Of the class of forbidden words like "horrendous" (*kdekudel*) and "dangerous" (*kengaol*) and "prohibited" (*mekull*), above them all is the word "sacred" (*meang*). And there is also the "sacredness of that which is sacred" (*engal er a meang*), which is above all the rest. The word "sacred" rests on top of all these other words, and the "sacredness of the sacred" (*engal*) rests on top of "sacred." When we break the law of the meetinghouse or the law of the village, we are fined; but there is no fine for violations of sacredness. We can also call the four children of Milad the "four new titleholders" (*teoa el becheklubak*), meaning that they are four new titleholders (*teoa el beches el rubak*). Now Rengulbai [chief of Imeliik] is not to be included in these four new chiefs, since he is female. But Imeliik does have a child, the village of Ngerard [i.e., Ngebuked], and so Mad [chief of Ngerard] is included among the four new chiefs, since he is the sister's son (*chebedel a kesol*). Now whereas the sacredness of Oreor remains with the *rubak* Ngirturong [chief of Imeiong], and the sacredness of Melekeok remains with Klang [house of Ngiraklang], the sacredness of the sacred is located in the public domain of Belau. And should we violate this, we are both cursed and fined.

These words were not spoken by Milad. Rather, it was Uchelianged (Foremost of Heaven) who issued them through the Ruchel, and it was the Ruchel who brought them here and who spoke at this place [Uchuladebong]. And this one word is the reason for many other things. So of all the villages in Belau, only Ngeremlengui has wives of the respected (*buch el chuong*), who are the wives of the four respected titleholders. Melekeok has Chebil Reklai [first female title] and Oreor has Bilung [first female title]. The reason for the difference is that Ngeremlengui has these four respected ones with no particular names assigned to them. Names like Ngiraklang and Ngirturong derive from the names of land parcels, just as do the names Ngirutelchii and Ngirasibong. These are just the four respected ones, and they do not have female relatives as respected, but rather their wives are in this role. In Ngeremlengui, in addition to the four respected ones, the other six titleholders are not to be respected, and consequently their wives are not wives of the respected. The other villages such as Oreor with its Bilung and Mirair [female titles] have female titleholders (*kldorolel a rubak*), and these women are the female relatives of the male titleholder. So in Ngeremlengui the wives of the titleholders are the female titleholders, and they take their names from the names of the houses [of their husbands]. When the wives of the respected titleholders come to a funeral, they take their seats at the opposite end of the meetinghouse from the male titleholders, with two on each side. They do not sit in the doorways assigned to the male titleholders. There, the female relatives of the titleholders have the responsibility to guard them. Old women, Blubult and Idub for instance, used to guard the meetinghouse and severely scold anyone who came near when the wives of these titleholders were there. But when one of the wives of the respected speaks, she must whisper and not use a loud voice.

When the Ruchel gods came to Ngerutechei after Milad had given birth to four sacred stones, they declared that the leading houses of Imeiong would henceforth be known by the collective label "the four respected ones." The particular titles associated with these four parcels of land were not created by the Ruchel at this moment; their action was rather to announce a new coordinated valuation of a preexisting arrangement. This contrasts sharply with other myths and stories which describe how various gods, including Uchelianged and the Ruchel, "plant" or invent titles de novo when forming a new chiefly council. At Uchuladebong, the Ruchel also confirmed Milad's quadripartite polity by legitimizing the homologous four-part political order of Imeiong, which then became the stable locus of the sacredness of Belau. Although Melekeok and Oreor, the second and fourth children of Milad, are established as villages geographically removed from their mother, the sacredness of these two villages remains behind at Imeiong. Here the terms "sacred" (*meang*) or "sacredness" (*engal*) refer to that abstract principle upon which rank is based.[3] In other words, since Melekeok's rank depends on its birth order in the sibling set of Milad's children, the sacredness of Melekeok is said to remain in Imeiong. The narrator of this text makes a consistent distinction between "sacredness" and "prohibition" (*mekull*), the former being grounded in presupposed rank, backed by the authority of gods, and resulting in the cursing of offenders; the latter being grounded in the active power of political position, backed by the authority of a title, and resulting in the fining of violators. On another occasion the narrator explained, "Prohibitions come out of the mouth of a *rubak*. If a *rubak* speaking formally says, 'That over there is hereby prohibited,' it is as if sacredness itself commands him to say this. But sacredness cannot come out of the mouth, only prohibitions." Thus that Melekeok's sacredness remains in Imeiong in no way implies that its titleholders lack independent power to create laws and impose financial penalties, or that people in Melekeok owe respect to the individual leaders or people of Imeiong.

This notion of "the sacred remains" is entirely consistent with a general Belauan pattern in which the first position in a ranked set of terms functions as the constitutive member of the set. For example, the principal house in a set of affiliated houses (*kebliil*) is at one level one house among many, and at a second level constitutive of the set considered as a unit. Similarly, a chiefly title has one assigned seat in the village council, but also represents the entire village in dealings with outsiders. The first position is thus instantiated and anchors all the lower-ranking elements in a series. In the context of Milad and Uchuladebong, this principle of hierarchy implies that Imeiong functions both as one of Milad's four children and as the instantiation of the sibling set taken as a totality. This, I believe, helps explain the conjuncture of the ideology of Imeiong's transcending interdistrict conflict and the notion that Belau's sacredness remains in Imeiong. Imeiong's immunity from political entanglement is not, then, grounded merely in its high rank among Milad's children but rather in its being the locus of the "sacredness of

---

3. Kubary (1900b:24) concludes that *meang* "does not include only the privileges of rank, but also the qualities which form the basis of this rank."

the sacred" of all Belau. Making war on Imeiong would be, therefore, a threat to the attacker's own rank.

So according to the narrator of this text, there is a direct connection between Imeiong's position as the firstborn of Milad and two pecularities of its internal political organization. First, in contrast to other cpaital villages where the most important rank distinction is drawn between the chief (*merredel*) and all other titleholders, the crucial split in Imeiong is between the four respected titleholders as a set and the rest. Second, of all the villages in Belau, Imeiong is the only one where wives of titleholders rather than matrilineally related women carry female titles.[4] Formally, these "wives of the respected" titles are formed by adding the female prefix Dirra- (*dil er a,* "women of/at") to the name of the husband's house: Dirraklang, Dirrturong, Dirrutelchii, and Dirrasibong.[5] Under normal circumstances senior women (*ourrot*) of a titled house exercise their authority in selecting a matrilineally strong male to carry the house's title. But since these women normally reside with their husbands in other villages, their power is not residentially anchored. In Imeiong, however, a female titleholder lives in the same household as the male titleholder but maintains matrilineal ties elsewhere. For example, Dirraklang lives in Imeiong at Klang but plays only a small role in decisions concerning Klang as a political unit.

For two years in the field I puzzled over these anomalies and remained especially attentive for any offered explanation. I was convinced—perhaps because so little else was making any sense—that there must be some significant connection between Imeiong's distinctive custom of having wives as female titleholders and its unique position as Milad's firstborn. Although these two traditions were often mentioned in the same breath (as in the text given above), I never heard an explanation that completely satisfied me. The three rationalizations I did record are as follows. First, Imeiong does not use the expression "female counterpart titleholder" (*kldorolel a rubak*), because this would imply that a titleholder's wife would exercise power in the affairs of a house with which she has only affinal connection—this, of course, pre-

---

4. According to Krämer (1917–29, 3:293), the "female titleholders" (*rubak el dil*) necessarily belong to the matrilineal line of their houses, while the "wives of titleholders" (*rebuch el rubak*) are only affinally linked.

5. People in Ngeremlengui refer to these women individually as "female titleholders" (*rubak el dil*) and collectively as "wives of the respected" (*buch el chuong*), rather than by the usual label "female counterpart titleholder" (*kldorolel a rubak*), a term derived from the word *kederaol,* "side of the canoe toward the beach." a *kldorolel a rubak* is thus a female counterbalance to the extended (male) outrigger of the ship of state. Krämer (1917–29, 3:293) gives a different etymology based on the word *kldelaol,* "motherhood," but I suspect that he simply misheard the distinction between *l* and *r.*

supposes rather than explains the distinctive title system. Second, women from lower-ranking villages within the district can marry into Imeiong's leading houses, and the respect which accrues to the wife of a titleholder would rub off on her house in Ngeremetengel or Ngchemesed—an interesting program for manipulating an ongoing custom. And third, Imeiong awards this special dignity to wives of titleholders because when the Ruchel came to legitimize the four leading houses as residences of the four respected ones they awarded this status to a category of titleholders without naming a particular list of individual titles. That is, it would be illogical for the village to have a list of specially designated female titles when its high-ranking male titles merely follow the names of land parcels—a very suggestive idea, but one which does not make clear the sought-after link to the Milad story.[6]

My own hypothesis about the structural connection between Imeiong's position in the Milad story and its system of female titles draws on all three of these explanations, as well as on the conclusions from chapter 3 concerning the cultural meaning of quadripartition. I think that simultaneity in narrative is a Belauan way of representing achieved stability, and that quadripartition in institutional arrangement represents historical maturity. Together the Milad story and the text given above about the Ruchel gods at Uchuladebong pavement signal a moment of cultural transformation whose justification lies in symbols of stable permanence and autochthonous integrity. The Milad polity is represented in sacred stones whose names follow the names of the four principal villages of Belau; the Ruchel distributed male and female respected titles at a raised stone platform in Ngerutechei, the name of which expresses perfectly this combination of presupposed order and foward-looking motion: Uchuladebong (Origin Point From Which We Go Forth), that is, go forth to become leaders of Belau. Both Milad's death at Ngeroach mountain, one of the highest points on Babeldaob, and the Ruchel's legitimization of preexisting land parcels in Imeiong suggest the autochthonous quality of these events, in contrast to many stories about migrations from foreign places and externally derived power. In other words, everything points to this mythological moment as a declaration of historical transformation without the assumption of external motivation or internal contingency.

6. As symbolic reinforcement for this ideology of undifferentiation among the four titleholders, the backrest stones standing at the four corners of Chemeraech square (where these titleholders reentered the village after leaving Ngerutechei) are not assigned or ranked. "The seats are not specifically designated, since they are simply the 'four to be respected' and their powers are exactly the same, and their wives, similarly, are the 'wives of the respected.'"

To this must be added the important point that both these stories are told from the point of view of Ngeremlengui, more particularly from the point of view of the capital village Imeiong, even though their range encompasses all of Belau. The narrative which claims that the sacredness of Oreor and Melekeok remains with the four respected titleholders of Imeiong echoes the Milad story's description of all the village stones except Imiungselbad (Imuings Stone) as being removed from their original position to more distant spots. This pattern, as has been noted several times, is not unusual: the highest-ranking term in a series legitimizes its position by insisting on its constitutive power.

With these points in mind the hypothesis can be stated simply: the Story of Milad and the narrative of Uchuladebong enable Imeiong to preserve an ideology of preeminent village rank by joining an affirmation of its constitutive role in a pan-Belauan siblingship polity with a complementary denial of actual engagement in affinal alliances with other important villages. Given the combination of matrilineal descent the virilocal residence in traditional Belau, senior women of a high-ranking house, including the one carrying the house's female title (*kldorolel a rubak*), marry into roughly equally high-ranking houses in other villages. And in general, the higher the rank of the house, the more vital that alliance be created outside the district, since the ensuing affinal exchange pattern will be proportionally intense and the need to avoid the financial penalty for "falling" (that is, for marrying down) will be more severe. As a result, chiefly houses in a district capital are likely not only to send their title-carrying females to marry important titleholders in rival districts, but also to receive title-carrying women as wives for their own male titleholders. Thus increasing local rank correlates with greater involvement in a network of distant affinal obligations.

Now for a village like Imeiong, which asserts that it is the resting place of the sacredness of all Belau, and that it is immune from military attack and generally aloof from the petty political struggles of Oreor and Melekeok, the existence of these affinal ties presents a potential threat to its transcendent position, "dwelling as if in the heavens" (i.e., Kerngilianged). The option of Imeiong's taking wives entirely from within the district—a well-documented regularity—does not resolve the problem about sending its own women with their female titles to reside elesewhere. An elegant solution, however, is to simultaneously transform in-marrying women into Imeiong women and to send its own women to other districts without female titles, by simply assigning female titles to the incoming wives rather than to the outgoing sisters of titleholders. In this way, powerful women from other villages carrying *kldorolel*-type titles (that is, matrilineal titles) who come to Imeiong are relabeled by titles derived from their new husbands' houses: Dirr-aklang, Dirrturong, etc. Their respected quality as *buch el chuong* then becomes a formal justification for isolating them from ongoing village politics: as the narrator observed, two matrilineally strong senior women named Blubult and Idub guard the seating positions of these women in the meetinghouse, where the female titleholders can only speak in whispers. A man related to the Ngerturong house once told me that the woman holding the female title Dirrturong is respected by the village, but should keep "as silent as a statue" when village affairs are being discussed.

A fiction of nonalliance is thereby perpetuated, enabling Imeiong to stress its consanguinally calculated rank as the eldest sibling among Milad's children without the evident impingement of affinally determined involvement with other districts' chiefly houses. In an interesting twist on the more common patrilineal ramage systems found in Oceania, the Milad myth asserts a village-based matrifilial consanguinity which is thus reinforced by a denial of house-based marital alliance. And finally, the presence of four respected male titleholders and four female wives of the respected, all bearing titles derived from Imeiong's original land parcels, reinforces the mythic connection between quadripartition, historical maturity, organizational integrity, and high rank. The terms of this solution recall the connection between extensive matrimonial alliance and an openness to planned development in medieval Japan, which Lévi-Strauss (1985:78) juxtaposes to the nostalgic self-reproduction encouraged by marriage among close kin in Fiji. In Belau, wide-ranging alliance is certainly an option for building political power, but only at the expense of admitting the necessity of its acquisition.

NGEREMETENGEL: SUBORDINATE VILLAGE OR EMERGENT CAPITAL?

From the perspective of high-ranking Imeiong, the villages of Ngeremetengel and Ngchemesed participate in district polity as sides of the mangrove channel allied to two principal houses in Imeiong, namely, Ngerturong and Klang. The assignment of these two member villages to two chiefly houses at the capital is consistent with the pervasive division of responsibility between chiefs Ngirturong and Ngiraklang and implies that people from these low-ranking villages have an obligation to contribute food, money, and labor to the prescribed social units at Imeiong. The clear rank differentiation reflected in this categorization is not, however, accepted in these terms by people from Ngeremetengel themselves, who point to the fact that for over a hundred years

Ngeremetengel rather than Imeiong has been the residence of successive titleholders from Ngerturong house and the center of commercial activity within the district. These conflicting understandings are manifested in contrasting narratives told by people from Imeiong and Ngeremetengel, stories which reveal predictably different assumptions about the link between historical processes and political rank.

Understanding these stories is further complicated by the fact that there are two adjacent mangrove channels leading to the general Ngeremetengel area (see map 4). The northern channel, named Ngerekebrong, leads to the landing place of the earlier village site named Beluurametengel (Village at the Descent), while the southern channel, named Oderderong, leads to Ngeremetengel proper, that is, the village visited by Semper in the mid-nineteenth century and more fully documented by Krämer in 1910 (1917–29, 3:149–50).[7] The distinction between the two village sites is frequently expressed in terms of their respective important houses, Dilubech and Mechoang: the older Beluurametengel is called the "village of Dilubech" and the newer Ngeremetengel site is known as the "village of Mechoang."[8]

The Imeiong version of the story places the history of Ngeremetengel in the context of a genre of traditions describing the migration (*omerael*) of houses and whole villages from the southern rock islands to Babeldaob. These people abandoned their homes after living conditions became intolerable because of warfare, lack of water, depopulation, threatening monsters, and natural catastrophes. In this case, people from the island of Ngerecheu near Ngemelis left their homes and under the leadership of chief Ucherecheu (Foremost of Ngerecheu) sailed north along the west coast of Babeldaob, where they finally entered Ngerekebrong channel. At that time there was no established village there, so Ucherecheu dispatched a man to Imeiong to ask permission from chiefs Ngirturong and Ngiraklang for his people to build a new village on the wooded slope above the channel. At first Ngirturong,

7. Actually, Captain Wilson also visited Ngeremetengel briefly on 12 October 1783 on his way from Imeiong back to Oreor. "About one o'clock all landed; and the King and his retinue, with our people, walked up the country about a mile, to a town called Aramalorgoo [Ngeremlengui], where was exhibited a dance of spearmen; after which the usual sort of refreshments were served to the company. They then returned to their canoes" (Keate 1788:179). Since Wilson gives only the district name and does not provide any geographical details, it is impossible to determine if his party entered the village at Ngerekebrong channel or at Oderderong channel.

8. After 1947 people moved into a third area of land reclaimed from the mangrove swamp by the refuse from a Japanese bauxite-rinsing plant located on a high rock above Ometubet river. People jokingly refer to this as the "swamp" or as the "third Ngeremetengel."

whose responsibility covered affairs arising from the direction of the lower sea to the south, did not grant the request, since no valuable had been paid for the rights sought. So only when Ucherecheu sent over two money pieces he had brought with him from Ngerecheu was permission granted.

The first piece of money, called Large Omrukl even though it was the smaller of the two, went to Ngerturong house to gain rights of entry (*olsisebel a beluu*). The larger piece of money, named Small Omrukl, was paid to Klang house as the cost of building roads and platforms in the new village, Beluurametengel. Work done to prepare a village for habitation is called "cutting the vine" (*oretel a kebeas*), after the name of the vinelike plant (*kebeas*) used to measure straight lines during house and road construction. According to Imeiong sources, neither the entrance-into-the-village money nor the cutting-the-vine money paid to Ngirturong and Ngiraklang actually purchased the land of Beluurametengel, a contention strongly denied by residents of present-day Ngeremetengel, for whom the money was indeed the legitimate purchase price of their village (see below).

In order to impress upon these new residents that their existence depended entirely on the goodwill of high-ranking Imeiong, Ngiraklang and Ngirturong informed the new residents that they were only permitted to fish in a small lagoon section near the shore and that they must regularly bring fish as tribute to Imeiong. They were allowed to cultivate taro in Ngeruilang swamp owned by Klang house, and part of their crop was required to be returned to this house. Only much later did they gain access to the larger taro swamp Chum (Snail) owned by people from Ngetechum village. Established at Beluurametengel under the haughty eye of Ngirturong, the people from Ngerecheu were given a new leader to head their local council. Ngiruturong and Ngiraklang conferred together at Imeiong and decided that it would be dangerous to have Ucherecheu continue as the chief, since he was a rich and powerful man who might some day gain enough strength to challenge their authority in the district. So these two chiefs appointed Ngiradilubech to be the new leader of Beluurametengel, and the house of this new *rubak* was named Dilubech (Sprung Up) to signal its sudden, artificial institution. This practice of deliberately altering the rank order of titleholders or of demoting a chief to a lesser position is a regular feature of migration stories and, especially in this case, illustrates the fragility and contingency of rank in noncapital villages.

In fact, migration legends depicting the stages of founding of Ngchemesed's houses show a structure parallel those dealing with Ngeremetengel. At present, the six titled houses of Ngchemesed are

Ngeremakiar (*kebliil* is named Ked), Mesebelau (*kebliil* is named Se-lau), Ngeriem, Ilild, Ngerechumengal, and Temoungil. But according to folklore, the fourth house Ilild was the original occupant of all the land now controlled by Ngchemesed. These people are related to peo-ple from Ngerebuuch in Ngeaur on the basis of the journey of Obakel-sechal, a man from Ngeaur who recovered from facial injuries caused by a bamboo spear (*ilild*) at Ilild. When he returned to Ngeaur he took with him the child who had nursed him back to health, and after her death the two villages exchanged "ancestral spirit money" (*udoud el bladek*) in memory of their linkage. Another group of people came from Ngeruangel, the now-submerged atoll north of Ngcheangel, via a small village named Ngedesiur, and they founded the house named Ngeriem, with its title Chaderuangel (Man from Ngeruangel). The houses of Ngeremakiar and Mesebelau were both established by people from Ngemelis island who returned to Babeldaob in search of their former relatives from Ngeruangel who had taken up residence in Ngchemsed. The leader of this return migration was the famous warrior Uchermelis (Foremost of Ngemelis), but upon his arrival the council at Imeiong removed him to the sixth position in rank and instituted Beches (New) as the new chief of Ngchemsed, a village now clearly under the sway of Imeiong.

More particularly, Ngchemsed is called a "village linked to Klang," because of a kinship connection between the houses of Ilild and Klang. Analogously, people of Beluurametengel are considered to be "children of the house of Ngerturong," since Ngirturong would use his own money to pay off their fines as he would for his own children.

The village of Beluurametengel flourished for an indeterminate peri-od in this low status of servants of Ngerturong house, until the decision of Ngiraklang to throw off the oppression of Uluang village (located on an elevated hillcrest southwest of Imeiong) gave the people of Beluurametengel an opportunity to make Imeiong indebted to their village (see a full account in chapter 7). Thanks to the consolidated efforts of warriors from allied villages (such as Ulimang, Ngellau, Ngeiungl, and Beluurametengel), Imeiong succeeded in burning Ulu-ang to the ground and in putting its residents to flight. And to repay the incurred debt, the council at Imeiong granted Beluurametengel three privileges (*klebkall*). First, when the titleholders of Imeiong as-semble at night in their meetinghouse at Orukei square, a person from Beluurametengel has the task of lighting the lamp. Second, if a funeral or some other customary activity is held in Imeiong, women from Beluurametengel can wear fiber rain hats only after Uchelebil, the female titleholder from Dilubech house, puts one on. And third, Ngirturong and Ngiraklang granted the village permission to use fruit from the mangrove trees growing at a nearby creak as their "taro patch." All three of these privileges are the historical signs of the assistance given by Beluurametengel to Imeiong in its campaign against Uluang, but they are at the same time marks of the condescending attitude of Imeiong: to light the lamp at Orukei, to wear rain hats while carrying taro from a great distance, and to have a mangrove tree as a taro patch are signs of being a dependent member village (*kekere el beluu*).

This paternal attitude on the part of Imeiong toward Beluurametengel (and by extension Ngeremetengel) is reflected in a document distributed by Imeiong chiefs to villagers as part of instruction in the late 1970s in traditional stories and customs, a section of which I translate below:

> When the people of Ngerecheu came, they landed at the shallow spot in front of Ngeremetengel and asked permission to enter the village. They paid out a valuable named Large Omrukl, which was the price of their entering the channel. So they entered at Ngerekebrong. After this the village was cleared, and they sent over another piece of money, Small Omrukl, as the cutting-the-vine payment for fixing up the village. The Large Omrukl went to Ngerturong and the Small Omrukl went to Klang. This village of Ngeremetengel is like a child of the house of Ngerturong, in that if there is some customary event at Ngerturong house they go fishing for them. They were only permitted to fish in front of Iungs [small rock in front of the village]. Ngirturong said to them, "Go fishing, and bring your catch here and then you will be permitted to fish at Ngeluong [in front of Imeiong]." In former times, if [people from Ngeremetengel] were fined, Ngirturong would pay their fine according to this pattern. They took money to stuff into Ngirturong's handbag, and then he paid their fine; and if it was a low-ranking person who had no money, he would just stick his hand inside Ngirturong's handbag and then depart. Ngirturong would then know that this person had no money, so he would take care of him.

The story of the founding of the village site at Oderderong channel parallels the story of Beluurametengel. A second migration of people from Ngerecheu followed the path created by their former village-mates, but when Renguul and his group approached Ngeremlengui they entered the southern channel in the hope of finding available land to settle on. Ngiradilubech gave permission for them to build their houses at this second site, and then the last inhabitants of Ngetechum village willed their taro patches (Chum and Omeklochel) to the new-comers. Renguul's house Mechoang became the most important house in the village, although Dilubech remained the overall leader in this area of the district. Over the centuries the distinction between the people of Dilubech and the people of Mechoang became blurred, especially since the latter group grew stronger, and houses from Beluurametengel started to relocate at Ngeremetengel. At some point Ngeremetengel was granted permission to build a permanent meetinghouse for its ti-tleholders, a privilege denied to Beluurametengel. The expansion of Ngeremetengel was further stimulated when Ngirturong Otobed (Banished) built a house for his high-ranking family at Ongerool on a parcel of land ceded from Mechoang house. Ngirturong's presence was also the reason that nineteenth-century traders made this village the head-quarters for their various commercial operations, and since this Ngir-turong simultaneously held the title Ngiraikelau in Oreor, this tie cemented the political alliance between the two districts.

The version of the founding of Ngeremetengel told by people of that village differs in important respects from the Imeiong version presented above, notably in linking the village's history to the wider context of dynamic shifts in political rank within Ngeremlengui as a whole and in reinterpreting the contemporary presence of chief Ngirturong in their village. In this version, Beluurametengel must be distinguished not only from the more recent village site at Ngeremetengel but also from an even earlier village named Omisaolmlai (Observe Canoes), the stone foundations of which can still be seen on the hillside just below the Japanese cannons pointing out to the western reef opening. It was the people of Omisaolmlai, not the people of Dilubech, who first came from the rock island Ngerecheu when that island was destroyed by warfare.

> When they arrived at Ngeremlengui there were no people living on the hillside above Ngerekebrong channel, so their leader Ucherecheu established his new village there. No money was paid to the chief of Imeiong, and no limitations were placed on land ownership and fishing rights, since Imeiong itself had not yet overthrown oppressive Uluang to emerge as the head of the district. A second independent migration from a different rock island near Tabermediu [south of Oreor] then arrived, and these were the people who founded Dilubech. But now when chief Ngiradilubech entered the channel at Ngerekebrong he had to get permission from Ucherecheu of Omisaolmlai. Although these two villages existed side by side, no connecting road was built between

them. Ngiradilubech refused to join Ucherecheu, because he would then lose his status as an independent leader. If Ngirturong and Ngiraklang come to Ngeremetengel they cannot go above [i.e., outrank] Ngiradilubech. Before the time when Imeiong was a strong village it was under the control of chief of Ngesisech village, and when the people of Ngesisech died out they came down to Imeiong and were under the authority of Imeiong. In just this way Ucherecheu took his village and went down to enter into the village of Dilubech, and he was then under Ngiradilubech, for he had been able to protect his own village or prepare food, should a visiting party arrive.

This version offers an explicitly dynamic view of the relationship between capital villages and member villages within a district, in direct contrast to Imeiong's own static view of its inherent rank as the result of the distribution of titles at Uchuladebong. In the dynamic view, village rank is not immune to the pressures of demography and the impact of political change. If the chief of a capital village relocates at a small village when his own becomes uninhabitable, underpopulated, or destroyed, or when he is banished from his home, he cannot then exercise the power of his title in the context of a new village. While he might continue to be respected until his death, his title will cease to possess the inherent sacredness (*meang*) which is the basis for that respect. Chiefly power is, in this view, localized at the title's traditional stone pavement, and capital village status reflects actual political strength rather than some ideology of sacred rank.

The village of Ngeremetengel (also called Oliau in chants and songs), the story continues, was not founded by Renguul of Mechoang house, but rather by a rich and clever man named Deluus, who acquired rights to the land of Mechoang by fooling the chiefs of Imeiong. Deluus and his people set out from Ngerecheu island and passed through Beliliou, Imeliik, and Ngchesar, and finally came to Ngersuul, a village on the east coast of Babeldaob. Deluus lived for a time in Ngersuul, while others in his party, including his sister Dildenguich, continued on to Melekeok, Chol, and then finally to Ollei in Ngerechelong, where Deluus's sister lived at the first house, Ukall.

Deluus and his sister both entered Ngeremlengui, though by independent paths: Deluus came to Ngeremetengel after passing through Ngetbang and Ngereklngong, while Dildenguich came to Imeiong to take the highest male title, Ngirturong, following an ancient *kebliil* path between Ukall and Ngerturong houses. While still in Ngereklngong, Deluus sent word to a fellow villager from Ngerecheu named Rebes for him to set sail with his people and for them to travel up the west coast until they sighted a small island with a hole pierced through the rock which stands directly in front of Oderderong channel. There they were to turn in to rejoin Deluus at Ngeremetengel. In order to secure rights to land and taro patches at Ngeremetengel, Deluus sent two pieces of money, a smaller piece called Large Omrukl and a larger piece called Small Omrukl, to Ngiraklang and Ngirturong in Imeiong as the price of the land of Mechoang. But since Ngirturong was at this time Dildenguich, the sister of Deluus—a fact carefully concealed from the other Imeiong titleholders—the money just circulated within the family. People in these two villages continued to live together with mutual understanding and friendship, and a sense of unity grew between them.

As a result of this intrigue, not only did the people related to Deluus own the land of Mechoang in complete independence from Ngiradilubech at neighboring Beluurametengel, but they also established a path between Mechoang and the chiefly house of Ngerturong in Imeiong through their relation to Dildenguich Ngirturong. According to this version, then, the reason that Ngeremetengel is the side of the channel of Imeiong, and the reason that a later Ngirturong titleholder left Imeiong to live at Ongerool near Mechoang, is not that Ngirturong automatically holds responsibility toward the lower sea (thus encompassing these immigrants from the rock islands), but that this early Ngirturong was herself related to the original founders of Ngeremetengel.

Not only did Ngeremetengel have a strong bond with Imeiong, but it also developed an equally strong tie with powerful Oreor village. This came about as the result of heroic deeds by two young men, Klasekl and Kladikm, from the houses of Dilubech and Mechoang, respectively. While they were on an expedition in the rock islands to collect resin for clay lamps, their food and water supply ran low, so they put in at Oreor. But as they walked up from the landing place into the village, they noticed that the paths were deserted and the houses boarded up. At Idid house they discovered an old woman, who explained, "My children, the reason this village appears empty is that a war party from the east coast and from Ngerdmau is threatening us, so the people of Oreor have all fled to Metukerariang in the rock islands." Klasekl and Kladikm decided to defend the village—coming to the aid of high-ranking people in distress is always a profitable venture—and managed to kill the leader of the war party and turn back the attack.

When the leaders of Idid and Ikelau houses returned to the village and learned what had happened, they listed the rewards for these two brave men:

From now on, if you sail to the rock islands, and should your supply of food, water, or betelnut run out, simply place an *olangch* on the hull of your canoe, and men from Oreor who pass by will see the *olangch* and provide you with whatever you need. Never forget the *olangch*. Also, if you come to Oreor you can dock at Kliis Oliau and wait for a messenger from Ibedul or Ngiraikelau to escort you into the village. If there is a dance taking place at the canoe shed at Delui landing, it is usually prohibited for anyone to enter, but you can use the *olangch* and go inside. But if someone fails to use the *olangch,* he will be considered a deceiver and will be killed. And if there is a feast in the village, you are permitted to attend. Place your *olangch* on whatever food you desire and the people from Oreor will give it to you.

This second version, told from the point of view of Ngeremetengel, has few elements in common with the first version. No mention is made of the grant of land and taro patches from Ngetechum to Mechoang; no connection is postulated between the original migration which landed at Ngerekebrong and the later one which landed at Oderderong. And more importantly, the two pieces of money are said to have been the purchase price of the village of Ngeremetengel rather than merely payment for the cost of building roads and platforms. And according to this version, the original title at Mechoang is Iechadrametengel rather than Renguul; Renguul was actually the leader of a small hamlet named Ii (Cave), located within the territory of Ngereklngong village, but when he was unable to meet his chiefly obligations at a ceremony for purchasing a meetinghouse this title was removed from Ii and brought to Mechoang. And finally, the special privileges extended by the leaders of Oreor to Ngeremetengel are the real reason that Oreor and Ngeremlengui are mutual friends, not the *kebliil* relationship between the high-ranking houses Ngerturong and Ikelau.

Apart from these details, however, this story contains a radically different theory about the nature of village foundation and about the link between village rank and chiefly rank. In place of an ideology of quadripartition and the implication of inherent rank found in the narrative about Uchuladebong, this storyteller from Ngeremetengel put forth a view based on the model of paths, according to which the four houses in a village are the result of chronologically layered processes rather than the product of instantaneous quadripartition institution by the gods.

I think that in olden times the villages in Belau did not each have four houses. In each migration there was only one leader, and if there were other men they were like the second and third mates on a ship. And when they arrived, they all lived together. And then later a completely different migration came, and so after a while there would be several "captains" [uses English word], and since no captain wanted to live under the authority of an earlier captain they would build an independent house. And so in this way there would come to be four houses [in a village]. But the four houses all were founded at different times.

This sensitivity to historical process extends to the broader issue of the development of Ngeremlengui's district polity. But in contrast to the comparison of stories about the founding of Ngeremetengel discussed above, where storytellers from the two villages presented distinct narratives, in this broader perspective of districtwide polity all the narratives I recorded were told by Imeiong people. So the distinction between a high-ranking perspective and a low-ranking perspective comes rather from differing interpretations placed on a unified set of stories. In particular, Ngeremetengel commentators seized upon the dynamic implications of two interlocking stories involving Imeiong, the first about the fall of Ngeremeskang village (see chapter 5) and the second about the destruction of Uluang village (see chapter 7), which together challenge some of the static assumptions of the Milad-Uchuladebong narrative.

According to the interpretation from Ngeremetengel people, the political development of the district has repeated the same process four times. First, when the earliest district polity centered around Ngeremeskang (the capital of the federation of tribute-paying villages called Kerngilianged) collapsed, its leader, Obak of Ibedechal house, abandoned the capital and went to live at Roisbeluu, near the large village Ngesisech, which then became the second capital of the reorganized district. And then Ngeremlengui emerged as a third political order under the leadership of chiefs Ngiraklang and Ngirturong only when Imeiong managed to defeat Uluang. And now that these Imeiong leaders have moved to Ngeremetengel, it is easy to make the analogy that they are, in fact, under the authority of Ngiradilubech, the local chief. Some people from Ngeremetengel told me that the presence of Ngiraklang and Ngirturong is proof that Ngeremetengel has become the new capital village.

While I was in the field the ambiguity of the presence of high-ranking families in the lower-ranking village was played out one night in competitive dancing. Dance troops from Imeiong and from Ngeremetengel alternated in performing songs, the texts of some of which rather pointedly referred to individuals and families in the district. At one point in the festivities, the Imeiong dancers sang a brief song taught to them by one of the Imeiong titleholders now residing in Ngeremetengel:

Dance Song of Imeiong

Ak mla er a Batkiekl el mei tia el eou me dechor er a ürengii Belau.
Kmal milsang e mo er ngii okuk e elecha e ak uluk er ngii.
Biusech a medak, melusech a renguk.
Oltitech e kau a mengerechir e ngak a mekerior el chad.
Ng chemoit a beluu, ng chemoit a blai.
E ko er a di mengedeoal el chad el mo kalel a tengadidik.

From the High-Jumping-Off-Place, I have come to this place
 below, where I stand and survey all Belau.
Looking carefully at it, I see my anchor and now I fix it fast here.
My eyes are wide awake, my spirit is fortunate.
Men of Ngaraoltitech club, you have come here and see me as a
 most unfortunate person.
My village is abandoned, my house is left behind.
And now I am like a homeless wanderer, who will someday be
 food for the kingfisher.

Whereas the titleholder himself recognizes that his relocation from the High-Jumping-Off-Place (i.e., Imeiong) has resulted in personal prosperity, the young men visiting from Ngaraoltitech club can only see him as a wanderer, to be pitied because his original village and house are abandoned.

What is important to note in comparing these "tales of two cities" is that the Imeiong perspective focuses on the negative implication of village migration traditions, namely, that successive journeys along a path involve a degree of contingency not part of the notion of the sacred remains found in the story of the origin of Imeiong's (and Belau's) cornerpost order. From Ngeremetengel's point of view, much of the traditional evidence about the dynamics of the district's political history—the fall of Ngeremeskang, the defeat of Uluang, the presentation of Small Omrukl and Large Omrukl, the abandonment of Imeiong's chiefly houses, and the overall rise of Ngeremetengel's commercial importance—points to a realistic conception of political rank as reflective of actual power and indexed by factors such as population, economic growth, and the residential presence of high-ranking titleholders. What gives the Imeiong perspective its legitimacy, however, is simply the fact that its version is the one taught in district schools, recited by chiefs at customary gatherings, used as evidence in land claims hearings, recorded in various local archives, and told as the official version to visiting anthropologists (cf. Feeley-Harnik 1978:411–12). Political rank thus depends in part on the control of historicizing *olangch* (narratives as well as stones) and in part on the strategic manipulation of the rhetorical implications of political models such as paths and cornerposts.

CHAPTER

7

The Story of Ngeremlengui

Despite the ideological claim that Imeiong, as the oldest child of Milad, stays away from the petty struggles of other villages as it looks down on all lower-ranking people with its air of superiority, many stories I heard in Ngeremlengui show that the village was constantly embroiled in interdistrict competition, warfare, alliances, exchange, and political intrigue, and that these intervillage relations were directly linked to the political conditions of the village's high-ranking cornerpost houses. This chapter narrates the story of Ngeremlengui from approximately 1700 to about 1900, the period during which the "classic" organization of titles, houses, councils, and clubs described in the previous chapters took shape, and during which the pattern of hierarchical relations between capital village and member villages within the district became consolidated. The five events which are the focal points of this narrative—three wars, one peace treaty, and one assassination—do not represent a selection on my part; rather, I present these events in much the same way as they were told, retold, and explained to me by local storytellers. In order to illustrate the rhetorical and poetic style of these traditions, I reproduce several verbatim texts, although I generally synthesize material collected from different Imeiong informants at different times. To increase intelligibility, at several points I also interweave explanatory information that would be presupposed by Belauan storytellers and their audiences; and to relate these stories to Western historical periods, I cite foreign documents which shed additional light on the narratives. Taken together, these stories flesh out the schematic analysis of mechanisms of intervillage relations reviewed in chapter 2 and give life to the normative description of Ngeremlengui's political organization presented in chapter 5. Of particular importance in all of these stories is the narrative device of concentrating on the *olangch*, such as

stones, trees, valuables, place names, titles, and customary privileges, all
of which function not just as signs of history, that is, as commemorative
markers of events, but also as signs in history, that is, as foci of ongoing
political struggle.

THE DESTRUCTION OF ULUANG

In light of the high status conferred upon Imiungs (or Imeiong) as the
first child of the goddess Milad and upon its four principal titleholders
as the four respected ones, it is surprising to hear stories which say that
the village was at one time enslaved by Uluang, a village located in the
shadow of Roismlengui mountain midway between present-day Imeiong and Ngeremetengel (see map 3). Today Uluang's impressive
house foundations and meetinghouse platforms can be seen on both
sides of the Japanese-built road which crosses the hillside between
Umad and Luul bridges.[1] The village's most spectacular features are
two terraced hills visible from almost any point in the surrounding
countryside.[2] The names of these two hills, Uudes (Navel) and Umerang (Truth), are also the names of the two highest-ranking houses in
Melekeok, a district on the other side of the island. Spanning the distance between Umerang and Uudes is a monumental stone square with
house platforms, a raised stone road, and other stoneworks. Three
meetinghouse foundations are easily located by their stone remains still
standing high above the grass: Tellach (Law) lies just to the north of
the modern road in a small strip of wooded land, Omekesebech (Self-
restraint) is located to the right of the road as it descends to Umad
channel, and an unnamed platform stands between the two hills at the
southwestern corner of Umerang hill. Lucking's (1984) recent archaeological survey has revealed fourteen house platforms in the village,
most of which are located on the sloping terraced apron which reaches
toward the swampland to the south. Finally, at the extreme southern
boundary of the complex is the taro swamp Ngeruuchel, created according to tradition by Milad herself.

The name Uluang is widely known today largely because this village
was a stopping place for a group of wealthy people who migrated from
Ngeruangel atoll, passed through Uluang, and eventually founded the
important house of Uudes in Melekeok. This migration story as recited

1. The present road passes to the north of the hills of Umerang and Uudes, while the
ancient path follows the outlines of the mangrove swamp to the south. In the process of
building roads and digging foxholes, the Japanese destroyed much of the old stonework
of Uluang.

2. A photograph is reproduced in Osborne 1966:163, fig. 52A.

by an elderly *rubak* from Melekeok is an excellent example of the important mnemonic function of place names in constructing a linear chain of social identity:

Story of the Migration of Uudes

The title Reklai started with a group of people from Ngeruangel who later moved to Ngcheangel. This group of people entered a passage called Uaingtuul and from there proceeded on to Ngeruudes. They did not stay long, for they moved again to Klubas, and then on to Ngerkebang. Ngeriungs in Rengoor was their next destination; however, they stopped there briefly before they went on to Ngerbelas, Orak, and then on to Ngerechur. When they arrived at Ngerechur, they lived in a house on top of a cave called Ngerusekluk. They left Ngerusekluk and moved to Ngerudecheong in Omisaears, then to the house of Ngesechei. In Ngsechei they started building their house in Orukil. They did not stay in Orukil very long, for they began to search for a suitable place to settle. They moved out of Orukil and traveled to Chol and stopped briefly at the house of Tengadik to drink water and exchange a few words, then continued their journey. They arrived in Ngurang, settled and stayed for a good length of time. They were not quite satisfied with what they found in Ngurang, so they moved out again and went to Ngeremlengui by way of Chebei and they climbed to a location called Uluang. In Uluang they started preparing for permanent living accomodation. They gathered rocks for house foundations and meetinghouses which can still be seen today. (PCAA, Melekeok File)

Although this portion of the migration story does not give any specific information concerning the role Imiungs played in the settlement of Uluang, it does go on to mention that, at least initially, the relationship between the newcomers and the inhabitants of Ngeremlengui (or Imiungs) was peaceful, if not cooperative. "These people lived there comfortably because when the people of Ngeremlengui went fishing they divided their catch with the people of Uluang. And there was one old woman who gave taro from her patch at Ngeruuchel." My informants from Ngeremlengui corrected this statement concerning the name of the taro patch: the women from Imiungs, in particular the women from the house of Klang, worked in the taro patch at Ngeruilang at Ngeremetengel. Because the sun would be comfortably at their backs in the morning and again in the afternoon, hardworking "wives of men" (*buch el sechal*) from Klang house were sent to work in Ngeremetengel, while lazy (*dengerenger*) women were told to work at a different taro patch named Ngedelchong (located on the other side of Ngesisech village toward Ngeremeskang) so they would face glaring sun both coming and going.

Soon, however, the residents of Uluang began to oppress their neighboring hosts. They walked haughtily over to Imiungs, took what they pleased, and molested the wives from high-ranking houses as they traveled to and from their taro patches. This relationship between Uluang and Imiungs was not that of two unequal members of a single village federation, in which the lower-ranking member sends prescribed tribute to the high-ranking member in return for military protection. Rather, the people of Uluang treated Imiungs as an enslaved village (*ker el beluu*) simply by seizing what they wanted in an arbitrary and demeaning manner. At no time were the two villages part of a stable federation headed by governing council. Rather, "laws" (*llach*) established at Imiungs had no relevance at all on the western side of Umad channel. Uluang had its own lawmaking body and named its meetinghouse Tellach (Law) in order to mock the law of Imiungs. They also derisively referred to their other meetinghouse as Omekesebech (Selfrestraint), since this was where they would detain the women from Imiungs whose tattoo designs indicated that they were of high rank.[3]

This relationship, in which Imiungs was the slave of Uluang, characterizes the political situation mentioned in other narrative accounts of both Melekeok and Oreor villages. According to these stories, each of these villages of Milad was also the victim of a fearless (*bekeu*), highranking (*meteet*), and wealthy (*merau*) neighbor: Ngerekebesang oppressed Oreor and Oliuch enslaved Melekeok. And as is shown below, in each case the enslaved village formed military alliances with other villages to overthrow the yoke of oppression. The final destruction of the three oppressive villages marked the consolidation of Imiungs, Melekeok, and Oreor, three of Milad's male children, as undisputed heads of their local districts. An informant clarified the connection between these political struggles and the tradition of Milad:

> I am going to tell you again the reason (for the relationship
> between Uluang and Imiungs). Uluang, Oliuch, and some other
> villages like Ngerekebesang had in them very strong people, and

3. The name Omekesebech comes from the verb *omekesebech*, a causative form based on the stem *sebech-*, "ability, permission, fitness, adjustment." The name of this meetinghouse can mean "self-restraint" or "self-control," an ironical label for the site of disrespectful violations of Imeiong's women. Alternatively, the sense could be "made adjusted" or "equalized," that is, the place where high-ranking women are mockingly brought to humiliation.

people who possessed many valuables. And then Milad distributed
the titles, so that Imiungs was the first—just like distributing
chiefly titles—and Melekeok was the second, and then Imeliik. This
is the reason that these other villages got so angry, saying, "We
have been senior, and yet we were not given the title to carry." The
words of Milad were only directed to her own children. And so
before the time of Milad, Imiungs, Oreor, and Melekeok were not
at all strong villages. In fact, they were just like children. But when
Milad spoke they started to carry the titles and became the leaders
of Belau. Uluang, Oliuch, and Ngerekebesang are not villages from
the time of Chuab, for they come after that. But they were villages
prior to the time of Milad. But of course all this happened a long
time ago.

This explanation suggests that the villages of Milad were in fact upstart
villages and not ancient loci of politico-sacred power, and that villages
such as Uluang, Oliuch, and Ngerekebesang countered the words of
Milad with the power of wealth, the tokens of which which originate
from outside Belau.

Uluang's wealth came not only from Ngeruangel and Ngcheangel,
the two northern atolls where traditions record the presence of valuables taken from wrecked ships, but also from the village of Ngerair on
the east coast of Babeldaob, where the wealthy woodcarver
Ngirarengais lived. Ngirarengais, who held the position of leadership in
Ngerair, had two sons, the first named Cherechar (Past) and the second
named Chelechang (Present). Upset that his mother habitually prepared a larger lunch basket for his spoiled younger brother, Cherechar
decided to leave Ngerair, but not before he stole his father's hidden
money purse. Cherechar crossed the hills of central Babeldaob and arrived at Tellach landing place at Uluang, where he met the village chief
Rungiil. At that time Rungiil was faced with a potentially embarrassing
lack of exchange valuables, since his village was about to collect money
to pay for concubines visiting from Ngerekebesang (an island next to
Oreor). In addition to the money (*oredem*) paid directly by each man to
a male relative of his lover, the village chief was obligated to provide a
bachel piece as the *olsechekiil* payment for the chief of the women's
village.

After the women were returned to Ngerekebesang, the Uluang men
prepared to sail there to complete the exchange ceremony (*desiil*). Cherechar, sensing Rungiil's desperate plight, hid his father's money inside
betelnuts, which were to be distributed to the men of Ngerekebesang.
And Rungiil, not knowing that his young friend had plans to bail him

out, paid a quick visit to Imeliik to ask his sister's husband Rebluud for money. With the famous *bachel* piece Bederiich in his handbag, Rungiil sailed across the lagoon to join his fellow villagers at Ngerekebesang.[4] The ceremony held the next morning surprised everyone involved: when the men of Ngerekebesang prepared their betelnut for chewing, they found the many *kluk* pieces previously hidden by Cherechar; and Rungiil's associates were delighted to watch him present the Bederiich piece as the *olsechekiil* payment for their hosts. From this time Uluang's reputation as a dangerously wealthy place spread widely. So proud were they of their riches that the leaders of Uluang engaged in competition to see whose collection of money could fill the top of a stone display table (*oleketokel*).

The use of money as a principal instrument of intervillage politics and as a sign of high rank is certainly one of the most important themes in narratives I collected in the field. As this story shows, payments such as the *oredem* and *olsechekiil* are the focus of the system of institutionalized concubinage which links Uluang and Ngerekebesang and their respective titleholders. The rapid circulation of the most valuable pieces, including the precious yellow curved prism sections (*bachel berrak*), among high-ranking houses was one way by which they were distinguished from the general population. The *kluk* pieces owned by Ngirarengais, the chief of Ngerair village in Ngiual, passed through his son Cherechar to Rungiil, chief of powerful Uluang village, and then to the leaders of Ngerekebesang. Also the Bederiich piece from Ngeremedengir, the first house in Chelechui village, was handed over by Rebluud to his wife's brother Rungiil, who then paid it out to chief Chesbangel of Ngerekebesang. While many high-ranking villages used the valuables of their leaders in various types of exchange and payment, only Uluang is said to have openly displayed its wealth in competition for filling a display table. The people of Uluang are said to have further flaunted their money by inserting feathers in drilled holes. (Money so decorated is called *olomel busech*, "planted with flowers.") These examples of wanton boasting of riches are extremely marked, in light of the normal secrecy, formality, and respect with which financial affairs are handled in Belau.

---

4. The name Bederiich comes from *bad*, "stone," and *-riich*, "reddish in color." Kubary (1895b:13) notes the subsequent history of this piece of money: "Fig. 2 shows a *bachel* of this sort, which is 25 mm. long and 17 mm. wide, and which bears the special name Bederiich. It was given to King Reklai of Melekeok by the Ngirturong of Ngeremlengui, on the occasion of a peace treaty between the two territories. Subsequently, in 1883, it came into my possession."

Rich in valuables and fearless in abusing the wives of Imeiong's titleholders, Uluang continued to oppress the surrounding villages, until Imiungs's two leaders, Ngiraklang and Ngirturong, formulated a plan to destroy this village. The following story tells about the culmination of the tense relationship between Uluang and Imiungs.

Story of the Destruction of Uluang

Dirraklang [wife of Ngiraklang] walked from Imeiong on her way to work in the taro patch, and there was a meetinghouse at Uluang named Omekesebech. The *rubak* were there when Dirraklang approached, and they called out to her, "Come over here!" When she went over there, they lifted up her grass skirt and looked at her private parts. If she was tattooed properly, they would say, "Come into the meetinghouse." So she stayed in the meetinghouse instead of going to work in the taro patch. When she finally returned to the village, Ngiraklang asked her, "What happened?" She told him, "You know very well that the men of Uluang inspected me and forced me to go into the meetinghouse where they all slept with me until it was evening." Ngiraklang really did not like this at all. And when the next day came and she went back to work in the taro patch, the very same thing happened. He really did not like this.

There was at that time a man from Ngerechelong living in Imeiong who was married to a woman who was a child of a man from Klang house [in Imeiong]. Ngiraklang knew that there was a fearless warrior living in Ngeiungl in Ngerechelong, so he spoke to this man [married into Klang], "Go to Ngerechelong and tell the *rubak* named Rimirech of Ngeiungl that the village located next to Ngiraklang is giving him a constant pain in the neck. Can you make Ngiraklang happy once again?" [When this message was delivered, Rimirech replied,] "Yes, indeed, but tell Ngiraklang that he should wait just a bit." And so Rimirech traveled to Ulimang and spoke to a brave man of Ulimang [named Ngirairung], and this brave man from Ulimang said, "Yes, but wait a while so I can talk to the men of Ngellau and ask them if we can help each other out in this affair." Ngellau is a village which is part of Ngiual, although it is very near to Ulimang.

So Ngirairung said to the men of Ngellau, "We are going to help Rimirech." So they traveled to Ulimang and then sent word to Rimirech. This man from Ulimang was highly skilled in the art of warfare—like Eisenhower. He told them, "Now you men will initiate the battle. And then the people of Ulimang will come after

you, and we will burn down the village." So the men of Ulimang
went to stay in Imeiong, and the men from Ngeiungl and the men
from Ngeremetengel combined and waged war together. When
they began the battle the people of Uluang came out to meet the
war party, and the men from the villages on the east coast, from
Ulimang and Ngellau, descended and burned down the village.
And it burned until there were no houses standing, and this is the
reason that Uluang was defeated. Uluang had been a very strong
village within Ngeremlengui. Imeiong was strong, too, but it was
not a village of lawless men like the men of Uluang, who liked to
do harm to the wives of the chiefs of Imeiong.

The destruction of Uluang, prompted by Imeiong's desire to be rid
of this oppressing neighbor and immediately caused by the violation of
the sanctity of chief Ngiraklang's wife, was accomplished by the coordinated assault led by Rimirech and Ngirairung. My informants described precisely how the attacking forces first drew Uluang's warriors
down to the channel while warriors from neighboring Ngeremetengel
rushed into the defenseless village. Although the battle plan was insti-
gated by the chiefs at Imeiong, the actual fighting was intentionally
made to appear as if Imeiong was not itself involved—the storyteller
commented that this "remaining above the fray" was consistent with
Imeiong's status as the oldest son of Milad.

Their village in flames, the inhabitants of Uluang fled in several directions. One group headed south over water and, after a long series of
intermediate stops, finally settled at Uudes house in Melekeok.

When the people escaped [from Uluang], some of them came to
the houses named Chedukl and Ngerungelang [in Imeiong]. They
carried the lineage god of their mother carved in wood to the
house. From there they started to plot their course again. Those
who were in the house of Ngerungelang returned again to
Medorem [in Imeliik]. And there is a place in Medorem called
Ngeruudes, which they named. From Medorem they entered the
house of Tonget, which is a house that belongs to Ongal [*kebliil*],
and then on to Ngchemliangel to the house of Klai and Sucheltei.
They remained in these two houses for a long time, but decided
again to move. They were inquiring about all the other places, but
finally found out that Ngerusar was good, not [*sic*] because of its
legends and stories, which were known all over Belau; so they
moved to the house of Klai and settled. When they were at the
house of Klai, the mother of Chelebebai was married to a man
from Ngerebodel in Oreor, and then moved to Ngeremid, and this

is why Chelebebai came to Ngeremid. The rest of the group that remained in Ngerusar proceeded on through the mangrove.[5] (PCAA, Melekeok File)

Another group headed by Ngiraumerang, the titleholder from Umerang house of Uluang, escaped to the north and stopped briefly to rest at a place in Ngeremeskang appropriately named Olenguurangiraumerang (Resting Place of Ngiraumerang).[6] Another man, named Rudimech, led a group of people from Uluang northwest to Ngerutoi in Ngerdmau district. It was this Rudimech who is said to have carried with him the famous stone display table mentioned in the story—contrary to Hidikata's (1973a:23) claim that the man's name was Arbedulratebelak.[7]

Two other individuals, a man Okerdeu and a woman Diluka, took refuge in Imeiong itself. Okerdeu carried one of the high-ranking titles of Uluang, and his name recalls the *olangch* his ancestors brought from Ngeruangel, namely, several *kerdeu* trees which they planted in different stops on their journey. When he left Uluang he first stopped at the house of Mengederaol in Ngerutechei and then came to Imeiong.[8] It

5. A slightly different route is traced in another account. "The clan of Uudes came from Ngeruangel, an island about seven miles from the northern tip of Ngcheangel. This group came from the east coast. The group that came from the west came from Uluang. They went to Medorem in Imeliik and then to Ngeremid in the house of Blosech, then to Ngerusar in the house of Tucheremel (Reklai's house), then they proceeded to the east coast and stopped at a corner of one of the mangrove areas outside Irrai called Klai. They anchored at this place which is just on the outskirts of Oikull and had their lunch and named this area Klai, after the name of the clan. From there they went to Melekeok" (PCAA, Melekeok File).

6. Kubary (1885:66) provides different information about the advent of Umerang house in Melekeok: "The house of Umerang, whose head, having been chased away from Chelab in Ngerard, landed here [in Melekeok] and was well received."

7. Hidikata (1973b:23) describes this display stone, which he saw in Ngerdmau: "Customarily the stand is made of wood from a single tree in either round or rectangular shape. . . . The small holes on the lower edge of the upper platform shown in the figures [fig. 24B] were said to be where the small shells called *besachel* were hung for decoration. It was also reported that in olden times wealthy families would line up their *udoud* [valuables] for measurement on this stand, but nevertheless it still probably functioned mainly as an offering stand for placing tribute to the gods." When I visited the same spot in 1980 the meetinghouse at Ngerutoi was no longer standing, but the area had been recently cleared of weeds. This display table stood where Hidikata had seen it, and on it lay the stone face of a Modekngei deity.

8. Tradition records that the *kerdeu* tree was carried from Ngeruangel and planted at several locations in Belau, including Ilild house in Ngchemesed, Inglai house in Ngetbang, and Ngerutelchii house in Imeiong. These houses are thus connected by the model of the path through these homologous signs. The title Okerdeu (*o-kerdeu*) also is the *olangch* of this same migration.

may seem surprising that this high-ranking man from Uluang would find welcome in Imeiong, but two things must be kept in mind. First, a village is usually enthusiastic in receiving high-ranking people, since its overall status could be raised by their presence and their money. Second, as noted above, the people of Uluang did not know that Ngiraklang and Ngirturong were directly responsible for recruiting the warriors Rimirech and Ngirairung, so they did not instantly rule out Imeiong as a place of refuge.[9] Left behind by her fleeing relatives, Diluka eventually found a home at Chedukl, the fifth-ranking house in Imeiong. And when she was old and weak, several people related to the former residents of Uluang now living at the house of Baulbei in Melekeok returned to Imeiong as part of a large visiting party and carried her back to Melekeok. When she died they buried her at the grave pavement of Baulbei, and her journey from Chedukl to Baulbei established a mutual house linkage between these two houses and between their respective titleholders, Iechadrachedukl and Renguul. The people of Chedukl then summoned Okerdeu from Ngerutechei to come to live at their house in Imeiong, since a path had been established between this fifth house and Uluang. As a result, to this day people of Chedukl house hold joint claim to the abandoned land parcels Uluang and Tellach and participate in customary exchanges with people from Baulbei house in Melekeok.

Custom demands that villages present valuable signs such as stones, money, names, privileges, or women to those who come to their rescue in times of crisis or who perform especially remarkable deeds of service. Chief Ngiraklang accordingly rewarded the participating villages for their assistance in defeating Uluang by giving up four sacred stones which had rested outside the chiefly meetinghouse at Orukei square in Imeiong. Two stones, named Dengarech (Lying Face Up) and Chebecheb (Lying Face Down), were given to Rimirech. These stones had originally come to Imeiong from Ngetechum, an ancient village located on the rocky cliff above Ngeremetengel.

Story of Dengarech and Chebecheb of Ngetechum

Dengarech and Chebecheb are two very valuable stones which came from Ngetechum, and there is a story about them. There was a man named Dengarech who walked with his face up in the air, and there was another man named Chebecheb who walked with his face to the ground. They were living at Ngetechum and got into an

---

9. A refuge stone, the Iingerturong (Cave of Ngerturong), stands in front of Ngerturong house.

argument. Dengarech was afraid and fled. And the other one who always faced to the ground pursued him all around Belau. He chased him completely around the island until they arrived back at Ngetechum. Dengarech then said, "Friend, we have arrived back at our point of origin (*uchud*) at Ngetechum." So when they had found their point of origin at Ngetechum their argument was over. The one facing up turned into a stone which faced up, and the other one turned into a stone which faced the ground. So the story goes that they completely encircled Belau, and when they got back to Ngetechum they said, "Friend, we are men of Ngetechum. Let's end the argument, so there will no longer be a fight." This is the story about Ngetechum.

Then Ngiraklang took two other precious stones and presented them to Rimirech, first the Imiungselbad (Imiungs Stone) representing the village of Imiungs as the child of Milad and second the smaller Imiungseldui (Imiungs Title) (photograph 5). In recognition of the skill and leadership provided by Ngirairung of Ulimang, Rimirech in turn handed over these paired stones to the people of Ulimang. And Ngirairung then gave them to the people of Ngellau who had assisted him. Today these two stones stand at the (now-abandoned) meetinghouse platform of Illai in Ngellau (just north of Ngiual).[10] Ngirairung kept the Dengarech and Chebecheb stones on behalf of the village of Ulimang. Together these four stones constituted the "repayment for their effort" to those villages that helped Ngiraklang finally throw off Uluang's oppression.

It is not at all ironical, in light of the nature of the movement of hierarchically ranked valuables, goods, and stones in Belauan culture and in light of the tension between static and dynamic perspectives on district political development, that the very moment Imiungs attains or fulfills its position as the sole leader of Ngeremlengui district is also the moment when the material embodiment of its sacred birthright, the Imiungselbad, is removed from Orukei square and taken to a rather insignificant village on the east coast. This is one example of a fundamental principle of Belauan culture, that a sign representing the first position in a hierarchical set of values (titles, money, stones, villages) frequently maintains its dominance by being isolated or concealed from everyday social activity. There is, in addition, no contradiction between the ideological notion that the sacredness of all Belau remains in Im-

---

10. Krämer (1917–29, 2:124) notes the related fact that the sixth title of the chiefly council of Ngellau is named Imiungs.

eiong (see chapter 6) and the historical fact that the physical embodiment of this sacredness has been hidden for generations in the underbrush of Ngellau. Isolation from ongoing social activity and from the
gaze of generations of individuals in fact guarantees the stability of the
sacredness embodied in these stones. The absence of this stone from the
sphere of social activity and consciousness means that the negative implications of historical contingency embedded in the story of Uluang
can be avoided. That is, storytellers from Imeiong explicitly deny that
Imeiong's defeat of Uluang and the consolidation of its position as the
capital of Ngeremlengui district led to the recognition of the village as
the first child of the goddess Milad. Imeiong's sacredness, they claim, is
not anything that could be achieved or lost. Rather, the claim is that
Uluang became hostile in the first place because the high rank endowed
upon Imeiong by the Ruchel gods at Ngerutechei challenged its own
long-standing prowess and renowned riches.

Part of the significance of the destruction of Uluang for these storytellers lies in their observation that the three sons of Milad, that is,
Imiungs, Melekeok, and Oreor, all emerged as capital villages of their
districts by overthrowing nearby enslaving villages through the coordinated effort of allied villages. Soon after the destruction of Uluang,
news of Ngirairung's talents reached the ears of the leaders of Melekeok
and Oreor. Reklai of Melekeok knew that Ngirairung could assist him
to end the oppression of Oliuch village, so he arranged for this brave
warrior to join forces with the men's club of Ulimang. Indeed, under
Ngirairung's leadership, Oliuch was destroyed and Melekeok emerged
as an independent capital of Ngetelngal district, and it no longer had to
send tribute to Oliuch. Oreor's two leaders, Kloteraol and Rubasech,
similarly asked for support from famous warriors from the rock island
area to to destroy Ngerekebesang, the then-powerful group of villages
located on an island directly west of Oreor.

> If the people from Ngerekebesang came to Oreor and it rained,
> they would pull down a house and discard it. They would just
> come to Oreor to play around, pull down a house, and use it as an
> umbrella. And so the people of Oreor became very angry. They
> went to look for Chemesiochel and other people from the rock
> islands to help them make war. But first after they went to get help
> these people destroyed Imeliik, and the people of Imeliik fled. And
> then the people of Oreor said, "Ngerekebesang is just over there.
> We really hate it, so let us get together to destroy Ngerekebesang."
> They then went to speak to the god of Ngerebeched village, saying
> "Come and help us." But this god said, "Very well, but if I help

you, you will have to give me this land." The land where the hospital stands today is now owned by Ngerebeched, but in ancient times it was owned by Oreor. So the god said, "If you are successful in the battle, give me this land to become the possession of Ngerebeched." They did make war and they were victorious. The *olangch* of this today is that there is a title from the council of Oreor which is a title in Ngerekebesang.

Drawing on the help of warriors from the rock islands (especially from Ngerengchol), these war leaders attached Ngerekebesang at the new moon. A bloody assault routed the enemy, who fled under hot pursuit all the way to Ngerechelong at the northern end of Babeldaob. The terms of settlement included payment of a valuable piece of money from Chesbangel, chief of Ngerekebesang, to the chiefs of Oreor. In return, Oreor reinstated Chesbangel as the second-ranking title and placed the Obakeraiuong title from Oreor in the reconstituted council, and high-ranking Idid house in Oreor sent a young woman to Ngere-kebesang to cement a marriage alliance.[11] (One aspect of the parallelism of these three wars of Imiungs, Melekeok, and Oreor not articulated by my informants is that in each case victory was obtained by the kind of coordinated intervillage political action that is the essence of the corner-post model of Milad's polity.)

Now the rhetorical danger in citing these parallel war stories is that they can easily be taken to suggest that the three sons of Milad earned their high rank through the contingencies of military victory, much the way Uluang, Ngerekebesang, and Oliuch had previously acquired their power. This implication is, however, strongly denied by people from Imeiong:

Uluang enslaved Imeiong; they took things from the people of Imeiong and also took the wife of the *rubak*. This is the reason Uluang got destroyed and is no longer a village. And also the village of Oliuch enslaved Melekeok, and this is why it got destroyed in warfare. Ngerekebesang also enslaved Oreor. All these villages which enslaved the other villages were destroyed in major battles. (But if Imeiong was high ranking, why did Uluang enslave it?) Yes, Imeiong was high ranking, but Uluang was fierce. Now I will tell you the reason. When Milad gave birth to the stone which remained behind [i.e, Imiungselbad], there were at that time

11. This transferred title was labeled the *olangch* of the victory, since Obakeraiuong now "guards" Ngerekebesang and is in an excellent position to impose swift punishment should any renewed aggressiveness emerge in the future.

already a lot of people, like the villages of Uluang, Oliuch, and Ngerekebesang, these fierce people. And so when the Ruchel gods distributed titles, Imiungs, the first child, became the leader. And it was this which these other villages disliked so much. The people of Oliuch did not want Melekeok to be the leader, since it was just like a newly born child. And Ngerekebesang said, "Oreor is a newly born child, but now it is the leader and carries the high title. Are we going to just sit by and endure this?" So Melekeok, Oreor, and Ngeremlengui were all opposed by these fierce villages. This is the reason for the term Imiungselbad: a stone (*bad*) cannot die, it remains forever.

These parallel battles are all thus successful defenses of sacred rank rather than wars of political conquest.

In addition to the sacred stones noted in both the story of Uluang and in the account of the distribution of titles at Uchuladebong (given in chapter 6), there is another *olangch* that functions to mark the transformation of Ngeremlengui's political organization. The earliest-remembered Ngiraklang titleholder was named Ngirasumang Chelungel, and it was his successor Ngirachosbesiang who performed the symbolic act that recorded the status reversal of Uluang and Imiungs as an accomplished fact (*mera el tekoi*).

When Ngiraklang Ngirasumang died, the people of Klang house brought a man from Ngcheangel named Ngirachosbesiang to become Ngiraklang. And it was this man who turned Umad bridge around. The end of Umad bridge, the end of the tree trunk, had been pointing toward Imeiong, since Uluang was such a powerful village. And while Ngirasumang held the title Ngiraklang it remained that way, but when he died this *rubak* from Ngcheangel became Ngiraklang, and he turned the bridge around.

Custom stipulates strict attention to the difference between the trunk end of the log (*uchul a kerrekar*) and the tip end of the log (*rsel a kerrekar*) in construction projects. For example, the reserved seating position for the head of a household is beneath the trunk end of the *orengodel* beam.[12] Added to this differential symbolic valuation of trunk and tip is the important notion of bridge, which played such an important role in the origin myths analyzed in chapter 4. A bridge is more than a link between two points on a line; it creates a path of articulation

12. Similar patterns of evaluation of trunk and tip are reported for Eastern Indonesia (Barnes 1974:68–68) and for Ponape (Riesenberg 1968:69).

between two separated places. And this articulation necessarily—at least before the use of concrete and steel—indexes the directionality of the rank vector, since a log has only one trunk end and one tip end. The bridge at Umad is not the only bridge in Ngeremlengui to have been intentionally reversed as a symbolic gesture. An early Ngirturong titleholder named Maui is said to have turned around the bridge at Ibai that crosses a stream between Imeiong and Ngerutechi. Maui's intent was to mark the transition in the location of Ngeremlengui's sacredness from Uchuladebong stone pavement in Ngerutechei to Orukei square in Imeiong.

THE WARS OF CHEMERUAOL

The rise of Imiungs as the capital of Ngeremlengui was soon challenged, but not by a rival village within the district. Rather the threat came from Chemeruaol, the younger brother of Ngiraklang Ngirasumang, the crippled old chief Captain Wilson met at Imeiong in 1783. This section tells the story of the war campaigns of Chemeruaol, a fearless warrior living at the high-ranking house of Ngedengcholl in Ngerdmau, the district immediately north of Ngeremlengui on the west coast of Babeldaob. These raids took place approximately five to ten years prior to Wilson's visit to Imeiong. Chemeruaol had not managed to obtain the chiefly title Beouch at Ngedengcholl house by the time the god Sechaltbuich arrived in Ngerdmau to seize village leadership from the legitimate titleholder. On account of strong opposition from men like Chemeruaol, Sechaltbuich fled to Ngersuul, where he plotted to organize a war party to kill Chemeruaol. At this same time, Chemeruaol's older brother Ngirasumang, who then carried the highest title Beouch, left Ngerdmau to take the chiefly title Ngiraklang in Imeiong. In need of some means to strengthen his vulnerable position in Ngerdmau and faced with the possibility of an attach upon his life, Chemeruaol began a series of raids against Imeiong, where his older brother lived. Traditions of Ngeremlengui record many of these raids in great detail, for the anger of Chemeruaol against his older brother struck at the heart of Imeiong's persistent claim to rank as the oldest child of Milad and also threatened to disrupt the important mutual house relationship between these two high-ranking houses, Ngedengcholl and Klang (Parmentier 1984:665–66).

During one of these raids, for example, Chemeruaol's warriors from Ngerdmau entered the channel at Ngeluong looking to take a head trophy. A sudden rainstorm forced them to take shelter within the channel. One of the warriors, named Ocherei, while waiting beneath a mangrove tree, was killed when a sharp branch from the tree fell on his head. The war party returned to Ngerdmau without a head by carrying the body of Ocherei, who thereupon received the epithet Bekeubngaol (Fierce Mangrove Tree) as a mocking reminder of his misfortune.

Several stories which narrate other raids on Ngeremlengui by Chemeruaol end with the formulaic warning from Ngiraklang to his "younger brother" (*ochellel*): "I am Ngiraklang and you cannot possibly wage war on Ngeremlengui. If you should happen to take a head, stay outside the village and then go home." After several unsuccessful attempts, Chemeruaol altered his strategy and decided to mount an all-out siege to destroy Ngeremlengui. First he traveled with his group of warriors to the other side of the island to recruit allies in villages belonging to Ngetelngal's side of heaven, including the villages of Melekeok, Ngchesar, Ngersuul, and Irrai. But in this period of Belauan history, Imeiong did not stand alone to face this impending attack, since Oreor and Imeiong had by then established a mutual defense pact.

> From very ancient times there was a relationship between Imiungs and Oreor, so that if a war party appeared at Imiungs, the people of Imiungs would carry a fire up to the place of the signal fire [on Chetiruir mountain], where the people of Oreor could see it. This meant that a war party was approaching and that Oreor should come to the defense of Imiungs. This pact was known only to the people of Imiungs and the people of Oreor.

Chemeruaol and the warriors from Ngaramedekodek club planned to attack Ngeremlengui from the south in the early morning on the third day after the full moon, when the moonlight rising over the hills would give just enough light for battle. They paddled on the high tide until their war canoes came to a shallow spot just behind Ngesebokel island near the entrance to Ngeremeduu bay (south of Ngeremlengui). Here they waited silently until morning. At daylight some people from Ngeremlengui spotted the anchored war canoes at Ngesebokel—some say that they were tipped off by an omen of war, or that Chemeruaol himself sent a threatening message to the leaders of Imeiong. One brave man named Ngiraitaoch from the house of Itaoch in Ngeremetengel climbed up to the top of a rocky cliff overlooking the bay and engaged Chemeruaol in a shouting match across the water. Chemeruaol cried, "Ngeremlengui, pack up your belongings and get the village ready, because tomorrow you will no longer be people of Ngeremlengui!" In retort Ngiraitaoch called out, "Stay where you are! You cannot come into this village, for if you do you will all be cursed." (This threat is based on the notion that they would be cursed for violating Imeiong's position as the locus of Belau's sacredness.) But Chemeruaol only continued more fiercely, "My friend, put your pots and utensils and all your possessions together, for by morning you will all be far away from here, and this village will belong to me."

Ngiraitaoch then went to Imeiong to report these events to Ngiraklang and Ngirturong, who in turn ordered members of the local men's club to climb Chetiruir mountain to light the signal fire to alert Oreor. A man from Oreor who was at the moment in the process of stealing betelpepper leaves from a tree near Meketii meetinghouse caught sight of the fire on Chetiruir (the two locations are approximately fifteen miles apart). He quickly climbed down and blew the conch-shell trumpet to notify chief Ibedul and the leaders of Oreor that their ally was under attack. The war cry went up throughout the village, and soon war canoes from nearby hamlets such as Ngerebeched, Ngerekebesang, and Ngeremid were on their way around Bkulengrill point to come to the defense of Ngeremlengui.

By the time the war canoes arrived at Ngesebokel, the tide had gone out far enough so that the canoes of Chemeruaol and his fellow warriors from Ngerdmau, Ngchesar, and Ngersuul were blocked inside the shallows where they had anchored the previous night. When the war canoes from Oreor drew near to Chemeruaol, a brave man named Ngirachelid shouted to his fellows, "Let me have him, and I will kill him." So they paddled close to his stranded canoe, where they observed Chemeruaol calmly singing a lullaby to his baby son whom he held cradled in his arms. Quickly Ngirachelid jumped into the water and ran across the shallows toward Chemeruaol, who placed his son in the hull of the canoe and jumped into the water. But when Chemeraol took his first step toward Ngirachelid, the sharp edge of a trochus shell cut his foot and the water around him turned red from the gushing blood. As Ngirachelid rushed up, Chemeruaol cried out, "Friend, end my life here. I do not want to die at the hands of a lesser man." So Ngirachelid struck him dead and the war party from the other side of heaven scattered in all directions. Some crossed Ngeremeduu bay and escaped overland to Ngersuul and Ngchesar. Others climbed up the steep slopes into Ngchemesed village. The warriors from Ngeremlengui pursued one Ngirangeang of Ngerdmau into the village, where they killed him and discarded his body at a place named Ucheriu. Two others were caught near Luul creek in Ngeremetengel, where the place named Iuau marks their graves.[13]

13. Krämer (1917–29, 4:137–38) gives a very short account of a battle which he dates at 1780 and which resembles the story reported here in several respects, although with a slightly different cast of characters and political circumstance: "The people of Melekeok had called together some villages to wage war on Oreor, but they did not ever

Oral traditions concerning the aftermath of this abortive assault tie in with several details of Captain Wilson's observations during his visit to Imeiong in 1783. Immediately after the battle, Ngiraklang Ngirasumang instructed the men's club of Imeiong to throw the head of Chemeruaol out at Tabelngas, a spot behind Klang house. When the flesh rotted away, Ngiraklang placed the skull of his younger brother below the door opening of his house for use as a spittoon and urinal. Wilson mentions that the skulls of warriors from Melekeok were on display at Orukei square:

> Captain Wilson enquired of the linguist the meaning of some
> human skulls he saw placed over the outside of doors at the ends of
> the great house [the meetinghouse]; he directly went and asked
> Rechucher [a chief from Oreor], who gave him the following
> account: That the *rubak* and principal men of Imiungs having gone
> on some particular occasion to another island, taking with them a
> considerable number of inhabitants, a party of the Ngetelngal
> people landed at their town, and killing many who could not
> escape into the woods, set their houses on fire; the news of which
> being brought to Ibedul, he immediately assembled his canoes and
> warriors, and went and attacked them before they had quitted the
> place; that being so unexpectedly beset, many were killed, and the
> rest fled, some in their canoes, and others into the woods; that the
> *rubak* and people of Imiungs returning at this juncture, few of the
> Ngetelngal people escaped; and that those were the heads of some
> of their Chiefs. This affair appeared not to have happened very
> long before, as the materials of the houses which had been
> destroyed looked still rather fresh, nor were overgrown with weeds
> at that time. (Keate 1788:174–75)

Although Wilson explicitly says that these skulls at Orukei were heads of warriors from Ngetelngal, contemporary informants insist that the

---

actually bring a war party because they were too weak. On account of this, they gave up their plans and plotted instead to destroy Ngeremlengui. When Ngirturong of Imiungs heard this news, he sent a boat to Ibedul, saying that Melekeok wanted to attack him soon, and that when they saw the signal fire at Roismlengui they should send help quickly. At the same time he ordered an old woman who lived on the mountain to light the fire when the enemy approached. Shortly thereafter warriors from Melekeok came, and the old woman immediately lit the fire on Chetiruir. At that moment a thief in Oreor was up in a tree and saw the fire and cried out, 'A great fire burns on top of Roismlengui! The fire is a bad sign.' Then Ibedul said, 'The warriors from Melekeok have attacked Ngeremlengui, so let us go there.' So the warriors went there and helped Ngeremlengui kill most of the people from Melekeok. On account of this Oreor and Imiungs are friends." The hostility between Ngeremlengui and Melekeok is discussed in detail below.

battle described was one of the campaigns of Chemeruaol, and that Wilson's labeling of the enemy as being from Ngetelngal simply reflects the fact that Chemeruaol recruited allies from villages allied to the other side of heaven. Also the fresh appearance of the village is attributed not to the rebuilding of houses after a fire but rather to the fact that the location of many houses and roads in Imiungs was changed through the labor of people of Ulong, who in repayment for lengthy hospitality restructured the layout of the village.

One of the variants of the story of Chemeruaol concludes by describing Imeiong's payment of money for Oreor's assistance.

> This was a very big battle, and many people were wiped out, and also many houses were burned down. In this battle the people from Ngeremlengui asked for assistance from the people of Oreor, who came to their aid. This was a very important war, and many war canoes from Oreor came to defend the village. When they arrived, the war canoe of Chemeruaol was blocked at a shallow spot near Ngesebokel, and Ngirachelid, a man from Oreor, killed Chemeruaol. The raiding party of Oreor was the reason that Ngeremlengui was not destroyed in this battle. After it was over, Ngiraklang and Ngirturong tied the knotted cord (*teliakl*) and collected together five *chelebucheb* pieces and *kldait* pieces. And when the knotted cord was completed, they sent for the people of Oreor, and Ibedul and his men's club took these pieces of money. Then Ngiraklang paid out another large *kldait* piece, and Beouch [chief of Ngerdmau] took it to make the peace at Ngerubong. After that there was no more war.[14]

It is also possible that the valuables mentioned in this account are identical with those described by Wilson on the basis of his observation of a ceremonial distribution (*boketudoud*) among chiefs from Imeiong, Oreor, and Ngebuked in 1783.

> The old *rubak* [Ngiraklang Ngirasumang Chelungel] distributed beads to the other *rubak,* in the following manner: The old *rubak* gave them to an officer in waiting, who advancing into the middle of the square, and holding them up between his forefinger and thumb, made a short speech, and with a loud voice called out the person's name for whom they were designed, and immediately ran

---

14. Other informants say that the payment of money to Beouch to make peace between Ngeremlengui and Ngerdmau belongs to a different story.

and gave them to him, and then returned in a slow pace to the old
rubak for the next, which was presented in the same manner.
(Keate 1788:176)

My informants stated that the "old *rubak*," a chief Wilson describes as
being carried from his house to the central square on a wooden litter,
was Ngiraklang Ngirasumang and that his epithet, Chelungel (Carried), reflects the feeble state of his body.

The story of the wars of Chemeruaol and the narrative of Wilson's
visit to Imeiong provide a rare glimpse of Ngeremlengui on the eve of
Western contact. By the 1780s Ngeremetengel village and Ngchemesed
villages were established members of the district headed by chiefs
Ngiraklang and Ngirturong at Imeiong. And Imeiong, in turn, belonged to an interdistrict alliance with Oreor which was opposed in
general to villages on the eastern coast of Babeldaob. Within Imeiong,
chief Ngiraklang held the position of leadership, played the most
important role in the political and financial negotiations of the district,
and was treated with deferential respect both by local villagers and by
Ibedul of Oreor, who distanced himself from Ngiraklang's presence by
letting his lower-ranking associate Rechucher act in his place.

That the subsequent political situation of the early nineteenth cen-
tury was not simply a matter of balanced alliances on each side of
Babeldaob is clearly illustrated in the next segment of the story of
Ngeremlengui, which tells about the complex interrelations among
Oreor, Imeliik, Ngeremlengui, Ngerdmau, Ngiual, and Melekeok.

THE SLAUGHTER AT BELOD

The story of the slaughter of a visiting party from Ngeremlengui at
Belod landing place in Ngiual takes place approximately twenty years
after the death of Chemeruaol and the visit of Captain Wilson. The
story illustrates more fully than the previous story the political relationships among major villages such as Oreor, Imeliik, Ngeremlengui,
Ngerdmau, Melekeok, and Ngiual. The version of this long narrative I
recorded tells the story from the point of view of Dirrengulbai Diluei, a
high-ranking and clever woman from Uchelkiukl, the highest-ranking
house of Imeliik, but the story line intersects several other well-known
stories, such as that of two lovers, Ngiramengerengei and Obirir, and
that of the struggle between two famous warrors, Bechab and Malsol.[15]

15. I taped the complete story of Belod several times during my stay and discussed the
implications and details of the narrative with many people in Ngeremlengui. Krämer
(1917–29, 4:275–80) gives an exceptionally full account of the same events, but I have
not used his version in the retelling here.

Diluei lived in Ngerekeai, the capital village of Imeliik district. Her house was near Kloulblai, the residence of her relative Rengulbai, the chief of Imeliik and leader of Uchelkiukl *kebliil*. Nearby lived her younger brother Chesou Ngiramellong, the sister's son of chief Rengulbai and potential heir to the high title at Uchelkiukl.[16] Chesou decided to move to Imeiong, where he entered the house of Ngerturong, since this house was in a mutual-house relationship with Uchelkiukl. He lived in Imeiong for a long time, working with the local men's club and participating in household affairs at Ngerturong. One day he returned home to visit his sister and mother's brother in Imeliik. When Chesou arrived, chief Rengulbai had gone to the shore to make coconut-fiber cord and his wife Dirrakloulblai was alone at the house.[17] "Come in, my child," she said to Chesou, "You must be very tired from your journey. Come in and have something to eat." Chesou replied, "Yes, I walked across the hills for a long time, and if you do have some food I will eat something."

Unfortunately, at that moment there was no fish in the house other than some crab meat Dirrakloulblai was saving for her husband. So she prepared taro and then said to Chesou, "We have no fish at all other than some crab left over from Rengulbai's lunch. But since you are so famished, go ahead and eat it, and when he returns I will fix him some coconut meat or *titemel*-leaf soup." When he finished eating, Chesou traveled back to Ngeremlengui. Rengulbai returned that evening and he told his wife to prepare his taro. He then noticed that the crab which he had been saving was gone. "What happened to my crab?" he demanded. She explained, "Ngiramellong [i.e., Chesou] visited while you were out, and he was so hungry that I gave it to him. He has returned to Ngeremlengui. Perhaps they needed him to do something at Ngerturong house."

In the next few days Rengulbai started overhearing vicious rumors about his wife and Chesou, rumors which were being intentionally circulated by some of the elders of Uchelkiukl, to the effect that his wife was Chesou's lover. The motive of these elders was to discredit Chesou, whose direct line to the Rengulbai title was stronger than their claims. And when Rengulbai overheard one of these senior men say, "I actually *saw* him sleeping with Rengulbai's wife," he decided to act before these rumors spread any further. So he called his trusted messenger, a man

16. These individuals appear on Krämer's (1917–29, 2:169) genealogical table for Ngerekeai (Imeliik).

17. In Ngerekeai the name of the highest-ranking clan is Uchelkiukl, while the name of the chief's house is Kloulblai; so Rengulbai's wife carried the house name, Dirrakloulblai.

named Beludes, and entrusted him with a message for Ngirturong of
Imeiong. The message was that Chesou should not live long enough to
return to Imeliik—meaning that Ngirturong should arrange to have
him killed.

A few days later, when the young men of Imeiong and Ngeremetengel were putting a new roof on the canoe shed at Chelsechei landing place, Ngirturong realized a perfect opportunity to carry out
Rengulbai's strategy. Conferring privately with two men, Malsol and
Ngiruburek, he plotted that when Chesou was up on top of his
canoe shed these two strong men would strike him with their hand
axes. There would be so much commotion as workers competed with
each other in stitching pandanus leaves that no one would notice the
murder. So according to plan, Chesou was killed at Chelsechei, and
they threw his body to the ground.

Ngirturong said to the men, "Take his body and dump it at Ordilsau
island in front of Mebechubel village. Then proceed on to Oreor to
notify Ngirngemeiusech that the body is at Ordilsau waiting to be
picked up." Ngirturong's order to have this man from Idid house pick
up Chesou's body was explained in terms of the bilateral paths linking
villages belonging to Milad's cornerpost political order: "Chesou was a
young man from Imeliik, so if the body had been taken directly to
Imeliik, then the path between Ngeremlengui and Imeliik would have
been severed. But by sending the body to Oreor the path between
Oreor and Imeliik was severed instead, and Ngeremlengui remained
above the conflict." This strategy of keeping Ngeremlengui, the oldest
child of Milad, out of intervillage disputes recalls the identical political
maneuver employed during the war against Uluang.

So they sailed first to Ordilsau and then on to Oreor with the message for Ngirngemeiusech. When Ngirngemeiusech and the men of
Oreor arrived at Ordilsau, they discovered the dead body of Chesou
exposed on the rocks at low tide. Ngirngemeiusech cursed the corpse:
"My young friend, you discarded your responsibilities at Imeliik and
took your handbag to a place other than Imeliik. Now you are dead and
you cannot ever become Rengulbai." That is, by living in the related
Ngerturong house in Imeiong, Chesou made himself vulnerable to the
power play of the elders of Uchelkiukl. Ngirngemeiusech was so out-
raged by what had happened that in his anger he spat on the body
before his men carried it back to Oreor.

When Diluei heard what had happened at Imeiong and at Ordilsau,
her first action was to send a piece of money to Oreor as the ransom
payment (*melkatk*) for the body of her brother. But after she had taken
care of the funeral and burial in Imeliik, she began to plot full-scale

revenge against the leaders of both Imeiong and Oreor. Shortly after the conclusion of the mourning period for Chesou, Diluei said to chief Rengulbai, "Prepare my traveling food (*telechull*) and send me off to Oreor, for I am going to become the wife of Ngirngemeiusech." This food package was prepared, and she sailed off to Oreor, where she soon married this Idid man.

The first step in her plan could now be put into operation. One day when she had gone to work in the taro patch at Kesuk, she suddenly abandoned her labor and ran back to Idid house. Ngirngemeiusech asked her, "What is the matter?" She replied, "I thought that the men of Idid were better behaved than this. They came down to the taro patch and tried to molest me there. So I had to run to get away." A few days later she tried the same deception once more, this time when she went to bathe at Kesol pool. Grass skirt in hand, she ran back to Idid and complained to her husband, "Those men of Idid must really want to show disrespect to you, for they know you are my husband. This time they tried to rape me at the bathing pool. I think it is time that we left this village and moved to some place on Babeldaob where young men do not grab at women and where they respect their elders." He could only agree and said, "We are not going to live here any longer. Let's find a new home on Babeldaob. Get your possessions ready and I will prepare the canoe for the journey." Diluei had successfully manipulated her husband by transferring the (invented) insult from herself to Ngirngemeiusech, who was not in a powerful enough position at Idid house to pursue the matter locally.

Early the next morning they loaded their possessions in the canoe at Delui landing place and set off toward Babeldaob. When their canoe passed in front of Imeliik, Diluei's husband asked, "Don't you want to settle here in your home village?" To his amazement she replied, "No, from here I could still see Oreor across the water." Later as they rounded Bkurrengel point, Diluei noticed a small sardine attached to the outrigger. "This sardine came from Oreor, and I really don't want it to accompany us any further. Turn the canoe around." They turned around and sailed all the way back to Oreor, where they discarded the offending sardine and then headed back toward Ngerdmau.

The couple finally settled in Ngerdmau, and the house Diluei ordered to be built at a place called Ngerutang had a peculiar design, with a surrounding stone wall and an extra door at the end. This style of construction was selected in order for their new house to imitate the house of the local village god Sechaltbuich. This violation of local privilege was designed to stimulate rumors which would spread their reputation beyond Ngerdmau district. Continuing her treachery, Diluei

sent word to chief Cheltuk Reklai of Melekeok, "My husband has constructed a very unusual house, like the house of the god. He respects
neither the gods nor the *rubak* of Ngerdmau. You should find a way to
kill him, for our house resembles that of Sechaltbuich, with a door
opening at each end. And our house is even taller than the god's house.
Quickly, before he does something to destroy this village and threaten
you, find a way to kill him. If you are successful, I will come to Melekeok and become your wife."

Reklai's willingness to cooperate with Diluei is grounded not only in
his eagerness to form an alliance with a woman from a powerful and
high-ranking house like Uchelkiukl, but also in the ancient path linking
these two characters: "This woman Dirrengulbai [Diluei] and her
brother [Chesou] were 'children' of Melekeok. They had ancestors
from Melekeok, from the fourth house Lukes. This is the reason Reklai
listened to her, because there was a path in ancient times. Had there not
been this path, Reklai would have wanted to marry a much-younger
woman." Reklai spoke to members of the local men's club, who then
went to Ngerdmau by night to kill Ngirngemeiusech. He was buried
there, and as soon as the funeral and mourning period were over Diluei
sent word to Reklai, "Come and bring me to Melekeok." The men of
Ngarachar (At Cost) club were dispatched to bring her to Melekeok,
where she became the chief's wife.

From her new residence in the capital of the other side of heaven
Diluei was finally in a position to accomplish revenge simultaneously
against both Oreor and Ngeremlengui. Each night when she went to
bed she tied her skirt around her legs. Every time Reklai tried to make
love she refused him, until one night Reklai finally asked her, "Is there
something bothering you, so that you do not want to sleep with your
husband?" "Reklai," she said, "I carry a great sorrow with me, and I
will not untie my skirt until this care is removed." Reklai replied, "Tell
me what it is so that I can do something about it." Then Diluei revealed
what she wanted. "I am thinking of that village on the western side of
the island [i.e., Imeiong]. If you don't make some plan to destroy it, I
will never sleep with you." Eager to claim his marital right, Reklai proclaimed, "Before the sun reaches its zenith tomorrow that village will be
destroyed."

At this period in the development of pan-Belauan district polity,
Ngeremlengui and Melekeok used to send visiting parties back and
forth (*kauklechedaol*). When it came time for a group of men from
Ngeremlengui to come to Melekeok, Reklai called together all the local
women, including the wives of the members of Ngaramelekeok council.
He instructed these women that while the men from Ngeremlengui

were being entertained in the meetinghouse, the wives of the titleholders, rather than the young girls, should carry food to them. He
further instructed that when they went to the meetinghouse these
women were to put on their oldest, most frayed skirts with only a small
purse underneath, so that when they stepped up into the building the
men sitting on the ground could see up their skirts. And so when the
visiting party arrived, these women did exactly this when they carried
food into the meetinghouse. Astounded at this degree of license, the
young men from Ngeremlengui sent word back to their villages, saying,
"Send everyone to Melekeok, for there is a most incredible thing going
on here."

Soon Melekeok was crowded with visitors from Ngeremlengui, and
Diluei proceeded to arrange the final act of this carefully orchestrated
drama. She had Reklai send a message to chief Ngirakebou of Ngchesar, saying, "Is there a cooking pot in Ngchesar large enough to contain
the boiled fish of Melekeok?" The meaning of this cryptic message was
simple: can the warriors from Ngchesar handle the total slaughter of
these visitors in Melekeok? But Ngirakebou did not accept the gambit
and sent word back, "No, there is not a pot large enough to hold Kerngilianged. Find some other village to do it." A similar message was
then sent to Chuodelchad, the female chief of Ngiual who replied,
"Yes, Ngiual can handle this.[18] We will expect you at the next full
moon."

The women of Melekeok continued to ply their astonished guests
with special food and fascinating entertainment until the day of departure arrived. Reklai announced to the assembled group, "Chuodelchad
of Ngiual has sent a message inviting all of you to stop off there on your
way home." They made their farewell speeches and then started to walk
across the hillside toward Ngiual. As soon as the men from Ngeremlengui were out of sight, war canoes from Melekeok set out to head
them off at Belod landing-place in Ngiual. But in the meantime
Chuodelchad had arranged to double-cross (*mengeblad*) Reklai and ruin
the plot of Diluei. She instructed the women of Ngiual to lay mulching
grass all over the stone road crossing the taro patch from Ngeasek to
Belod landing. Fighting broke out as soon as the visiting party arrived,
and the men from Ngeremlengui were trapped at Belod. As they fled
down the road to safety, the women of Ngiual were waiting for them
and yelled, "Jump into the taro patch and cover yourselves with mulch-

18. At this time Ngiual was subject to the oppression of Ngerard. Not only did
Ngerard demand tribute from Ngiual, but warriors from Ngerard repeatedly killed all
high-ranking male children. To avoid further bloodshed, the village decided to give the
position of leadership to Chuodelchad, the female titleholder at Ngerueos house.

ing grass." This alone saved the lives of many of the ambushed young men.

A famous warrior from Sibong house in Imeiong named Ngiramengerengei had not been part of the original visiting party in Melekeok, for he had been spending time with his lover Obirir of Beliliou at their favorite trysting spot in the rock islands. As soon as he returned to the village, he learned that his friends were trapped at Belod. He ran across the forests and hillsides of central Babeldaob and came out at Ngiual. Chuodelchad was the first to catch sight of him as he entered the village: "Friend, come over here! Where are you coming from? What is your name?" "I am Ngiramengerengei," he informed her. Over the clamor of battle she shouted back, "Come into my house, for many are being slain at this very moment. If you go down to the channel you too will perish. Many who took flight are being concealed beneath the mulching grass in the taro patch."

So he dashed into her house, climbed up onto the rafter beam, and demanded, "Who is still fighting?" "Ngiraitaoch and a few others," she answered. Minutes later he asked again, "Who is still alive?" "The pride of Ngeremlengui are all dead except Ngiraitaoch, who stands alone on the field of battle." Hearing the name of his closest friend pronounced, Ngiramengerengei jumped down from his hiding place and said, "Give me some betelnut." She gave it to him, and then he demanded once more, "Give me some turmeric (*reng*)." Chuodelchad, frightened at his sudden anger, took out the turmeric from the Ngerueos house supply and Ngiramengerengei quickly smeared this symbol of courage and might on his face, grabbed his spear, and ran toward Belod landing. But by the time he arrived, his friend Ngiraitaoch had already been killed, and in a short time he too was slain by Melekeok warriors. Many were buried where they perished at Belod, but Chuodelchad sent for the body of Ngiramengerengei, which she took care to bury at the grave pavement in front of Ngerueos house.

Upon learning of the fate of their warriors, Ngirturong and Ngiraklang called a meeting of the village and created a new men's club, calling it Ngarabelod (At Belod) in memory of those who had perished in Ngiual. Soon this newly named club began pressuring Ngirturong for permission to conduct a revenge raid against Ngiual. But when word of this desire leaked out, Chuorueos, then leader of Ngiual, instantly sent his messenger to Ngeremlengui to present a valuable to Ngirturong. The still-bitter men's club was not pleased with this collusive *kelulau,* but there was nothing more they could do.

Ngarabelod continued to be the name of Imeiong's strongest club until the American period, when Obak of Ngeredelolk, chief of Beliliou, petitioned the leaders of Imeiong for the name. Ngeredelolk and Imeiong villages are related at "people with common ancestral spirits" (*klauchad er a bladek*), so the gift of this club name was thought to be proper repayment for assistance rendered by men from Beliliou during a building project in Ngeremlengui. A man who witnessed this name-giving ceremony recalled an additional gift which symbolized in material form this reinforced intervillage friendship.

> The titleholders of Imeiong agreed that on account of the ancestral spirits from olden times the name Ngarabelod should be given to them. So (personal name) announced, "The *rubak* are agreed. Take the name Ngarabelod." The men from Beliliou were so overjoyed that they sounded the metal gong which had been used during the work project. But then they said, "We have no real *olangch* of this." So we said to them, "Then take the gong with you back to Beliliou as the *olangch*." They returned to Beliliou, and the two villages began to be even more closely related.

Another *olangch* of this tragic battle was the custom that whenever a men's dance was held during a large feast, dancers from Klang and Ngerturong houses were not permitted to emerge onto the dance floor until the men of Sibong house, the house of brave Ngiramengerengei, had been annointed with turmeric brought specially from Ngerueos house in Nigiual. (Once, when the required turmeric was not available at this crucial moment, a young man from the village had to run all the way to Ngiual and back before the dancers could come out.) It is interesting to note that in the modern story of name giving, the men of Beliliou ask for a "real *olangch*," that is, some physically permanent reminder in addition to the historically laden name Ngarabelod, just as in the context of the aftermath of the Belod war the people of Imeiong adopted both the new club name and the highly visible practice of using imported turmeric as markers of the tragic event.

The numerous elements of political strategy and intervillage relationships found in this story of the slaughter at Belod constitute a mini-ethnography of Belau around 1800 and illustrate many of the generalizations presented in earlier chapters. That young Chesou left the village where as an "offspring of woman" he held a strong claim to the chiefly title Rengulbai demonstrates clearly the level of competition generated among senior males (*okdemaol*) of ranking houses over important titles. Chesou was apparently trying to use service to the related *kebliil* house of Ngerturong as a way to establish a future claim to the Ngirturong title, since his chances of overcoming local opposition at Uchelkiukl seemed small. Ngirngemeiusech's being so easily fooled by Diluei's trickery can perhaps be explained by this Oreor man's eagerness to become allied with such a powerful house, where his children would be in line to become Rengulbai, and by his sense that this future alliance with Uchelkiukl in Imeliik would in the end be a pathway for valuables to flow into Oreor. This strategic marriage supports Kubary's (1873:193) claim that rank endogamy was so prevalent in nineteenth-century Belau that the heads of all the principal houses were "cousins." Diluei's intentional violation of Ngerdmau's status system by constructing a house rivaling that of the village god shows the importance of this kind of symbolism of privilege (*klebkall*) and reminds us that the term "god" (*chelid*) refers, not to some insubstantial supernatural being, but rather to a powerful religious leader whose political power in many villages (especially Ngerdmau, Chol, and Irrai) often exceeded that of the chiefly titleholders.

As far as interdistrict political relations are concerned, the story exemplifies the multiple coding of paths, cornerposts, and sides discussed in previous chapters. Chesou's body was removed from Imeiong and taken to Oreor rather than directly back to his home in Imeliik. One storyteller explained this in terms of the Milad polity, pointing out that Imeiong's gesture was intended to avoid an overtly hostile relationship between Ngeremlengui and Imeliik, the daughter of Milad. Remaining above the fray, Ngeremlengui maintained its position as immune to dispute (*chelechelakl*). And while the initial events of the story involve the siblingship relationship among the villages of Oreor, Imeliik, and Imeiong, the final battle at Belod implies a level of side-of-heaven confederation on the eastern side of Babeldaob. Reklai turned first to Ngchesar and then to Ngiual—the two villages flanking Melekeok—to do the dirty work on behalf of Diluei. Clearly, however, side-of-heaven solidarity around 1800 did not compel either chief Ngirakebou or chief Chuodelchad to do Reklai's bidding. Their independent actions point to a degree of political independence which would not be possible by the end of the century. Similarly in the western side of heaven, lines of alliance between Ngerdmau, Imeiong, and Oreor are shown to have been relatively open and without any degree of blind loyalty or forced subordination to Oreor.

A final point was highlighted for me in 1980, when I traveled to Ngiual with several men from Ngeremlengui in order to photograph the sacred stone Imiungselbad. Located not more than one mile apart, Imiungselbad, symbolic of Ngiual's assistance to Imeiong in the destruction of Uluang, and the stonework at Belod landing, recalling Ngiual's effort to save the lives of the men in the men's club of Ngeremlengui, stand today as powerful reminders that the sides-of-heaven polity of the nineteenth century was not the only political organization operative in Belauan history.

THE PEACE OF OLOUCH

As the stories about Chemeruaol and the war at Belod indicate, the orientation of Ngeremlengui's foreign policy at the close of the eighteenth century was divided between its peaceful alliance with Oreor and a relation of "settled enmity" (Robertson 1876–77:46; i.e., *kaucherecharo*) with Melekeok. And in the mid-nineteenth century, Oreor and Ngeremlengui formed twin loci of the western side of heaven, balance against Melekeok's Ngetelngal federation on the eastern side of heaven. But as Reklai's machinations on behalf of Diluei reveal, this east/west split did not imply that Ngirturong of Imeiong and Reklai of Melekeok were not engaged in various forms of direct, reciprocal political relations during this period. This section traces the development of formalized mutual hostility between these two villages of Milad from the post-Belod period until the final declaration of the "peace of Olouch." Of particular concern is to see how this hostility at the interdistrict level became implicated in the parallel mutual-hostility relationship between Ngiraklang and Ngirturong, the highest-ranking titleholders in Imeiong village.

Throughout much of the nineteenth century, a state of declared war (*lloched*) existed between Ngeremlengui and Melekeok. This is expressed in political language by the phrase "Olouch is severed." Olouch is a forest just east of Ngeremeskang where the main path between Imeiong and Melekeok passes, and the name came to stand for the political "path" between these two powerful villages, just as Klai path stands for the relationship between Oreor and Melekeok, Keanges path for that between Imeliik and Oreor, and Kebtot path for that between Ngesias and Ngeredelolk. War parties departing from Imeiong toward Melekeok climb up Klailchutem ridge and then travel through Ngeremeskang to Olouch, where the war party leader of the group makes the final decision as to which members will make the final assault on the hills above Melekeok.

> When the men go out as a war party, they first travel to Olouch. There the bravest man along with us tests our abilities. He examines the soles of our feet and then says, "Friend, you just stay here and guard the path." Those young men who are afraid just stay behind at Olouch, while the rest proceed on to Ngerulmud. Again, the leader will make an inspection and tell a few of us to

remain there, and only a few of the bravest men will be included in the actual raiding party. From there we proceed to Olebechel Chedeng, which faces Ibesachel hill. At this point the war party consists of only the bravest men like Ngiracheungel and Chetmengeed.

Coming across the forests of central Babeldaob in the opposite direction, raiding parties from Melekeok enter Imeiong through Klailchutem ridge, Ngesisech village, or along the trail passing between the peaks of Roismlengui range.

Raids for head trophies were conducted either in complete secrecy or by mutual arrangement between chiefs Ngirturong and Reklai. If, for example, Reklai was faced with some financial obligation incurred in the exercise of his political function as head of Ngaramelekeong council, and if he did not at the moment hold the proper *chelebucheb* piece (the medium of chiefly politics), he could arrange to acquire the needed money by sending his messenger to Imeiong carrying his broken thatching needle.

> Taking heads is the way *rubak* earn money, although the *rubak* of Ngeremlengui used it as a means of taking revenge. There have only been a few heads taken in Melekeok, and Melekeok has taken a few here. Several of these head trophies were asked for by means of a political strategy called the "politics of the thatching needle." When there is no *chelebucheb* money at the house of Uudes [Reklai's house], this needle is sent to Ngirturong to request a head. Ngirturong then looks around for a man who has no relatives in the village and calls to him, "Come in, my friend. Tomorrow morning I want you to come back here to my house." And so Dirrturong [Ngirturong's wife] then prepares some taro and fish and sets out betelnut and tobacco for him. When he arrives at the house Ngirturong tells him, "Go out to Ngeremeskang to collect betelnut for me." But before he goes out warriors from Melekeok have already arrived there and are lying in wait for him. So when he arrives they cut off his head and carry it back to Melekeok. When the dancing is over, Reklai adds these *chelebucheb* valuables to his handbag and then sends his messenger to Ngirturong, saying, "Ngirturong, thank you very much." The broken thatching needle is significant because it is the sign (*olangch*) that Reklai has been upset by a particular situation and is looking for a head trophy. When the warriors return to Melekeok, the man who actually took the head is given only the finest food to eat, and he is treated royally. He eats pig and chicken, but no fish. And when

they go to dance in Ngiual, he sits under the door beam of the meetinghouse. The women of Ngiual know that the man sitting there is the bravest one, who took the head, and so they will try to arrange a midnight meeting with him. These women fight with each other over the man, for they know that they will have a good time.[19]

Secret cooperation between Reklai and Ngirturong is also called "the strategy of playing catch" (*ongaitonget el kelulau*), named after the children's game in which a firebrand is tossed quickly back and forth. A well-known story which illustrates this particular political technique involves a man named Meduchrutechei of Ngerutechei, who foiled the plans of Reklai and Ngirturong.

Story of Meduchrutechei

Meduchrutechei (Skilled of Ngerutechei) was a very powerful man, as strong as Samson, and this is the reason his name was Meduchrutechei. He was the chief of the village of Ngerutechei and held the title Ucherutechei. He was so strong that they called him Meduchrutechei. Reklai asked for a head, since he did not have any more *chelebucheb* pieces. He prepared the thatching needle and sent it to Ngirturong. Ngirturong saw it and thought, "Who is around that I can sacrifice for Reklai?" He tried to think of someone who no longer had any living relatives, and he finally picked out the person and sent word for him to come to speak with Ngirturong. Ngirturong told Dirrturong to prepare specially made taro, as well as fish, drink, and lots of betelnut for him to chew. The man was invited to dine, and when they finished Ngirturong

---

19. This secret strategy is described from the point of view of Melekeok as follows: "[Reklai] sends his messenger who carries the needle (*rasm*) made out of the stem of the betelnut tree or any other kind of firm tree; the messenger gives the needle to Ngirturong and then informs him: Reklai has something to say. Should the needle be broken (*chelam*), Ngirturong would then send out Ngaratebelik club of Ngeremlengui to Olouch . . . and they will wait there for one of the enemy who is to be killed and taken as a *blebaol* [head trophy]. Should this enemy be captured, they would take him back to Ngeremlengui and go to dance with the head at the dock of Ngerekemais at a place called Chemrert. If the needle is broken in half (*chelemuul*), this means that a war party is approaching. And those enemies whose heads have been captured are taken to a specific place. If the needle is not broken, this means that the message concerns good news for the people. This needle is like a code between Ngirturong and Reklai" (PCAA, Melekeok File). Other stories mention this same strategy used between Ibedul and Reklai; in one case Reklai requests that Ibedul sacrifice a man related patrilaterally (*ulechell*) to Idid house with the expression: *motobedii a bkul a chimam*, "send out the person at your elbow."

said to him, "Go to Ngeremeskang and cut down some betelnut for me to chew." But even before he could go to Ngeremeskang this other man, Meduchrutechei, had gone there to look for fiber cord to use in constructing fish traps. He had a feeling that something unusual was in the air when he arrived at Ngeremeskang. He thought that perhaps men from Melekeok had come to look for a head. He put his trap aside and used the fiber cord to pull down the tops of trees, and when the people of Melekeok who were hiding saw this man toppling over trees they became frightened. Meduchrutechei continued to topple huge trees, and the men watching him thought, "He must be a very brave man, and he is so strong." So they fled back to Melekeok. When Reklai found out what had happened, he sent another messenger to scold Ngirturong, saying, "Why, when I asked for a head, did you send Meduchrutechei?" Ngirturong replied, "I do not know what happened. I did send a man, but this other man must have arrived there first." So this was a rather big insult or cause of shame for Reklai.

Another formalized path between Ngeremlengui and Melekeok which ran counter to this state of declared warfare was called the Raelburech (Path of Ngeburech), after the name of Ngeburech hamlet near Melekeok. Men from Ngeburech would spy on the chiefs from Melekeok and then cross the forest of central Babeldaob to report on Reklai's war plans. This cooperative relationship, which contradicts the normal hostile relations between the respective districts, is described in the following account of the migration of the people of Ngeburech. When Captain Wilson's ship ran aground near Ulong, southwest of Oreor, this island was no longer inhabited. The fate of the people of Ulong is recorded in a narrative describing an assault led by two warriors, Terebkul of Beliliou and Uchermelis of Ngemelis. By planning their attack with the setting sun in the eyes of the men defending Ulong who were assembled along Ikesakes reef, these two valiant men were able to destroy the island, which had for some time oppressed other small islands in the rock islands area.[20] The people of Ulong fled northeast to Ngerekebesang, where their leader Osilek had previously cemented an alliance with chief Uchelkebesadel. Another group split up, with some people going up the east coast of Babeldaob to the small

20. The war strategy of Terebkul and Uchermelis is the origin of the proverbial expression: *ko er a mekemedil a Ulong el dob er a kebesengei,* "like the war at Ulong, which came in the evening" (McKnight 1968:18).

village of Ngeburech near Melekeok and others going up the west coast to Ngeremlengui. This latter group remained for a long time in Imeiong, although they never lost their sense of identity as people related to those who had settled in Ngeburech—both groups being "related through Ulong" (*kauchad er a Ulong*). So in time they decided to rejoin their former village mates, and they petitioned Ngaraimeiong council for permission to leave. Permission was granted, but since these people did not have the large piece of money required to repay the debt they owed to Imeiong for years of hospitality, they offered to rebuild the stone roads and platforms of the village. At this early date, many of the houses of Imeiong (more properly, Imiungs) stood on the open hillside running from Ingesachel (Ascent) and Ikrel (Outside) south of the present village down to the beginning of the mangrove channel which flows past Umad bridge. When the people of Ulong finished moving the stones from this elevated location down closer to Ngerdong channel, they departed and traveled overland to Ngeburech, a small village near Melekeok.

This migration of Ulong people through Imeiong to Ngeburech is the reason for an important warfare strategy used by the leader of Imeiong against Melekeok. Since Ngeburech was a village within the Ngetelngal federation, it would normally be expected to contribute warriors to any war party assembled to attack an enemy. But if the war party was ordered to attack Ngeremlengui, one of these men from Ngeburech would act as a spy (*rabek*) and travel by night through the dense forests that separate Melekeok and Ngeremlengui to warn the people of Imeiong that their village was in danger. This strategy was described by an informant from Ngeremlengui:

> There is a village in Melekeok named Ngeburech, and these people have a very unusual path to Ngeremlengui. When they come they do not travel by the real path—there is just one path between Ngeremlengui and Melekeok. When they come from Ngeburech to Ngeremlengui, they conceal themselves by following what we call the Raelburech. These people are spies, because when they are in Melekeok they hear about the plans of the men's clubs and they know what Reklai's decision in response is. If the decision is to send out a war party, then one of these people waits around until dark and then comes to Ngeremlengui following this Raelburech. He comes directly to the house of Ngirtutelchii [third title in Imeiong] in order to notify him of the plan. But when he gets to the house he speaks in a secret language, for if there are other

people at the house, Ngirutelchii will ask, "Who are they?" And this person will reply, "We are they." He will wait beneath the house until there are no people present and then enter the house without lifting up the woven door mat. He will then repeat the message for Ngirutelchii, "There has been a decision by the men's club of Melekeok to send out a war party to come here. They have asked permission from Reklai and he has agreed to it. They will enter the village by the path at Itab, or at Ngesisech, or at Chemeraech." When Ngirutelchii has been informed, he says to the man, "Have something to eat and drink some coconut syrup." And then this man returns to Ngeburech following Raelburech trail.

And when Ngirutelchii gets up in the morning he will go to Orukei square and speak to Ngirturong and Ngiraklang, saying, "Call together the *rubak* for a conference." They will then discuss this affair which has been planned in Melekeok, and since three different paths were mentioned, they will gather the men's clubs from both side channels. And then the *rubak* address the young men: "There are three paths by which the war party might enter. Which club is going to guard these paths?" One of the clubs replies, "We will guard on the first path." And another of the clubs replies, "We will guard the second path." And another club replies, "And we will guard the third path." The other three clubs will stay behind in the village, but should there be a war cry, then they will rush out to assist. No one from Melekeok knows that the people from Ngeremlengui are prepared for the arrival of their warriors.

This account highlights two important points, the first concerning political paths and the second concerning the division of responsibility among cornerpost titleholders in Imeiong. First, the friendship tie between Ngeburech and Imeiong had to be expressed secretly, because it did not "pass through" (*okiu*) the proper level of political organization, that is, through the chiefly representatives of the two villages. Rather, the path of the people of Ngeburech passed literally as well as symbolically through the untraveled forest where no trace of the linkage remained, where the trail did not become progressively more distinct, and where no traveler could be seen making the journey. Second, the text is an excellent example of the specific responsibility assigned to Ngirutelchii, the third-ranking title in Ngaraimeiong council.

In ancient times Ngirutelchii had the responsibility to defend against war parties if there was an open state of war between Ngeremlengui and Melekeok. Also, Ngirutelchii had command of the timing for sending out a raiding party. It is also his job to inform the other *rubak* that the time has come for a war party to go out. And he also informs them that the village is prepared to defend against warriors coming here.

A second relationship of mutual hostility which intensified during the second half of the nineteenth century was that between Ngirturong and Ngiraklang of Imeiong. From the genealogies of titleholders of these two houses it is clear that both Ngerturong and Klang houses were often unable to find suitable men from within Imeiong itself to carry these high titles, so "mutual houses" in other villages were drawn on to recruit new titleholders (Parmentier 1984). As the stories about Chemeruaol and Belod show, and as Captain Wilson's narrative confirms, Ngiraklang still held the leadership of the village in 1800, but by the time of Semper's visit in 1860 and Cheyne's stay in 1864, Ngirturong Otobed (Banished) had reestablished residence at a place named Ongerool in neighboring Ngeremetengel and from there had begun to challenge the authority of Ngiraklang (Cheyne 1863–66: 28 July 1864).[21] The reasons behind the decision of Ngaraimeiong council to banish Ngirturong Otobed are not entirely clear, and the nature of his path to Ongerool is given radically different interpretations by various contemporary storytellers. According to one opinion,

> If a person from Ikelau house in Oreor becomes Ngirturong, he lives here at Ongerool house, while a person from within Ngeremlengui who becomes Ngirturong will live at Ngerturong house in Imeiong. If the man is from Oreor, he lives at Ongerool and then walks over to Imeiong to confer with the *rubak* there, and then he returns to Ngeremetengel. The reason that these Oreor people and one of the [Ngirturong] titleholders fled [from Imeiong] and came into the channel of Ngeremetengel and asked for some land to build a house is, I think, that Ngirturong committed some serious offense (*delengerenger*) against the *rubak* of Imeiong. This happened a long time ago. About six men have held the title Ngirturong since then. It was Ngirturong Otobed (Banished) who was banished. He came to Ngeremetengel and asked for land belonging to Mechoang house, and this is why Ongerool is located right next to Mechoang. But Ngirturong had no land of his own here, and once he was banished he was just like a low-ranking person, as if he no longer held the title. So he built a very large house here and made up the name Ongerool (Storehouse).

21. This man is also referred to as Ngirturong Mladeraterreter (Died from Sickness). Kubary (1873) notes that he held the title Ngiraikelau in Oreor and died in 1872.

Living at Ngeremetengel, Ngirturong had easier access to the growing commercial activities of foreign merchants, closer contact with his relative and business partner Ngiraikelau of Ikelau house in Oreor, and strong relations with the locally powerful Mechoang house, which ceded land for the construction of Ongerool. By the 1860s Ongerool and its subsidiary houses had become the new official "house of the title" of Ngirturong; and the three Ngirturong titleholders who shared kinship ties to Ikelau are all buried at the grave pavement at Ongerool rather than at the traditional site at Ngerturong grave pavement in Imeiong.

This relocation of the grave pavement not only signals the growing split between Ngiraklang and Ngirturong as rival leaders of Ngaraimeiong council, but also marks the beginning of Ngeremetengel's emergence as the point of contact between Ngeremlengui district and the West, a process which continued throughout the nineteenth century and which was finalized during the Japanese administration when the colonial police station and bauxite plant were constructed there.

The hostility between these two high-ranking Imeiong titles and the warfare between the villages of Imeiong and Melekeok are not independent phenomena, for the foreign policy of Ngeremlengui is the political strategy of its leaders, whether Ngirturong or Ngiraklang. So internal conflict over the succession to and rank position of these two titles is bound to have repercussions in the district's political relations with Melekeok. And conversely, the success of the *kelulau* aimed at Melekeok and Oreor directly effects the standing of these Imeiong titleholders.

Between the time of Ngirturong Ngirngotel, when the path of Olouch first became severed, and the time of Ngirturong Remengesau, when peace between Ngeremlengui and Melekeok was concluded, more than a dozen raiding parties traveled overland between the two districts. Ngaratelebkatl club of Melekeok was the first war party to enter Ngeremlengui to capture a head. In the early part of the century there was a small village named Cheloitelbeluu (Abandoned Village) located on the banks of the Ngeremeskang river. Only a few families remained in the village to keep up the gardens. Warriors from Melekeok armed with clubs and adzes met no opposition as they descended upon this lonely outpost. They cut off the heads of several of the residents and then fled with their trophies across the hillside back to Melekeok. This attack severed the path of Olouch and forced the surviving people of Cheloitelbeluu to abandon their homes and gardens and come to Ngerutechei village, where they joined Ngemes house.

For the next twenty or thirty years, clubs from Ngeremlengui and Melekeok stalked each other's villages in hopes of finding a lone women in the taro patch, a family left unprotected, or a solitary fisherman who could be dispatched without risk. Ngaraboes (Rifles) club of Melekeok, so called because they were armed with imported rifles, which continued to pour into the islands, took the head of the son of Ngiratemaloi of Ngesisech, whom they caught alone up a coconut tree at Irisong bathing pool. Ngaraboes club returned shortly afterwards to kill an unsuspecting young man from Ngerumesemong house in Ngerutechei as he returned from a midnight tryst with his lover on Kesekim hillside above Imeiong.

But when the same club made more ambitious plans to destroy the whole village of Roisbeluu, Reklai Temol of Melekeok opposed the plan by telling the club, "You may not go there, for Roisbeluu is a dangerous/holy (*kengaol*) place. My own father was from there, and for this reason you will not be able to destroy it. If you go there you will be killed." But the club refused to heed this warning, and when they attacked Roisbeluu, one of their own men was struck down by a spear. His compatriots abandoned him for dead, and when the people of Ngeremlengui came upon him, he shouted, "I am not a man from Melekeok! I am from Imeliik." Not fooled by this ruse, one of the warriors from Ngeremlengui shouted back, "Oh no; we saw you come from Melekeok," and then speared him to death.

Concubines living in clubhouses were easy targets for these raids, for they were often left alone when local men were away fishing or doing village labor. Once the men of Ngaraboes club sneaked up on Diberdii clubhouse at Chemeraech square in Imeiong, and when they learned that club members had gone to Ngeremetengel to assist in the construction of a new canoe house, they cut off the head of one of the concubines who had fallen asleep. Just then two men from Imeiong returned from work and chased the Ngaraboes warriors, who escaped over the hill waving their guns and carrying the head of this unfortunate woman from Imeliik.

After each of these raids, young warriors from Ngeremlengui, either with or without the consent of Ngaraimeiong council, plotted a revenge attack against one of the smaller villages in the opposite Ngetelngal federation. Each of these raids is remembered for its particular strategy and for the name of especially brave or clever leaders. Under the leadership of Ngiracheungel of Ngchemesed, for example, the warriors of Ngeremlengui took advantage of inside knowledge that a particular house in Ngeburech hamlet near Melekeok was the site of frequent domestic quarrels, and that whenever the people of Melekeok would rush up to investigate the shouting they would find only fighting within the house. So when the Ngarabelod war party attacked and cut off the heads of the man, his wife, and their child, no one in the village responded to their cries and no one gave chase to the fleeing warriors.

A small group of warriors, including a man from Ngerutechei named Ngiracholengau and a man from Ngerechelong living in Imeiong, planned an attack on Blissang, a small village near Melekeok. Ngiracholengau was related to people in Blissang, and during one of his visits there he had noticed that one house stood alone near the edge of the forest. In order to mark the trail to the house, he went into the forest and collected luminescent mushrooms, which he placed in a line leading to the front door of the house. Upon returning to Ngeremlengui, he called together his fellow club members at Didelbad stone bridge in Imeiong (where headhunting plans were made under cover of night) and told them, "We can easily take a head at Blissang because I have arranged a way to do it. When we go there at night we will be able to find the path leading to the house, since I have lined it with mushrooms."

The next night they waited in the woods near Blissang until the couple had gone to bed. The group decided that one of their party would enter the house by lifting up the floorboards and then kick down the door to let in the second, while the third would stand outside in case they met opposition. When the first warrior penetrated the house he found the couple sleeping, but before he could spear them both the woman suddenly awoke and screamed, "War! War!" The village of Blissang was thereby alerted, and men rushed up to the house, where the third warrior cried out to them, "People of Blissang, rest easy! Imiungs has arrived and the fighting will last until morning. If you try to fight us now in the darkness, you will all perish. Come back in the morning when we can see each other and fight then." But this was just to gain time, and the three men grabbed the heads and ran through the woods back to Ngeremlengui.

Then a group of five men from Ngaramecherocher (Salty) club of Ngchemesed under the leadership of fearless Ngiracheungel attacked Ngchesar, a village on the other side of Babeldaob south of Melekeok. A young man named Marsil pleaded with Ngiracheungel to be allowed to join the war party, and the older men were not able to dissuade him. When they came upon a man from Ngcheangel living near Mesengebang path leading into Ngchesar, Ngiracheungel speared him, and then in order to share the glory with his associates he ordered another man to cut off the Ngcheangel man's head.[22] Ngiracheungel also found

---

22. Some versions note that Ngiracheungel's attack was carefully planned to kill the man living at Mesengebang, the same person who earlier had taken the head of the concubine sleeping at Diberdii.

a small child at the house and gave the boy to young Marsil to guard until the battle was over. In his eagerness to take his first war trophy, Marsil cut off the child's head, not knowing that Ngiracheungel intended to take the child home to raise him as his son.

Similar stories from Ngeremlengui tell of one head taken at Omiomelketau near Imeiong, two taken in Ngersuul village, and one unsuccessful raid by Ngarabelod club armed with guns purchased from the merchant O'Keefe.[23]

Throughout this period of reciprocal headhunting raids between Ngeremlengui and Melekeok, Ngirngotel held the title Ngirturong and Temol held the title Reklai in the two capital villages. At the death of Ngirngotel a young man named Remengesau (who was related to Oreor's second-ranking house, Ikelau) became the new Ngirturong. This Remengesau, the son of Ibedul and a woman from powerful Ikelau house, altered the course of the *kelulau* which Ngeremlengui had been following for decades by sending word to Reklai Temol, "Reklai, I am still a young man, but have I have become the chief. I want very much for there to be peace between us." Remengesau's aggressive pursuit of peace was in part conditioned by a sense of confidence, in that the active trade between Ngeremlengui and European merchants had recently brought a large supply of guns into his hands. Reklai sent a messenger with his reply, "Very well, but Reklai still has one score to settle with respect to the *kelulau*. Reklai is a very old man, and unless the score is settled, he cannot be washed clean in terms of the *kelulau*. When this is taken care of Melekeok will be the side channel of Ngeremlengui." The meaning of these cryptic words was clear to Ngirturong: unless Reklai was allowed to destroy one more village, no peace would be possible.

Ngirturong considered the various small hamlets within Ngeremlengui and decided to sacrifice Ngetmadei, because there were only a few people left in this inland village, and because it was isolated from the main road between Imeiong and Ngeremetengel. So he sent word to Melekeok to inform Reklai, "It has all been arranged. The village of Ngetmadei is yours to bathe yourself in." Reklai responded to this with the message, "Then all is set. A club from Ngchesar will come to destroy Ngetmadei." Ngchesar had previously petitioned Reklai for this opportunity to revenge the head taken earlier in their village by warriors from Ngeremlengui. To complete his collusive strategy Ngir-

23. Of all the raids recalled by my informants, only two involved rifles. O'Keefe sold forty rifles to Ngarabelod club; these were distributed to ten warriors from each of the four principal houses of Imeiong. The Spanish and German administrations conducted careful searches to collect all imported firearms; during the Japanese period a final search was carried out.

turong recalled his own warriors who were guarding Ngetmadei, so when the attack came men from Ngchesar easily killed three old men and one child and then burned down their houses. By the time Ngira-cheungel and his Ngarabelod club were alerted, they were too late to catch up with the warriors from Ngaramerikl club of Ngchesar, who swam to safety across the Ngeremeskang river.

Back in the village one hotheaded man named Chelsengel, suspicious that a secret *kelulau* between Ngirturong and Reklai was in operation, pointedly challenged his own chief: "He is the one that unleashed this flood upon our village! Kill him at once!" Ngirturong pleaded for his life, "Friend, I may have been at fault, it is true. But first let us bury the people who have perished at Ngetmadei." After the funeral Remengesau Ngirturong left Ngeremlengui in a self-imposed banishment (*dmik*) and took up residence at Ikelau house in Oreor, where he carried the title Ngiraikelau. For two years Imeiong was without a Ngirturong. Finally Ngiraklang and Ngaraimeiong council sent word to Oreor to tell Remengesau that all was forgotten, and that the rash young man Chelsengel had been out of place in speaking so harshly in front of such a high-ranking superior. Accepting this conciliatory *kelulau*, Remengesau visited his father Ibedul at Idid house and told him: "Father, I am going to return to Imeiong, and I intend to conclude peace at Olouch." Ibedul gave his son one *chelebucheb* valuable to use to "make the path peaceful."

The peace conference between Ngirturong Remengesau and Reklai Temol took place at Olouch on the border between Ngeremlengui and Melekeok. These two chiefs lived there in temporary camps for over a month, while women from Imeiong and Melekeok supplied the two parties with food carried daily all the way from their home villages. In their daily sessions, the older Temol instructed the younger Remengesau in the finer points of political strategy and traditional wisdom. When all was agreed upon, Ngirturong gave an *chelebucheb* piece of the *kluat* class to Reklai, who returned an equally valuable piece (some say the very same piece) to Ngirturong. Temol's parting words to Remengesau were: "You have become my younger brother (*ochellek*), and when I die, come and bury me. Then Okemii [the landing at Melekeok] will be your side channel." To which Remengesau replied, "I will, and from now on Chelsechei [the landing at Imeiong] is the side channel of Melekeok."

These two men and their parties returned home, and the peace of Olouch was established for the first time. Temol's wish that Remengesau bury him was not, however, fulfilled, since only a few years later Remengesau was himself killed while fishing with explosives. And so it was Temol, by then a very old man, who came to Ongerool house in Ngeremetengel to bury his "younger brother." Mourning at the grave of his political ally, Reklai said, "Young friend, I thought you would bury me, and now I have come to bury you. Our brotherhood (*klodam*) is over."

The words exchanged between Remengesau and Reklai are part of the political language used by village chiefs in their negotiations and presuppose an understanding of both the sides-of-heavens polity and the siblingship model of villages derived from the Story of Milad. In saying that Imeiong's landing place would be the side channel of Melekeok, Remengesau meant that from the time of this peace forward the two villages would no longer be associated as warring sides of heavens, but rather as a balanced, cooperative unit divided into two sides of a single mangrove channel. Temol's point here was achieved by a recontextualization of the model of sides from heavens to channels, that is, from the pan-Belauan context to the village context, rather than by an application of a different sociopolitical metaphor. And his words at Remengesau's funeral, that these two chiefs had become brothers, were an allusion, not to a fictive kinship relationship between these individuals, but to the brotherhood of Imiungs and Melekeok villages as sons of the goddess Milad.

THE ASSASSINATION OF NGIRACHEUNGEL

This new *kelulau* established by Ngirturong Remengesau and Reklai Temol had immediate effects on their respective villages even before the accidental death of Remengesau in approximately 1890. When the trader O'Keefe's ship *Lilla* ran aground north of Ngerechelong in 1880, villages on the eastern side of Babeldaob were accused of destroying the vessel and plundering its cargo. With the willing assistance of Ibedul and the other titleholders of Oreor, O'Keefe pressed formal charges against Melekeok. As a result, Reklai was required to pay 4,600 pounds sterling, a fine which he neither understood nor was capable of paying (Grove 1891; Kubary 1885:139–40). Unable to come up with the payment either in cash or in produce such as copra, pearl shells, trepang, and turtle shells, Reklai and the residents of Melekeok fled from their homes when British warships came to bombard their village in 1882 (East 1885:311–12). As Kubary describes these events,

> Remembering the fate of the second to last Ibedul of Oreor, who had been shot on orders of the English, Reklai ran away and the whole land after him, and for such unheard of behavior the whole

village, eight large *bai* [meetinghouses] and all the dwelling houses,
were burned down, the *bai* being blown up with dynamite![24] The
people of Oreor triumphed and extorted money secretly, loading
their canoes with plunder under the protection of the men-of-war.
The punishment was not lifted and was to be paid nine months
later, when respónsibility for failure would fall on Reklai. This was
the last *benged* [siege] in Palau. (Kubary 1885:140)

The irony of Kubary's last sentence is lost on those who do not realize
that *benged el mekemad* (sieges) waged by Belauans had ended when
Ngeremlengui and Melekeok concluded peace at Olouch. Only foreign
intervention perpetuated the wholesale destruction of villages for political ends.

People from Melekeok did not flee at random when the shelling
began; they came to Ngeremlengui under the protection and assistance
of their newly found friend, Ngirturong Remengesau. The following
text, dictated by a *rubak* who held the same title Kubary had carried
ninety years earlier, tells the story from Melekeok's point of view.

There was a ship aground near Melekeok, which the people from
Ngerechelong visited first and said, "Let's go get our things in it."
They got things in it and left to stay in a cave at Ngerechur with
sailors. However, there was a big box which the ship's compass was
hidden in. There was a man who sat on it to protect and watch it,
so out of curiosity they kicked the man and took it, that made
O'Keefe very furious toward the natives. So he sent word to Oreor
to report the damage to his ship, at the same time he charged
people to pay certain amounts to him. It didn't take long when the
Spanish ship came in from Oreor, with some other people in
Oreor whom they dropped at Ngerecheluu who started to burn
houses. So they put a bomb under the *bai* [meetinghouses] and
blew them up. So the people from Melekeok started running away
to the mountains. During that time Temol was Reklai. They ran all
the way to the mountain Elbraikiu, they built houses and stayed
there. Ngirturong from Ngeremlengui heard about them, so he
gathered his people and said, "Go bring the eggs." Meaning bring
Reklai and his people to come and stay with us. So Reklai and his
people stayed at Ngeremlengui for a while. Then the folks from

24. In his official report on the incident, Captain East (1882) insists that he ordered
his men to burn down only Reklai's house and the meetinghouse, but that an energetic
men's club from Oreor (summoned to Melekeok to aid the provisioning of the British
ship) set fire to private houses.

Ngeremlengui together with them built temporary houses at Melekeok for them to stay. Melekeok was damaged very greatly, since it was considered as a ruling place or village. (PCAA, Melekeok File)

From the point of view of Ngeremlengui, this offer of protection to Melekeok was prescribed by the notion that the former village is the "older brother" of the latter. When the people of Melekeok arrived at the forest on the outskirts of Imeiong, the leader of Melekeok's men's club sent his messenger to confer with Ngirturong. This message was shockingly forceful, given the fact that Melekeok had just been destroyed: "Make room, or else we will enter the village and kill someone." Ngirturong responded to these strong words with an expression showing his recently acquired political skills: "Go tell Louch that the eggs of Melekeok have come to the grouper fish." The meaning of this *kelulau* is that in its fragile condition Melekeok is safe from the warriors of Oreor's Ngarametal club, for if they should try to reach them now, their hands would be cut by the dangerous grouper fish, that is, by Ngeremlengui. So after Melekeok was rebuilt, with the assistance of Ngeremlengui's men's clubs, Reklai Temol sent a large *bachel* valuable named Nglalemulekl to Remengesau for the "village reconstruction payment."[25]

Remengesau's peaceful overture to the "eggs" of Melekeok stands in sharp contrast to the ambitious and violent "politics of fire" he pursued within Ngeremlengui. As the son of Ibedul by a high-ranking woman from Ikelau and as the new "younger brother" of Reklai Temol, he had little cause to fear challenge based on social rank from the titleholders in Imeiong's first house, Klang. Remengesau further strengthened his position as a "powerful man" (*mesiich el chad*) by expanding his trading establishment at Ongerool in Ngeremetengel. He hired men from Yap, Tobi, and even the Philippines to work for him in return for tobacco and subsistence needs. But then a man named Ngiracheungel, known throughout Belau for daring feats of bravery in battle and for a self-confident and often vicious nature, took the Ngiraklang title on the relatively weak basis of being the son of a previous Ngiraklang titleholder, rather than on the basis of being an offspring of women from Klang house. At this particular moment Klang was seriously weakened by the departure of several of its senior women to Chol village, leaving only a few offspring-of-men members remaining in Imeiong. But in

---

25. Kubary (1885:137) notes that Oreor performed the same role when it reestablished the residents of Ngebuked after their village was destroyed.

spite of his lack of strong matrilineal status, Ngiracheungel became a well-respected titleholder. He is remembered for walking armed with his gun alongside local women as they went to and from distant taro patches.

Competition between the two principal houses of Ngerturong and Klang reached a climax when Remengesau commissioned two Yapese men named Belaluk and Beuch, then living in Ngeremetengel, to kill Ngiracheungel. (An informant dated this event at 1885, the year prior to the beginning of the Spanish administration.) One day when Ngiracheungel had gone fishing at Sebungel, a short distance off the coast of Imeiong, these Yapese men came upon him and shot him. At first Ngirturong ordered his messenger Dingelius to have Ngiracheungel's body unceremoniously thrown into the sea, but a high-ranking woman from Klang opposed this insult to the sanctity of the Ngiraklang title (*meang er a klngiraklang*). Before the crowd which gathered in the village after the murder, she commanded them as "people of Imeiong" (in contrast to "residents of Imeiong") to prepare a proper funeral and then to bury Ngiracheungel at the grave pavement at Duab, one of the satellite houses affiliated with Klang.

The political situation immediately after this event was tense while Remengesau waited to see if the male elders and senior women of Klang would summon another man to take the title. Fearful that the same thing would happen again, these people of Klang chose rather to let the title remain vacant for a time, which gave Remengesau several opportunities to claim the prescribed food portion (*deliukes*) of the village chief.

> Ngirturong killed Ngiracheungel in order to become the higher-ranking *rubak,* but he could not accomplish this by simply declaring that he was higher-ranking, since he lived in fear of Ngiracheungel. There would certainly have been a major conflict if he had just said, "I outrank you." So by plotting the murder he automatically became the higher-ranking man. After this there was a long period of time without a replacement for Ngiraklang. The council never made any official pronouncement to recognize Ngirturong's supremacy, but whenever there was a customary event which involved giving out food portions to the various *rubak,* Ngirturong took the portion designated for Ngiraklang [i.e., the first portion]. This happened perhaps three or four times before there was a general awareness in Imeiong that Ngirturong was the first title in Imeiong. This is called "seizure of the title." During Krämer's visit no one told him anything about the events which led up to this change in rank.

This informant's knowledge of the information Krämer received concerning this event is absolutely correct, for as Krämer himself notes, "The Ngiraklang no longer has any power; it passed long ago to the second Ngirturong" (1917–29, 2:144). That this seizure was only the formal ratification of a gradual process in which Ngiraklang's power became eroded through the successful external political alliances concluded by leaders from Ngerturong house is supported by Kubary's observation from the 1870s: "In Ngeremlengui the No. 1 title in the chief village of Imiungs is Ngiraklang; but the supreme leadership of the whole land [Ngeremlengui] was seized by the head of the Turong [Ngerturong] family, Ngirturong, who really should be chief No. 2" (1885:80).[26] And finally, it was Remengesau's violation of the sacredness of the Ngiraklang title rather than his murder of a particular individual which led people in the village to say that his own accidental death was the result of his being "cursed by sacredness."

Considering the importance of this title usurpation for understanding the history of Ngeremlengui, it is fortunate that there is extant the Chant of Ngiracheungel, which describes the political implications of Remengesau's actions in terms of the *kelulau* of the district. Being extant is not, however, the same as being readily interpretable, since the allusive style and archaic vocabulary of chiefly chants (*chesols*) are today often beyond the grasp of most middle-aged Belauans and are almost impossible to put into coherent English. The Chant of Ngiracheungel was composed in approximately 1914 by a woman named Lotelel, who came to Ngeremlengui from Ngerard. After invoking the ancestral spirits (*oltuubladek*) of the village, she dictated the words that the spirits spoke through her, line by line, to several old women of Imeiong. The texts available today come from two men who studied the chant from these women.[27]

26. In the 1870s Kubary (1873:210) observed that Ngirturong, living then in Ngeremetengel rather than Imeiong, "ruled all of Ngeremlengui." At that time Ngirturong also held the second title in Oreor, Ngiraikelau. Captain Stevens (1867) even refers to Ngirturong as "a Chief and King" of Ngeremlengui, although his general attitude was that Ngirturong's actual status was less than this projected image.

27. I studied the chant during several intensive sessions in 1978 and 1979 from one of these men, who is the present Ngiraklang titleholder. We both benefited from the fact that the ethnomusicologist Yamaguchi had made an excellent tape of the chant as sung by the late Santos Ngodrii Kloteraol, a brilliant expert on chanting. This tape is broadcast almost biweekly over the local radio station. Unfortunately the English translation that Yamaguchi gives is only a rough paraphrase (presumable made through Japanese) of the words Kloteraol sings. Another translation is available in PCAA, Ngeremlengui File.

Chant of Ngiracheungel

Ser a lekiei a Ngirturong e ng di melebekla a kelulul me a
   Uchelngebard a melechor er a Imiungs.

Kemiu a rubekul a Sechesob e ng dikea be mkldibel e ak dmu chelei me
   lekong me lebo ltutuu er a rengmiu a meang el kelulau a kelulul a
   ngebard.

Me kau a mocha er a dui me ke omekall er a beluu me ko mo mekelii a
   meserii me ng di melalemalt e ruba me lak dekoll.

Ngiuei Imiungs el ngura a mlai el chuodel kung me te mo rouar e te mo
   tongii me ng oltak a kelulau el mo tmurk er a Delui. A
   Ngaremeketii a ngar er ngii me te mo otiriked e te omes a meang el
   kelulau a kelulul a ngebard.

Ngiuei Imiungs e ruba a dikea a chemedii me ng di blechakl e mengetut
   e mei merrechokl.

Olbilmeai ng techa a chelid el ngar er eou el mo ulterkii e medei e ng
   dikea a tebechelel me a Imiungs a blechakl.

Obilmeai ng techa a chelid el ngar er eou el mo ulterkii e medei me ke
   ngoura a Imiungs e rubak el mo chebecheb.

Ngiuei Imiungs e ruba ng dikea kedung e ng sorir a ngebard e kid a di
   merrechokl.

Kom milechellii a ldengerenger el omtok er a kelulau el ngar er kemiu e
   me er eou e domekellomes a rengmiu e dolemelubet.

While Ngirturong was still living, his *kelulau* proceeded with head
   bent low, but then Uchelngebard (Foremost of the West) made
   Imiungs haughty.

You elders of Sechesob no longer gather together, and so I tell you
   now that the marvelous *kelulau* which has entered your hearts is
   Western *kelulau.*

Now that you are going to take the title and navigate the village,
   you must trim the sails to keep it on a straight course, *rubak,* so
   that we will not capsize.

Imiungs is a boat in dire need of repair, which is now being taken
   out. They gather together ropes to tie it together, and they place
   the *kelulau* on board and land at Delui, where Ngarameketii
   examines it carefully, and they see that this marvelous *kelulau* is
   Western *kelulau.*

Imiungs, *rubak,* no longer has anyone who can repair it, and so it
   floats freely, drifting out to sea as its sails flutter down.

Obilmeai, which god do you entreat to descend and die, so that
   without a mooring pole Imiungs just drifts?

Obilmeai, which god do you entreat to descend and die, so you
could destroy Imiungs, *rubak,* so that it turns upside down?
Imiungs, *rubak,* no longer has law-abiding people, for everyone
favors Western ways, and we all flutter downward.
You have given birth to lawbreakers who oppose the *kelulau* which
legitimately belongs to you and who have brought it down low.
Let our hearts be enlightened and let us be absolved of these
wicked things.

This chant is spoken from the perspective of the ancestral spirit
(*bladek*) of Ngiraklang Ngiracheungel, who looks down upon Imeiong
and warns the elders of Sechesob (the poetic name for Klang house)
that the imported *kelulau* brought into the village by Ngirturong Remengesau is not the legitimate *kelulau* which is the birthright of Imeiong. It is rather the *kelulau* of the West, the politics of guns and hired
assassins. The most important responsibility of the new village leader is
to steer the ship of state so that it does not capsize, but this has become
difficult because Imeiong is in drastic need of repair, having lost its
captain who alone possessed the skill to repair its tattered sails. And in
spite of the precarious condition of the village, Imeiong is now planning on transporting this recently discovered foreign *kelulau* to Delui
landing place in Oroer, where the members of Ngarameketii council
will examine it carefully to see whether or not the people of Imeiong
have all been led into lawlessness. The chant closes with a plea for
wisdom, a plea that the village can put off the wicked ways of the West
and return to the *kelulau* appropriate to Imeiong's status as the firstborn of Milad.

From the institution of its four respected titles by the Ruchel gods to
the murder of its chief Ngiraklang Ngiracheungel by hired assassins, the
story of Imeiong's intradistrict and interdistrict political relations involves the village's struggle to legitimize and defend its preeminent
position in the face of internal and external pressures which make this
effort increasingly impossible. Continuing to assert its status as "older
brother" to other villages and claiming to house the sacredness of all
Belau, Imeiong asserts a history which appears to us as profoundly
ahistorical, in the sense that it constantly denies the village's engagement in political turmoil. Imeiong refuses to acknowledge the contingent implications of certain historical processes and to allow any
olangch of political change to penetrate its ideology of superiority. The
progression of economically dominant villages within Ngeremlengui
(Ngeremeskang, Imeiong, Ngeremetengel) is dismissed as sharply as
the notion that Imeiong "achieved" its status as capital village by defeat-

ing Uluang. And similar wars of district consolidation in Ngetelngal and Ngerekldeu are cited as parallel defenses of the polity instituted by Milad, rather than as evidence for pan-Belauan political development. Even Imeiong's sideline role in the struggle to harness Western economic and military power during the late-eighteenth and nineteenth centuries is viewed not in terms of its concrete ineffectiveness but rather in terms of its legitimizing passivity.

In a context of the growing domination of Belauan politics by the two sides of heaven, Imeiong persists in interpreting events according to the model of four cornerposts. Imeiong's title system itself, with wives rather than sisters of *rubak* taking female titles, implies a focus on village endogamy over interdistrict alliance, and this draws on the ideology of pan-Belauan consanguinity among the children of Milad. The repulsion of Chemeruaol is taken to be a reaffirmation of the *kebliil* solidarity between Klang and Ngedengchol houses and as the assertion of an older brother's authority to suppress a rebellious younger brother, rather than as a foreshadowing of Imeiong's military dependence on Oreor. The independence of village chiefs on the eastern side of heaven displayed in the narrative about the revenge of Diluei suggests that Reklai and Ibedul did not rule over monolithic confederations. The headhunting raids reciprocated by Imeiong and Melekeok also indicate that the path between Oreor and Melekeok was not the only important axis in Belau. And finally, the usurpation of village leadership by Ngir-turong is considered to be the result of imported *kelulau* rather than the expression of the rising importance of Ngeremetengel's commercial concerns. It is also seen as a result of the powerful alliance between Ngerturong and Ikelau houses in the face of the demographic weakness of Klang house, which awarded its high title to local child-of-man candidates rather than to non-local child-of-woman individuals.

✲

Conclusion

In concluding his assessment of recent efforts toward a rapprochement between history and anthropology, Cohn (1981) observes that one of the ironic consequences of this disciplinary division is that the historians' history, narrowly grounded in the authoritative archive of written testimony, and the anthropologists' history, too often based on the assumptions about timeless, archaic society, deal with completely different temporal fields. In studies of situations of colonial contact, for example, the former begins at the moment of discovery, while the latter typically "ends with the coming of the destructive other—the Europeans" (1981:252). In an effort to avoid this unfortunate complementary distribution, I have concentrated on showing how the postcontact period in Belau has been interpreted as the sequential focusing on different models of historical narration, while demonstrating that these rhetorical idioms are themselves explicable in terms of internally generated cultural principles.

Furthermore, I have made liberal use of both Belauan testimony from stories, chants, and exegesis and Western eyewitness and documentary evidence. Contrary to Price's (1980) claim that the class of historical evidence consciously produced by the people being studied must be sharply separated from documentary materials whose original recording and preservation were unintended, my procedure has been to relate the two categories in order to grasp the function of these historicizing signs in particular contexts of social action. In fact, far from being dismissible on the grounds of being culturally mediated or ideologically tainted, the "political myths" of Belau have proven to be priceless for understanding the motivations behind different positions in the political hierarchy. In other words, the analysis of indigenous signs, models, and meanings has not assumed that these "cultural templates," to use a phrase employed by Hanson and Hanson (1983:191), can be viewed in the abstract, apart from their instantiation in particular political struggles. So our analytical options are not restricted to the verifiable positivist account of events as they "actually happened," constructed according to "critical tests," using "sophisticated techniques of chronological reconstruction," and isolating out "possible factors of distortion" (Mercer 1979), and some mystified emic concept of the past, since much of what does happen in social life involves the processual realization of "indigenous perspectives on the nature of change and time" (McDowell 1985:31).

In speaking of any cultural phenomena, one can never consider "what happens" apart from uncovering the meaningful categorizations that specify the significance of events for social actors. This claim is merely a generalization of the position taken by the Boas-Sapir tradition, which insisted for the study of language on careful attention to actors' subjective valuation of their language as the key to uncovering the dimension of "psychological reality." Languages, and by extension other cultural codes such as "history" in the sense used here, are not objects capable of being investigated through positivistic techniques limited to the synchronic perspective. Rather, they are essentially historical objects "maintained through the subjectivity of the native others, at each moment part of an unbroken transmission of subjective intuitions" (Silverstein 1984:10).

This is not the same thing, however, as declaring that people are always fully aware of all the relevant dimensions of the "what" of history, only that their interpretation will always be relevant to an adequate anthropological analysis, since it is this understanding which forms the basis for history as a locally realized social process and as a socially constituted form of collective subjectivity. Belauan islanders who looked in amazement at the sailing ships and then steam vessels that arrived at their harbors did not at first comprehend the purposes of these voyages and obviously did not grasp the mechanical principles behind the cannon fire which immediately become decisive in their interdistrict warfare. But that these European visitors were categorized as parallel to the Ruchel gods who, according to myths, made periodic migrations through the archipelago, that the colorful explosion of British fireworks on the eve of battle was compared to the activity of the war god Orekim whose natural embodiment is the rainbow, and that the worthless baubles distributed by various foreign captains were considered to be valuable tokens of wealth cannot be ignored in any account of what happened in instances of contact, warfare, and exchange.

Moreover, in addition to these examples of the hermeneutic subsumption of contingent event by categorical structure, it is also important to realize that many of these moments of the contextual realization of cultural values enter into Belau's own historical discourse by being recorded in narratives, depicted in rafter carvings, commemorated in stones of various kinds, and labeled by names of places, groups, and persons. The absence of writing should never be taken as an absence of permanent historical markers.[1] And the diagrammatic patterning (binary, linear, gradational, and quadripartite) of the deployment of these historical markers offers additional evidence for the significance attributed to the events referred to. As we have seen, a roster of four titles proclaims a village to be a mature and integral political unit, while a group of similar objects (trees, titles, graves) distributed widely in space points to a previous linkage due to sequential migration.

For future generations, then, knowledge of the past is entirely mediated by these historical markers and organizational diagrams and, more specifically, by the politically motivated actions of sign creators and preservers—the carving of a stone, the composition of a chant, the institution of a deferential protocol, or the presentation of an exchange valuable. The receiving generation is not confined, however, to the automatic or neutral transmission of these records to its heirs, but is also capable of actively shaping the course of the historicizing process. History, seen as a diachronically realized semiotic system, is not a process of transparent causal determination, with past events having a unidirectional cumulative effect. History, rather, is fundamentally reconstructive (cf. Comaroff 1985:253), with each generation subject to the influence of its ancestors' historicizing actions, yet imposing its own representations on these inherited signs and patterns, and finally transmitting in turn a particular determination to future generations.[2] Of course historical signs can even be rendered mute: sacred stones are thrown into the lagoon or remain hidden beneath forest underbrush, exchange valuables are locked in banks, and rafter beams are left to rot when the meetinghouse decays or is blown down by a typhoon. More interesting, though, are cases in which these signs themselves become engaged in social activity because of their representational function and

---

1. There is a tendency for theorists of the relationship between semiotics and history to concentrate almost exclusively on linguistic, if not written, representation; see, for example, Haidu 1982; Finlay-Pelinksi 1982; Williams 1985. Even scholars of Southeast Asian and Austronesian megaliths often tend to overlook the historical function of stones when they focus on their role in transmitting fertility and in calendrical calculation; see Wheatley 1983:58–62.

2. See Parmentier 1985b for a discussion of the Peircean framework for this argument.

become thereby modified, either physically through alteration in their semiotically relevant properties or conceptually through the sedimenting potential inherent in contexts of action to contribute a subtle revaluation to the sign's meaning.

Many of the ethnographic arguments in the preceding chapters involve the effort to link the level of abstract categorization, exemplified in the various diagrammatic icons, and the level of context-specific social activity by focusing on the complex role of *olangch* as the permanent signs which function as present evidence of a significant past.[3] These signs lie between schema and practice because they instantiate general patterns of meaningful order—forming systems of elements arranged as balanced sides, linear series, graded hierarchies, or coordinated quadripartitions—and because, having arisen in certain contexts in the past, they continue to undergo political manipulation (e.g., narratives) and social reconstitution (e.g., exchange valuables). Furthermore, I have distinguished two overlapping functional modalities by the terms "signs of history" and "signs in history." As signs of history, *olangch* represent the past as history in the sense of providing an explicit classification in terms of these four differentially valued analogical schemata: for example, Milad's stone children remain after the flood in the four cornerpost villages as representatives of the new world of pan-Belauan polity. They are thus essentially referential symbols implicated in overlapping iconic patterns. As signs in history, *olangch* are those historical signs whose token instantiations themselves become the objects of sociopolitical interest because of their value as reified embodiments of historicity: for example, the emblematic Imiungselbad is presented to Ngellau village in payment for military assistance. In a modified Peircean vocabulary, these signs in history are indexical symbols on the basis of their token-level contiguity with ongoing social processes. In Belau, *olangch* look in these two directions, toward the typifying role of schemata and toward the sedimenting role of practice.

Central to this ethnographic account of the "sacred remains" of Ngeremlengui are three canonical texts which present in explicit form Imeiong village's understanding of the nature of political transformation. First, the narrative about the distribution of cornerpost titles at Uchuladebong is grounded in the parallelism between Imeiong's quadripartition and the pan-Belauan cornerpost polity established by Milad.

---

3. *Olangch* cited in previous chapters include titles, names, specially designed weapons, gravestones and burial position, exchange valuables, the wristband placed on a small child, sacred stones of various sorts, ritual prerogatives, distinguishing marks on the hull of a canoe, trees planted from nonlocal saplings, the direction of bridge logs, a chief's broken thatching needle, and a metal gong.

Second, the funeral chant composed after the assassination of Ngiracheungel Ngiraklang expresses sorrow at the apparent revolution in political technique, from the subtle rhetoric embodied in the whispers of chiefs to the excesses of imported guns. And finally, the "closely guarded story of Ngeremlengui" was dictated for the purpose of contemporary historical preservation and is shaped by the feeling that Imeiong has reached its "final turning point." Together these three texts provide important clues for comprehending the ideology of history characteristic of Imeiong: first, that quadripartition is a unifying theme of this capital village's intensional reconstruction and projection of its history; and second, that the village is the anchor, axis, and pronouncer of political change, both for Belau as a whole (through the notion of the sacred remains) and for Ngeremlengui district (whose name means "Place of Molting"). If quadripartition implies the coordinated stability of culturally constituted order, axial transformation expresses Imeiong's claim to be the "official" historicizing force in Belau.

But this is not simply a matter of local pride or self-proclamation. Prior to my arrival in the field, for example, skilled carpenters and experts in mythology were employed to construct a traditional-style meetinghouse for the museum in Oreor. Called Ngesechel a Cherechar (Reminder of the Past), this building (see photograph 3) was designed as a unifying pan-Belauan sign of history. It certainly was this, until it became also a sign in history when it was vandalized and then burned to the ground during recent political struggles. The craftsmen still tell the story of how, at the dedication ceremony for Ngesechel a Cherechar, a Ngeremlengui spokesman mistakenly labeled the cornerpost seating positions with Imeiong's titles rather than with the names of Belau's cornerpost villages! Also, when chief Ngirturong was appointed to the position of head of the House of Chiefs in the national legislature, many people commented to me that this was appropriate, given Imeiong's high rank as the oldest child of Milad. And when Belauans living in Guam returned home to join the debate over the draft constitution, they began their circumnavigation of the archipelago by coming first to Ngeremlengui, which was pronounced "our mother, from whence we can enter every other village." Finally, when an inquisitive ethnographer stated his intention to explore Belauan traditions, he was sent to Ngeremlengui and recorded his finding in a book about that district's sacred remains.

English-Belauan Glossary

ancient times: *irechar*
archaic world: *mechut el renged*
capital village: *klou el beluu*
chief of village: *merredel er a beluu*
cornerpost: *saus*
cursed by sacredness: *delebeakl er a meang*
doormat concubines: *uulech*
east coast: *desbedall*
era of Milad: *rengedel a Milad*
external sign: *olangch*
female counterpart titleholder: *klderolel a rubak*
foreign policy: *kelulau*
four cornerposts: *eoa el saus*
four respected ones: *teoa el chuong*
headhunting raid: *mekemad, ururt*
head of the village: *btelul a beluu*
head trophy: *blebaol*
high-ranking: *meteet*
historical marker: *olangch*
house affiliation network: *kebliil*
house of senior woman: *blil a ourrot*
house of the title: *blil a dui*
lesser title: *kekere el dui*
letting out the dancers: *tuobed er a ruk*
looks upon the title: *melanges er a dui*
lower sea: *eou el daob*
low-ranking: *chebuul, kekere*
make the path peaceful: *omudech er a rael*
migration story: *cheldecheduch er a omerael*
money collection: *boketudoud*
mutual adversaries: *kaucheraro*

mutual friendship: *kausechelei*
mutual hostility: *kaucheraro*
new world: *beches el belulchad*
offspring of men: *ulechell*
offshoot of the turmeric root: *chebedel a kesol*
offspring of women: *ochell*
oppressing village: *otingaol el beluu*
path: *rael*
people of Imeiong: *rechad er a Imeiong*
permanent sign: *olangch*
political discourse: *kelulau*
political strategy: *kelulau*
politics of fire: *kelulau er a ngau*
polity of Milad: *rengedel a Milad*
privilege: *klebkall*
public land: *chutem buai*
reminder of the past: *ngesechel a cherechar*
repayment for effort: *cheral a sulir*
residents of Imeiong: *rekiei er a Imeiong*
sacredness: *meang, engall*
sacred remains: *meang a medechel*
sacred stone: *meang el bad*
sail rope concubine: *klemat el mengol*
secondary council: *uriul el klobak*
seizure of the title: *omerober er a dui*
side legs: *bita el oach*
side of heaven: *bita el eanged*
side of the mangrove channel: *bita el taoch*
side of the meetinghouse: *bita el bai*
side of the village: *bita el beluu*
siege: *benged el mekemad*
sister's son: *chebedel a kesol*
slave village: *ker el beluu*
tribute: *tenget*
upper sea: *bab el daob*
valuable: *udoud*
village land: *chutem beluu*
village reconstruction payment: *osumech beluu*
visiting party: *klechedaol*
west coast: *kiukl*
wives of men: *buch el sechal*
wives of the respected ones: *buch el chuong*
words of the village: *tekoi er a beluu*
woven pandanus hat covering: *dekedekel a btelul*
year of the east wind: *rekil a ongos*
year of the west wind: *rekil a ngebard*

Place Names

Babeldaob: largest island in archipelago
Babelngas: rocky promontory near Imeiong
Bailrulchau: stone pillars in Ngerechelong
Beliliou: southern island district
Belod: landing place at Ngiual
Beluuraklngong: village in Ngeremlengui
Beluurametengel: village in Ngeremlengui
Beluusung: village in Ngerechumelbai
Bungelkelau: poetic name for Ngersuul
Chedebsungel: house in Ngibtal
Chedukl: house in Imeiong
Chelsechei: landing place in Imeiong
Cherenguul: poetic name for Oreor
Chetiruir: mountain in Ngeremlengui
Chol: village in Ngerard
Debellelangalekdmeoang: terraced hill near Ngeremetengel
Delui: landing place of Oreor
Dilubech: first house in Beluurametengel
Duab: house in Ulechetong
Ibedechall: first house in Ngeremeskang
Idid: first house in Oreor
Ikelau: second house in Oreor
Imeiong: capital village of Ngeremlengui (= Imiungs)
Imiungs: capital village of Ngeremlengui (= Imeiong)
Imeliik: district in southwestern Babeldaob
Imul: village in Imeliik
Irrai: district in southern Babeldaob
Klang: second house in Imeiong
Mechoang: house in Ngeremetengel
Mederemel: rocky promontory near Imeiong
Meketii: meetinghouse in Oreor

Melekeok: capital village of Ngetelngal
Melengel: landing place in Imeiong
Mengellang: capital village of Ngerechelong
Ngcheangel: northern atoll district
Ngchemesed: village in Ngeremlengui
Ngchemlianged: village in Beliliou
Ngchesar: district on eastern side of Babeldaob
Ngeaur: southern island district
Ngebei: village in Ngerechelong (= Ngebiul)
Ngebuked: capital village of Ngerard
Ngeburech: village in Ngetelngal
Ngeiungel: village in Ngerechelong
Ngellau: village in Ngerechelong
Ngeluong: mangrove channel leading to Imeiong
Ngemelis: reef island west of Beliliou
Ngerard: district on western side of Babeldaob
Ngerbungs: poetic name for Imeliik
Ngerdmau: district on western side of Babeldaob
Ngerduais: small island off the coast of Irrai
Ngerebau: village in Ngerechelong
Ngerebesek: forest in Ngeremlengui
Ngerechelong: district in northern Babeldaob
Ngerecheu: rock island
Ngeredelolk: village in Beliliou
Ngeredubech: village in Imeliik
Ngerekeai: capital village of Imeliik
Ngerekebesang: island west of Oreor
Ngerekebrong: channel leading to Beluurametengel
Ngerekldeu: district south of Babeldaob
Ngereklngong: village in Ngeremlengui
Ngeremasech: village in Ngeremlengui
Ngeremeduu: bay between Ngeremlengui and Ngetbang
Ngeremeskang: ancient capital of Ngeremlengui
Ngeremetengel: village in Ngeremlengui
Ngeremid: village in Ngerekldeu
Ngeremlengui: district on western side of Babeldaob
Ngeremobang: second house in Ngeremeskang
Ngerengchol: rock island
Ngeroach: mountain peak in Ngeremlengui
Ngerringal: poetic name for Ngerard
Ngersuul: village on eastern side of Babeldaob
Ngerturong: first house in Imeiong
Ngeruangel: submerged northern atoll
Ngerubong: path between Ngeremlengui and Ngerdmau
Ngeruburek: house in Nglabang hamlet
Ngeruikl: village in Ngeaur

Ngeruktabel: rock island
Ngerusar: village on eastern side of Babeldaob
Ngerutechei: village in Ngeremlengui
Ngerutelchii: house in Imeiong
Ngesisech: village in Ngeremlengui
Ngetbang: district on western side of Babeldaob
Ngetechum: village in Ngeremlengui
Ngetelngal: district on eastern side of Babeldaob
Ngetmadei: village in Ngeremlengui
Ngetmel: village in Ngerechelong
Ngibtal: submerged island off coast of Ngiual
Ngiual: district on eastern side of Babeldaob
Ngkeklau: village in Ngerard
Nglabang: hamlet near Imeiong
Oderderong: channel leading to Ngeremetengel
Odesangel: poetic name for Beliliou
Oikull: village in Irrai
Okemii: landing place at Melekeok
Oliuch: village in Ngetelngal
Ollei: village in Ngerechelong
Omekesebech: meetinghouse in Uluang
Omisaolmlai: village in Ngeremlengui
Ongerool: house in Ngeremetengel
Oreor: capital village of Ngerekldeu
Orukei: central square in Imeiong
Raelburech: path between Imeiong and Melekeok
Rois: village on Ngeaur
Roisbeluu: village in Ngeremlengui
Sibong: house in Imeiong
Teliko: house in Ngeredubech
Tellach: landing place in Uluang
Toachelmlengui: western reef passage
Tublai: first house in Ngebuked
Uchelkiukl: first house in Ngerekeai
Uchuladebong: stone pavement in Ngerutechei
Ulechetong: hamlet near Imeiong
Ulimang: village in Ngerard
Ulong: island southwest of Oreor
Uluang: village in Ngeremlengui
Umerang: house in Melekeok; terrace in Uluang
Uudes: first house in Melekeok; terrace in Uluang

❧

References

Alkire, William H. 1972. Concepts of Order in Southeast Asia and Micronesia. *Comparative Studies in Society and History* 14:484–93.

———. 1977. *An Introduction to the Peoples and Cultures of Micronesia.* 2d ed. Menlo Park, Calif.: Cummings.

———. 1980. Technical Knowledge and the Evolution of Political Systems in the Central and Western Caroline Islands of Micronesia. *Canadian Journal of Anthropology* 1:229–37.

———. 1984. Central Carolinian Oral Narratives: Indigenous Migration Theories and Principles of Order and Rank. *Pacific Studies* 7:1–14.

Aoyagi, Machiko. 1979. *Bitang Ma Bitang* (Two Halves), *Eual Saus* (Four Corners) and Mechanical Confusion in Palauan Socio-Political Organization. In Humio Kusakabe, ed., *Cultural Anthropological Research on the Folk Culture in the Western Caroline Islands of Micronesia in 1977,* pp. 19–38. Tokyo: Tokyo University of Foreign Studies.

———. 1982. The Geographical Recognition of Palauan People. In Machiko Aoyagi, ed., *Islanders and Their Outside World: A Report of the Cultural Anthropological Research in the Caroline Islands of Micronesia in 1980–1981,* pp. 3–34. Tokyo: St. Paul's (Rikkyo) University, Committee for Micronesian Research.

Athens, J. Stephen. 1983. The Megalithic Ruins of Nan Madol: Archaeology and Oral History Join Forces in a Pacific Island. *Natural History* (December):51–60.

Bamler, A. 1900. Vokabular der Tamisprache. *Zeitschrift für afrikanische, ozeanische und ostasiatische Sprachen* 5:217–53.

Barnard, Edward C. 1980. *"Naked and a Prisoner": Captain Edward C. Barnard's Narrative of Shipwreck in Palau, 1832–1833.* Ed. Kenneth R. Martin. Sharon, Mass.: Kendall Whaling Museum.

Barnes, R. H. 1974. *Kédang: A Study of the Collective Thought of an Eastern Indonesian People.* Oxford: Clarendon Press.

———. 1979. Lord, Ancestor and Affine: An Austronesian Relationship Name. *Nusa* 7:19–34.

Barnett, H. G. 1949. *Palauan Society: A Study of Contemporary Native Life in the Palau Islands*. Eugene: University of Oregon Publications.
——. 1970. Palauan Journal. In George D. Spindler, ed., *Being an Anthropologist: Fieldwork in Eleven Cultures*, pp. 1–31. New York: Holt, Rinehart and Winston.
Barraud, Cécile. 1979. *Tanebar-Evav: Une société de maisons tournée vers le large*. Cambridge: Cambridge University Press.
Barthes, Roland. 1986 [1967]. The Discourse of History. Trans. Richard Howard. In *The Rustle of Language*. pp. 127–40. New York: Hill and Wang.
Bateson, Gregory. 1958. *Naven: A Survey of the Problems Suggested by a Composite Picture of the Culture of a New Guinea Tribe Drawn from Three Points of View*. 2d ed. Stanford: Stanford University Press.
Beauclair, Inez de. 1963. Some Ancient Beads of Yap and Palau. *Journal of the Polynesian Society* 72:1–10.
Becker, Carl L. 1955. What are Historical Facts? *Western Political Quarterly* 8:327–40.
Beidelman, T. O. 1971. Lévi-Strauss and History. *Journal of Interdisciplinary History* 1:511–26.
Bellwood, Peter. 1979. *Man's Conquest of the Pacific: The Prehistory of Southeast Asia and Oceania*. New York: Oxford University Press.
——. 1980. Plants, Climate and People: The Early Horticultural Prehistory of Austronesia. In J. J. Fox, ed., *Indonesia: The Making of a Culture*, pp. 57–74. Canberra: Research School of Pacific Studies, Australian National University.
——. 1983. New Perspectives on Indo-Malaysian Prehistory. *Bulletin of the Indo-Pacific Prehistory Association* 4:71–83.
Bender, Bryon W. 1971. Micronesian Languages. In Thomas A. Sebeok, ed., *Current Trends in Linguistics*. Vol. 8. *Linguistics in Oceania*, pp. 426–65. The Hague: Mouton.
Benjamin, Walter. 1968. *Illuminations*. New York: Schocken Books.
Berde, Stuart. 1973. Contemporary Notes on Rossel Island Valuables. *Journal of the Polynesian Society* 82:188–205.
Bernart, Luelen. 1977. *The Book of Luelen*. Ed. and trans. John L. Fischer, Saul H. Riesenberg, and Marjorie G. Whiting. Pacific History Series no. 8. Honolulu: University Press of Hawaii.
Biersack, Aletta. 1982. The Logic of Misplaced Concreteness: Paiela Body Counting and the Nature of the Primitive Mind. *American Anthropologist* 84:811–29.
Blair, Emma Helen, and James Alexander Robertson, eds. 1906. *The Philippine Islands, 1493–1898*, vol. 41. Cleveland: Arthur H. Clark.
Blust, Robert. 1976. Austronesian Culture History: Some Linguistic Inferences and Their Relation to the Archaeological Record. *World Archaeology* 8:19–43.
——. 1979. Proto–Western Malayo–Polynesian Vocatives. *Bijdragen tot de Taal-, Land- en Volkenkunde* 136:205–51.

————. 1980a. Austronesian Etymologies. *Oceanic Linguistics* 19(1–2): 1–189.

————. 1980b. Early Austronesian Social Organization: The Evidence of Language. *Current Anthropology* 21:205–26.

————. 1980c. Notes on Proto-Malayo-Polynesian Phratry Dualism. *Bijdragen tot de Taal-, Land- en Volkenkunde* 136:215–47.

————. 1981. Dual Divisions in Oceania: Innovation or Retention? *Oceania* 52:66–79.

Bohannan, Laura. 1958. Political Aspects of Tiv Social Organization. In John Middleton and David Tait, eds., *Tribes Without Rulers: Studies in African Segmentary Systems*, pp. 33–66. London: Routledge and Kegan Paul.

Brown, D. E. 1973. Social Classification and History. *Comparative Studies in Society and History* 16:437–47.

Browning, Robert L. 1833–36. Notes on the South Sea Islands on Board the U.S. Ship "Vincennes," 1833–1836, J. H. Aulick Commander. Browning Family Papers. Library of Congress, Washington, D.C.

Capell, A. 1941. *A New Fijian Dictionary*. Sydney: Australasian Medical Publishing Company.

Chapman, Peter S. 1968. Japanese Contributions to Micronesian Archaeology and Material Culture. In I. Yawata and Y. H. Sinoto, eds., *Prehistoric Culture in Oceania: A Symposium*, pp. 67–82. Honolulu: Bishop Museum Press.

Charbonnier, G. 1969 [1961]. *Conversations with Claude Lévi-Strauss*. Trans. John and Doreen Weightman. London: Jonathan Cape.

Ch'en, Ch'i-lu. 1968. *Material Culture of the Formosan Aborigines*. Taipei: Taiwan Museum.

Cheyne, Andrew. 1962. Letters, British Schooner "Acis," Manila Bay, 9 September 1862. Public Record Office, London, Admiralty 1/6006.

————. 1863–66. Journal Aboard the Brigantine "Acis," November 1863 to February 1866. Typescript of original manuscript, Palau Community Action Agency, Koror.

————. 1971. *The Trading Voyages of Andrew Cheyne, 1841–1844*. Ed. and trans. Dorothy Shineberg. Pacific History Series no. 3. Honolulu: University of Hawaii Press.

Christie, Anthony. 1961. The Sea-locked Lands: The Diverse Traditions of South East Asia. In Stuart Piggott, ed., *The Dawn of Civilization*, pp. 277–300. London: Thames and Hudson.

Claessen, Henry J. M. 1984. Internal Dynamics of the Early State. *Current Anthropology* 25:365–70.

————. 1986. Kingship in the Early State. *Bijdragen tot de Taal-, Land- en Volkenkunde* 142:113–27.

Clark, Roger, and Sue Rabbitt Roff. 1984. *Micronesia: The Problem of Palau*. Minority Rights Group Report no. 63.

Clyde, Paul Hibbert. 1935. *Japan's Pacific Mandate*. New York: Macmillan.

Cohn, Bernard S. 1961. The Pasts of an Indian Village. *Comparative Studies in Society and History* 3:241–49.

————. 1981. Anthropology and History in the 1980s: Toward a Rapprochement. In Theodore K. Rabb and Robert I. Rotberg, eds., *The New History: The 1980s and Beyond*, pp. 227–52. Princeton: Princeton University Press.

Colani, Madeleine. 1935. *Les Mégalithes du Haut-Laos*. 2 vols. Paris: Publications de l'Ecole Française d'Extrême-Orient.

Collingwood, R. G. 1926. Some Perplexities about Time: With an Attempted Solution. *Proceedings of the Aristotelian Society* 26:135–50.

————. 1956. *The Idea of History*. New York: Oxford.

————. 1965. *Essays in the Philosophy of History*. Austin: University of Texas Press.

————. 1970 [1939]. *Autobiography*. Oxford: Oxford University Press.

Comaroff, Jean. 1985. *Body of Power, Spirit of Resistance: The Culture and History of a South African People*. Chicago: University of Chicago Press.

Coulter, John Wesley. 1957. *The Pacific Dependencies of the United States*. New York: Macmillan.

Craib, John L. 1983. Micronesian Prehistory: An Archaeological Overview. *Science* 219: 922–27.

Craib, John L., and Nancy L. Farrell. 1981. On the Question of Prehistoric Rice Cultivation in the Mariana Islands. *Micronesica* 17:1–9.

Cunningham, Clark E. 1965. Order and Change in an Atoni Diarchy. *Southwestern Journal of Anthropology* 21:359–82.

Davidson, Janet. 1985. New Zealand Prehistory. *Advances in World Archaeology* 4:239–91.

Delano, Amasa. 1817. *A Narrative of Voyages and Travels in the Northern and Southern Hemispheres*. Boston: E. G. House.

Dempwolff, Otto. 1934–38. *Vergleichende Lautlehre des austronisischen Wortschatzes*. 3 vols. Berlin: D. Reimer.

Dening, Greg. 1966. Ethnohistory in Polynesia: The Value of Ethnohistorical Evidence. *Journal of Pacific History* 1:23–42.

————. 1980. *Islands and Beaches: Discourse on a Silent Land, Marquesas 1774–1880*. Honolulu: University Press of Hawaii.

Douglas, Bronwen. 1982. "Written on the Ground": Spatial Symbolism, Cultural Categories and Historical Process in New Caledonia. *Journal of the Polynesian Society* 91:383–415.

Downs, R. E. 1955. Head-hunting in Indonesia. *Bijdragen tot de Taal-, Land- en Volkenkunde* 111:40–70.

Duby, Georges. 1980. Memories With No Historian. *Yale French Studies* 59:7–16.

Durkheim, Emile, and Marcel Mauss. 1963 [1903]. *Primitive Classification*. Trans. Rodney Needham. Chicago: University of Chicago Press.

Dyen, Isidore. 1965. *A Lexicostatistical Classification of the Austronesian Languages*. International Journal of American Linguistics Memoir no. 19. Baltimore: Waverly Press.

————. 1971. Review of *Die Palau-Sprache und ihre Stellung zu anderen indo-*

nesischen Sprachen by Klaus Pätzold. *Journal of the Polynesian Society* 80:247–58.

East, J. W. 1882. Letter of Proceedings, H.M.S. "Comus" at Koror, Pelew Islands, 23 April 1882. Public Record Office, London, Admiralty 1/6618.

———. 1885. An Expedition to the Pelew Group of the Caroline Islands in 1882. *Colborn's United Service Magazine* 114:304–14.

Ehrlich, Paul, and Moses Mekoll. 1984. *Koror: A Center of Power, Commerce and Colonial Administration.* Micronesian Archaeological Survey Report no. 11. Saipan: Office of the High Commissioner, Trust Territory of the Pacific Islands.

Errington, Shelly. 1983. The Place of Regalia in Luwu. In Lorraine Gesick, ed., *Centers, Symbols, and Hierarchies: Essays on the Classical States of Southeast Asia,* pp. 194–241. Monograph Series no. 26, Yale University Southeast Asia Studies.

Evans-Pritchard, E. E. 1940. *The Nuer: A Description of the Modes of Livelihood and Political Institutions of a Nilotic People.* Oxford: Oxford University Press.

Eyde, David B. 1969. On Tikopia Social Space. *Bijdragen tot de Taal-, Landen Volkenkunde* 125:40–63.

Feeley-Harnik, Gillian. 1978. Divine Kingship and the Meaning of History among the Sakalava of Madagascar. *Man* 13:402–17.

Feinberg, Richard. 1980. History and Structure: A Case of Polynesian Dualism. *Journal of Anthropological Research* 36:361–78.

———. 1982. Structural Dimensions of Sociopolitical Change in Anuta, S.T. *Pacific Studies* 5:1–19.

Feldman, Jerome A. 1979. The House as World in Bawömataluo, South Nias. In Edward M. Bruner and Judith O. Becker, eds., *Art, Ritual and Society in Indonesia,* pp. 127–89. Papers in International Studies, Southeast Asia Series no. 53. Athens: Ohio University Center for International Studies, Southeast Asia Program.

Finlay-Pelinksi, Marike. 1982. Semiotics or History: From Content Analysis to Contextualized Discursive Praxis. *Semiotica* 40:229–66.

Firth, Raymond. 1967. *The Work of the Gods in Tikopia.* London School of Economics Monographs on Social Anthropology nos. 1 and 2. London: Athlone Press.

———. 1969. Tikopia Social Space: A Commentary. *Bijdragen tot de Taal-, Land- en Volkenkunde* 125:64–70.

———. 1979. The Sacredness of Tikopia Chiefs. In William A. Shack and Percy S. Cohen, eds., *Politics in Leadership.* New York: Oxford University Press.

Firth, Stewart. 1973. German Firms in the Western Pacific Islands, 1857–1914. *Journal of Pacific History* 8:10–29.

Foley, William. 1980. History of Migrations in Indonesia as Seen by a Linguist. In J. J. Fox, ed., *Indonesia: The Making of a Culture,* pp. 75–80. Canberra: Research School of Pacific Studies, Australian National University.

Force, Roland. 1959. Palauan Money: Some Preliminary Comments on Material and Origins. *Journal of the Polynesian Society* 68:40–41.

———. 1960. *Leadership and Cultural Change in Palau.* Fieldiana: Anthropology no. 50, Chicago: Chicago Natural History Museum.

Force, Roland, and Maryanne Force. 1961. Keys to Cultural Understanding. *Science* 133:1202–6.

———. 1965. Political Change in Micronesia. In Roland W. Force, ed., *Induced Political Change in the Pacific*, pp. 1–16. Honolulu: Bishop Museum Press.

———. 1972. *Just One House: A Description and Analysis of Kinship in the Palau Islands.* Bernice P. Bishop Museum Bulletin no. 235. Honolulu: Bishop Museum Press.

Fortes, Meyer. 1945. *The Dynamics of Clanship among the Tallensi: Being the First Part of an Analysis of the Social Structure of a Trans-Volta Tribe.* Oxford: Oxford University Press.

———. 1969. *Kinship and the Social Order: The Legacy of Lewis Henry Morgan.* London: Routledge and Kegan Paul.

Fox, C. E. 1924. *The Threshold of the Pacific: An Account of the Social Organization, Magic, and Religion of the People of San Cristoval in the Solomon Islands.* London: Kegan Paul, Trench, Trubner & Co.

Fox, James J. 1971. Sister's Child as Plant: Metaphors in an Idiom of Consanguinity. In Rodney Needham, ed., *Rethinking Kinship and Marriage,* pp. 219–52. Association of Social Anthropologists Monograph no. 11. London: Tavistock.

———. 1979. "Standing" in Time and Place: The Structure of Rotinese Historical Narratives. In A. Reid and D. Marr, eds., *Perceptions of the Past in Southeast Asia,* pp. 10–25. Canberra: Asian Studies Association of Australia.

———. 1980a. Introduction. In James J. Fox, ed., *The Flow of Life: Essays on Eastern Indonesia,* pp. 1–18. Harvard Studies in Cultural Anthropology no. 2. Cambridge: Harvard University Press.

———. 1980b. Retelling the Past: The Communicative Structure of a Rotinese Historical Narrative. *Canberra Anthropology* 3:56–66.

Fox, Robert B. 1979. The Philippines during the First Millennium B.C. In R. B. Smith and W. Watson, eds., *Early South East Asia,* pp. 227–41. New York: Oxford University Press.

Friedman, Jonathan. 1985. Our Time, Their Time, World Time: The Transformation of Temporal Modes. *Ethnos* 50:168–83.

Geertz, Clifford. 1980. *Negara: The Theatre State in Nineteenth-Century Bali.* Princeton: Princeton University Press.

Germany, Reichstag. 1903. Denkschrift über die Entwickelung der deutschen Schutzgebiete in Afrika und in der Südsee, 1901/1902. *Stenographische Berichte über die Verhandlungen des Reichstages.* Berlin: J. Sittenfeld. (Trans. in HRAF.)

Gifford, E. W., and D. S. Gifford. 1959. *Archaeological Excavations in Yap.* Anthropological Records no. 18:2. Berkeley: University of California Press.

Glover, I. C., B. Bronson, and D. T. Bayard. 1979. Comment on "Megaliths" in South East Asia. In R. B. Smith and W. Watson, eds., *Early South East Asia*, pp. 253–58. New York: Oxford University Press.

Golson, Jack. 1972. The Remarkable History of Indo-Pacific Man: Missing Chapters from Every World Prehistory. *Search* 3:13–21.

Goodenough, Ward. 1957. Oceania and the Problem of Controls in the Study of Culture and Human Evolution. *Journal of the Polynesian Society* 66:146–55.

———. 1986. Sky World and This World: The Place of Kachaw in Micronesian Cosmology. *American Anthropologist* 88:551–68.

Goodman, Grant K., and Felix Moos, eds. 1981. *The United States and Japan in the Western Pacific: Micronesia and Papua New Guinea*. Boulder, Colo.: Westview Press.

Goody, Jack. 1978. Oral Tradition and the Reconstruction of the Past in Northern Ghana. In B. Bernardi, C. Ponti, and A. Triulzi, eds., *Onti Orali: Antropologia e Storia*, pp. 285–95. Milan: Franco Angeli.

Gross, David. 1981–82. Space, Time, and Modern Culture. *Telos* 50:59–78.

Grove, Stanhope. 1881. Reporting Proceedings, H.M.S. "Lily," Hongkong, 10 February 1881. Public Record Office, London, Admiralty 1/6575.

Gumerman, George J., David Snyder, and W. Bruce Masse. 1981. *An Archaeological Reconnaissance in the Palau Archipelago, Western Caroline Islands, Micronesia*. Center for Archaeological Investigations Research Paper no. 23. Carbondale: Southern Illinois University at Carbondale.

Haidu, Peter. 1982. Semiotics and History. *Semiotica* 40:187–228.

Hanson, F. Allan. 1983. Syntagmatic Structures: How the Maoris Make Sense of History. *Semiotica* 46:287–307.

Hanson, F. Allan, and Louise Hanson. 1983. *Counterpoint in Maori Culture*. London: Routledge and Kegan Paul.

Harrisson, Tom. 1964. 100,000 Years of Stone Age Culture in Borneo. *Journal of the Royal Society of Arts* 112:74–91.

Hayden, Brian. 1983. Social Characteristics of Early Austronesian Colonisers. *Bulletin of the Indo-Pacific Prehistory Association* 4:123–34.

Heekeren, H. R. van. 1958. *The Bronze-Iron Age in Indonesia*. The Hague: Martinus Nijhoff.

Heine-Geldern, Robert. 1942. Conceptions of State and Kingship in Southeast Asia. *The Far Eastern Quarterly* 2:15–30.

———. 1945. Prehistoric Research in the Netherlands Indies. In P. Honig and F. Verdoorn, eds., *Science and Scientists in the Netherlands Indies*, pp. 129–67. New York: Board for the Netherlands Indies, Surinam, and Curaçao.

Henrickson, Paul R. 1968. Two Forms of Primitive Art in Micronesia. *Micronesica* 4:39–48.

Henry, Teuira. 1928. *Ancient Tahiti*. Bernice P. Bishop Museum Bulletin no. 48. Honolulu: Bishop Museum Press.

Heyerdahl, Thor. 1958. *Aku-Aku*. Chicago: Rand McNally.

Hezel, Francis X. 1971. Spanish Capuchins in the Carolines. *Micronesian Reporter* 19(2): 36–40, 19(3): 36–42.

———. 1978. The Role of the Beachcomber in the Carolines. In Neil Gunson, ed., *The Changing Pacific: Essays in Honour of H. E. Maude,* pp. 261–72. Melbourne: Oxford University Press.

———. 1979. *Foreign Ships in Micronesia.* Saipan: Trust Territory Historic Preservation Office.

———. 1983. *The First Taint of Civilization: A History of the Caroline and Marshall Islands in Pre-Colonial Days, 1521–1885.* Pacific Islands Monograph Series no. 1. Honolulu: University of Hawaii Press.

Hezel, Francis X., and Maria Teresa del Valle. 1972. Early European Contact with the Western Carolines: 1525–1750. *Journal of Pacific History* 7:26–44.

Hidikata, Hisakatso. 1973a [1940]. *Palauan Kinship.* Micronesian Area Research Center Publication no. 1. Agana, Guam: Garrison and McCarter.

———. 1973b [1956]. *Stone Images of Palau.* Micronesian Area Research Center Publication no. 3. Agana, Guam: Garrison and McCarter.

Hobart, Mark. 1978. The Path of the Soul: The Legitimacy of Nature in Balinese Conceptions of Space. In G. B. Milner, ed., *Natural Symbols in South East Asia,* pp. 5–28. London: University of London, School of Oriental and African Studies.

Hockin, John P. 1803. *A Supplement to the Account of the Pelew Islands.* London: G. and W. Nichol.

Hogbin, H. Ian. 1963. *Kinship and Marriage in a New Guinea Village.* London School of Economics Monographs on Social Anthropology no. 26. London: Athlone Press.

Holden, Horace. 1836. *A Narrative of the Shipwreck, Captivity and Sufferings of Horace Holden and Benj. H. Nute . . . on the Pelew Islands, in the Year 1832.* Boston: Russell and Shattuck.

Hooper, Antony. 1981. *Why Tikopia Has Four Clans.* Royal Anthropological Institute of Great Britain and Ireland, Occasional Paper no. 38.

Hose, Charles, and William McDougall. 1912. *The Pagan Tribes of Borneo.* 2 vols. London: Macmillan.

Intoh, Michiko. 1981. Reconnaissance Archaeological Research on Ngulu Atoll in the Western Caroline Islands. *Asian Perspectives* 24:69–80.

Iyechad, Gwenda, and Frank Quimby. 1983. Belau: Super-port, Fortress or Identity. In *Politics in the Pacific Islands,* vol. 3, *Politics in Micronesia,* pp. 100–130. Suva, Fiji: University of the South Pacific, Institute of Pacific Studies.

Izui, Hisanosuke. 1965. The Languages of Micronesia: Their Unity and Diversity. *Lingua* 14:349–59.

Jacobs, Hubert. 1980. Father Francisco Miedes Discovers the Caroline Islands before They Are Discovered. *Archivum Historicum Societatis Iesu* 49:393–416.

Jansen, H. J. 1977. Indigenous Classification Systems in the Ambonese Moluccas. In P. E. de Josselin de Jong, ed., *Structural Anthropology in the Netherlands,* pp. 101–15. The Hague: Martinus Nijhoff.

Johannes, Robert. 1981. *Words of the Lagoon: Fishing and Marine Lore in the Palau District of Micronesia.* Berkeley: University of California Press.

Josephs, Lewis S. 1975. *Palauan Reference Grammar.* PALI Language Texts: Micronesia. Honolulu: University Press of Hawaii.

Kaneshiro, Shigeru. 1958. Land Tenure in the Palau Islands. In J. de Young, ed., *Land Tenure Patterns: Trust Territory of the Pacific Islands,* vol. 1, pp. 288–336. Guam: Office of the Staff Anthropologist, Trust Territory of the Pacific Islands.

Kaudern, Walter. 1938. *Ethnographical Studies in Celebes.* Göteborg: Elanders Boktryckeri Aktiebolag.

Keate, George. 1788. *An Account of the Pelew Islands . . . from the Journals and Communications of Captain Henry Wilson, 1783.* London: G. Nichol.

———. 1820. *The History of Prince Lee Boo.* Dublin: C. Crookes.

Keesing, Felix. 1941. *The South Seas in the Modern World.* New York: John Day.

Kesolei, Katherine, ed. 1971. *Palauan Legends,* no. 1. Koror: Palau Community Action Agency.

———. 1975. *Palauan Legends,* no. 2. Koror: Palau Community Action Agency.

Kirch, P. V. 1980. Burial Structures and Societal Ranking in Vava'u, Tonga. *Journal of the Polynesian Society* 89:367–71.

Kituai, A. 1974. Historical Narratives of the Bundi People. *Oral History* 2:8–16.

Klee, Gary A. 1972. The Cyclic Realities of Man and Nature in a Palauan Village. Ph.D. diss., University of Oregon.

———. 1976. Traditional Time Reckoning and Resource Utilization. *Micronesica* 12:211–46.

Klingman, Lawrence, and Gerald Green. 1950. *His Majesty O'Keefe.* New York: Charles Scribner's Sons.

Koskinen, Aarne A. 1963. On the Symbolism of "the Path" in Polynesian Thinking. In *Linking of Symbols: Polynesian Patterns 1,* pp. 57–70. Helsinki: Finnish Society for Missionary Research.

Krämer, Augustin. 1908. Studienreise nach den Zentral- und Westkarolinen. *Mitteilungen aus den Deutschen Schutzgebieten* 21:169–86.

———. 1917–29. *Palau.* 5 vols. In G. Thilenius, ed., *Ergebnisse der Südsee-Expedition, 1908–1910.* Hamburg: Friederichsen. (Part. trans. in HRAF.)

Kruijt, A. C. 1914. Indonesians. *Hastings Encyclopaedia of Religion and Ethics* 7:232–52.

Kubary, J. S. 1873. Die Palau-Inseln in der Südsee. *Journal des Museum Godeffroy* 1:177–238. (Trans. in HRAF.)

———. 1885. Die sozialen Einrichtungen der Pelauer. In *Ethnographische Beiträge zur Kenntnis der Karolinischen Inselgruppe und Nachbarschaft,* pp. 33–150. Berlin: Asher. (Trans. in HRAF.)

———. 1985a. Die Industrie der Pelau-Insulaner. In *Ethnographische Beiträge zur Kenntnis des Karolinen Archipels,* pp. 118–299. Leiden: P. W. M. Trap. (Trans. in HRAF.)

————. 1985b. Über das einheimische Geld auf der Insel Yap und auf den Pelau-Inseln. In *Ethnographische Beiträge zur Kenntnis des Karolinen Archipels*, pp. 1–28. Leiden: P. W. M. Trap.

————. 1900a. Die Todten-Bestattung auf den Pelau-Inseln. In A. Bastian, ed., *Die Mikronesischen Kolonien aus ethnologischen Gesichtspunkten*, vol. 2, pp. 37–48. Berlin: Asher. (Trans. in HRAF.)

————. 1900b. Die Verbrechen und das Strafverfahren suf den Pelau-Inseln. In A. Bastian, ed., *Die Mikronesischen Kolonien aus ethnologischen gesichtspunkten*, vol. 2, pp. 1–36. Berlin: Mittler. (Trans. in HRAF.)

————. 1969 [1888]. *The Religion of the Palauans*. Woodstock, Md.: Micronesian Seminar.

Kurashina, Hiro, et al. 1981. Prehistoric and Protohistoric Cultural Occurrence at Tarague, Guam. *Asian Perspectives* 24:57–68.

Kurashina, Hiro, and Russell N. Clayshulte. 1983. Site Formation Processes and Cultural Sequence at Tarague, Guam. *Indo-Pacific Prehistory Association Bulletin* 4:114–22.

Kusakabe, Humio. 1979. Inclination in Cardinal Direction in the Western Caroline Islands, Micronesia. In Humio Kusakabe, ed., *Cultural Anthropological Research on the Folk Culture in the Western Caroline Islands of Micronesia in 1977*, pp. 1–7. Tokyo: Tokyo University of Foreign Studies.

Labby, David. 1976. *The Demystification of Yap: Dialectics of Culture on a Micronesian Island*. Chicago: University of Chicago Press.

Lancy, David F., and Andrew W. Strathern. 1981. "Making Twos": Pairing as an Alternative to the Taxonomic Mode of Representation. *American Anthropologist* 83:773–95.

Latukefu, Sione. 1968. Oral Traditions: An Appraisal of Their Value in Historical Research in Tonga. *Journal of Pacific History* 3:135–43.

Layard, John. 1942. *Stone Men of Malekula: Vao*. London: Chatto & Windus.

Leach, Edmund R. 1973. Structuralism in Social Anthropology. In David Robey, ed., *Structuralism: An Introduction*, pp. 37–56. Oxford: Clarendon.

Lessa, William A. 1962. An Evaluation of Early Descriptions of Carolinian Culture. *Ethnohistory* 9:313–403.

————. 1975. *Drake's Island of Thieves: Ethnological Sleuthing*. Honolulu: University Press of Hawaii.

————. 1980. *More Tales from Ulithi Atoll: A Content Analysis*. Folklore and Mythology Studies no. 32. Berkeley: University of California Press.

Lévi-Strauss, Claude. 1966 [1962]. *The Savage Mind*. Chicago: University of Chicago Press.

————. 1970. A Confrontation. *New Left Review* 62:57–74.

————. 1976. *Structural Anthropology*, vol. 2. Trans. Monique Layton. New York: Basic Books.

————. 1983. Histoire et Ethnologie. *Annales: Economies, Sociétés, Civilisations*. No. 4:1217–31.

————. 1985. *The View from Afar*. New York: Basic Books.

Lévi-Strauss, Claude, Marc Augé, and Maurice Godelier. 1976 [1975]. Anthropology, History and Ideology. *Critique of Anthropology* 6:44–55.

Liep, John. 1983. "This Civilising Influence": The Colonial Transformation of Rossel Island Society. *Journal of Pacific History* 18:113–33.

Lingenfelter, Sherwood G. 1975. *Yap: Political Leadership and Culture Change in an Island Society.* Honolulu: University Press of Hawaii.

Lowie, Robert H. 1917. Oral Tradition and History. *Journal of American Folk-Lore* 30:167–67.

Lucking, Laurie Jo. 1984. An Archaeological Investigation of Prehistoric Palauan Terraces. Ph.D. diss., University of Minnesota.

Lyman, H. S. 1902. Recollections of Horace Holden. *Quarterly of the Oregon Historical Society* 3:164–217.

McBryde, Isabel. 1979. Ethnohistory in an Australian Context: Independent Discipline or Convenient Data Quarry? *Aboriginal History* 3:128–51.

McCluer, John. 1790–92. Journal of a Voyage to the Pelew Islands in the H. C. "Snow Panther." Typescript of original British Museum manuscript, Palau Community Action Agency, Koror.

McCutcheon, Mary. 1978. Taro Cultivation in Palau: A Study of Extensification. Paper presented at the Annual Meeting of the American Anthropological Association, Los Angeles.

McDowell, Nancy. 1985. Past and Future: The Nature of Episodic Time in Bun. In Deborah Gewertz and Edward Schieffelin, eds., *History and Ethnohistory in Papua New Guinea*, pp. 26–39. Oceania Monograph no. 28. Sydney: University of Sydney.

MacGaffey, Wyatt. 1978. African History, Anthropology, and the Rationality of Natives. *History in Africa* 5:101–20.

McHenry, Donald F. 1976. *Micronesia: Trust Betrayed.* New York: Carnegie Endowment for International Peace.

McKinley, Robert. 1976. Human and Proud of It: A Structural Treatment of Headhunting Rites and the Social Definition of Enemies. In G. N. Appell, ed., *Studies in Borneo Societies: Social Process and Anthropological Explanation*, pp. 92–126. Special Report no. 12. Center for Southeast Asian Studies, Northern Illinois University.

———. 1979. Zaman dan Masa, Eras and Periods: Religious Evolution and the Permanence of Epistemological Ages in Malay Culture. In A. L. Becker and A. A. Yengoyan, eds., *The Imagination of Reality: Essays in Southeast Asian Coherence Systems*, pp. 303–24. Norwood, N.J.: Ablex.

McKnight, Robert K. 1958. Palauan Names. In J. E. de Young, ed., *The Use of Names in Micronesia*, pp. 16–54. Anthropological Working Papers no. 3. Guam: Office of the Staff Anthropologist, Trust Territory of the Pacific Islands.

———. 1960. Competition in Palau. Ph.D. diss., Anthropology Department, Ohio State University.

———. 1961. *Mnemonics in Pre-literate Palau.* Anthropological Working Papers, no. 9, pp. 1–36. Guam: Office of the Staff Anthropologist, Trust Territory of the Pacific Islands.

———. 1968. Proverbs of Palau. *Journal of American Folklore* 81:3–33.

———. 1970 [1964]. *Orachl's Drawings: Palauan Rock Paintings.* Micronesian Research Working Papers no. 1. Saipan: Trust Territory of the Pacific Islands.

―――. 1975. Rigid Models and Ridiculous Boundaries: Political Development and Practice in Palau, circa 1955–1964. In Daniel T. Hughes and Sherwood G. Lingenfelter, eds., *Political Development in Micronesia*, pp. 37–53. Columbus: Ohio State University Press.

―――. 1977. Commas in Microcosm: The Movement of Southwestern Islanders to Palau, Micronesia. In M. D. Lieber, ed., *Exiles and Migrants in Oceania*, pp. 10–33. Honolulu: University Press of Hawaii.

―――. 1978. Nanyo Paradaisu: Images of Life in the Western Carolines. In *Toshi Maruki Exhibition: Island Ways, Impressions from the Micronesia of 1940*. Koror: Palau Museum.

McKnight, Robert K., and Adalbert Obak. 1960. Taro Cultivation in the Palau District. In *Taro Cultivation Practices and Beliefs*. Part 1, *The Western Carolines*, pp. 1–49. Guam: Office of the High Commissioner, Trust Territory of the Pacific Islands.

McManus, Edwin G. 1977. *Palauan-English Dictionary*. Ed. and expand. Lewis S. Josephs. PALI Language Texts: Micronesia. Honolulu: University Press of Hawaii.

Mander-Jones, Phyllis, ed. 1972. *Manuscripts in the British Isles Relating to Australia, New Zealand, and the Pacific*. Honolulu: University Press of Hawaii.

Manhard, Philip W. 1979. *The United States and Micronesia in Free Association: A Chance to Do Better?* National Security Affairs Monograph Series no. 79-4. Washington, D.C.: National Defense University, Research Directorate.

Masse, W. Bruce, David Snyder, and George J. Gumerman. 1984. Prehistoric and Historical Settlement in the Palau Islands, Micronesia. *New Zealand Journal of Archaeology* 6:107–27.

Matthews, W. K. 1949–50. Characteristics of Micronesian. *Lingua* 2:419–37.

Meares, John. 1790. *Voyages Made in the Years 1788 and 1789 from China to the North-West Coast of America*. London: Logographic Press.

Meeking, Charles W. 1846–47. Journal of the Cruise of the "Orotava," 1846–1847. National Library of Australia, Canberra, MS. 1676.

Meller, Norman. 1969. *The Congress of Micronesia: Development of the Legislative Process in the Trust Territory of the Pacific Islands*. Honolulu: University of Hawaii Press.

Mercer, P. M. 1979. Oral Tradition in the Pacific: Problems of Interpretation. *Journal of Pacific History* 14:130–53.

Miller, Joseph C. 1980. Introduction: Listening for the African Past. In J. C. Miller, ed., *The African Past Speaks: Essays on Oral Tradition and History*, pp. 1–59. Hamden, Conn.: Archon Books.

Milner, G. B. 1952. A Study of Two Fijian Texts. *Bulletin of the School of Oriental and African Studies* 14:346–77.

Miyatake, M. 1933. *Mikroneshia Gunto Parao no Dozoku to Shimago Tekisuto*

(Texts of the Local Customs and Languages of Belau in the Micronesian Archipelago). Nara Prefecture. (In Japanese, with transliterated Belauan texts by Ngiraked.)

Mosko, Mark S. 1985. *Quadripartite Structures: Categories, Relations, and Homologies in Bush Mekeo Culture.* Cambridge: Cambridge University Press.

Murdock, George P. 1948. Anthropology in Micronesia. *Transactions of the New York Academy of Science* 1:9–16.

———. 1968 [1964]. Genetic Classification of the Austronesian Languages: A Key to Oceanic Culture History. In Andrew P. Vayda, ed., *Peoples and Cultures of the Pacific*, pp. 81–94. Garden City, N.Y.: Natural History Press.

Nooy-Palm, Hetty. 1979. *The Sa'dan-Toraja: A Study of Their Social Life and Religion.* Vol. 1, *Organization, Symbols and Beliefs.* The Hague: Martinus Nijhoff.

Nufer, Harold F. 1978. *Micronesia under American Rule: An Evaluation of the Strategic Trusteeship (1947–77).* Hicksville, N.Y.: Exposition.

Obak, Adalbert, and Robert K. McKnight. 1969. Kedam: The Palauan Kite. *Lore* 19(2): 49–57.

Oda, Shizuo. 1981. The Archaeology of the Ogasawara Islands. *Asian Perspectives* 24:111–138.

Oliver, Douglas, ed. 1951. *Planning Micronesia's Future: A Summary of the United States Commercial Company's Economic Survey of Micronesia, 1946.* Cambridge: Harvard University Press.

Onvlee, L. 1983 [1949]. The Construction of the Mangil Dam: Notes on the Social Organization of Eastern Sumba. In P. E. de Josselin de Jong, ed., *Structural Anthropology in the Netherlands: A Reader*, pp. 150–63. Dordrecht: Foris.

Orbell, Margaret. 1975. The Religious Significance of Maori Migration Traditions. *Journal of the Polynesian Society* 84:341–47.

Osborne, Douglas. 1958. The Palau Islands: Stepping Stones into the Pacific. *Archaeology* 2:162–71.

———. 1966. *The Archaeology of the Palau Islands: An Intensive Survey.* Bernice P. Bishop Museum Bulletin no. 230. Honolulu: Bishop Museum Press.

———. 1979. *Archaeological Test Excavations, Palau Islands, 1968–1969. Micronesica*, Supplement 1.

Palau District Planning Office. 1977. *Existing Conditions: Ngaremlengui Municipality.* Koror: District Planning Office.

Palau Museum. n.d. *Palauan Folktales.* 2 vols. Koror: Palau Museum.

Parmentier, Richard J. 1981. The Sacred Remains: An Historical Ethnography of Ngeremlengui, Palau. Ph.D. diss., Anthropology Department, University of Chicago.

———. 1984. House Affiliation System in Belau. *American Ethnologist* 11:656–76.

———. 1985a. Diagrammatic Icons and Historical Processes in Belau. *American Anthropologist* 87:840–52.

———. 1985b. Signs' Place *in Medias Res:* Peirce's Concept of Semiotic Mediation. In Elizabeth Mertz and Richard J. Parmentier, eds., *Semiotic Media-*

tion: Sociocultural and Psychological Perspectives, pp. 23–48. Orlando, Fla.: Academic Press.

———. 1985c. Times of the Signs: Modalities of History and Levels of Social Structure in Belau. In Elizabeth Mertz and Richard J. Parmentier, eds., *Semiotic Mediation: Sociocultural and Psychological Perspectives,* pp. 131–54. Orlando, Fla.: Academic Press.

———. 1986a. Mythological Metaphors and Historical Realities: Models of Transformation of Belauan Polity. *Journal of the Polynesian Society* 95:167–93.

———. 1986b. The Political Function of Reported Speech: A Belauan Example. Manuscript.

———. 1986c. Tales of Two Cities: The Rhetoric of Rank in Ngeremlengui, Belau. *Journal of Anthropological Research* 42:161–82.

Pätzold, Klaus. 1968. *Die Palau-Sprache und ihre Stellung zu anderen indonesischen Sprachen.* Berlin: D. Reimer.

Paullin, Charles O. 1910. Early Voyages of American Naval Vessels to the Orient. *U.S. Naval Institute Proceedings* 36:707–34.

Pawley, Andrew, and Roger C. Green. 1984. The Proto-Oceanic Language Community. *Journal of Pacific History* 19:123–46.

PCAA (Palau Community Action Agency). 1974a. *A Rubekul Belau.* Publication no. 4. Koror: Palau Community Action Agency.

———. 1974b. *Dui Ma Klobak er Belau.* Koror: Palau Community Action Agency.

———. 1976–78. *A History of Palau.* 3 vols. Koror: Palau Community Action Agency.

Peirce, Charles Sanders. 1931–35. *Collected Papers of Charles Sanders Peirce.* Ed. Charles Hartshorne and Paul Weiss. Cambridge: Harvard University Press.

———. 1977. *Semiotic and Significs: The Correspondence between Charles S. Peirce and Victoria Lady Welby.* Ed. C. S. Hardwick. Bloomington: Indiana University Press.

Peralta, Jesus T. 1980. Ancient Mariners of the Philippines. *Archaeology* 33(5): 41–48.

Peralta, Jesus T., and Rey Santiago. 1979. Petroglyphs in the Singnapan Basin Reflect the Southeast Asia Past: Did They Have a Ritual Function? *Archipelago* 6(54): 13–17.

Plumb, J. H. 1971 [1969]. *The Death of the Past.* Boston: Houghton Mifflin.

Price, Barbara. 1980. The Truth Is Not in Accounts but in Account Books: On the Epistemological Status of History. In Eric B. Ross, ed., *Beyond the Myths of Culture: Essays in Cultural Materialism,* pp. 155–80. New York: Academic Press.

Price, Willard. 1944. *Japan's Island of Mystery.* New York: John Day.

Purcell, David C., Jr. 1967. Japanese Expansion in the South Pacific, 1890–1935. Ph.D. diss., University of Pennsylvania.

Ranney, Austin, and Howard R. Penniman. 1985. *Democracy in the Islands: The Micronesian Plebiscites of 1983.* Washington, D.C.: American Enterprise Institute for Public Policy Research.

Rattray, R. S. 1923. *Ashanti*. Oxford: Oxford University Press.

Raven, H. C. 1926. The Stone Images and Vats of Central Celebes. *Natural History* 26:272–82.

Riebe, Inge. 1967. Anthropomorphic Stone Carvings on Unea Island. *Journal of the Polynesian Society* 76:374–78.

Riesenberg, Saul H. 1968. *The Native Polity of Ponape*. Smithsonian Contributions to Anthropology no. 10. Washington: Smithsonian Institution Press.

Riesenfeld, Alphonse. 1950. *The Megalithic Culture of Melanesia*. Leiden: Brill.

Ritzenthaler, Robert E. 1954. *Native Money of Palau*. Milwaukee Public Museum Publications in Anthropology no. 1.

Robertson, Russell. 1876–77. The Caroline Islands. *Transactions of the Asiatic Society of Japan* 5:41–63.

Rosaldo, Renato. 1980. Doing Oral History. *Social Analysis* 4:89–99.

Routledge, David. 1985. Pacific History as Seen from the Pacific Islands. *Pacific Studies* 8:81–99.

Sahlins, Marshall D. 1958. *Social Stratification in Polynesia*. American Ethnological Society Monograph no. 29. Seattle: University of Washington Press.

———. 1976. *Culture and Practical Reason*. Chicago: University of Chicago Press.

———. 1981. *Historical Metaphors and Mythical Realities: Structure in the Early History of the Sandwich Islands Kingdom*. Association for Social Anthropology in Oceania Special Publication no. 1. Ann Arbor: University of Michigan Press.

———. 1983a. Other Times, Other Customs: The Anthropology of History. *American Anthropologist* 85:517–44. Reprinted in Sahlins (1985b).

———. 1983b. Raw Women, Cooked Men, and Other "Great Things" of the Fiji Islands. In Paula Brown and Donald Tuzin, eds., *The Ethnography of Cannibalism*, pp. 72–93. Washington, D.C.: Society for Psychological Anthropology.

———. 1985a. Hierarchy and Humanity in Polynesia. In Antony Hooper and Judith Huntsman, eds., *Transformations of Polynesian Culture*, pp. 195–218. Memoir no. 45. Auckland: The Polynesian Society.

———. 1985b. *Islands of History*. Chicago: University of Chicago Press.

Sakiyama, Osamu. 1979. Genealogical Identification of Languages in the Western Carolines. In Humio Kusakabe, ed., *Cultural Anthropological Research on the Folk Culture in the Western Caroline Islands of Micronesia in 1977*, pp. 9–17. Tokyo: Tokyo University of Foreign Studies.

Salii, Lazarus E. 1973. Liberation and Conquest in Micronesia. In Ronald J. May, ed., *Priorities in Melanesian Development*, pp. 41–44. Canberra: Research School of Pacific Studies, Australian National University.

Sayes, Shelley Ann. 1984. The Paths of the Land: Early Political Hierarchies in Cakaudrove, Fiji. *Journal of Pacific History* 19:3–20.

Schneider, David M. 1949. The Kinship System and Village Organization of Yap. Ph.D. diss., Harvard University.

Schulte Nordholt, H. G. 1971 [1966]. *The Political System of the Atoni of Timor*. Trans. M. J. L. van Yperen. Verhandelingen van het Koninklijk Instituut voor Taal-, Land- en Volkenkunde no. 60. The Hague: Martinus Nijhoff.

Seligman, C. G., and Horace C. Beck. 1938. Far Eastern Glass: Some Western Origins. *Bulletin of the Museum of Far Eastern Antiquities* 10:1–64.

Semper, Karl. 1982 [1873]. *The Palau Islands in the Pacific Ocean*. Trans. Mark L. Berg. Guam: University of Guam, Micronesian Area Research Center.

Shuster, Donald R. 1980. Palau's Constitutional Tangle. *Journal of Pacific History* 15:74–82.

———. 1982a. More Constitutions for Palau. In *The Politics of Evolving Cultures in the Pacific Islands*, pp. 81–89. Laie, Hawaii: Institute for Polynesian Studies, Brigham Young University–Hawaii Campus.

———. 1982b. State Shinto in Micronesia during Japanese Rule, 1914–1945. *Pacific Studies* 4:20–43.

———. 1983. Elections in the Republic of Palau. *Political Science* 35:117–32.

Shutler, Richard, Jr., and Jeffrey C. Marck. 1975. On the Dispersal of the Austronesian Horticulturalists. *Archaeology and Physical Anthropology in Oceania* 10:81–113.

Silverstein, Michael. 1976. Shifters, Linguistic Categories, and Cultural Description. In Keith H. Basso and Henry A. Selby, eds., *Meaning in Anthropology*, pp. 11–55. School of American Research Advanced Seminar Series. Albuquerque: University of New Mexico Press.

———. 1984. The Diachrony of Sapir's Synchronic Linguistic Description; or, Sapir's "Cosmographical" Linguistics. Paper presented at the Edward Sapir Centenary Conference, National Museum of Man, Ottawa, Canada.

Simmons, D. R. 1970. Palau Cave Paintings on Aulong Island. *Records of the Auckland Institute and Museum* 7:171–73.

Smith, Bernard. 1960. *European Vision and the South Pacific, 1768–1850*. London: Oxford University Press.

Smith, DeVerne Reed. 1981. Palauan Siblingship: A Study in Structural Complementarity. In Mac Marshall, ed., *Siblingship in Oceania: Studies in the Meaning of Kin Relations*. pp. 225–73. Association for Social Anthropology in Oceania Monograph no. 8. Lanham, Md.: University Press of America.

———. 1983. *Palauan Social Structure*. New Brunswick: Rutgers University Press.

Solheim, W. G. 1964. *The Archaeology of Central Philippines*. Manila: Bureau of Printing.

Sopher, David E. 1964. Indigenous Uses of Turmeric (*Curcuma domestica*) in Asia and Oceania. *Anthropos* 59:93–127.

Spear, Thomas. 1981. Oral Tradition: Whose History? *History in Africa* 8:165–81.

Spencer, J. E. 1963. The Migration of Rice from Mainland Southeast Asia into Indonesia. In Jacques Barrau, ed., *Plants and the Migrations of Pacific Peoples*, pp. 83–89. Honolulu: Bishop Museum Press.

Spencer, J. E., and G. A. Hale. 1961. The Origin, Nature, and Distribution of Agricultural Terracing. *Pacific Viewpoint* 2:1–40.

Spoehr, Alexander. 1957. *Marianas Prehistory.* Fieldiana: Anthropology no. 48. Chicago: Field Museum of Natural History.

Spriggs, Matthew. 1982. Taro Cropping Systems in the Southeast Asian-Pacific Region: Archaeological Evidence. *Archaeology in Oceania* 17: 7–15.

Sproat, M. N. 1968. *A Guide to Subsistence Agriculture in Micronesia.* Agricultural Extension Bulletin no. 9. Saipan: Trust Territory of the Pacific Islands.

Stevens, Charles E. 1867. Report of Proceedings at the Pellew Islands, in the Matter of the Murder of Andrew Cheyne, Master of Schooner "Acis." H.M.S. Perseus at Sea, North Pacific Ocean, 16 April 1867. Public Record Office, London, Admiralty 1/6006.

Swellengrebel, J. L. 1960. Introduction. In W. F. Wertheim, ed., *Bali: Studies in Life, Thought, and Ritual,* pp. 1–76. The Hague: W. van Hoeve.

Takayama, Jun. 1979. Archaeological Investigations of PAAT-2 in the Palaus. In Humio Kusakabe, ed., *Cultural Anthropological Research on the Folk Culture in the Western Caroline Islands of Micronesia in 1977,* pp. 81–101. Tokyo: Tokyo University of Foreign Studies.

———. 1981. Early Pottery and Population Movements in Micronesian Prehistory. *Asian Perspectives* 24:1–10.

———. 1982a. Archaeological Research in Micronesia during the Past Decade. *Indo-Pacific Prehistory Bulletin* 3:95–114.

———. 1982b. A Brief Report on Archaeological Investigations of the Southern Part of Yap Island and Nearby Ngulu Atoll. In Machiko Aoyagi, ed., *Islanders and Their Outside World: A Report of the Cultural Anthropological Research in the Caroline Islands of Micronesia in 1980–1981,* pp. 77–104. Tokyo: St. Paul's (Rikkyo) University, Committee for Micronesian Research.

Tambiah, S. J. 1976. *World Conqueror and World Renouncer: A Study of Buddhism and Polity in Thailand Against a Historical Background.* Cambridge Studies in Social Anthropology no. 15. Cambridge: Cambridge University Press.

Terrell, J. E., and G. J. Irwin. 1972. History and Tradition in the Northern Solomons: An Analytical Study of the Torau Migration to Southern Bougainville in the 1860s. *Journal of the Polynesian Society* 81:317–49.

Tetens, Alfred. 1958. *Among the Savages of the South Seas: Memoirs of Micronesia, 1862–1868.* Trans. Florence M. Spoehr. Stanford: Stanford University Press.

Thomas, William L., Jr. 1968 [1967]. The Pacific Basin: An Introduction. In Andrew P. Vayda, ed., *Peoples and Cultures of the Pacific,* pp. 3–26. Garden City, N.Y.: Natural History Press.

Toomin, Philip R., and Pauline M. Toomin. 1963. *Black Robe and Grass Skirt.* New York: Horizon.

Tryon, D. T. 1984. The Peopling of the Pacific: A Linguistic Appraisal. *Journal of Pacific History* 19:147–59.

Useem, John. 1946. *Report on Yap and Palau.* U.S. Commercial Company, Economic Survey. Honolulu.

———. 1947. *Economic and Human Resources, Yap and Palau, Western Caroline Islands*, 3 vols. Honolulu: U.S. Commercial Company.

———. 1949. *Report on Palau*. Coordinated Investigations in Micronesian Anthropology Report no. 21. Washington: Pacific Science Board.

Ushijima, Iwao. 1982. The Control of Reefs and Lagoons: Some Aspects of the Political Structure of Ulithi Atoll. In Machiko Aoyagi, ed., *Islanders and Their Outside World: A Report of the Cultural Anthropological Research in the Caroline Islands of Micronesia in 1980–1981*, pp. 35–76. Tokyo: St. Paul's (Rikkyo) University, Committee for Micronesian Research.

U.S. Army, Chief of Engineers. 1956. *Military Geology of Palau Islands, Caroline Islands*. Intelligence Division, Office of the Engineer, Headquarters United States Army Forces Far East.

Valencia, Antonio de. 1892. Las Islas Palaos. *Boletin de la Sociedad Geográfica* 33:393–433.

Valeri, Valerio. 1982. The Transformation of a Transformation: A Structural Essay on an Aspect of Hawaiian History (1809–1819). *Social Analysis* 10:3–41.

———. 1985. *Kingship and Sacrifice: Ritual and Society in Ancient Hawaii*. Trans. Paula Wissing. Chicago: University of Chicago Press.

Van der Dussen, W. J. 1981. *History as a Science: The Philosophy of R. G. Collingwood*. The Hague: Martinus Nijhoff.

Van der Kroef, Justus M. 1954. Dualism and Symbolic Antithesis in Indonesian Society. *American Anthropologist* 56:847–62.

Van Ossenbruggen, F. D. E. 1983 [1916]. Java's *monca-pat*: Origins of a Primitive Classification System. In P. E. de Josselin de Jong, ed., *Structural Anthropology in the Netherlands: A Reader*, pp. 30–60. Dordrecht: Foris.

Vansina, Jan. 1965 [1961]. *Oral Tradition: A Study in Historical Methodology*. Trans. H. M. Wright. Chicago: Aldine.

———. 1985. *Oral Tradition as History*. Madison: University of Wisconsin Press.

van Wouden, F. A. E. 1968 [1935]. *Types of Social Structure in Eastern Indonesia*. Trans. Rodney Needham. Koninklijk Instituut voor Taal-, Land- en Volkenkunde Translation Series no. 11. The Hague: Martinus Nijhoff.

Vessel, A. J., and Roy W. Simonson. 1958. Soils and Agriculture of the Palau Islands. *Pacific Science* 12:281–97.

Vidich, Arthur. 1949. *Political Factionalism in Palau: Its Rise and Development*. Coordinated Investigations in Micronesian Anthropology Report no. 23. Washington: Pacific Science Board.

Vincent, James M., ed. 1973. *Micronesia's Yesterday: Illustrations for an Understanding of Micronesia's History*. Saipan: Trust Territory of the Pacific Islands, Department of Education.

Vitarelli, William. 1984. United States Educational Policies in Micronesia. In Catherine Lutz, ed., *Micronesia as Strategic Colony: The Impact of U.S. Policy on Micronesian Health and Culture*. Occasional Papers no. 12. Cambridge, Mass.: Cultural Survival, Inc.

Walleser, Salvator. 1913. *Palau-Wörterbuch, I: Palau-Deutsch; II: Deutsch-Palau*. Hongkong: Typis Societatis Missionum ad Exteros.

Walleser, Sixtus. 1913. Religiöse Anschauungen und Gebräuche der Bewohner von Jap. *Anthropos* 8:607–29, 1044–68. (Trans. in HRAF.)

Walsh, D. S., and Bruce Biggs. 1966. *Proto-Polynesian Word List 1*. Teo Reo Monographs. Auckland: Linguistic Society of New Zealand.

Walsh, D. S., and W. Hadye Lini. 1981. Veveven bwatun tauvwa, ata la vanua Raga: A Story about the Beginning of Creation, from Raga Island. In J. Hollyman and A. Pawley, eds., *Studies in Pacific Languages and Cultures in Honour of Bruce Biggs*, pp. 361–82. Auckland: Linguistic Society of New Zealand.

Ward, R. Girard, ed. 1966. *American Activities in the Central Pacific, 1790–1870*, vol. 1. Ridgewood, N.J.: Gregg.

Wessing, Robert. 1979. Life in the Cosmic Village: Cognitive Models in Sundanese Life. In Edward M. Bruner and Judith O. Becker, eds., *Art, Ritual and Society in Indonesia*, pp. 96–126. Papers in International Studies, Southeast Asia Series no. 53. Athens: Ohio University Center for International Studies, Southeast Asia Program.

Wheatley, Paul. 1965. Agricultural Terracing. *Pacific Viewpoint* 6:123–44.

———. 1971. *The Pivot of the Four Quarters: A Preliminary Enquiry into the Origins and Character of the Ancient Chinese City*. Chicago: Aldine.

———. 1983. *Nāgara and Commandery: Origins of the Southeast Asian Urban Traditions*. Research Paper nos. 207–208. Chicago: Department of Geography, University of Chicago.

White, Hayden V. 1972. The Structure of Historical Narrative. *Clio* 1:5–9.

———. 1975. Historicism, History, and the Figurative Imagination. In *Essays on Historicism, History and Theory*. Beiheft 14:48–67.

Williams, Brooke. 1985. *History and Semiotics*. Toronto Semiotic Circle Monograph Series no. 4. Toronto: Victoria University.

Wilson, James. 1799. *A Missionary Voyage to the Southern Pacific Ocean Performed in the Years 1796, 1797, 1798 in the Ship Duff*. London: T. Chapman.

Woodin, Edward. 1851–52. Log of the Barque "Eleanor," 1851–1852. Microfilm of original manuscript in State Library of Tasmania, Hobart.

———. 1861–63. Log of the Schooner "Lady Leigh," 1861–1863. Microfilm of original manuscript in State Library of Tasmania, Hobart.

Yamaguchi, Osamu. 1967. The Music of Palau: An Ethnomusicological Study of the Classical Tradition. M.A. thesis, University of Hawaii.

Yanaihara, Tadao. 1940. *Pacific Islands under Japanese Mandate*. London: Oxford University Press.

Yawata, Ichiro. 1930. On the Sites of Ancient Villages in Palau Island (Caroline Ils.). *Geographical Review of Japan* 6:1–13.

Zorc, David R. 1978. Proto-Philippine Word Accent: Innovation or Proto-Hesperonesian Retention? In S. A. Wurm and L. Carrington, eds., *Proceedings of the Second International Conference on Austronesian Linguistics*, pp. 82–113. Canberra: Australian National University Press.

Index